The Farm Shop Cookbook

Christine McFadden

A.   Absolute Press

First published in Great Britain in 2009 by
Absolute Press, an imprint of
Bloomsbury Publishing Plc

Absolute Press
Scarborough House
29 James Street West
Bath BA1 2BT
Phone 44 (0) 1225 316013
Fax 44 (0) 1225 445836
E-mail info@absolutepress.co.uk
Website www.absolutepress.co.uk

This paperback edition first published 2013.

Publisher Jon Croft
Commissioning Editor Meg Avent
Designers Matt Inwood and Claire Siggery
Publishing Assistant Andrea O'Connor
Editor Anne Sheasby
Photographer Cristian Barnett
Props Stylist Jo Harris
Food Stylist Linda Tubby (except page 144)

ISBN: 9781906650810

Printed in China by C&C Offset Printing Co., Ltd

A catalogue record of this book is available from the
British Library.

A note about the text
This book was set using Helvetica Neue and Century.
Helvetica was designed in 1957 by Max Miedinger of
the Swiss-based Haas foundry. In the early 1980s,
Linotype redrew the entire Helvetica family. The result
was Helvetica Neue. The first Century typeface was cut
in 1894. In 1975 an updated family of Century typefaces
was designed by Tony Stan for ITC.

Bloomsbury Publishing
50 Bedford Square, London WC1B 3DP
www.bloomsbury.com

Contents

Introduction

I remember with great fondness my first visit to a farm shop. We had just moved to the wilds of West Dorset and had been out for a celebratory dinner. Driving home down unfamiliar country lanes we passed a small farm shop that appeared to be open despite the late hour. Intrigued, we went in and found a bunch of people who all seemed to know each other, buying this and that, and putting money in an honesty box in the fridge. The owners were nowhere to be seen. We asked what time the shop closed. 'When they go to bed,' we were told.

We came away with frozen trout, local goat's cheese, a carton of the best-ever strawberry ice cream, quail's eggs, unpasteurised thick Jersey cream, locally produced muesli, organic potatoes and spanking-fresh sprouting broccoli – at ten o'clock on a weekday evening, far from a city centre. The farm shop in question has gone on to win awards, expand its premises, and now keeps more conventional opening hours. The sheer quality and variety of the produce on sale remains the same, however, and it is this that makes farm shops so special.

Many people, myself included, are increasingly opting for fresh local produce and therefore use farm shops for a significant proportion of their food shopping. The food is not necessarily cheaper, but it is generally of very good quality. The better farm shops grow their own fruit and vegetables and harvest them on a daily basis. Food doesn't come much fresher than this unless you pick it yourself at a Pick-Your-Own farm. Here you can buy the best in the field, when it's ripe and ready to eat.

You'll invariably find really tasty fruit and vegetable varieties that simply don't last long enough to survive the supply chain and shelf-life demanded by the supermarkets. You may also come across juices made from named varieties of apples or pears, cider, wine and beer, as well as cut flowers and bedding plants. On sale also may be anything from artisan-made bread, pies and cakes to fish, game and meat, and dairy products and eggs.

This book is not about individual farm shops or producers (see **Resources**, page 284–286, for details of how to locate them). Instead it focuses on all the fantastic produce you can buy, what you need to know about it and how best to cook it. Some items like potatoes and carrots are familiar staples, but I have tried to show you how to bring out their best and hopefully inspire you with new ideas. Other items may come as a bit of a surprise – buffalo, goose eggs or squirrel, for example. Again, my intention has been to encourage you to be open to culinary adventures. In the process of testing the recipes, I have had to do the same myself.

Christine McFadden *January 2009*

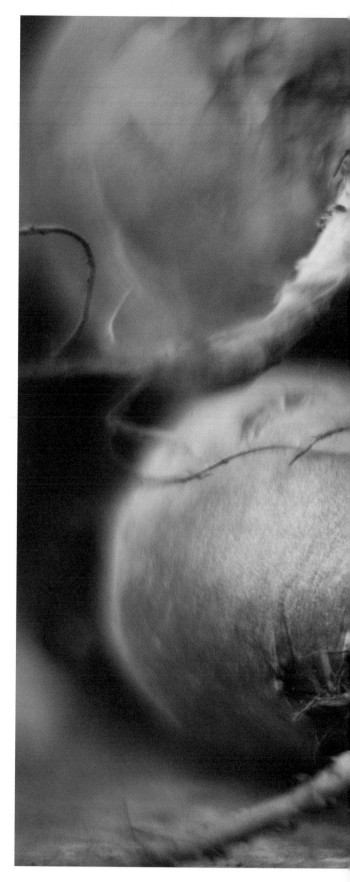

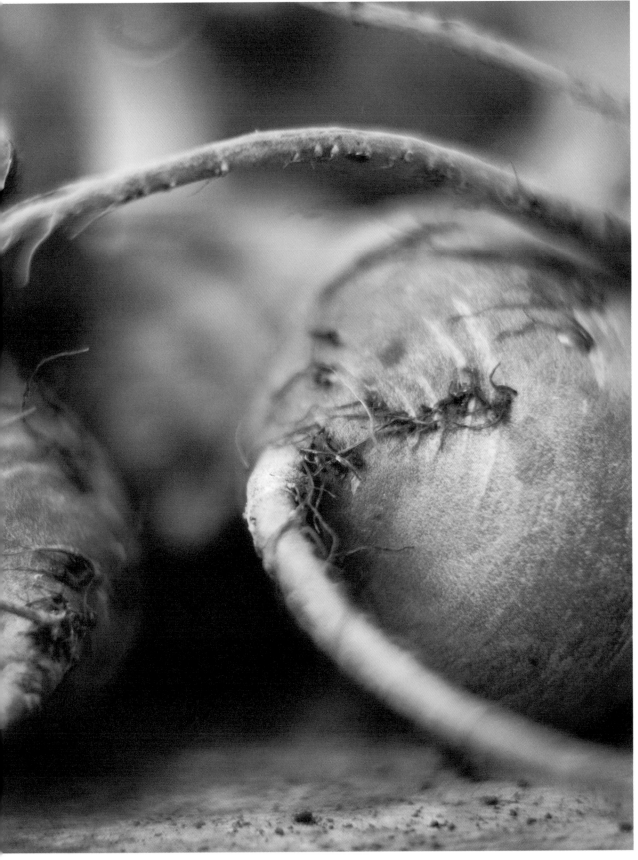

The success of the farm shop

Farm shops vary enormously from genuine farm outlets where produce has been picked that morning, to those that stock imported tomatoes and a surfeit of scented candles. Some are small enough to operate from sheds; others are veritable emporia located in stylish converted barns. Many boast tearooms, restaurants, farm trails, craft workshops, fishing facilities and holiday cottages.

The first date back to the seventies. They were few and far between and sales usually took place at the farm gate. Fast forward forty years and the numbers jump to more than 1700, a growth rate that currently outstrips any other type of food shop. The reasons for this are complex. Farmers have been encouraged to diversify and in the process, many have become adept at retailing. Since no middle-men are involved, the farmers get more for their goods, and artisan producers have a chance to keep their traditional skills alive.

As far as consumers are concerned, farm shops give people a taste of the dream depicted by bucolic TV programmes. At a deeper level, serious food scares have made consumers think hard about the provenance of their food and how it is produced.

At yet another level, there is growing awareness of environmental issues. Buying direct from the farm reduces food miles (though this is a double-edged sword if you think of the cost of getting to and from the farm). There is certainly less waste – farmers sell good food regardless of irregularities in size, shape or colour; supermarkets reject it on these counts. Since much of the produce is sold loose, unnecessary food packaging is kept to a minimum.

A key factor, however, is the ultimate difference between buying from a farm shop and a supermarket. At a farm shop you can have a direct dialogue with someone who is likely to have grown, reared, caught, milled or made the goods on sale, often on the farm where the shop is located. The food is fully traceable and the farmer can tell you about it, from the parentage of livestock, the breed, and why he or she chose to rear it, to how crops have been grown and fertilised, and which varieties do best in the local soil conditions and micro-climate.

This upsurge in popularity inevitably means that the term 'farm shop' is being used as a marketing tool. So-called farm shops are popping up in unlikely locations many miles from mud and tractors, whereas a genuine one will be attached to a working farm, selling goods produced on the farm itself or supplied by local producers. Genuine farm shops will also be accredited by FARMA, the National Farmers' Retail and Markets Association (see **Resources**, page 284–286)..

How to use the book

Each entry in the A–Z section includes notes on the UK season, varieties, shopping notes, preparation and storage. The information is necessarily brief so it is also worth bearing in mind the following:

UK season

Climate varies from region to region and, with the effect of global warming, the weather is becoming less predictable. This means that the season may be shorter or longer, earlier or later than I have indicated. Use the dates in the individual entries and the chart on pages 290–291 as a guide and then check with your farm shop or Pick-Your-Own farm to find out what's available locally.

Fruit and vegetable varieties

Thanks to consumer demand, an increasing number of fruit and vegetables are now identified according to variety: 'Cox's Orange Pippin' apples, or 'Duke of York' potatoes, for example. There is, however, a whole underclass of produce, such as rhubarb, celeriac and peas, that are not yet honoured with varietal marketing; these are simply given a generic name. Not wishing to exclude these, I have suggested varieties for all the fruit and vegetables in the book. I have personally sampled many of them at tasting trials, while producers and food writer colleagues have recommended others. Some varieties have won awards or have another interesting attribute that makes them especially worth seeking out.

Pick-Your-Own farms are the best places for finding a wider choice of varieties of a particular fruit or vegetable. In the case of non-PYO farms, it's always worth asking the farm shop manager to identify specific varieties on sale.

Storing fresh produce

In most cases it's best to eat fruit and vegetables on the day you buy them. The decomposition process starts immediately after harvesting. Though edible, produce gradually starts to dehydrate and wilt, and there are subtle changes to flavour – it may become sourer or sweeter or starchier. Sometimes storage is unavoidable, however, so I have given brief guidelines for this in every section. It is also worth taking on board a few key principles to help keep your produce in peak condition.

Different types of fruit and vegetables have different storage requirements. Soft berries and tomatoes should ideally be kept at room temperature. The chill of the fridge simply dulls their flavour and, once chilled, the flavour is never quite the same even when the fruit returns to room temperature. Similarly, the fridge is not a good place for storing onions, winter squash and root vegetables, such as potatoes. These are best kept in a well-ventilated drawer (wicker or perforated metal is ideal), or, better still, a larder, cellar or dry shed.

Most people assume that the fridge operates at a uniform temperature. The reality is that every fridge has warmer, cooler or more humid zones, and these in turn are better for different types of produce. Apples and grapes are fine in the colder part, others need the moderate zone, while the majority last best in the humidity of the salad drawer. It's worth investing in a fridge thermometer so you can see how the different zones of your fridge vary in temperature.

Packaging is another storage-related issue. Nowadays, environmentally conscious farm shops provide brown paper bags for fruit and vegetables. It's a good idea to keep your produce in its paper bag, even if you put it in the fridge. Paper absorbs moisture, providing the slightly humid but well-ventilated atmosphere that many vegetables need. In some cases a sealed plastic bag is preferable; watercress and herbs, for example, need an enclosed moist environment. That said, too much moisture can cause mould. If you have washed produce before storing it, make sure you dry it well, then wrap it in paper towels to absorb excess moisture in the bag.

The recipes

The recipes in this book are a broadly based collection that shows off the versatility of British produce. We are a multi-ethnic society and, as a result, our cooking and the ingredients we use have adapted to a melting pot of influences. You'll therefore find recipes from around the world as well as British classics and many that are my own invention. Some are written in full, others are just ideas to inspire you.

Whatever the recipe, I have tried to show you how to make the best of the ingredient: when to buy it, which varieties or breeds are particularly worth looking for, and how to store and prepare the ingredient once you get it home.

With few exceptions, the ingredients used in the recipes can be found in farm shops. Stocks vary, however, depending on the location and size of the shop. Large farm shops are on a par with delicatessens or small supermarkets; others have a more limited selection. The goods on sale will also reflect the type of farm the shop is attached to – a dairy farm, beef farm, fruit farm or an arable farm, for example.

It's always a good idea to be flexible and see what a farm shop has on the shelves before you decide on a recipe. You may want to take this book with you so you can flick through it and see what you could make with what is available. The following is a guide to the basics:

Butter
Use unsalted butter for preference. It has a cleaner flavour than salted butter, and is especially good for desserts.

Cream
Use double, whipping or single cream as specified. I choose to buy organic cream as it is relatively free from pesticide residues.

Herbs
Herbs are fresh unless specified otherwise. I have used flat leaf parsley in preference to curly. It is easier to clean and has a more pleasing texture, but it's fine to use curly parsley if you wish.

Milk
Use whole milk unless specified otherwise. I choose to buy organic milk as it is relatively free from pesticide residues.

Oils
For frying and roasting, I have specified UK-grown rapeseed oil rather than other vegetable oils. A relative newcomer to the market, rapeseed oil is cold-pressed and rich in all-important omega-3 essential oils. By using it, you will be reducing food miles and boosting your health.

Salt
In most cases I have used sea salt flakes, either whole or lightly crumbled between your finger and thumb. Added just before serving, they provide crunchy texture and delicious bursts of flavour on the tongue. Free-flowing table salt is fine for seasoning dishes such as soups and casseroles in which the salt dissolves during cooking.

Spices
Whole spices, including pepper, are a must if you want bright zesty flavours. Once ground or crushed, they quickly lose their distinctive aroma and flavour. Grind as needed, using a mill for pepper and a mortar and pestle for other spices.

Vinegars
Balsamic vinegar: a speciality from Modena in northern Italy, this is terrific for deglazing pans, as a marinade, and as a seasoning for anything from game to strawberries. In salad dressings, use it sparingly as a condiment rather than as a replacement for ordinary vinegar. The quality varies enormously. 'Aged' balsamic vinegar is the one to use when you want a thick syrupy glaze. It is expensive but a little goes a long way. For everyday use, choose a medium-priced vinegar preferably labelled 'di Modena'. Cheap balsamic vinegar is not worth buying.
Cider vinegar: since cider apples grow in the UK, I have used this vinegar in preference to grape-based vinegar.

Measurements
• Use proper measuring spoons: 1 teaspoon = 5ml, 1 tablespoon = 15ml.
• All spoon measurements are level unless otherwise stated.
• Where I specify 'a handful' or 'a good pinch' or no measurement at all, I want to encourage you to use your own judgement and taste buds.
• All eggs, fruit and vegetables are medium unless stated otherwise.
• Oven temperatures and timings are approximate. No two ovens are alike and thermostats are rarely accurate. If you are using a fan-assisted oven, or one that combines grilling with circulated air, reduce the time and/or temperature according to the manufacturer's instructions.

Cooking vegetables
Since many of the recipes in this book are based on vegetables, it is worth preparing and cooking them in ways that will make the most of their delicious flavours. Certain

cooking techniques work best with specific vegetables, and there are a few tricks of the trade that come in handy at the preparation stage:

• Regardless of cooking method, use vegetables of a similar size or cut them into even-sized pieces so that they cook at the same rate. This is particularly important when steaming and stir-frying.
• Aim to cook vegetables soon after cleaning, peeling and chopping. Cut surfaces can discolour and develop off flavours if left to stand.
• When roasting or frying vegetables, give them plenty of room. If you overcrowd the pan, they will steam in their own moisture rather than browning and crisping. Use two pans or cook in batches if necessary.
• Remember that vegetables continue to cook after they have been removed from the heat. To keep them crisp and tender, remove from the heat when slightly underdone.

Steaming

I steam almost all vegetables and find it a particularly worthwhile technique for porous or delicate types such as sprouting broccoli, asparagus and cauliflower. The vegetables are not in direct contact with the liquid, so they do not become waterlogged. They also keep their bright colours, crisp texture and much more flavour. Steaming is a healthier way of cooking, too, since fewer nutrients leach into the cooking water.

If you have never tried steaming, it's worth investing in a 'universal' steamer insert. This is a capacious perforated container with a stepped base that will fit into the top of most saucepans regardless of size. For small quantities, you can use a compact fold-out steamer that sits in the bottom of the saucepan above the boiling liquid.

Boiling

This is a good method for root vegetables, or for blanching any dense-textured vegetable prior to stir-frying. Remember that the turbulent action of boiling can break up the texture of floury potatoes. It's best to start them off in cold water and, once boiling point is reached, turn down the heat so they cook at a gentler pace.

Also worth bearing in mind is that potatoes absorb water during boiling and, depending on variety, can become rather sodden. Some cooks argue that it is better to boil potatoes in their skins so the water cannot penetrate. I have tried boiling the same variety with and without skin and cannot honestly detect any noticeable difference.

Grilling

This works well for moist vegetables such as asparagus, courgettes and tomatoes, and even baby broad beans in their pods. The direct heat of the grill quickly seals in the juices and crisps the exterior, creating deliciously intense flavours.

For stovetop grilling you will need a heavy-based cast-iron pan, preferably with ridges for producing appetising brown stripes.

Roasting

The dry heat of the oven caramelises natural sugars in squash and pumpkin, onions and root vegetables, making them deliciously brown and sticky in the process. It's best to use a shallow roasting tray rather than a high-sided roasting tin, so that the heat can circulate unimpeded

Apples

The National Fruit Collection at Brogdale in Kent lists nearly 2000 varieties of British apple but only a handful of these end up on the shelves. Farm shops, however, are great places for buying varieties that you rarely find elsewhere, particularly those that are special to a particular region. Many are oddly shaped and have strange-sounding names, but don't be put off. There are some real beauties to be enjoyed – crisp and juicy with subtle flavours unique to the type of apple (see **Varieties to look for**). Some are redolent of almonds or pear drops, while others have a whiff of peach or apricot. Gleaming red 'Rubens' has exquisite pink-tinged flesh, while 'Christmas Pearmain' is almost yellow. You should be able to find the true 'Cox's Orange Pippin' rather than the 'Queen Cox' – favoured by supermarkets on account of its more uniform colour. You might also come across cider apples. They are far too tart to eat but they give cider an unsurpassable flavour.

Apples continue to ripen after harvest; the flesh softens and dries, and the texture becomes mealy. To halt the process, supermarket apples are often refrigerated and kept in controlled-atmosphere storage. The drawback is that once apples reach the shelves, the ripening process accelerates and even firm-fleshed varieties start to soften quickly. Your best bet is to buy from a farm shop. Depending on season, the apples are likely to have been freshly picked or will have been stored in cool, well-ventilated storage sheds.

Cooking

After months of luscious summer fruit, it's easy to forget how good an apple can be – crisp, sweetly acidic and aromatic, and close to perfection eaten either alone or with a slice of good British cheese. Once autumn is under way, though, other ideas spring to mind.

Raw apples can be sliced and added to salads. I think their all-important crunch is better in savoury rather than fruit salads. They are lovely in a **goose salad with celery, apple and citrus fruit** (page 121), and an essential component in Waldorf salad – a retro mix of walnuts, sliced celery and eating apples, preferably red-skinned, tossed with mayonnaise.

I have never understood the peculiarly British habit of classifying apples as cookers and eaters. Unless you are specifically after the soft acidic flesh of a cooking apple, most eating apples are perfectly suited to cooking. Choose one with a good balance of sweetness and acidity such as 'Gravenstein', rather than one that is very sweet.

An iconic British dish made with cooking apples is baked apple. As famed food writer Elizabeth David wrote in 1962, 'There is no more chilling dish in the whole repertory of English cooking than those baked apples in their macintosh skins'. I have to agree – mushy acidic flesh bursting from leathery skin is not nice.

UK season
• September–April depending on variety.

Varieties to look for
Cooking apples:
• *'Bramley Seedling'*, green-red flushed skin, acidic flesh. Perfect for apple pie.
• *'Howgate Wonder'*, large, mottled red-green skin. Sharp when cooked, mild and sweet enough to eat raw.
• *'Grenadier'*, misshapen, lumpy green skin. Superb when cooked, excellent for pies and jam.
• *'Arthur Turner'*, large round, yellow-red flushed skin. Soft smooth flesh when cooked. Good in sauces and purées.

Dessert apples:
• *'Christmas Pearmain'*, pleasant aromatic fruity flavour. Juicy crisp flesh.
• *'Claygate Pearmain'*, pear drop aroma, almondy flavour. Crisp flesh, excellent balance of sweetness and acidity.
• *'Cox's Orange Pippin'*, strong apple aroma, unsurpassed fresh flavour. Good crunch, excellent balance of sweetness and acidity. The classic English apple.
• *'Gravenstein'*, juicy crisp flesh, strong flavour, good balance of sweetness and acidity.
• *'Ingrid Marie'*, punchy flavour with hint of aniseed. Crisp fine-textured flesh, good crunch.
• *'Rubens'*, sparkling flavour, pink-tinged fine-textured flesh.

Shopping notes
• Choose firm apples with no sign of bruising, cuts or other damage. Don't bother with any that feel soft or flabby.
• Apples should be pleasantly aromatic.
• Don't worry if the skin feels greasy. This is a natural waxy coating.

Cooking apples are far better peeled, thickly sliced and packed into a homely double crust pie (**English Apple Pie with Sweet Spices**, below), or relegated to savoury sauces and purées. Their soft fluffy flesh is just the job for **horseradish and apple sauce** (page 141) to go with mackerel, or **mint-flavoured apple sauce** to go with roast pork or duck. Quarter, core, peel and chop one or two cooking apples. Heat in a covered pan with a splash of water and some chopped mint. Allow to boil but keep stirring to prevent sticking. Once reduced to a mush, remove from the heat and whisk away any remaining lumps with a fork. Stir in a small knob of butter and a sprinkling of sugar if you prefer to take the edge off the tartness.

Moving on to dessert apples, they are excellent in a number of savoury dishes. Try them in **Partridge with Braised Red Cabbage, Apples and Juniper** (page 180), or **Braised Pheasant with Apples and Somerset Cider Brandy** (page 190), or in a creamy cider-based sauce (**Black Pudding with Caramelised Apple, Sage and Cider,** page 42). They are at their most delicious, however, thinly sliced in an open-faced French-style tart, or, albeit combined with cooking apples, in **Two-Apple Pizza with Walnuts** (page 17).

Storing
• Store loosely wrapped in a paper bag in the fridge for 1–2 weeks.
• Bring to room temperature as required.

Preparation
• *For a pie or compôte*: slice first into quarters, remove the core and lastly the peel. If peeled first, the exposed flesh browns more easily.
• *For a fruit salad*: slice in a way that reflects the profile of the apple i.e. vertically in thin segments.

English Apple Pie with Sweet Spices

Based on a recipe from *Great Dishes of the World* by the late Robert Carrier, this splendid double-crust pie has always been a favourite.

Line a lightly greased deep 23-cm pie dish with the pastry, reserving about one-third for the top crust. Preheat the oven to 200°C/gas 6. Quarter, core and peel the apples, then slice into thick segments.

Combine the sugars, flour and spices and rub a little of this mixture into the pastry base. Add the lemon and orange zest to the remaining sugar mixture. Arrange a layer of apple slices in the bottom of the pastry case, and sprinkle with a few sultanas and some of the sugar mixture. Repeat the layers until the pie is richly filled.

Sprinkle with the orange juice and dot with butter. Fit the top crust over the apples, pressing the edges together and fluting them. Decorate with the trimmings, and cut slits in the top to release steam. Brush with beaten egg yolk and bake for 35–40 minutes.

Cook's notes
• Use your creative skills to decorate the pie with attractive leaves, berries and flowers cut from the pastry trimmings.
• The pie is sublime served hot with very cold **Clotted Cream Ice Cream** (page 88).

ready-made shortcrust pastry 450g
cooking apples 4, weighing about 675g in total
sugar 75g
dark muscovado sugar 40g
plain flour 1 tbsp
freshly grated nutmeg $^{1}/_{8}$ tsp
ground cinnamon $^{1}/_{4}$ tsp
lemon grated zest of $^{1}/_{2}$
orange grated zest of $^{1}/_{2}$, plus 1–2 tbsp juice
sultanas 50g
butter a knob
beaten egg yolk to glaze

Serves 6

Two-Apple Pizza with Walnuts

There is no reason why a pizza cannot be sweet. The principles are the same as for a savoury one: very high heat and a light topping that allows the base to cook through and become crisp. I have combined two kinds of apple – fluffy cooking apples and dense-fleshed dessert apples (see **Cook's notes**).

First make the dough: sift the flour and salt into a warmed bowl and add the yeast. Make a well in the centre and stir in the rapeseed oil and water. Keep stirring, gradually drawing in the flour from around the edge. Once you have a soft cohesive dough, knead for at least 10 minutes until it feels silky and springy. Place in an oiled bowl, turning once so the surface is coated. Cover with cling film and leave to rise in a warm place for 1–2 hours until doubled in size.

Preheat the oven to 240°C/gas 9. Quarter, core and peel the cooking apples. Roughly chop and put in a small saucepan with the lemon zest and a splash of water. Cover and simmer over low heat for 7 minutes, shaking the pan to prevent sticking, until the apples have disintegrated to a purée. Stir in the cinnamon, sugar and butter, and whisk until smooth.

Quarter, core and peel the dessert apples, then slice each piece lengthways into very thin segments, sprinkling with lemon juice as you prepare them.

Roll out the dough to a 30-cm circle and place on a perforated pizza pan. Pinch up the edges to make a raised rim and lightly brush with walnut oil. Spread the apple purée thinly over the base. Arrange the segments on top in concentric circles. Brush lightly with oil and sprinkle with sugar.

Bake for 15 minutes until the apple segments begin to blacken at the edges. Scatter the walnuts over the top and bake for 2 minutes more. Sprinkle with a little more sugar and serve right away.

Cook's notes
• Instead of the ubiquitous 'Bramley', look for other varieties of cooking apple such as 'Howgate Wonder' or 'Arthur Turner'. For dessert apples, try the richly-perfumed 'Claygate Pearmain' or 'Ingrid Marie' (see **Varieties to look for**, page 14).
• A perforated pizza pan allows heat to get to the pizza base and make it crisper. If you don't have one, use a baking sheet instead and cook for a few minutes longer.

cooking apples 2, weighing about 450g in total
lemon finely grated zest of $^1/_2$
ground cinnamon $^1/_4$ tsp
sugar to taste
butter a knob
dessert apples 4–5 small, weighing about 400g in total
lemon juice
walnut oil or **rapeseed oil** for brushing
shelled 'wet' walnuts 25g, halved

for the dough
unbleached strong white flour 225g
salt 1 tsp
easy-blend dried yeast 1 tsp
rapeseed oil 1 tbsp
tepid water 125–150ml

Serves 8

Asparagus

The appearance of the first British asparagus is a highlight of the culinary calendar. The season is tantalisingly brief, lasting just eight weeks from early May; there is no second crop. Some farmers are trying to extend the season by growing asparagus in polytunnels but as food writer Charles Campion states, 'The best asparagus always has to be grown quickly in the open air, then cut by hand and eaten as soon as possible.'

Farm shops are good places to find asparagus in tip-top condition – dewy-fresh and flab-free rather than jet-lagged. Better still, pick your own; you may get your fingernails dirty but that is a small price to pay for the treat in store.

Asparagus growers exist all over the country though they are concentrated in Kent, Lincolnshire and Worcestershire. There is an annual asparagus festival in the Vale of Evesham (see **Resources**, page 284–286) where you can taste and compare different varieties.

Cooking

Let's quickly dispense with the myth that you need a special asparagus kettle in which the stems stand upright in boiling water while the tips cook in the steam above. This comes from the days when all vegetables were routinely subjected to at least 20 minutes boiling. Had you cooked asparagus this way, the tips would have certainly disintegrated by the time the stems were cooked. Nowadays we cook vegetables differently, for as brief a time as possible.

Asparagus can be lightly boiled, steamed or grilled. Of the two wet methods I prefer steaming; the spears don't get waterlogged and they keep their colour better. The choice between steaming or grilling depends on the thickness of the spears; some are as thin as pencils, others as fat as fingers. Slender spears develop a wonderfully intense flavour when steamed, and they shrivel when grilled. Conversely, fat spears are lovely grilled but become watery when steamed.

Whichever way you choose, keep it quick. Steam for 4 minutes or until the thickest part of the stem is just tender; grill for about 7 minutes, tossed in oil, until just nicely charred.

Served alone, steamed asparagus needs an emollient dressing. Warm hollandaise sauce is traditional; simplest and nicest is melted butter. Other options are a lemony vinaigrette or good-quality mayonnaise.

Once you are sated with spears on their own, try them in other dishes. Asparagus has a special affinity with eggs; try **Asparagus and Pea Frittata** (page 20), or use it in a tart or quiche. Steamed spears are sublime as soldiers for dipping in a very fresh, soft-boiled organic egg, or to top creamy scrambled eggs.

Grilled or steamed, asparagus is excellent as a side dish with salmon or scallops. It is also the perfect addition to salads, especially with bacon and Parmesan (**Grilled Asparagus Salad with Bacon and Parmesan**, page 20), or paper-thin slices of air-dried ham or smoked salmon. Chopped into shorter lengths, the spears add colour and texture to a stir-fry, pasta or risotto (**Spelt and Asparagus**, page 238).

UK season
• May–June.

Varieties to look for
• *'Connover's Colossal'*, award-winning variety renowned for flavour, bright green spears with purple tips.
• *'English sprue'*, very thin spears usually sold loose. Good in stir-fries or puréed for soup.
• *'Pacific'*, long spears, excellent sweet flavour.
• *'Stewart's Purple'*, purple spears that keep their colour when steamed. Exceptionally sweet and tender.

Shopping notes
• Choose firm crisp spears with tightly closed tips. They should be the same thickness so that they cook evenly.
• Check the tips for traces of slimy rot.
• The cut ends will be dry but they shouldn't be wrinkled or wizened – a sign of age.

Storing
• Once harvested, asparagus deteriorates really quickly, so use on the day you buy it if possible.
• Otherwise, trim the ends and store upright in a jug of water loosely covered with a plastic bag. Keep in the fridge for up to 2 days.

Preparation
• Release the spears from their bundles when steaming. They will cook more evenly when spread out.
• Remove the inedible woody end by bending the stem about 2cm from the bottom until it snaps.
• Unless the spears are old and tough there is no need to peel the remaining end of the stem, as some recipes suggest.

Grilled Asparagus Salad with Bacon and Parmesan (page 20)

Grilled Asparagus Salad with Bacon and Parmesan

This is so quick to make – ideal for unexpected visitors who end up staying on for a meal. Grilling the asparagus gives it a richer flavour that goes really well with the meatiness of bacon and Parmesan.

Snap the woody ends from the asparagus and discard. Place the spears in a single layer on a roasting tray and sprinkle with enough olive oil to lightly coat. Season with sea salt and plenty of freshly ground black pepper. Grill for 7 minutes, turning halfway through.

While the asparagus is cooking, heat a large non-stick frying pan. Fry the bacon without any oil for 3–4 minutes until crisp. Remove from the pan and drain on paper towels.

Arrange a handful of salad leaves on individual serving plates. Dribble with a little olive oil and the merest soupçon of sea salt and black pepper, bearing in mind the saltiness of the bacon. Pile the asparagus, bacon and Parmesan wafers on top.

Cook's notes
• To make the dish more substantial, add softly boiled egg halves or quail's eggs and a scattering of crisply fried breadcrumbs.
• As an alternative to bacon you could use strips of smoked salmon.

asparagus 700g
extra-virgin olive oil
sea salt
freshly ground black pepper
thin dry-cured streaky bacon or pancetta 12 rashers
mixed salad leaves such as mizuna, wild rocket, beet leaves and baby chard
Parmesan cheese 40g, shaved into wafers

Serves 4 as a light meal or starter

Asparagus and Pea Frittata

This combines the best of early summer produce – new season asparagus and fresh green peas. The vegetables are very lightly cooked so that they keep their crisp texture and glorious fresh colour.

Snap the woody ends from the asparagus and discard. Chop the stems into 1-cm pieces and the tips into 2.5-cm pieces. Steam with the peas over boiling water for 3 minutes. Remove from the heat and reserve.

Beat the eggs and season with the salt and plenty of black pepper.

Heat a 24-cm non-stick frying pan over medium heat. Add the olive oil and butter, and fry the spring onions for 2 minutes. Stir in the peas and asparagus. Pour in the eggs, stirring to distribute the vegetables evenly.

Cover and cook over medium-low heat for 10–12 minutes or until almost set. Place under a preheated grill and cook for another 3–5 minutes or until the top is set. Turn out onto a serving plate and cut into wedges. Serve hot or warm with a green salad.

Cook's note
• I like the peas and asparagus to be only just cooked. If you prefer them softer, steam for an extra minute or two.

asparagus 8 spears
peas 350g, podded
eggs organic, 8
salt ½ tsp
freshly ground black pepper
olive oil 1 tbsp
butter a large knob
spring onions 8, trimmed and finely sliced
leafy green salad to serve

Serves 4 as a light meal or 8 as a starter

Bacon and Gammon

The terms bacon and gammon are sometimes used interchangeably, as are gammon and ham. Though all three are made with cured pork, there are technical differences: bacon comes from the back, sides and belly of the pig, gammon is the hind leg, and ham is the term used for gammon once it has been cooked. Sometimes bacon is smoked as well as cured – a process that gives it a distinctive salty flavour and a brighter colour. Cured bacon that has been matured but not smoked is called 'green' bacon and has a milder flavour.

Of the two basic curing methods, dry-curing by massaging the meat with salt, saltpetre and seasonings, produces a superior meatier flavour. Wet-curing by injecting or soaking with brine produces unappetising white sediment that oozes from the bacon as it cooks.

Farm-produced bacon is usually dry-cured – the traditional slow method that produces lovely crisp bacon. At one time each region had its own special cure and many still do. The Suffolk cure, for example, is sweet, while in Dyfed, South Wales it is distinctively salty, and in Wiltshire it is mild. These traditional cures are a world apart from mass-produced bacon and are to be savoured for their authenticity.

Cooking

Cooking traditional dry-cured bacon is an entirely different experience to cooking mass-produced bacon. Traditional bacon has a wonderfully rich flavour and remains dry in the pan. In contrast, mass-produced bacon wrinkles badly and produces so much liquid that it stews rather than fries. It is impossible to use in the same way.

Streaky bacon is usually thinly sliced and fatty enough to sizzle without adding any oil to the pan. It is lovely cut into crisp snippets and tossed with **pasta and savoy cabbage** (page 136) or in **Grilled Asparagus Salad with Bacon and Parmesan** (page 20). It also adds texture and contrasting colour to salads – try it in **Wilted New Zealand Spinach Salad with Bacon and Bantam Eggs** (page 169). Uncooked streaky rashers are often used to bard lean game birds during roasting, although the bird will end up tasting of bacon, which I'm not sure is a good thing.

Back bacon is leaner and more robust than streaky and just right for a bacon sandwich (**The Ultimate Bacon Sandwich**, page 22). Long rashers make a flavour-rich lining for the base of a terrine (**Pork and Herb Terrine**, page 99), while lardons, or small cubes of fatty bacon provide mellow background flavour to soups and stews (**Coq au Vin**, page 78).

Thick gammon steaks are superb grilled or fried and served with parsley sauce (**Gammon Steaks with Parsley Sauce**, page 23). Whole gammon joints can be boiled or, more accurately, very gently simmered to make cooked ham. Once cooked, you can coat the meat in a pungent syrupy glaze as in **Glazed Ham with Membrillo and Mustard** (page 137) and finish it off in the oven.

See also **Ham** (page 136)

Bacon to look for

• *Denhay Farms, Dorset:* dry-cured smoked back. Mildly smoked, slightly sweet, thin crisp rashers.
• *Ginger Pig, Grange Farm, North Yorkshire:* smoked thick streaky, long back, short back. Balanced salt and sugar cure, sizzles well, fatty.
• *Graig Farm Organics, Powys:* organic short back or long back. Good porky flavour, hint of juniper.
• *Maynards Farm, Shropshire:* traditional dry-cured back, Staffordshire Black, wild honey back, oak-smoked back.
• *Northfield Farm, Rutland:* smoked dry-cured long back. Sizzles well, slightly sweet, fatty.
• *Sillfield Farm, Cumbria:* Ayrshire Middle, traditional salt cure. Faultlessly balanced cure, impressive rich flavour.

Shopping notes

• Bacon should have clean white fat and reddish-pink meat.
• Don't buy if the meat looks dark and dry – it may have been sliced some time ago and exposed to the air.
• The rind should be thin and pliable; the colour will depend on the type of cure.

Storing

• Store vacuum-packed bacon in the fridge for up to 2 weeks. Once opened, use within 3–4 days.
• Store gammon steaks in the fridge for 3–5 days, and whole joints for 1 week.

Preparation

• Snip bacon rind at intervals or remove completely if you find it too chewy.
• Soak gammon joints in water for 12–24 hours to remove excess salt, changing the water once or twice. Drain and cover with fresh water when ready to cook.

Serving size

• Bacon: 3–4 rashers serves 1.
• Gammon, boned and rolled: 2kg serves 6; 2.8–3kg serves 8–10; 4kg serves 12–16.

The Ultimate Bacon Sandwich

The Ultimate Bacon Sandwich

Rough and ready though they may be, bacon sandwiches must be made just so – exactly the right bacon (back rather than streaky), white bread, good butter for spreading and some kind of sharp-tasting condiment.

Snip the bacon rind with scissors, or cut off completely – it can be quite chewy. Heat a ridged frying pan or stovetop grill over medium heat without any oil. Lay the rashers in the pan and cook each side for 2–3 minutes until nice and stripy (the second side will need less time).

Thickly spread the bread with butter and arrange the bacon on two of the slices. Add a dollop of HP sauce and put the other two slices on top. Slice in half diagonally and tuck in.

Cook's notes
• This is a rare culinary occasion when ordinary pre-sliced white bread comes into its own. It is the perfect foil for crisp rashers of bacon and absorbent enough to blot up the grease. Some would argue that a classic farmhouse bloomer does a good job too.
• Condiment options include tomato ketchup, English mustard, home-made **Piccalilli** (page 58) or **Rhubarb and Cranberry Chutney** (page 226).

dry-cured green back bacon 6 fairly thick rashers
white bread 4 slices
unsalted butter at room temperature, for spreading
HP sauce or other condiment

Makes 2 sandwiches

Gammon Steaks with Parsley Sauce

An old-fashioned dish that deserves resurrecting. Farm shops usually have nice thick gammon steaks that come from pampered pigs.

To make the parsley sauce, melt the butter in a frying pan or wide saucepan over medium-low heat. Add the shallot and gently fry for 2–3 minutes until soft but not coloured.

Stir in the flour away from the heat, then cook, stirring, for 1 minute. Reduce the heat to low and whisk in the stock and milk. Keep whisking until the sauce starts to bubble. Stir in the parsley and add the lemon juice, mustard powder, white pepper and a pinch of salt. Simmer very gently, stirring often, for 20 minutes.

While the sauce is simmering, cut the rind (but not the fat) off the gammon steaks. Slash the fat at 2-cm intervals. Brush the steaks with oil on both sides and season with black pepper but no salt. Heat a ridged frying pan or stovetop grill over high heat. Cook the steaks on one side for 5–6 minutes, reducing the heat once they start to colour. Turn and cook the other side for 5 minutes. Place on warm serving plates and pour the sauce over them.

Cook's note
• Curly parsley doesn't get much of a look-in these days but I think it is the right kind to use for parsley sauce.

unsmoked gammon steaks 4, 1.5–2cm thick, weighing about 200g each
rapeseed oil for brushing
freshly ground black pepper

for the parsley sauce
unsalted butter 25g
shallot 1, finely chopped
plain flour 3 tbsp
ham or **chicken stock** 200ml
whole milk organic, 200ml
curly parsley trimmed and chopped to make 2 tbsp
lemon juice a squeeze
mustard powder $1/2$ tsp
freshly ground white pepper
salt

Serves 4

Barley

Barley is one of the world's oldest grains, hugely adaptable to environment and used in the cuisines of countries as far afield as Scotland, Poland and Iran. Together with oats and spelt, it's a rich source of fibre, especially the cholesterol-lowering soluble type, and packed with vitamins and minerals.

In the kitchen, barley is a culinary multi-tasker though hugely under-rated. We think of it in terms of Scotch broth and homely stews, but tend to overlook its potential in more stylish dishes. Its lovely nutty flavour and pleasantly chewy texture work well in anything from risottos and salads to desserts and breads.

There are two main types of barley: pot and pearled. They are interchangeable in most dishes, so it is a matter of whether you prefer the juicy chewier grains of pot to the soft and swollen pearled.

Cooking

Barley couldn't be simpler to cook. Just rinse in water to get rid of surface starch then put in a saucepan with $2\frac{1}{2}$ cups of liquid to 1 cup of barley. Cover, bring to the boil, then simmer gently until tender and chewy but not mushy. Pearled barley takes 35–45 minutes, and pot barley 75 minutes or more, depending on the age of the grain.

I like to jazz up barley with robust ingredients as in **Barley with Celery, Preserved Lemon and Spices** (page 25). Also good are finely chopped chillies or fresh ginger root, fiery harissa sauce and oven-dried tomatoes. They all complement barley's natural sweetness, which, in turn, mellows the stronger flavours. Provided there is plenty of liquid, uncooked barley can be added to soups. It will provide body and thicken the liquid. Try it instead of spelt in **Celery and Dill Soup with Spelt** (page 63).

Another favourite is a **lamb and barley risotto**, or *orzotto* as it is correctly called in Italy. Heat 850ml good-quality chicken stock and keep it simmering in a small saucepan. Using a wide deep pan, fry 450g cubed boneless lamb or mutton in 2 tablespoons of rapeseed oil until brown. Remove from the pan and set aside. Next, soften 1 finely chopped onion in the same pan. Stir in 200g pearled barley and keep stirring until the grains are heated through and shiny. Sprinkle in 100ml white wine, stir until the liquid is absorbed, then add a ladle of stock. Keep stirring and adding small amounts of stock until it is all used up. Tip the lamb back into the pan and season with salt and black pepper. You can also throw in a handful of frozen peas if you like. Heat through, then cover and leave to stand for 3 minutes. Transfer to a warm serving dish and sprinkle with chopped mint or flat leaf parsley.

Barley is good in salads too. Toss cooked barley with **thinly sliced grilled duck breasts**, coarsely grated carrot, spring onions, toasted walnuts, orange zest and a tangy ginger dressing made by squeezing the juices from fresh ginger root into vinaigrette. Leave at room temperature for an hour before serving.

See also **Flour** (page 108)

Types of barley

Pot barley, Scotch barley: beige-coloured whole grains minimally processed to remove inedible husk. Superior to pearled barley in texture and flavour but needs lengthy soaking and cooking.

Pearled barley: whole grain barley polished to a pearly white. Needs no soaking. Can be cooked like rice or spelt.

Cracked barley or grits: whole grain or pearled barley that has been cut into smaller pieces.

Barley flakes: whole grain or pearled barley that has been steam-rolled and dried. Use like rolled oats as a hot cereal, or add to muesli or use in baking.

Shopping notes

• Buy packaged barley that is well within the 'use by' date.

• If buying loose barley, buy in quantities that you will use within a few months.

Storing

• Keep in an airtight container in a cool dark cupboard or in the fridge.

• Never mix a new batch with an old.

Preparation

• Rinse in several changes of water to get rid of dust.

• Soak pot barley for 3–4 hours before cooking.

Barley with Celery, Preserved Lemon and Spices

This is adapted from food writer Jenni Muir's erudite book *A Cook's Guide to Grains*. As Jenni says, preserved lemon and other bright-tasting aromatics lift homely barley and celery out of the ordinary.

Preheat the oven to 180°C/gas 4. Put all the ingredients in a casserole and stir to mix. Cover and bake for 1–1$\frac{1}{4}$ hours or until the barley is tender, and most, but not all, of the liquid has been absorbed – the dish should still be reasonably moist. Remove from the oven, fish out the herbs, and give the barley a quick stir before serving.

Cook's notes
• For a richer flavour and chewier texture use pot barley instead of pearled. The cooking time will be longer and you may need to add more stock.
• The stock and preserved lemon make this quite salty, so there's no need to add any salt.
• If you don't have any preserved lemon, use a little more lemon juice and add a pinch of salt.

hot vegetable or **chicken stock** 1 litre
pearled barley 175g, rinsed
celery stalks 3, destringed and thinly sliced crossways
preserved lemon 1, deseeded and finely chopped
lemon juice 1 tbsp
rapeseed oil 1$\frac{1}{2}$ tbsp
thyme 2 sprigs
fresh bay leaf 1
black peppercorns $\frac{1}{2}$–1 tsp, crushed
coriander seeds 1 tsp, crushed
garlic clove 1, crushed

Serves 4 as a side dish or 2–3 as a vegetarian main course

Beef

Buying beef direct from the farm gives you access to top-notch meat from pedigree provenance. If you are used to anything less, the sheer beefiness and succulence of meat from native British breeds is a revelation. All kinds of factors contribute to this: not just breed, but also rearing, grazing and the way the animal is slaughtered.

Rare breeds

When it comes to quality, breed is certainly a factor (see **Beef to look for**). Beloved of Americans are Aberdeen-Angus and Hereford, both renowned for their terrific eating quality, but there are many, many more. The Longhorn with its massive pitchfork horns was the breed that reputedly made English roast beef famous, and there is the sleek White Park, knighted 'Sir Loin' by King James I in honour of the meat. The Rare Breeds Survival Trust (see **Resources**, page 284–286), guardian of pure-breed beef, also includes on its register Dexter, Devon, Galloway, Highland, Lincoln Red, Red Poll, Shorthorn, Sussex and Welsh Black. These breeds need a market for their meat if they are to survive. The more customers who seek it out, the greater the hope of the meat remaining on the culinary map.

Suckler herds

The best beef comes from suckler herds that are raised purely for beef production. The herds have high standards of welfare and, unlike dairy-cross cows, are completely traceable. They are allowed to grow at a slower rate, grazing mainly or entirely on grass and natural forage such as herbs, seed heads, wild flowers, even seaweed, which produces flavoursome meat with soft yellow fat. Some of the sturdier breeds are hardy enough to winter out of doors – Longhorns and certain Scottish breeds, for example. They build up an insulating marbling of fat within the muscle, which in turn gives the meat a superior flavour. Beef from warmer regions is usually leaner and lighter in flavour.

Slaughter and butchery

Regardless of pedigree and provenance, beef will not be at its best unless the animal has been humanely treated at slaughter; meat from a frightened animal will be tough and dry. One farmer I know takes his Longhorns to the slaughterhouse and times the visit to avoid queues. His animals are quietly led in and go to a relatively peaceful death, as is evident in the quality of the meat. Proper hanging or maturing is also essential. Twenty one days or even longer is the norm for maximum tenderness and flavour to develop.

Farm shops with a dedicated butchery are likely to have a good choice of cuts available since they have a vested interest in getting rid of the whole animal. Cooked with care, a cheaper cut can be every bit as tasty as an expensive steak. The most hard-working parts of the animal – the leg, neck and shoulder – are the toughest, and need slow patient cooking to bring out their best. The most tender and therefore the priciest cuts come from the least-used muscles along the back – the fillet, loin and rib sections.

Beef to look for

'*Aberdeen Angus*', rich red flesh, well-marbled, excellent flavour.
'*Dexter*', rich dark flesh, high level of marbling, punchy flavour.
'*Galloway*', very dark flesh, light marbling, strong gamey flavour, melt-in-the-mouth texture.
'*Gloucester*', rich red close-grained flesh, chewy but tender.
'*Hereford*', rich red flesh, high level of marbling, great depth of flavour.
'*Lincoln Red*', well-marbled flesh when mature, excellent flavour.
'*Longhorn*', dark close-grained flesh, good marbling, rich flavour.
'*Red Poll*', rich red flesh, close-grained, well-marbled, tender.
'*Welsh Black*', brownish-red flesh, lean but with some marbling, rich beefy flavour.
'*White Park*', rich red flesh, chewy but tender, strong distinctive flavour.

Shopping notes

• Look for dark red meat – a sign that it has been properly hung. Meat that is pillar-box red or dripping with blood probably hasn't been hung long enough.
• Meat should be slightly moist but not wet. It should smell fresh or of nothing at all.
• External fat should feel firm and waxy to touch.
• Steaks and joints for roasting should have a visible marbling of fat. During cooking this will melt, basting and flavouring the meat as it does so.
• Choose a cut suitable for the dish:
Stewing: blade, brisket, chuck, shin, skirt.
Braising and pot roasting: brisket, silverside, topside.
Grilling and frying: steaks – rump, sirloin, T-bone, porterhouse, skirt or 'onglet'.
Roasting: fillet, fore rib, rolled sirloin.

Cooking

Of all the ways of cooking beef, roasting springs to mind first. For success, follow three all-important rules of thumb: first, for flavour choose a bone-in joint; second, give the meat a preliminary 20–30 minute sizzle at a high temperature; third, let it rest for at least 30 minutes after cooking to allow the juices that have come to the surface to flow back through the meat.

So, for a **rib roast** for 6–8 people you'll need a three-rib joint weighing about 2.7kg. Place it in a roasting tin, fat-side up, and massage well with rapeseed oil. Season all over with salt and black pepper and lightly dust the fat side with flour. Roast at 220°C/gas 7 for 30 minutes then reduce to 170°C/gas 3. Cook for a further 15 minutes per 500g for medium-rare. (Deduct 5 minutes per 500g for rare, or add 5 minutes per 500g for well-done.) Baste with the juices from time to time. Remove the meat from the oven and put it in on a warm platter or carving board. Loosely cover with foil and leave to rest for at least 30 minutes before you serve up. Meanwhile, cook your chosen vegetables. Finally, deglaze the roasting tin with stock, wine or vegetable cooking water, and stir in the juices that have flowed from the meat.

Steak

Though it's hard to beat a mighty roast, a perfectly cooked steak has to be one of life's treats. Choose from the cuts listed in **Shopping notes:** rump and sirloin are especially flavoursome and T-bone gives you a bone to gnaw as well as a good chunk of sirloin on one side and a smaller piece of fillet on the other. A porterhouse steak has an even bigger piece of fillet attached. On its own, I think fillet is a bit flavourless and soft, and needs a sauce to perk it up. Skirt steak is a little-known cut hanging from below the ribs of the animal. Loose-textured, chewy and full of flavour, it is the classic French bistro steak served with *frites*.

Steak is one of the simplest and quickest dishes to prepare, but it's also easy to mess up. Regardless of cut, the trick is temperature and timing. Make sure the meat has lost its chill when you start to cook (see **Preparation**). Pan-frying is the best way to cook an average 2cm-thick steak; grilling is more suitable for heftier cuts or those containing a bone. Have the pan (or grill) good and hot before you put in the meat. Lightly brush the meat on both sides with oil rather than putting oil in the pan. Season with salt and black pepper after anointing with oil. Don't cook too many steaks at once; the pan temperature will drop and the meat will stew rather than sizzle.

When you're ready to go, drop your prepared steak into the very hot pan or slide it under the preheated grill and time each side as follows: rare $2^1/_2$ minutes, medium-rare $3–3^1/_2$ minutes, medium 4 minutes, well-done 6 minutes. Allow an extra minute per side for thick T-bone and porterhouse steaks. Once cooked, leave the steak to rest for 5 minutes before serving.

Storing

• Store on the bottom shelf of the fridge so raw juices cannot drip onto other food.
• Remove wrapping and store in a shallow dish, loosely covered with foil. Large joints will keep for 5 days; steaks and small joints 2–3 days. Mince should be eaten within 24 hours.
• If vacuum-packed or in a rigid plastic container, leave unopened until ready to cook.

Preparation

• Remove from the fridge 1–2 hours before cooking. The meat will heat and brown more evenly if it starts off at room temperature.
• Rub salt into roasts and thick-cut steaks an hour before cooking to produce a beefier flavour.
• Snip the fat on steaks at intervals to stop it shrinking and curling.

Serving size

• Boneless: 250g serves 1.
• Bone-in: 375g serves 1.

Burgers

A home-made beefburger with a nicely charred crust and juicy interior is another meaty treat. Again, there are tricks of the trade. First, don't use ready-minced beef unless you can be sure of provenance and cut. Mince the meat yourself, or ask the butcher to do it. For succulence and flavour, choose a slightly fatty cut, not necessarily a pricy one. As long as they are trimmed of sinew, blade and brisket are fine, especially from a pedigree breed such as Galloway (see **Beef to look for**). Allow about 150–200g per burger.

Second, don't add garlic, onion, parsley or Worcestershire sauce; if the meat is top-notch you won't need to. Just gently shape it into rounds at least 2.5cm thick, lightly brush with oil and season the outside before frying. Start off with a hot pan before adding the meat. Once the burger is sizzling, don't be tempted to keep peeking underneath or press with a spatula (the latter squeezes out juices, and compacts the meat, the former stops a crust forming). For medium to medium-rare, cook for 4–5 minutes on one side then flip and cook for 2–3 minutes more. The exact time will depend on the thickness of the burger.

Braising and stewing

Though roasting and frying produce lip-smacking beef, don't miss out on moist cooking methods. Pot roasting (**Old-Fashioned Beef Pot Roast**, page 29) is just as good in its own way, producing full-bodied juices and moist, tender meat. Hearty stews and casseroles, such as *boeuf bourguignonne* or Hungarian goulash, are also delicious.

See also **Oxtail** (page 175), **Steak and Kidney Pie** (page 153)

Old-Fashioned Beef Pot Roast

It's worth using meat from a pure breed (see **Beef to look for**, page 26), even for a pot roast. The flavour will be outstandingly beefy and slow cooking in a covered pot will produce a succulent tender joint.

Dry the meat thoroughly, rub with sea salt flakes and make about twenty slits all over the surface with the tip of a knife. Poke garlic slices and rosemary leaves into the slits, using the knife tip to embed them. Leave to stand for 1 hour.

Preheat the oven to 140°C/gas 1. Heat a heavy-based casserole over medium-high heat. Add the rapeseed oil and when it is very hot, brown the meat on all sides, turning with tongs. Put the meat on a plate and reduce the heat to medium. Add the butter and gently fry the onion until soft and golden. Add the carrot and celery and fry until soft.

Put the meat back in the casserole with any juices that have accumulated. Pour in the wine and bubble briskly for a minute or two. Add the stock, thyme sprigs and bay leaf, and season with freshly ground black pepper. Bring to the boil, cover with a tight-fitting lid and put in the oven. Cook at a trembling simmer for 3–3$\frac{1}{2}$ hours, turning the meat every 30 minutes or so.

When the meat is very tender, lift it onto a warm dish and leave it to rest for 15 minutes, loosely covered with foil.

Blot up any fat from the braising liquid with paper towels and strain the liquid into a saucepan, pressing the vegetables hard with the back of a wooden spoon. Bring the strained liquid to the boil, adding any juices that have flowed from the meat. Let it reduce slightly, then check the seasoning.

Carve the meat diagonally and arrange in overlapping slices on a warm serving platter. Pour some of the sauce over the meat and serve the rest in a jug.

Cook's note
• The amount of stock depends on the diameter of the casserole. There should be enough liquid to come no more than one-third of the way up the meat.

rolled brisket or **silverside** 1.25kg
sea salt flakes
fat garlic cloves 2, thinly sliced
rosemary 1 sprig
rapeseed oil 2 tbsp
butter a knob
onion 1 small, finely chopped
carrot 1 medium, diced
celery 2 tender stalks, diced
red wine 250ml, such as Côtes du Rhone
meat stock, preferably home-made, 300–425ml
thyme 2 sprigs
fresh bay leaf 1
freshly ground black pepper

Serves 4

Herb-Crusted Barbecued Fillet of Beef

This is an expensive treat that will elicit cries of euphoria – succulent beef fillet with a dark brown crust and rosy pink interior, scented with herbs and fragrant smoke from the barbecue.

Place the meat in a shallow dish and massage with the olive oil. Sprinkle with the sea salt, black pepper and herbs, rubbing them in with your fingertips. Cover and leave to marinate in the fridge for 2 hours. Bring the meat to room temperature at least 1 hour before you want to cook it.

Light the barbecue and wait until the coals are covered with a film of ash (about 40 minutes). The fire is ready when you can hold your hand over the coals and count slowly to 5 before you have to remove it. Push some of the coals to one side to make a slightly cooler coal-free zone. Brush the grate with oil.

Place the meat on the grate and cook, giving it a quarter turn every 2 minutes, until brown and crusty on the outside. Move to the cooler part of the fire and cover with the lid. Cook for 16–18 minutes for rare, or 20–25 minutes for medium-rare.

Move the meat onto a board, loosely tent with foil and leave for 15 minutes. Carve diagonally into 1-cm thick slices, and serve with the juices and accompaniments.

Cook's notes
• Make sure your piece of meat is an even thickness along the entire length.
• It's best to check the internal temperature of the middle of the meat with an instant-read thermometer. It should register 50°C for rare, and 60°C for medium-rare.
• If your barbecue doesn't have a lid, use a large upturned roasting tin instead.

whole beef tenderloin 1, weighing about 900g
olive oil 1 tbsp plus extra for brushing
sea salt flakes $\frac{1}{2}$ tbsp
coarsely ground black pepper 1 tsp
mixed herbs (rosemary, oregano, thyme, flat leaf parsley) chopped to make 4 tbsp

to serve
English mustard or **horseradish**
green salad
new potatoes

Serves 4

Beetroot

Beetroot must be one of the most under-rated of vegetables, and it deserves better. It's packed with health-promoting vitamins and minerals, it has a rich earthy flavour, it's easy to cook and it comes in glorious colours – the familiar garnet red and also golden yellow, albino white and stunning pink and white stripes.

Farm shops usually sell beetroot in bunches with the leaves still attached. It remains a mystery why so many other shops sell it pre-cooked, vacuum-packed and, worse still, drowned in malt vinegar. It's so easy to cook at home and tastes so much better that way.

Cooking

My favourite way with beetroot is to bake it in a **foil parcel with herbs and olive oil**, either in the oven or on the barbecue. The bulbs cook in their own steam, producing wonderful concentrated flavours and fragrant oily juices. Scrub well and chop off all but a short length of stalk and root. Toss the bulbs in olive oil and place one or two on a square of thick foil. Add a thyme sprig, sea salt flakes and freshly ground black pepper. If you like a touch of heat, add a pinch of dried chilli flakes too. Wrap loosely but seal well, and bake at 190°C/Gas 5 for about 1 hour, depending on size. The beets are ready when you can pierce the parcel with a skewer.

Beetroot marries well with Eastern European and Scandinavian flavours – think buttermilk and soured cream, and 'northern' herbs such as caraway, dill and juniper. Creamy borscht, the national dish of Ukraine, is the quintessential beetroot soup. Less well known is Polish **chlodnik**, a beautiful pink and green chilled soup that I like to serve with bowls of plump prawns and hunks of dark rye bread. Lightly steam 3 small finely diced beetroot and their sliced leaves until just tender. Cool and mix with 450ml chilled and defatted chicken or vegetable stock, 150ml buttermilk, a chunk of deseeded and diced cucumber, 4 chopped spring onions, 2–3 tablespoons each of chopped dill and chives, 1 tablespoon of lemon juice, and some salt and black pepper. Chill for at least 3 hours. Garnish with thinly sliced radishes and slices of lemon. Serve as is or with prawns and bread.

Salty, pungent or bitter flavours are good with beetroot too. Combined with horseradish, it makes a stunning fuchsia-red relish **Horseradish and Beetroot Relish** (page 142) that is excellent with fatty smoked fish such as eel or mackerel. Alternatively, try it raw and coarsely grated in a salad with walnuts, crumbled goat's cheese and slightly bitter leaves such as chicory and radicchio.

UK season
• June–November.

Varieties to look for
• *'Boltardy'*, early variety, deep red, sweet and mildly earthy flavour.
• *'Burpee's Golden'*, glowing golden roots, great flavour.
• *'Chioggia'*, light red skin with pink and white-ringed flesh. Best eaten raw, colour fades when cooked.

Shopping notes
• Look for small-to-medium beets with leaves attached. Small beets are sweeter; large ones can be fibrous.
• Flesh should be firm rather than flabby, and free from blemishes and bruises.

Storing
• Keep unwashed bulbs loosely wrapped in a paper bag in the fridge for up to 1 week.
• Remove the leaves before storing, leaving a short length of stem attached. Leave the whiskery roots intact.

Preparation
• Wash the bulbs just before cooking, taking care not to damage the skin.
• To prevent staining cook whole and unpeeled. The skin slips off easily once cooked.

Colourful Beets with Roasted Shallot and Chilli Dressing

Slice the bulbs lengthways to give them a more stylish profile.
The dressing is pungent and goes well with the sweet young beetroot
and slightly bitter leaves.

Preheat the oven to 220°C/gas 7. Trim all but 1cm of stalk from the
beetroots and any very long roots. Plunge into a large saucepan of
boiling water, bring back to the boil, then simmer briskly for about
30 minutes or until just tender. Drain and leave to cool slightly.

While the beetroots are cooking, make the dressing: wrap each
shallot in foil, place in a small roasting tin and roast in the oven for
15 minutes. Add the chillies and roast for another 10–15 minutes or
until the shallots feel soft and the chillies start to blacken.

Peel the shallots, roughly chop the flesh and put in a blender.
Remove the skin and seeds from the chillies. Roughly chop the flesh of
one of them and add this to the blender together with the lemon juice,
olive oil and seasoning. Whizz until thick and smooth, then set aside.
Slice the remaining chilli into very small neat squares.

When the beetroots are cool enough to handle, slip off their skins
leaving the stalk in place. Take care not to damage the flesh. Slice in
half lengthways using a sharp knife.

Arrange the salad leaves on a serving plate with the sliced beetroots
on top. Sprinkle with sea salt flakes, a grinding of black pepper and the
reserved chopped chilli. Spoon the dressing over the top.

Cook's notes
- Use dark red beetroots if you can't find other colours.
- If you don't have banana shallots use 4 small shallots instead.

yellow, white, pink and red beetroots
12, no more than 4cm in diameter
**young dandelion leaves, New Zealand
spinach** or **rocket** 4 small handfuls
sea salt flakes
coarsely ground black pepper

for the dressing
banana shallots 2, unpeeled
mild green chillies such as New Mexican or
Anaheim, 2
lemon juice of $^1/_2$
extra-virgin olive oil 8 tbsp
sea salt flakes
freshly ground black pepper

Serves 4 as a starter

Bison and Buffalo

Farms shops are increasingly turning to speciality meats such as bison and buffalo. Although the terms are used interchangeably, 'bison' refers to the gigantic American bison (*Bison bison*) with its trademark hump, and 'buffalo' is the correct term for the longer-horned domesticated Asian water buffalo (*Bubalus bubalis*).

Grazing almost entirely on grass and natural forage, these hefty beasts tick all the right boxes for provenance and health. They are genetically pure species totally free from BSE and they thrive without growth promoters and unnecessary use of antibiotics. The lean and tender meat is significantly higher in protein and valuable minerals, and lower in saturated fat than almost any other red meat.

Water buffalo are valued for their milk as well. UK buffalo farms produce mozzarella to equal the best of Italian. They also sell hard cheeses, ice creams, naturally thick yogurt and calcium-rich pasteurised milk for drinking (see **Resources**, page 284–286).

Cooking

The rich dark meat is best cooked in a way that reflects its campfire origins – simple grills and roasts are ideal. Most beef recipes are suitable, though there are a few basic changes. Being ultra-lean, bison and buffalo meat doesn't sizzle in the same way as a juicy joint of beef or steak. If cooked at a high temperature, it tends to scorch or dry out. When roasting, skip the high-heat start and roast at a steady 170°C/gas 3. Grill or fry at a slightly lower temperature and for a shorter time. Always baste well, particularly when frying.

The meat should be cooked rare to medium-rare. If well-done, it will be dry, chewy and lacking in flavour. There is no internal marbling of fat to keep it juicy, so treat steaks like beef fillet and preferably serve with a sauce.

For a gustatory treat, try **bison au poivre**. The soft texture and full-bodied juices of the meat, the heat and crunch of peppercorns and the richness of cognac-spiked cream amount to culinary euphoria. Rub two 2.5-cm thick steaks with olive oil, sea salt flakes and $1\frac{1}{2}$ tablespoons of mixed black and white peppercorns. Leave at room temperature for 1 hour, turning once. Brush a heavy-based frying pan with a film of oil and place over medium-high heat. Drop in the steaks and cook for $1\frac{1}{2}$–2 minutes a side for rare, and $2\frac{1}{2}$–3 minutes for medium-rare. Remove from the pan and leave to rest in a warm place for 5 minutes. To make the sauce, sizzle a knob of butter in the same pan, scraping up any sediment. Add a generous splash of cognac and set it alight. Once the flames have died down, swirl in the best part of a small pot of whipping cream and any juices from the meat. Bubble until thickened, then pour over the steaks.

Shopping notes

• Bison and buffalo come in cuts similar to beef (page 26).
• The meat is expensive but with its intense rich flavour a little goes a long way.

Storing

• Store on the bottom shelf of the fridge so raw juices cannot drip onto other food.
• Remove wrapping and store in a shallow dish, loosely covered with foil. Large joints will keep for 5 days; steaks and chops 2–3 days. Mince should be eaten within 24 hours.
• If vacuum-packed or in a rigid plastic container, leave unopened until ready to cook.

Preparation

• Remove from the fridge 1–2 hours before cooking. The meat will heat and brown more evenly if it starts off at room temperature.
• Rub salt into roasts and thick-cut steaks an hour before cooking to produce a meatier flavour.

Serving size

• Boneless: 250g serves 1.
• Bone-in: 375g serves 1.

Blackberries

Whether cultivated or wild, blackberries are one of a dwindling number of truly seasonal fruits; they tell me that summer is on its way out and autumn awaits. Like all soft fruit, blackberries are best eaten on the day you buy or pick them. If you don't have access to blackberry-laden hedgerows, you can find them freshly harvested at PYO farms. There may even be thorn-free varieties to make picking your own easier (see **Varieties to look for**).

Cooking

Blackberries are exquisite just as they are, perhaps with a dusting of sugar or a spoonful of cream. They also go hand-in-hand with apples in pies and tarts – the one adding colour, the other substance, both adding balanced sweetness and acidity. A handful or two are delicious stirred into rice pudding or tucked between slices of bread in bread and butter pudding. They also go well with dairy foods and eggs – try them laced with *eau-de-vie* in a batter pudding (**Blackberry Batter Pudding with Eau-de-Vie**, page 36) or swirl them into cream to make a beautiful lavender-coloured fool.

For a **richly coloured sauce** to serve with pancakes or ice cream, simmer a saucepan of blackberries with sugar (about 100g for every 400g blackberries) for 15 minutes until soft and thickened. Whizz to a purée in a food processor and push through a fine sieve if you want to get rid of the seeds.

Blackberries are good in savoury dishes too. I like them stuffed into the cavity of roasted game birds, particularly **grouse** (page 130) – they offset the richness of the meat and tint the gravy a magnificent royal purple. They also look very stylish floated in a glass of chilled prosecco.

UK season
• Late July–early October.

Varieties to look for
• *'Helen'*, thorn-free early variety with long conical fruits. Good all-round flavour.
• *'Kotata'*, thorn-free variety with long glossy fruits. Outstanding flavour.

Shopping notes
• If buying in punnets look for plump, dry, dark berries that are fairly firm.
• Check the base of the punnet for signs of mushy fruit.

Storing
• Avoid storing in the fridge if possible – the chill dulls the flavour. If kept cool and dry blackberries should last for a day or two.

Preparation
• Briefly dunk in cold water to get rid of dust and insects.
• Drain well and dry thoroughly on paper towels.

Blackberry Batter Pudding with Eau-de-Vie

This is an easy-to-make boozy pudding based on a Russian recipe. The berries are soused with *eau-de-vie* – a colourless spirit distilled from fruit. Larger farm shops often have an interesting selection of artisan fruit liqueurs that would be perfect for this recipe.

Preheat the oven to 150°C/gas 2. Put the berries in a shallow baking dish and sprinkle with the liqueur, if using, and 2 tablespoons of the sugar. Bake for 20–30 minutes until the berries are thoroughly heated through.

Meanwhile, beat the eggs and the remaining 1 tablespoon of sugar until pale and creamy. Fold in the flour and soured cream. Pour the mixture over the berries and return the dish to the oven.

Bake for 45–50 minutes until pale golden and firm to touch. Sprinkle with a little more sugar before serving.

Cook's note
• If you can't find blackberry *eau-de-vie*, use Kirsch or another fruit liqueur.

blackberries 450g
blackberry *eau-de-vie* 1–2 tbsp (optional)
caster sugar 3 tbsp, plus extra for sprinkling
eggs organic, 2 large
plain flour 1 tbsp
soured cream 300ml

Serves 4–6

Blackcurrants

Just the smell and feel of blackcurrants epitomise for me the quintessential summer fruit. Sun-warmed, plump and inky-black, they are superb when freshly picked and minimally packaged – farm shops or PYO farms are the best source. The season is tantalisingly short and needs to be relished, though it is not necessarily met with the same enthusiasm that we have for other summer fruits. Perhaps there are too many associations with Ribena or cough sweets rather than glorious summer puds.

Cooking

The flavour of blackcurrants is so fiercely concentrated that they must be cooked with a copious amount of sugar to make them edible. Regardless of sugar, I still find them too acidic to use alone in pies and tarts, preferring them mixed with apples or pears. Used in moderation, blackcurrants marry well with other soft fruits in summer pudding (see **Raspberries**, page 220).

The strident flavour is soothed by the rich softness of cream – think mousses and fools, or try gorgeous purple **Blackcurrant and Mint Ice Cream** (page 39). Alternatively, make a richly coloured **sweet-sharp sauce** for spooning over chilled desserts such as panna cotta. Put 300g blackcurrants and 100g sugar in a small saucepan with a splash of water and bring to the boil. Simmer for 5 minutes until the currants are split and the juices flowing. Serve as is if you like solid bits, or purée and push through a sieve.

Blackcurrants are well suited to jellies – both shimmering and wobbly (**Grown-Up Blackcurrant Jelly with Cassis**, page 39), or for spreading thickly on toast. They also make good partners to game and duck. Try them in a superb **savoury sauce** blended with pan juices from the meat. Reduce 5 tablespoons of red wine vinegar and a spoonful of red- or blackcurrant jelly to a glaze. Stir in 250ml strong home-made stock, 300g blackcurrants, 2 teaspoons of sugar, and a little salt and black pepper. Simmer for a few minutes, adding any pan juices from the meat. Push through a sieve into a clean saucepan. Add a spoonful or two of the debris to give texture to the finished sauce. Reheat gently, swirl in a knob of butter and check the seasoning.

UK season
• June–August.

Varieties to look for
• *'Pixley Black'*, plump currants, superior flavour.

Shopping notes
• Look for plump dry currants without any traces of mould.
• Check the base of the punnet for signs of seepage from mushy fruit.

Storing
• Like all soft fruit, blackcurrants are best eaten on the day you buy them.
• The currants are prone to mould so make sure they are kept dry.
• Avoid storing in the fridge as the chill dulls the flavour.

Preparation
• Leave the currants attached to the strings until ready to cook.
• Briefly dunk in cold water to get rid of dust and insects. Drain well and dry on paper towels.
• Use the tines of a fork to strip the currants from the strings.
• There is no need to remove the dry brown tips – just sieve them after cooking.

Grown-Up Blackcurrant Jelly with Cassis

Grown-Up Blackcurrant Jelly with Cassis

A very intense jelly that encapsulates the essence of blackcurrants.

Heat the blackcurrants and sugar in a saucepan over medium-low heat, stirring, until the juices start to flow. Purée in a blender then push through a fine sieve to get rid of the pips. Add the cassis and enough water to make the mixture up to 900ml.

Put 6 tablespoons of water in a small bowl and sprinkle the gelatine over the surface. Leave for 10 minutes until spongy, then heat over a pan of hot water until completely dissolved.

Add the dissolved gelatine to the blackcurrant mixture, mixing thoroughly. Pour into a large wetted mould, or individual moulds, then cover with cling film and chill for several hours until set.

To turn out, run the tip of a knife round the edge of the mould. Invert over a plate – the jelly should slide out in one piece. Decorate with sprays of redcurrants and serve with softly whipped cream.

Cook's note
• If the jelly is reluctant to leave the mould, dip into hot water for a few seconds, or cover with a tea towel wrung out in hot water.

blackcurrants 450g, (see **Preparation**)
caster sugar 175g
cassis 1–2 tbsp
powdered gelatine 2 tbsp
redcurrants to decorate
whipped Jersey cream organic, to serve

Serves 6

Blackcurrant and Mint Ice Cream

This is so easy to make – just cream and blackcurrants. The flavour is stunning, as is the colour.

Put the blackcurrants in a saucepan with 3 tablespoons of the sugar – no need to add any water as there will be enough clinging to the fruit after rinsing. Cook over medium heat for a few minutes or until the currants collapse. Tip the mixture into a bowl.

Stir in the mint, lemon juice and the rest of the sugar. Press with a potato masher to break up the currants. Leave until cold then chill in the fridge for at least 1 hour.

Lightly whip the cream to the soft peak stage. Fold into the blackcurrant mixture. Churn and freeze in an ice cream machine. Once thickened, store in the freezer to harden.

Cook's notes
• If you prefer your ice cream without any pips and bits of skin, push the cooked currants through a fine sieve, pressing hard with the back of a wooden spoon to extract maximum pulp.
• If you don't have an ice cream machine, follow the directions for still-freezing Quince and Ginger Sorbet (page 213)

blackcurrants 250g (see **Preparation**)
sugar 140g
mint finely chopped to make 6 tbsp
lemon juice of ½
whipping cream organic, 250ml

Makes about 700ml

Black Pudding

Black pudding is a heavy-duty sausage made with boiled pig's blood, bound with cereal and encased in a length of intestine, similar to the French *boudin noir* or Spanish *morcilla*. What these sausages have in common besides the blood is that they all evolved from a commendable need to use every single bit of the pig once it was butchered.

Black pudding has undergone a renaissance in recent years, cropping up on smart restaurant menus all over the country. It varies from region to region and butcher to butcher. Depending on the mix, it can be spicy or mild, coarse or fine. Black pudding has always been popular in the north of England – particularly Lancashire where the food markets and farm shops are the place for the connoisseur. Black pudding is also popular in Scotland and Ireland.

Cooking

A good black pudding is coarse-textured and studded with nice big pieces of fat. Once sliced and in the pan, the fat melts and the filling tends to disintegrate. The trick to keeping the pudding intact is to slice it thickly (about 2cm), use a hot pan, preferably non-stick, and allow enough time for a crust to build on the underside before you fry the other side. Once the second side is crusty, quickly remove the slices from the pan before the filling dries out.

For a splendid Sunday brunch it's hard to beat crusty chunks of black pudding with **buttery scrambled eggs and chives**; the flavours are as stunning as the colours. For two people you will need 225g thickly sliced black pudding and 4 eggs. Fry the pudding as above without adding any oil – the fat will soon start to flow. Allow about 2 minutes a side over medium heat, then blot on paper towels and keep warm while you scramble the eggs.

Black pudding is also good fried with a few slices of apple or pear and some cream swirled in (**Black Pudding with Caramelised Apple, Sage and Cider**, page 42). With a handful of robust leaves, it makes a wonderful autumn salad – try adding a few fried slices to the **Warm Duck Breast Salad** (page 94) or to **Warm Salad of Pheasant Breasts with Wet Walnuts and Bacon** (page 189). With the casing removed, black pudding can be crumbled into a risotto or added to a bean-based stew.

Shopping notes
• Look for coarse-textured pudding studded with nuggets of fat.
• Check that it is well within the 'use by' date.

Storing
• Keep loosely wrapped in the fridge for up to 2 weeks, depending on the 'use by' date.

Preparation
• Black pudding is already cooked but is best reheated.

Black Pudding with Caramelised Apple, Sage and Cider (page 42)

Black Pudding with Caramelised Apple, Sage and Cider

This is a gorgeous combination of flavours – sweet buttery apples and slightly spicy black pudding swirled with cider and cream.

Heat one-third of the butter in a heavy-based frying pan. Fry the apple segments over medium-low heat, turning, until golden. Remove from the pan and keep warm.

Add another third of the butter to the pan, turn the heat to medium and fry the black pudding slices for about 3 minutes a side, turning them carefully so that they don't disintegrate. Set aside and keep warm.

Wipe out the pan with paper towels. Soften the shallot and sage leaves in the remaining butter for 3–4 minutes.

Pour in the stock and cider, then raise the heat and simmer briskly until reduced by half. Season with sea salt flakes and plenty of freshly ground black pepper. Add the cream and bubble for another minute, then return the apple slices to the pan. Sprinkle with the parsley and serve with the black pudding slices.

unsalted butter 50g
dessert apples 2, peeled, cored and cut into 8 segments
black pudding 4 thick slices
shallot 1, chopped
sage leaves 4, shredded
chicken stock 50ml
organic dry cider 50ml
sea salt flakes
freshly ground black pepper
single cream organic, 4 tbsp
flat leaf parsley leaves chopped to make 1 tbsp

Serves 2 as a light meal

Blueberries

Originally a wild fruit from the woodlands of North America and Canada, blueberry plantations have been thriving in the UK since the 1950s and there are now a number of specialist farms dotted around Dorset and East Anglia. These are the place to go for huge bags of berries rather than expensive little punnets. You can pick as many as you can carry, sample different varieties and they'll be cheaper too.

Cooking

A bowl of sweet and tangy blueberries sprinkled with sugar and served with thick cream has to be the most exquisite of desserts. They are also delicious scattered over breakfast yogurt or muesli, or added to a stylish **Compôte of Dark Fruits in Spiced Syrup** (page 196) or **summer pudding** (**Raspberries**, page 220). They look stunning suspended in a sparkling jelly made with dilute elderflower cordial instead of water.

Blueberries tend to lose flavour when cooked but the juice that bursts forth adds glorious colour to chilled desserts, tarts and cakes. Try them in the scrumptious **Blueberry Muffins** (page 45), or for a technicolour dessert, serve scoops of **Blueberry Sorbet** (page 45) with **Fresh and Dried Strawberry Sorbet** (page 249).

Sharpened with lemon, blueberries make a versatile **sauce for ice cream or cheesecake**. Put 450g plump blueberries in a saucepan with 100g sugar and 1 teaspoon of finely grated lemon zest. Stir over medium heat until the blueberries start to soften and produce juice. Mix 2 teaspoons of cornflour and the strained juice of a lemon to a smooth paste. Stir this into the blueberry mixture and bring to the boil. Simmer for a few minutes, stirring, until thickened. Once cool, the sauce can be kept in the fridge for a few days until needed.

UK season
• July–September.

Varieties to look for
• *'Brigitta'*, large light blue berries that keep well. Sweet, slightly tart flavour.
• *'Legacy'*, medium-to-large light blue berries. One of the best-flavoured varieties.
• *'Northblue'*, plump navy-blue berries that keep well. Sweet flavour.
• *'Patriot'*, very large medium blue berries. Outstanding flavour.

Shopping notes
• If buying in punnets, look for firm plump berries with a healthy bloom and no whiskers of mould.
• Check the base of the punnet for signs of seepage from mushy fruit.

Storing
• Store unwashed in the fridge for 4–5 days.

Preparation
• Wash only when ready to eat. Drain well and pat dry with paper towels.

Blueberry Muffins

Blueberry Muffins

There is nothing like baking blueberry muffins to make one feel that all is well with the world. Soft, moist and oozing with purple juice, they are the culinary equivalent of a comfort blanket.

Preheat the oven to 200°C/gas 6. Place twelve paper muffin cases in a 12-cup muffin tray.

Sift the flour, baking powder and salt into a large bowl. Beat the butter and sugar together until fluffy. Gradually beat in the eggs, vanilla extract and orange zest. Beat in the milk and the flour mixture a little at a time, then fold in the blueberries.

Divide the batter evenly among the muffin cases. Bake for about 20 minutes or until risen and golden, and a skewer inserted into the centre comes out clean. Place on a wire rack and leave to cool.

Cook's note
• The amount of sugar used here is quite low – the blueberries provide quite a bit of sweetness. If you would like a definite sweet flavour, increase the sugar to 125g.

plain flour 250g
baking powder $2\frac{1}{2}$ tsp
salt $\frac{1}{2}$ tsp
unsalted butter 115g
caster sugar 100g
eggs organic, 2, lightly beaten
vanilla extract 1 tsp
orange finely grated zest of 1
whole milk organic, 250ml
blueberries 200g

Makes 12

Blueberry Sorbet

Blueberries have a stunning colour and are packed with nutrients, but the flavour is sometimes bland. For this sorbet you need top-notch berries with a bit of oomph.

Put the sugar and water in a saucepan. Stir over medium heat until the sugar has dissolved. Bring to the boil briefly, then remove from the heat and leave to cool.

Put all but 100g of the blueberries in a food processor with the cold syrup, the lemon juice and a pinch of salt. Whizz thoroughly until smooth. Push through a fine sieve to get rid of pips and skin (optional).

Lightly crush the reserved blueberries and stir into the mixture. Cover and chill for at least 2 hours.

Churn and freeze in an ice cream machine. Once thickened, store in the freezer to harden.

Cook's notes
• It may seem odd to season a sweet dish with salt, but it rounds out and accentuates the flavours just as it does in savoury dishes.
• If you don't have an ice cream machine, follow the directions for still-freezing Quince and Ginger Sorbet (page 213).

sugar 115g
water 4 tbsp
blueberries 550g
lemon juice 2 tbsp
salt a pinch

Makes about 900ml

Broad Beans

Though I admit to a liking for frozen broad beans, there is nothing quite like the first fresh pods of early summer for putting a spring in a cook's step. Farm shops are usually quick off the mark with an early June crop. Make the most of this – the beans are sweet and tender, at their freshest and best. As the season wears on, flavour and texture gradually change, eventually culminating in mealy monsters with bulbous pods.

Cooking

If there is a drawback to broad beans it is the disappointingly small yield per pod: 2kg unpodded beans produces a mere 450g beans – enough for 4. There is also the fiddly but necessary task of removing the skin surrounding the bean itself (see **Preparation**).

If the beans are very young and tender – no bigger than your little finger – you can skip the preparation and cook them Middle Eastern-style, steamed whole for about 5 minutes. Eat them, pods and all, tossed in melted butter or olive oil, or try the recipe on page 48.

Larger specimens, no more than 18–20cm long, can be **grilled in their pods** over a barbecue or on a ridged frying pan or stovetop grill. The beans will be especially tasty since they will have steamed inside the pod. Brush the pods with oil, then spread them out in a single layer and grill for about 7 minutes, turning with tongs halfway through. Once the pods start to brown, open one up to check the state of the beans within – they should be just tender. Snip off one end and squeeze out the beans (you will need gloves to protect you). Discard the pods and serve the beans simply tossed with melted butter, sea salt flakes, snipped garlic chives or summer savory and wisps of lemon zest.

Podded young broad beans need no more than steaming or boiling for 2–3 minutes; larger ones will need 5–6 minutes. Serve them dressed and seasoned as above. They are perfect with **Gammon Steaks with Parsley Sauce** (page 23) alongside some plainly boiled potatoes. Or mix barely cooked beans with pasta shapes, olive oil, garlic, lemon zest, shaved Parmesan or pecorino, and a generous amount of chopped herbs. Another option is to simmer blanched beans in cream, black pepper and tarragon until the cream has slightly reduced and thickened. Briefly blanched broad beans with nuggets of sizzled bacon and chopped spring onions are also good.

Then there are the salads. Lightly cooked young beans tossed with crumbled feta cheese, inky-purple Kalamata olives and a dribble of grassy extra-virgin olive oil are worthy of a still-life painting. Equally beautiful, with different shades of green, is a **salad of broad beans**, shredded green cabbage, kohlrabi cut into matchsticks, shredded spring onions, chives and pumpkin seeds. Dress with extra-virgin sunflower oil and a few drops of lemon juice. Top with hard-boiled quail's eggs and you have a meal made in heaven.

UK season
• Mid–June–September.

Varieties to look for
• *'Green Windsor'*, stubby variety, deep green beans, good for freezing.
• *'Stereo'*, early season, very small white beans. Pods can be eaten when very young.
• *'The Sutton'*, heritage dwarf variety, fine-flavoured.

Shopping notes
• Choose smooth, even-shaped pods 12–15cm long.
• Very small pods, 5–6cm long, can be cooked and eaten like mangetout.

Storing
• Store loosely packed in a paper bag in the fridge for 2–3 days.
• Once podded, cook within 1 hour before the beans start to discolour.

Preparation
• Snap the pods open and remove the beans.
• Remove the leathery outer skin by nicking it with your fingernail and pinching one end. Otherwise plunge in boiling water for 2–3 minutes, rinse in cold water, then slip off the skins.

Warm Salad of Baby Broad Bean Pods, Grilled Cherry Tomatoes and Feta (page 48)

Broad Bean Bruschetta with Summer Savory and Goat's Cheese

You will need fingernail-sized beans for this. Get your guests to help with podding and skinning.

Steam the beans or cook in boiling salted water for 3 minutes until just tender. Drain, sluice under cold running water, then slip off the skins.

Toss the denuded beans with the olive oil, lemon juice, most of the summer savory, and a little sea salt and freshly ground black pepper. Whizz briefly to a chunky purée in a blender or food processor.

Toast the bread on both sides, preferably under the grill for a crisper result. While still warm, rub one side with the cut garlic clove and drizzle with olive oil. Cut each slice in half, then spread the bean mixture over the top. Add a small dollop of goat's cheese and sprinkle with more sea salt and the rest of the summer savory.

podded small broad beans 400g (about 1.7kg in their pods)
extra-virgin olive oil 2 tbsp, plus extra for the bread
lemon juice 2 tsp
summer savory finely chopped to make 2 tsp
sea salt flakes
freshly ground black pepper
sourdough bread 4 thick slices from a small loaf
garlic clove 1, halved
fresh goat's cheese 4 tbsp

Serves 4 as a snack

Cook's notes
• Summer savory is the perfect herb for broad beans – the flavours really complement each other. It is grown as a companion plant to discourage black fly. Lemon thyme is a good substitute.
• Not to be confused with rinded goat's cheese, fresh soft goat's cheese is snowy white and easy to spread. It is widely available in farm shops but if you can't find any, use ricotta cheese instead.

Warm Salad of Baby Broad Bean Pods, Grilled Cherry Tomatoes and Feta

Make the most of the very first beans of the season. Barely emerged from the flowers, the pods are tender enough to eat and can be enjoyed just like French beans or runner beans. There will be more pod than bean but the flavour is delicious.

Preheat a ridged frying pan or stovetop grill. Grill the tomatoes for about 5 minutes or until slightly blackened, crushing them lightly with the back of a wooden spoon.

Meanwhile, steam the broad beans in their pods for 5–6 minutes until just tender. Tip into a bowl and toss with just enough olive oil to coat, the garlic chives and lemon zest.

Arrange on serving plates with the tomatoes. Sprinkle with feta cheese, crumbled sea salt flakes and coarsely ground black pepper. Serve right away while still warm.

cherry tomatoes 10
baby broad beans unpodded, 200g, flower stalks removed
extra-virgin olive oil
garlic chives roughly chopped to make 2 tsp
lemon zest $\frac{1}{2}$ tsp
feta cheese 40g, crumbled
sea salt flakes
coarsely ground black pepper

Serves 2 as a starter

Cook's note
• If you can't find garlic chives, which are broad and flat, use ordinary chives instead.

Brussels Sprouts

Brussels sprouts are divisive – you either love them or hate them. Those in the anti-camp no doubt have distressing memories of over-cooked monstrosities. Prepared and cooked with care, though, sprouts are a delightful vegetable. The colour is a beautiful green, the flavour satisfyingly meaty and very slightly sweet, and the texture just the right side of tender-crisp.

Farm shops are the place to find sprouts at their best – still attached to a length of stalk to keep them in tip-top condition. Sometimes there is a crown of leaves at the top of the stalk. These are perfectly edible, albeit slightly fibrous, and can be cooked just like cabbage.

Cooking

Brussels sprouts can be boiled, steamed, stir-fried or, better still, microwaved, which keeps them particularly crisp and bright green. Whichever method you choose, it's important not to overcook them or they will develop that all-too-familiar sulphurous flavour.

When you are boiling sprouts, or any other green vegetable, keep the pan uncovered otherwise acids in the steam will gather under the lid and drip onto the vegetables. This, in turn, changes the colour to an unappetising khaki. If you are steaming them you will of course need a lid, but it's a good idea to lift it every so often to allow the acid-laden steam to escape.

Traditionally, sprouts are cooked with chestnuts to serve with the Christmas turkey. I find this a rather stodgy combination and prefer the crunch of crisp buttery breadcrumbs and punchy flavours such as lemon or lime zest, green or white peppercorns, spring onions, coriander or ginger as in the recipes on page 50.

UK season
• October–March.

Varieties to look for
• *'Evesham Special'*, heirloom variety with good solid buttons.
• *'Noisette'*, heirloom variety with small buttons and a nutty flavour.
• *'Rubine'*, glamorous sprout with striking red buttons and foliage.

Shopping notes
• Look for firm, compact buttons with sprightly leaves and no yellowing or brown spots.
• Brussels sprouts should smell fresh without any whiff of sourness.
• If sold off the stalk, make sure the base isn't dried out or discoloured.

Storing
• Store in a paper bag in the fridge for no more than 2 days.

Preparation
• Trim the stem but not right up to the leaves or they will fall off during cooking.
• Don't bother making a cross-cut in the base; it is a myth that this speeds up cooking. All it does is allow water to penetrate further, making the sprouts soggy in the process.

Stir-fried Brussels Sprouts with Ginger, Chilli, Lime and Coriander

This will convert even the most entrenched sprout-hater. The seasonings really cut through the sprouty flavour, resulting in a clean-tasting spicy dish.

Briefly blanch the Brussels sprouts, either in boiling water or a steamer basket set over boiling water. Remove after 2 minutes, reserving the cooking water. Slice the sprouts vertically into quarters.

Heat a large frying pan over medium-high heat, then add the groundnut and sesame oils. Stir-fry the shallot, ginger, chilli and garlic for 3 minutes or until the garlic is just starting to colour.

Add the sprouts and a good splash of the reserved cooking water. Season with sea salt and freshly ground black pepper, then stir-fry for 2–3 minutes until the sprouts are just tender but still bright green. Stir in the lime juice and coriander, and cook for a few seconds more.

Brussels sprouts outer leaves and tough stalks trimmed, 450g
groundnut oil 2 tbsp
toasted sesame oil 1 tbsp
shallot 1, finely chopped
fresh ginger root 2-cm piece, finely chopped
green chilli $1/4$, deseeded and finely chopped
garlic clove 1, finely sliced
sea salt flakes
freshly ground black pepper
lime juice of $1/2$
coriander leaves sliced to make 2 tbsp

Serves 2 with noodles or rice as a vegetarian main course, or 4–6 as a side dish

Brussels Sprouts with Green Peppercorns, Lemon Zest, Chives and Golden Crumbs

Crunchy crumbs, zesty seasonings and an indecent amount of butter add much-needed interest to the homely sprout.

Resisting any temptation to cut crosses in their bases, plunge the sprouts into a large saucepan of boiling water, or steam in a basket set over boiling water, for 8–10 minutes. When the sprouts are just about tender, drain and set aside.

While the sprouts are cooking, heat a large heavy-based pan over medium heat. Add half the butter and, when it is sizzling, add the bread crumbs. Stir them around the pan for 3–4 minutes until golden and crisp. Season with a sprinkle of sea salt flakes and some freshly ground black pepper. Drain on paper towels and keep warm in a low oven.

Wipe out the pan and melt the remaining butter over medium heat. Add the garlic and green peppercorns. When the garlic is just beginning to colour, tip in the sprouts, raise the heat a little and sizzle until just beginning to brown at the edges. Sprinkle with lemon juice and stir in the chives. Tip into a warm dish and strew with hot buttery crumbs.

Brussels sprouts outer leaves and tough stalks trimmed, 450g
unsalted butter 80g
breadcrumbs (from a stale loaf) 40g
sea salt flakes
freshly ground black pepper
garlic clove 1, thinly sliced
dried green peppercorns $1/2$ tsp, lightly crushed
lemon juice a squeeze
chives snipped to make 2 tbsp

Serves 4 as a side dish

Cabbage

The most benevolent and sturdy of crops, cabbages offer a cornucopia of colours, texture and flavours, and health benefits besides. They come in a rich palette ranging from deep emerald greens and royal purples to the palest of creams. The leaves may be deeply blistered like the Savoy, or smoothly etched with veins like the January King. Flavours are equally diverse, ranging from the peppery lightness of Chinese cabbage to the full-on meatiness of the Savoy.

Cooking

In the hands of a loving cook, the cabbage can be a feast for a king. The rule of thumb is a short cooking time for crispness and colour, or very long cooking to bring out sweetness. It's a good idea to cook green cabbage uncovered, otherwise acids in the steam will gather under the lid and drip onto the leaves below, changing the colour to an unappetising khaki. If you are steaming cabbage you will of course need a lid, but it's a good idea to lift it every so often to allow the acid-laden steam to escape. When cooking red cabbage add a little lemon juice or vinegar to the cooking liquid to keep the colour bright.

As a nation, we are not very adventurous with cabbage. For inspiration we should look to France and Eastern Europe where slow-cooked dishes bring out cabbage's hidden sweetness, and to Asia where spices, soy sauce and the heat of the wok temper its forthright flavour.

For me there is no finer dish than steamed Hispi cabbage anointed with butter, a few wisps of lemon zest, chopped fresh dill or coriander and freshly ground white pepper (preferable to black in this case). It really hits the spot, especially when served with pork.

Robustly flavoured spring greens are excellent sliced and blanched, then added towards the end of cooking to a casserole of slow-cooked cannellini beans, tomatoes and spicy chorizo sausage. Otherwise toss them with softened onion and garlic and crisp croûtons fried in olive oil and dusted with brick-red pimenton – a type of Spanish paprika.

Slowly cooked with onion, apples and port, red cabbage is the classic accompaniment to roast goose or pork, or try it braised with partridge (**Partridge with Braised Red Cabbage, Apples and Juniper**, page 180). It's also good stir-fried, though it will need preliminary blanching to soften it. Fry with sliced onion and chopped hazelnuts or walnuts, then moisten with stock and a splash of cider vinegar. A few cranberries or pomegranate seeds add brilliant nuggets of colour.

I also like cabbage in salads. It adds bulk and texture and, unlike delicate leaves, is tamed rather than overwhelmed by a strong dressing. Red cabbage makes a feisty coleslaw (**Red Slaw with Radish Sprouts, Smoked Cheese and Lemon Yogurt Dressing**, page 53). Also good is coarsely shredded white cabbage marinated in cider vinegar, salt and sugar with chillies and red onion – it becomes tinged a beautiful pink from the onion. Once the cabbage has lost some of its bounce, add cooked waxy new potatoes and dress with extra-virgin sunflower oil, black pepper and chives.

UK season
- *Spring cabbage:* April–June.
- *Winter cabbage:* November–March.
- *Red Cabbage:* August–June.
- *Spring greens:* year-round.
- *White Cabbage:* year-round.

Varieties to look for
- *'January King'*, winter cabbage, deep-green leaves etched with pink or red veins, dense round heart. Rich flavour. Long slow cooking brings out sweetness. Use in a rustic soup or stew.
- *'Hispi'*, cone-shaped spring cabbage, loosely packed apple-green leaves. Sweet and tender, best lightly cooked or in salads and stir-fries.
- *'Savoy'*, blistered dark blue-green leaves. Full satisfying 'cabbage' flavour, slightly pungent and mustardy. Excellent stuffed or cooked slowly in soups and stews, otherwise lightly steamed or boiled. A good all-rounder.

Shopping notes
- Look for heads that feel heavy for their size without any limp or yellowing outer leaves.
- Don't buy cabbage that has been stripped of its outer leaves.
- Leaves should squeak when you rub them together.

Storing
- An uncut fresh cabbage will keep in a roomy plastic bag in the fridge for up to 1 week.
- Once cut, wrap the unused portion in cling film and store in the salad drawer of the fridge. Use within 1–2 days.

Preparation
- Use as many of the dark green outer leaves as possible. They are tasty and packed with nutrients.
- Cut away the tough stalks by slicing either side of the stalk up into the leaf.
- For wedges, quarter the head lengthways and cut out the core. To shred, slice the wedges crossways into thin ribbons.

White and Green Cabbage with Coconut, Chillies and Ginger

Based on a traditional recipe from Kerala in south-west India, this is a great way of livening up cabbage.

Put the spice paste ingredients in a blender or food processor. Add a splash of water to moisten, then whizz to a purée.

Heat a large, heavy-based frying pan over medium-high heat and add the vegetable oil. Fry the mustard seeds until they start to crackle, then add the curry leaves. Sizzle for a few seconds. Reduce the heat to medium, add the onion and fry until golden. Season with the crushed peppercorns, then stir in the spice paste, shredded cabbage and spring greens. Pour in the water, stirring well so the cabbages are covered with the paste.

Cover and cook over low heat for 7–10 minutes, stirring now and again to prevent sticking. When the cabbage and spring greens are tender, add the coconut flakes, coriander and lime juice. Stir for a minute or two to heat through.

vegetable oil 3 tbsp
mustard seeds 1 tsp
curry leaves fresh, frozen or dried, 15–20
small onion 1 or **banana shallots** 2, sliced
black peppercorns $^{1}/_{2}$ tsp, crushed
white cabbage $^{1}/_{4}$, core removed, leaves shredded
spring greens 200g, tough stalks removed, leaves shredded
water 100ml
toasted coconut flakes 4 tbsp
coriander leaves sliced to make 3 tbsp
lime juice of $^{1}/_{2}$

for the spice paste
creamed coconut 50g sachet, melted
green chilli 1, deseeded and roughly chopped
fresh ginger root 2.5-cm piece, chopped
garlic cloves 2, sliced
small onion 1 or **banana shallots** 2, finely chopped
salt $^{1}/_{2}$ tsp
cumin seeds 1 tsp
ground turmeric $^{1}/_{2}$ tsp

Serves 4–6 as a side dish

Red Slaw with Radish Sprouts, Smoked Cheese and Lemon Yogurt Dressing

Red cabbage has a peppery flavour that marries well with smoked cheese and pungent radish sprouts.

Quarter the cabbage, cut out the core and shred the leaves very finely. Halve the onion lengthways and slice into thin crescents. Quarter and core the apple (do not peel), then slice crossways into segments. Slice the carrots into very thin matchsticks.

Put the prepared vegetables and apple in a bowl and sprinkle with a squeeze of lemon juice and some crumbled sea salt flakes. Toss well, then leave for 30 minutes or until slightly softened. Drain off any liquid that may have accumulated. Stir in the dressing and scatter the cheese and radish sprouts over the top.

Cook's notes
• Look for Applewood Smoked or Westcombe Smoked Traditional Cheddar. The flavour is not overly strong since they are naturally smoked over oak chippings.
• If you prefer cheese that has not been smoked, use a crumbly white variety such as Lancashire or Gorwydd Caerphilly (page 68) or a blue one such as Buxton Blue or Dorset Blue Vinny (page 67).

Variation
• For a different colour scheme, use green cabbage, spring onions and a green-skinned apple. Use kohlrabi instead of carrot, and mustard and cress instead of radish sprouts.

Serves 4 as a light meal

red cabbage preferably organic, 1 small
red onion 1 small
red-skinned dessert apple 1
carrot 1 medium
lemon juice a squeeze
sea salt flakes
Lemon Yogurt Dressing (page 278)
smoked cheese 40g, cubed
(see **Cook's notes**)
radish sprouts a handful

Carrots

Carrots are one of the great root vegetables. Bite into one that has been recently dug and I guarantee you will be bowled over by its sheer fresh sweetness and 'carrotiness'. Organic carrots are even better; they really do seem to have the edge on non-organic carrots, and in taste trials they consistently come out top.

Carrots come in surprising shapes and sizes, and different colours: purple, yellow or white as well as regulation orange. The more unusual colours are rarely found in supermarkets but it's worth looking for them in farm shops. Raw or cooked, they look stunning on the plate.

Cooking

Carrots are background ingredients that make everything taste better. They enhance soups and stews, are essential in stock, and give flavour and moistness to carrot cake. They come into their own when cooked with ingredients that either blend or contrast with their natural sweetness, and in ways that concentrate the flavour. Try frying them in thin diagonally-cut slices as in **Sticky Carrots with Ginger Glaze** (page 55). The sugars caramelise beautifully, producing appetisingly crisp and blackened carrots. Roasting carrots in the oven, either around a joint of meat or mixed with other root vegetables, produces a similar effect.

Braising is another method that brings out the natural sweetness. Cook small whole carrots or sliced larger ones in a small amount of water with some butter, a pinch of sugar, and salt and black pepper. The water will eventually evaporate, leaving a rich syrupy glaze. Sharpen with a few drops of lemon juice, and, if you like, sprinkle with chopped mint or chives.

Moving from sweet to contrasting sour, grated raw carrots are wonderful in a **Middle Eastern salad** with a sharp lemony dressing. Coarsely grate about 450g young carrots, preferably organic, and stir in 3 tablespoons of chopped coriander or flat leaf parsley and a handful of toasted pine nuts. Make a dressing with the juice of a small lemon, 1 crushed garlic clove, $\frac{1}{2}$ teaspoon of crushed cumin seeds, a pinch of dried chilli flakes, some sea salt and freshly ground black pepper. Whisk in 3 tablespoons of rapeseed oil or extra-virgin sunflower oil. Pour over the carrots and toss well.

Crunchy little batons of carrot are good dipped into humus or guacamole. Carrots make a delicious dip themselves, lightly cooked and puréed with garlic, ginger, lemon juice, olive oil and seasonings. Blended with fresh orange juice and apple, they also make one of the most healthy and palatable juices – a great kick-start to the day.

UK season
• May–December.

Varieties to look for
• *'Chantenay Red'*, short stumpy carrot with good 'carroty' flavour.
• *'Nantes'*, cylindrical, blunt-ended, no core.
• *'Yellowstone'*, sunshine yellow, large and crunchy.

Shopping notes
• Buy unwashed carrots if possible (soil acts as a protective barrier), preferably stored in a paper sack to exclude light.
• Check that they are firm and not sprouting rootlets through the skin.
• Don't buy any that are green around the top or have soft brown bruises, cracks or small holes – a sign of pest invasion.

Storing
• Freshly picked carrots, loosely wrapped in a paper bag will keep in a cool airy place or the fridge for a week.
• Baby carrots should be used within 1–2 days.
• If you have bought carrots with leaves, remove them before storing. Leaves may give the impression of freshness, but they deprive the roots of moisture.

Preparation
• Carrots usually need peeling unless they are very young. Use a swivel peeler to shave away a paper-thin amount of skin.
• Large old carrots may have a tough woody core that no amount of cooking will soften. If you suspect this is the case, quarter the carrot lengthways and prize out the core.

Sticky Carrots with Ginger Glaze

This must be the best way of cooking carrots: fried in buttery ginger-infused juices until caramelised and tender-crisp. The flavour is intensely sweet, savoury and pungent all at the same time – lovely with venison or roast pork.

Peel the carrots and slice into diagonal-cut ovals about 5mm thick. Pound the chopped ginger root, peppercorns, sugar and sea salt flakes to a paste using a mortar and pestle. Toss the carrots in the paste, turning with your hands until evenly coated.

Heat a large non-stick frying pan over medium-high heat. Add the oil and butter and when sizzling nicely, toss in the carrots and any paste left in the bowl. Spread out the carrots in a single layer. Fry for $2\frac{1}{2}$ minutes then start turning them with tongs. Keep turning them, one by one, until they are all starting to colour at the edges.

Pour in the stock and swirl the carrots in it. Simmer for a few minutes until reduced to a syrupy glaze. Season with extra salt if necessary.

Cook's notes
• A 23–24-cm diameter pan will take the carrots in a single layer. If you don't have a pan this size, fry the carrots in batches, returning cooked carrots to the pan when you add the stock.
• Be vigilant towards the end of frying. You may need to turn down the heat a little.

carrots preferably organic, 4 large
ginger root 4-cm piece, finely chopped
black peppercorns $\frac{1}{2}$ tsp
sugar 1 tsp
sea salt flakes large pinch
rapeseed oil 2 tbsp
butter a large knob
chicken or vegetable stock 150ml

Serves 3 as a side dish

Cauliflower

Once a familiar staple, this iconic British vegetable is in danger of vanishing from our plates. Many farmers are abandoning it altogether as it is no longer an economically viable crop. The pressure from supermarkets to reduce the price is simply too much, and cauliflower is not the easiest of crops to grow.

I make no apologies for including more than the usual number of recipes here. We should make the most of this national treasure.

Cooking

Cauliflower comes in glorious colours – glowing purple, orange and acid green Romanesco with its curious spiralling curds. Although the colour fades a little during cooking, these flamboyant varieties are great in cauliflower cheese (**Green Cauliflower Cheese with Blue Vinny and Tomatoes**, page 57).

Cauliflower benefits from the rich flavours of dairy products and contrasting crisp textures. Try steamed florets fried in butter with garlic, breadcrumbs, lemon zest, and perhaps some lovage or thyme. Use plenty of butter and breadcrumbs, making sure both the cauliflower and breadcrumbs are golden, and season well with sea salt flakes and freshly ground black pepper.

A simple but delicious **warm vegetable salad** can be made with lightly steamed cauliflower and slim green beans, tossed with chopped hazelnuts, garlic chives, plenty of black pepper and a garlicky dressing – a delicious starter in its own right or an accompaniment for plainly grilled fish.

Cauliflower makes a great curry (**Cauliflower Coconut Curry**, page 57). The florets add substance and texture, while curry spices and tomatoes add appetising colour. It is also good cooked **Mediterranean-style**. Gently fry onions, garlic and tomatoes until well amalgamated, then pour the resulting sauce over a quartered steamed cauliflower. Add pitted black olives and a topping of breadcrumbs, olive oil, chopped flat leaf parsley and seasoning. Bake at 200°C/gas 7 until the topping is crisp.

Roasting really concentrates the flavour and avoids the institutional smell that sometimes pervades when cauliflower is boiled or steamed. Toss wedges of large Romanesco or white cauliflower in 4 tablespoons of olive oil and season with sea salt flakes and freshly ground pepper (preferably white). Spread out on a non-stick roasting tray, cover the tray with foil and roast at 240°C/gas 9 on the bottom shelf of the oven for 20–25 minutes. Remove the foil after 10 minutes, and flip the wedges after about 20 minutes once the bases are nicely browned. Sizzle some paper-thin slices of large garlic in olive oil with $\frac{1}{4}$ teaspoon of dried chilli flakes and a few chopped sage leaves, and pour this over the cauliflower before serving. Alternatively, sprinkle with lemon zest, chopped flat leaf parsley and shavings of Parmesan.

Cauliflower Coconut Curry

Cauliflower is excellent in curries, and larger farm shops usually have a selection of the necessary spices. Don't be put off by the list of ingredients – the curry is very easy to make and reheats well.

Cut the cauliflower into quarters and remove the tough stalk. Break the quarters into florets and steam for 8–10 minutes until barely tender. Slice each floret into small pieces.

Heat the rapeseed oil in a heavy-based casserole over medium-high heat. Add the mustard seeds and as soon as they start to crackle, add the cumin seeds and asafoetida, if using. Stir for a few seconds, then add the onion and chilli. Reduce the heat to medium and fry, stirring for 6–8 minutes, until the onion is golden.

Stir in the turmeric and garam masala. Fry for a few seconds then add the chopped tomatoes, stock, cauliflower and shredded greens. Season with the salt and black pepper and bring to the boil. Cover and simmer for 15 minutes until the cauliflower and greens are tender.

Stir in the coconut flakes and coriander just before serving.

Cook's notes

• Asafoetida is a strange-smelling powder that adds an onion-like flavour to vegetable dishes. You can sometimes find it in farm shops that stock Bart Spices products, otherwise it is easy to find in Indian food shops.

cauliflower 1 small, leaves removed
rapeseed oil 2 tbsp
mustard seeds 1 tsp
cumin seeds 1 tsp
asafoetida (optional) a pinch
onion 1, chopped
green chilli 1, deseeded and chopped
ground turmeric $^1/_2$ tsp
garam masala 1 tsp
chopped tomatoes 400g can
vegetable or **chicken stock** 200ml
spring greens or **cabbage leaves** 75g, shredded
salt $^1/_2$ tsp
freshly ground black pepper $^1/_4$ tsp
toasted coconut flakes a handful
coriander leaves chopped to make 3 tbsp

Serves 2 as a vegetarian main course or 4 as a side dish

Green Cauliflower Cheese with Blue Vinny and Tomatoes

Made with creamy Blue Vinny cheese and brilliant green Romanesco cauliflower, this is a colourful and tasty version of traditional cauliflower cheese.

Cut the Romanesco into quarters, discarding the tough stalks. Steam for 3 minutes until only just tender, and set aside. Preheat the oven to 180°C/gas 4.

Melt the butter in a saucepan over low heat. Sprinkle in the flour and cook, stirring, for about 2 minutes until very smooth. Heat the milk in a separate pan until it starts to bubble, then gradually whisk it into the flour mixture. Remove from the heat and stir in the mustard, seasoning, and Blue Vinny cheese. Stir until the cheese has melted.

Break the Romanesco quarters into smaller chunks, then put in a baking dish. Pour the sauce over, then arrange the spring onions and tomato slices on top. Sprinkle with the breadcrumbs, grated Parmesan and a little olive oil. Bake for 20 minutes or until golden and bubbling.

Romanesco cauliflowers 2 small, weighing about 800g in total
butter 60g, plus extra for the topping
plain flour 4 tbsp
whole Jersey milk organic, 600ml
Dijon mustard $^1/_2$ tsp
salt
freshly ground white pepper
Blue Vinny or **other mild blue cheese** 150g, coarsely grated
spring onions 4, finely sliced
tomatoes 6, sliced
breadcrumbs (from a day-old loaf) 50g
Parmesan cheese 25g, freshly grated
extra-virgin olive oil for sprinkling

Serves 4 as a vegetarian main course

Piccalilli

Cauliflower is a major ingredient in this classic mixed vegetable pickle, flavoured with mustard and turmeric. Unbeatable for perking up a ham sandwich or cold meats.

Remove the leaves and tough stalks from the cauliflower. Break the curds into small florets, then chop them roughly. Put them in a non-reactive bowl with the rest of the vegetables. Dissolve the salt in the water and pour the solution over the vegetables. Cover with a plate to keep everything submerged. Leave in a cool place overnight or for up to 2 days.

Mix the cornflour and spices to a smooth paste with a little of the vinegar. Pour the rest of the vinegar into a saucepan and stir in the spice paste and sugar.

Drain the vegetables and add them to the vinegar mixture. Bring slowly to the boil, stirring to make sure the sugar and spices are dissolved. Simmer uncovered for 35–40 minutes, or until the vegetables are cooked to your liking. They should be tender but still with a bit of crunch and not at all mushy.

Pour into warmed sterilised jars and seal. Leave to cool, then store in a cool dry place, or, once opened, in the fridge.

Cook's notes

• The pickle will taste harsh at first so allow 2 weeks for the flavours to mellow. After that it gets better and better.
• You can use any combination of vegetables as long as it includes cauliflower and onions. Try green beans or some diced marrow or cucumber. You need a total of 1kg once the vegetables are trimmed or peeled.

cauliflower 1 medium
green pepper 1, deseeded and diced
red pepper ½, deseeded and diced
onions 4 small, chopped
gherkins 3, chopped
salt 175g
water 2 litres
cornflour 3 tbsp
dry mustard 1 tbsp
ground turmeric 2 tbsp
ground ginger 1 tbsp
cider vinegar 750ml
caster sugar 125g

Makes about 1.4kg

Celeriac

With its drab skin and Medusa-like tangle of roots, celeriac is an indisputably ugly vegetable. But it is also delicious – the vegetable to use when you want the fresh flavour of celery as well as the starchy comfort of potato. As the name implies, it is related to celery (and also parsley) but is grown for its root rather than the stem.

Supermarkets tend to sell celeriac straight-jacketed in cling film, denuded of whiskers and roots, and much of its character too. In farm shops you are more likely to find the whole plant, freshly dug, with an appetising celery-like aroma coming from the slightly damp skin.

Cooking

Celeriac is among the most under-rated of winter vegetables, yet it is so versatile. If you are unfamiliar with it, start off with a **celeriac and potato mash**. Boil or steam a half-and-half mix of celeriac and potato chunks until tender (they can share the same pan).This should take 25–30 minutes. Drain, mash to a purée and stir in plenty of butter, nutmeg, parsley and seasoning. For a full-on experience, leave out the potato and enrich the mash with double cream and sharpen it with lemon juice. This makes a fine accompaniment to **Roast Saddle of Wild Boar** (page 277) or venison.

Alternatively, a few chunks add refreshing flavour to a hearty casserole, or try roasting pieces of celeriac around a leg of pork or a duck. They will soak up the meaty juices and develop a rich complex flavour.

Celeriac also makes a **superb soup**, simple to prepare but deeply satisfying. Cut a medium-sized celeriac into small cubes, then soften in a large saucepan with a generous knob of melted butter, a fresh bay leaf and a finely chopped onion. After 15 minutes or so, pour in 900ml good chicken or vegetable stock. Cover and simmer for 30 minutes until tender. Whizz to a purée, then reheat gently with a spritz of lemon juice, 1 tablespoon of chopped fresh dill, and a little salt and black pepper. Pour into bowls and top with a swirl of soured cream and a few chopped toasted hazelnuts.

Celeriac marries well with mustard. Try sautéing cubes until golden, then finish them in a piquant mustard sauce (**Pan-Fried Celeriac with Dill and Mustard Sauce**, page 60). Or use raw celeriac in the French classic **celeriac rémoulade**. Coarsely grate 1 small celeriac and toss with the juice of 1 lemon, some sea salt and plenty of freshly ground black pepper. Leave to stand for 30 minutes to rid the flesh of some of its bounce. Once slightly softened, stir in 150ml mayonnaise, 2 teaspoons of Dijon mustard and 1 tablespoon of chopped herbs – chives, parsley or dill are good. I like to serve this with **crisply fried black pudding** or grilled sausages.

Grated, cut into matchsticks or sliced paper-thin, the raw flesh also makes a robust salad, especially with other clean-tasting crunchy ingredients such as apples, carrots and walnuts. Try it instead of kohlrabi in **Kohlrabi, Apple and Watercress Salad with Walnuts** (page 155).

UK season
• October–April.

Varieties to look for
• *'Giant Prague'*, heirloom variety with large roots. Excellent fried, roasted or in soups.
• *'Prinz'*, award-winning organic variety with smooth light skin. Good raw or cooked.

Shopping notes
• Celeriac should be firm, without any soft spots or other damage.

Storing
• Store in a cool dark airy place, or in a paper bag in the fridge for 2–3 weeks.

Preparation
• Scrub under running water to remove any clods of earth.
• Slice vertically into quarters and trim the knobbly ends.
• Remove the peel with a small sharp knife closely following the contours of the root. Slice, dice or grate the flesh according to the recipe.
• Once cut, plunge into acidulated water to prevent browning, or, if destined for a salad, stir straight into the dressing.

Chargrilled Celeriac Salad

Grilling celeriac slices on a ridged stovetop grill pan, or even on the barbecue, brings out the full flavour.

Using a large sharp knife, slice the celeriac in half vertically. Reserve one piece for another use, and slice the other vertically in half again. Trim the root end and remove the peel. Slice each piece crossways into 2–3-mm slices, keeping them an even thickness. Measure the olive oil into a bowl and toss the slices in it as you work.

Heat a ridged stovetop grill pan over medium-high heat. Arrange a few celeriac slices on the grill in a single layer. Grill for 2 minutes until starting to colour on the underside – keep lifting to check progress as the slices can burn quite easily. Lower the heat if necessary. Turn with tongs and grill for another minute. Repeat with the rest of the slices.

Toast the hazelnuts in a small pan over medium heat with some of the oil left in the bowl.

Pile a mound of salad leaves in the centre of each serving plate. Arrange the celeriac slices attractively on top and scatter with the hazelnuts. Sprinkle a few drops of balsamic vinegar and a trickle of hazelnut oil over the top. Season with a little crumbled sea salt and freshly ground black pepper.

Cook's notes

• Try to slice the celeriac evenly. If one end of the slice is thicker, it won't cook at the same rate as the thinner section, which, in turn, might burn.

• Use a mixture of robust leaves such as mustard, rocket, spinach and mizuna. Farm shops usually stock mixed bags of leaves.

• If you don't have hazelnut oil, use extra-virgin olive oil instead. Or try walnut oil and replace the hazelnuts with walnuts.

celeriac 1 small head, weighing about 350g
extra-virgin olive oil 5 tbsp
shelled hazelnuts 2 tbsp, roughly chopped
mixed salad leaves 2–3 handfuls
balsamic vinegar a splash
hazelnut oil a splash
sea salt flakes
freshly ground black pepper

Serves 2–3 as a starter

Pan-Fried Celeriac with Dill and Mustard Sauce

Unctuously rich and creamy, this is excellent with pork chops or boiled gammon.

Slice the prepared celeriac into $1\frac{1}{2}$-cm cubes. Place in a bowl and sprinkle with the lemon juice as you work.

Heat a heavy-based frying pan over medium heat, then swirl in the olive oil and butter. Add the celeriac cubes, tossing to coat. Season with the dill seeds, sea salt and black pepper. Fry for 10 minutes, turning with tongs, or until soft and evenly browned. Remove to a warm serving dish.

Pour off most of the fat from the pan. Stir in the stock and bubble over high heat, stirring until reduced. Pour in the cream and cook for 1 minute until slightly thickened. Stir in the mustard and cook for a few seconds more. Pour the sauce over the celeriac, stirring to coat. Sprinkle with the chopped dill.

celeriac 1 medium head (about 500g), quartered, trimmed and peeled
lemon juice of $\frac{1}{2}$
olive oil 1 tbsp
unsalted butter a large knob
dill seeds $\frac{1}{2}$ tsp
sea salt
freshly ground black pepper
chicken or **vegetable stock** preferably home-made, 125ml
Jersey whipping cream organic, 150ml
Dijon mustard 1 tsp
dill or **flat leaf parsley** chopped to make 1 tsp

Serves 2–4 as a side dish

Celery

Farm shops tend to sell imported green celery, neatly trimmed and incarcerated in plastic – it certainly doesn't fill you with excitement. That said, you occasionally come across dirty heads of home-grown celery, blanched until white, with fat fleshy stalks and a sweeping crown of leaves. These are definitely worth buying; every part from the coarse outer stems to tender hearts and verdant leaves can be put to good use in one way or another.

Cooking

Celery is essential for a well-flavoured stock and the tender inner stalks are lovely to nibble on, dipped in sea salt, with a platter of cheese. It also adds crunch to a salad as in **Celery, Pear and Walnut Salad with Blue Vinny Cheese** (page 63), and the small inner stalks are perfect for muddling a Bloody Mary. Cooked celery, however, has unfortunate connotations with waterlogged braised celery that used to be served in old-fashioned hotels.

For inspiration we need to look to Italy where celery is considered something of a delicacy. Destringed, chopped and lightly steamed, green celery adds texture and colour to a risotto. The chopped leaves and diced inner stalks can be sizzled with anchovies or pancetta, garlic and a little chopped chilli and used to garnish a soup or pasta dish. Celery is also an essential ingredient in *soffrito*, an aromatic mixture of celery, onions, carrots and herbs stewed in oil that forms the base of so many Italian dishes.

I like celery destringed and cut diagonally into thick chunks and steamed with spinach. The contrast in colour and texture is particularly pleasing. It is also delicious braised in **Barley with Celery, Preserved Lemon and Spices** (page 25).

UK season
• July–October.

Shopping notes
• Look for compact heads with crisp stalks and plenty of black soil round the base.
• Don't bother with heads that are stringy, devoid of leaves, or have brown marks on the outer stalks.

Storing
• Keep tightly wrapped in foil in the fridge for up to 1 week.

Preparation
• Trim the leaves but keep a few to use as a garnish or to add flavour to a meaty casserole.
• Cut off the root and separate the stalks. Scrub the stalks to get rid of soil and grit.
• Use a swivel peeler to remove fibrous strings.
• Slice or dice according to the recipe.

Celery, Pear and Walnut Salad with Blue Vinny Cheese

Celery, Pear and Walnut Salad with Blue Vinny Cheese

Elegantly curled strips of celery add flavour and all-important crunch to an autumn salad.

Trim the celery and remove the strings with a swivel peeler. Cut into 8-cm pieces, then slice lengthways into very thin strips. Put in a bowl of iced water and leave to curl in the fridge for at least 2 hours.

Next make the dressing: briefly whizz the cheese, olive oil and soured cream in a blender until smooth. Tip into a bowl and stir in the vinegar and the grated onion. Season with sea salt and black pepper.

Quarter the pears and remove the cores. Slice each quarter lengthways into four segments. Toss in a bowl with the lemon juice to prevent browning.

Arrange the salad leaves on a serving platter. Drain the celery and pears, and arrange attractively on top. Sprinkle with a little crumbled sea salt, then spoon over the dressing. Scatter the cheese and walnuts over the top, drizzle with a little olive oil and season with coarsely ground black pepper.

Cook's note
• If you're short of time and don't mind straight celery strips, leave out the 2-hour stint in the fridge.

tender celery stalks 4
red-skinned pears 2
lemons juice of 1
mixed salad leaves such as baby spinach, rocket and mizuna, 200g
sea salt flakes
Dorset Blue Vinny cheese 75g, crumbled
shelled walnuts preferably 'wet', 50g, halved
extra-virgin olive oil for drizzling
coarsely ground black pepper

for the dressing
Dorset Blue Vinny cheese 100g, crumbled
extra-virgin olive oil 5 tbsp
soured cream 4 tbsp
white wine vinegar 1 tbsp
onion 1 small, finely grated
sea salt flakes
freshly ground black pepper

Serves 6 as a starter or light meal

Celery and Dill Soup with Spelt

A sludge-coloured but fortifying soup brought to life by a lavish shower of fresh dill and some tasty garnishes. The soup puts to good use an entire bunch of celery, including the coarse outer stalks – as edible as the virginal inner stalks once the strings have been removed.

Put the spelt in a small saucepan with 500ml of the stock. Cover, bring to the boil, then reduce the heat to low and simmer very gently for 30 minutes until the spelt is tender but still a bit chewy.

While the spelt is cooking, melt the butter in a large saucepan and stew the onions and celery for about 10 minutes until just soft. Season with salt, black pepper and a couple of pinches of nutmeg. Pour in the remaining stock, bring to the boil, then simmer for 20 minutes.

Remove from the heat and purée about two-thirds of the mixture in a food processor. Tip back into the pan and stir in the spelt and its cooking liquid. Reheat gently, then add the dill and check the seasoning. Ladle into bowls and garnish with a blob of soured cream, pancetta snippets and a few chopped celery leaves.

Cook's notes
• This is exceptionally delicious with a spoonful of the **Stilton Pâté** (page 69). Use to garnish instead of soured cream.
• If you don't have any spelt, use rice or pearled barley instead.

pearled spelt 85g, rinsed
chicken or **vegetable stock** preferably home-made, 1.5 litres
butter 50g
onions 2, chopped
celery 1 large head, trimmed, destringed and diced
salt
freshly ground black pepper
freshly grated nutmeg 2 good pinches
dill trimmed and chopped to make 6 tbsp

to garnish
soured cream
fried pancetta snippets
celery leaves from the inner stalks, chopped

Serves 6

Chard

Curiously, chard has never really taken off in Britain although it is popular in the rest of Europe and is certainly available in UK farm shops. It is an almost year-round crop except for between-season months in spring and autumn.

Chard is a delicious treat, especially early in the year when it makes a change from cabbage and kale. The flavour is rich and complex, rather like spinach but with more depth. Some varieties have spectacularly coloured stems ranging from fuchsia pink to sunset yellow, set off by dark green puckered leaves. Swiss chard is less flamboyant with smooth grass-green leaves and wide white stems that remind me of cricket pads.

Cooking

With chard you get two vegetables – the fat juicy stems that can be cooked as a separate dish, and the green leaves that are steamed or boiled in the same way as spinach. You can also cook them together, as in **Bright Lights Chard Gratin** (page 65), although the stems need slightly different treatment.

I like to make a **salad of brightly coloured stems** with chunks of buttery avocado, buffalo mozzarella and a garlicky lemon dressing. For two people you will need about 225g stems (use the leaves in another dish). Trim a sliver from each side – the edges can be a little stringy – then slice diagonally into neat 2-cm pieces. Blanch for $1\frac{1}{2}$ minutes – no longer or you will lose the bright colours. Quickly make a dressing with a crushed garlic clove, sea salt flakes, freshly ground black pepper, 1 tablespoon of lemon juice and 3 tablespoons of extra-virgin olive oil. Drain the stems and immediately toss with the dressing. Arrange a couple of handfuls of salad leaves on plates – baby spinach is good – and scatter with the slightly warm stems, neatly diced avocado and shredded mozzarella cheese. Spoon over the dressing and serve right away.

Also good is a **stir-fry with enoki mushrooms and jasmine rice**. Slice 4 leaves of red-stemmed chard crossways into thin ribbons. Slice the stems thinly as well. Cut the root off a small clump of enoki mushrooms (or use 85g sliced button mushrooms). Cook 115g jasmine rice. Meanwhile, heat 2 tablespoons of groundnut oil and gently fry 1 garlic clove, a small piece of fresh ginger root and a sliver of fresh red chilli, all very finely chopped. Add the chard stems and the mushrooms and shunt around the pan until wilted. Add the leaves, then cover and cook over low heat for 5 minutes, stirring now and again. Add a few splashes of water or stock if the vegetables look dry. Remove the lid, raise the heat and stir in 2 teaspoons of shoyu (Japanese soy sauce). Stir-fry for 2–3 minutes until the chard is cooked to your liking. Divide the rice between two plates and serve with the vegetables on top.

UK season
• June–August, October–April.

Varieties to look for
• *'Bright Lights Chard'*, puckered dark green leaves with yellow, red or pink stems.
• *'Rhubarb Chard'*, puckered dark green leaves with burgundy-red stems.
• *'Swiss Chard'*, flat green leaves with wide white stems.

Shopping notes
• Look for glossy leaves with plenty of bounce and no signs of yellowing. Stalks should be firm without any bruising or cut marks.

Storing
• Chard needs a moist atmosphere. Store unwashed and untrimmed in damp paper towels in a roomy plastic bag in the salad drawer of the fridge. Use within 1–2 days.

Preparation
• Wash and trim only when ready to cook. Dunk in several changes of water to remove grit.
• Strip stems from leaves by folding the leaf in half so upper surfaces touch, then grasp the stem and pull firmly towards tip. Slice stems as per recipe.
• Stack larger leaves and slice into ribbons or as per recipe.

Bright Lights Chard Gratin

Stems and leaves are cooked separately in a rich gratin topped with bubbling cheese and crisp breadcrumbs.

Slice the ends off the chard stems and discard. Using a sharp knife, cut along each side of the stem to separate them from the leaves. Slice the stems lengthways into thin strips, then crossways into finger-length pieces.

Stack the leaves and roll into a wad. Slice crossways into 1cm ribbons. Preheat the oven to 200°C/gas 6.

Bring a saucepan of salted water to the boil. Blanch the chard stems for 2 minutes. Place the leaves in a steamer basket set over the stems, and steam for 2 minutes. Drain the stems and set aside.

Heat a large heavy-based frying pan over medium heat. Add the olive oil and when it sizzles, gently fry the onion for a few minutes until soft but not browned. Add the garlic and chilli flakes, cook for a minute, then add the chard leaves. Season with sea salt, black pepper and a smidgen of freshly grated nutmeg. Remove the pan from the heat.

Smear a medium-sized baking dish with about half the butter. Tip half the leaves and onion mixture into the base, arrange the stalks in an even layer on top, then cover with the remaining leaves. Dot with a few dabs of butter, then sprinkle with both the cheeses and the breadcrumbs. Dot with the remaining butter, season with a little more sea salt and freshly ground black pepper. Bake in the oven for 20–25 minutes until the chard is tender and the topping crisp.

Cook's note
• Make the most of British cheeses such as Lancashire or Caerphilly. They melt well so can be used instead of Emmenthal.

chard with coloured stems 1 bunch, weighing about 450g
olive oil 2 tbsp
red onion 1 small, thinly sliced
garlic cloves 2, lightly crushed
dried chilli flakes $1/4$ tsp
sea salt flakes
freshly ground black pepper
freshly grated nutmeg
butter 75g
Emmenthal cheese 100g, coarsely grated
mozzarella cheese 50g, coarsely grated
breadcrumbs (from a day-old loaf), 50g

Serves 2–3 as a light meal or 6 as a side dish

Cheese

There has been a renaissance of cheese-making in the UK; we are producing a phenomenal amount, both new and traditional, outstripping the growth of continental cheeses. Indeed, we have probably reached the point where there is a British or Irish alternative to most of the well-known continental cheeses that we cook with. Some of our cheeses – Single Gloucester and Stilton, for example – have been awarded PDO (Protected Designation of Origin) status by the EU. This is a real badge of honour and means that the cheese is made only in its geographic area of origin and complies with stringent regulations governing the way it is produced.

An increasing number of our cheeses are artisan-made and often available only locally or in specialist shops. Farm shops are the place to find such cheeses, especially if you are interested in provenance. The cheese may have been made on the farm itself using milk from its own dairy herds (see **Milk**, page 164). There will often be samples for you to try, and the cheese-maker may well be there to talk about the product.

The majority of cheeses are made with cow's milk, though goat's, sheep's and even buffalo's milk cheeses have taken off in the past few years. Regardless of milk, cheeses come in a range of textures, flavours and degrees of maturity. They can be classified in a number of ways – according to milk type or region, for example – but, as cheese diva Juliet Harbutt suggests, classifying according to the rind or covering is a good pointer to the type of cheese within.

Fresh cheese

These cheeses are too young to have developed a rind, though soft varieties are often wrapped in leaves or rolled in ash or herbs to give them character.

Cheeses to look for:

Devon: Vulscombe, unpasteurised, goat's milk, vegetarian. Topped with a bay leaf. Moist creamy texture, fresh lemon flavour. Use in dips, spreads, cakes and tarts.

Dorset: Woolsery Greek-Style Fiesta, goat's milk, vegetarian. Crumbly wet texture, delicate flavour, less salty than feta. Use in salads, pizza or as a topping for soups.

Monmouthshire: Pant Ys Gawn, goat's milk, vegetarian. Texture similar to cream cheese, clean fresh citrus flavour. Use in spreads, salads, cakes and tarts.

Somerset: Mozzarella, stretched curd, unpasteurised buffalo's milk, vegetarian. Use raw in salads or melted in lasagne and pizza.

Staffordshire: Innes Button, unpasteurised goat's milk, vegetarian. Mousse-like texture, beautiful sweet citrus flavour with hint of almonds. Available in pink peppercorn, rosemary, ash and natural finishes.

Soft-white

These have a typical Brie-like velvety white rind. The rind on unpasteurised varieties is dotted with reddish-brown marks known as ferments.

Shopping notes

• Buy cheese for the table in quantities that you will use within a day or two.

Fresh Look for: moist texture, fresh clean smell. Avoid: yellowish-brown liquid, grey fuzzy mould, bitter smell.

Soft white Look for: undulating rind, creamy texture. Avoid: dry or brittle rind, excessively runny or chalky texture, ammonia-like aroma.

Semi-soft Look for: undulating red-orange rind, creamy texture. Avoid: dried pale or dark rind, excessively runny or chalky texture.

Blue cheese Look for: even veining, fatty buttery texture. Avoid: yellowish, uneven or sparse veining, dry crumbly texture.

Hard cheese Look for: good colour, supple or firm texture. Avoid: dry granular texture.

Storing

• All cheeses need a damp and cool environment. Store fresh cheeses in the cold part of the fridge, between 2°–4°C. Others are best kept at 8°–10°C, preferably in a cool larder.

• If you have to keep cheese in the fridge, put it in the warmest part – the top shelf or the salad drawer – wrapped in foil, greaseproof or waxy paper. These preserve moisture and allow the cheese to breathe; plastic makes them sweat. Alternatively, store unwrapped in a ventilated 'cheese-keeper' box.

Preparation

• Allow table cheese to come to room temperature an hour or two before eating to allow the flavour to develop. Keep covered with a clean damp cloth if necessary.

• Crumbly or soft cheeses such as mozzarella, are easier to grate if you put them in the freezer for 10 minutes beforehand.

Cheeses to look for:
Carmarthen: Pont Gar Garlic and Herbs, vegetarian. Set-custard texture, incredibly rich and creamy, mild flavour of garlic and herbs. Also available smoked.
Carmarthen: Talley Mountain, goat's milk, vegetarian. Dense texture, rich flavour redolent of almonds and marzipan.
Devon: Sharpham, unpasteurised, vegetarian. Creamy, like butter in the mouth, mild flavour.
Oxfordshire: Farleigh Wallop No. 2, goat's milk, vegetarian. Dense and creamy when young, runnier with age. Herbaceous flavour with subtle hint of thyme and mushrooms.

Semi-soft, rind-washed
Brownish-orange to grey-brown leathery rind. Some are washed in brine or alcohol which creates a sticky orange rind.

Cheeses to look for:
Berkshire: Wigmore, unpasteurised sheep's milk, vegetarian. Very smooth texture, intense rich meaty and floral flavours.
Ceredigion: Celtic Promise, brine-washed, unpasteurised, vegetarian. Supple smooth texture, spicy fruity pungent flavour. Good melting cheese.
County Cork: Durrus, unpasteurised, vegetarian. Silky smooth, compact, runnier with age. Earthy buttery flavour redolent of apples, nuts, smoke.
Gloucestershire: Stinking Bishop, rind-washed in perry (pear cider), vegetarian. Smooth spoonable texture, distinctive pungent flavour and aroma.
Somerset: Ogleshield, unpasteurised, brine-washed. Firm slightly chewy texture, complex fruity savoury flavour. Excellent melting cheese, especially over potatoes.

Blue
Sticky damp rind, sometimes soft, gritty or crusty.

Cheeses to look for:
Berkshire: Barkham Blue, vegetarian. Buttery, melt-in-the-mouth texture, rich tangy flavour. Perfect with a juicy pear.
Derbyshire: Buxton Blue PDO, vegetarian. Crumbly texture, mild flavour. Use in salads, soups, sauces and spreads.
Dorset: Blue Vinny, unpasteurised, vegetarian, made from semi-skimmed milk. Moist and crumbly. Lovely in salads, tangy sauces and dressings, or stirred into polenta.
Nottingham: Colston Bassett Stilton DOC, vegetarian. Creamy texture, intense spicy tangy flavour. Use in salads, soups and sauces.

Hard

Dense, waxy rind, sometimes oiled, basket-woven or cloth-covered.

Cheeses to look for:

Dyfed: Gorwydd Caerphilly, unpasteurised. Crumbly moist supple texture, fresh slightly earthy flavour with hint of citrus. Good melting and grating cheese, ideal for toasted cheese and Welsh rarebit.

East Sussex: Duddleswell, unpasteurised, sheep's milk. Firm flaky texture, sweet caramel flavour. Use for grating. Good substitute for pecorino.

Lancashire: Kirkham's Lancashire, soft crumbly texture, salty tang. Good melting cheese, ideal for toasted cheese, pizza toppings.

Leicestershire: Red Leicester Aged, vegetarian. Firm flaky texture, well-rounded nutty butterscotch flavour. Use for grilling and grating.

Gloucestershire: Single Gloucester, PDO, supported by the Slow Food movement. Firm, moist texture. Buttery, slightly sweet-sharp flavour. Use for grilling and grating.

Shropshire: Appleby's Coloured Cheshire, unpasteurised, vegetarian, traditional clothbound. Flaky texture, tangy citrus flavour. Ideal for melting, grilling or enriching sauces.

Somerset: Montgomery's Extra Mature Cheddar, supported by the Slow Food movement, cloth-bound, unpasteurised. Firm but supple texture, rich, fruity herbaceous flavour. Use for grilling, grating, enriching sauces. Lovely with apples and celery.

Sussex: Ashdown Foresters Smoked, vegetarian, smoked over oak chips. Smooth rich texture, subtle and natural smoky flavour. Use in salads and egg dishes.

Cooking

Though cheeses are best enjoyed as part of a cheese board, or simply eaten with bread, fruit or celery, they are also major players in cooked dishes. They make fantastic toppings and fillings, they add rich flavours, and can even be used in desserts and cakes.

Cheeses with good melting qualities are probably the most useful. Hard cheeses are ideal for gratins and tarts (**Tomato Tart**, page 257), and they blend easily into **béchamel sauce** (page 164). Rinded goat's cheese is excellent grilled, while powerfully pungent Ogleshield is ideal for raclette or fondue. Stretchy mozzarella cheese makes a good topping for lasagne or pizza (**Pizza Bianca** variation, page 109).

But beware: if overheated, cheese will coagulate and separate from the fat, at which stage it's beyond rescue. When adding cheese to a sauce, heat it slowly without boiling, and be gentle when browning cheese under the grill. Hard cheeses tolerate higher temperatures than softer ones, which is the reason why Parmesan and Gruyère are so useful. Cheddar is usually thought of as a good melting cheese, but in fact Lancashire and Caerphilly are better.

Intensely flavoured hard cheeses add richness to sauces and egg dishes. Shaved or grated, they make a tasty condiment for rice, pasta or vegetables, as in **Roasted Banana Shallots with Sage, Parmesan and Crisp Breadcrumbs** (page 236). They also make well-flavoured pastry and cakes (**Caerphilly Curd Cake**, page 70). Firm blues like Stilton or Blue Vinny crumble easily enough to be whisked into sauces as in **Green Cauliflower Cheese with Blue Vinny and Tomatoes** 57), or creamy dressings as in **Celery, Pear and Walnut Salad with Blue Vinny Cheese** (page 63). Softer types such as Barkham Blue make unctuous soups and creamy pasta sauces. When seasoning a dish, bear in mind that blue cheeses can be quite salty and that heat will accentuate this.

Fresh soft cheeses add moisture and background lemony flavour, blending easily into soups and pasta sauces and adding substance to fillings. They are the main ingredient in a number of dips and spreads such as **Broad Bean Bruschetta with Savory and Goat's Cheese** (page 48) and **Stilton Pâté with Celery and Walnuts** (below). They make a healthy alternative to cream and can be used in salad dressings instead of mayonnaise. Without fresh soft cheeses, there would be no cheesecake and we'd miss out on a wide range of desserts such as tiramisu and heart-shaped *coeur à la crème*.

Stilton Pâté with Celery and Walnuts

Moist blue cheese, crisp celery and freshly cracked walnuts are the perfect ending to a meal. Here, I have combined them as a starter in a richly flavoured creamy pâté that will hit the spot with cheese lovers. The servings are small – a little goes a long way.

Put the Stilton in a food processor with the soft cheese, cream and wine, and pulse a few times until smooth. Tip the mixture into a bowl and mix in the walnuts, celery, celery leaves, chives and nutmeg. Season with a generous grinding of white pepper and some crumbled sea salt flakes.

Spoon into small ramekins, cover and chill for 2 hours or more. Garnish with a walnut quarter and a tiny sprig of celery leaf, and serve with hot toast.

Cook's note

• The pâté is great on grilled steaks – it will melt into a rich and tangy sauce. It's also good with pasta or swirled into soup such as **Celery and Dill Soup with Spelt** (page 63).

Stilton cheese 200g, diced
soft cheese 175g
single cream 2 tbsp
full-bodied white wine or **sherry** 2 tbsp
shelled walnuts 40g, roughly chopped
celery small tender stalks with leaves, diced to make 4 tbsp
celery leaves chopped to make 2 tbsp
chives chopped to make 2 tbsp
freshly grated nutmeg 2 large pinches
freshly ground white pepper
sea salt flakes
toasted sourdough or **ciabatta** to serve

to garnish
walnut quarters
tiny sprigs of celery leaves

Serves 4–6 as a starter

Goat's Cheese and Caramelised Onion Tart

This is based on a recipe from Matt Cook, former head chef at The Bull Hotel in Bridport, Dorset. Mild-flavoured goat's cheese gives the tart a lemony tang, as does the soured cream in the pastry. Golden sticky onions provide just the right touch of sweetness.

To make the pastry, put all the ingredients in a food processor and pulse until the mixture forms a dough. Knead lightly, then wrap in cling film and chill for 30 minutes.

Preheat the oven to 180°C/gas 4. Lightly grease a 4-cm deep, 24-cm loose-based tart tin. Roll out the pastry very thinly and use to line the tin. Press a rolling pin over the top to trim off surplus dough. Line the base with foil and weigh down with baking beans. Bake blind for 10 minutes, then remove the foil and beans. Reduce the oven temperature to 170°C/ gas 3 and bake 5 minutes more or until just pale golden.

Meanwhile, gently heat the milk until steaming but don't let it boil. Gradually whisk it into the beaten eggs. Season with sea salt flakes and freshly ground black pepper.

Spread the caramelised onions in the base of the pastry case. Sprinkle with the goat's cheese and pour in the milk and egg mixture. Bake for 30–35 minutes, checking regularly, until puffed up and golden.

Cook's notes
• You will need a soft mild crumbly goat's cheese such as Vulscombe or Pant Ys Gawn (see **Fresh Cheese**, page 66)
• Use ordinary yellow onions for the caramelised onions. Red ones are a bit too sweet.

whole milk organic, 450ml
eggs organic, 3, lightly beaten
sea salt flakes
freshly ground black pepper
caramelised onions (page 172)
crumbly goat's cheese 125g, coarsely grated (see **Cook's notes**)

for the pastry
plain flour 150g
unsalted butter 100g, chilled
soured cream, 4 tbsp
salt a pinch

Serves 4 as a light meal, or 6 as a snack

Caerphilly Curd Cake

A traditional Welsh cooked cheesecake made with moist crumbly Caerphilly, creamy curd cheese, dried apples and raisins.

Preheat the oven to 180°C/gas 4. Grease a deep 20-cm round cake tin with butter and line with baking parchment. Sift the flour and baking powder together.

Put the two cheeses, the sugar and vanilla extract in a food processor. Blend until smooth, gradually adding the eggs. Tip the mixture into a large bowl. Add the raisins and dried apples, then fold in the flour, mixing well.

Spoon the mixture into the prepared cake tin. Bake for 1 hour or until a skewer inserted into the middle of the cake comes out clean. Leave to cool in the tin for 10 minutes, then turn out and leave to cool on a wire rack.

Cook's note
• Curd cheese is similar to cream cheese but is lower in fat and lighter-textured. It is sometimes called medium-fat soft cheese.

butter for greasing
self-raising flour 115g
baking powder 2 tsp
Caerphilly cheese 225g, grated
curd cheese 225g
light muscovado sugar 115g
vanilla extract 1 tsp
eggs organic, 3, lightly beaten
raisins 115g
dried apples 85g, finely chopped

Serves 8

Goat's Cheese and Caramelised Onion Tart

Cherries

Once an integral part of our culture and landscape, British cherries have seen a steep decline in the past forty years. Happily a revival is under way, spearheaded by food writer Henrietta Green's Cherry Aid campaign and supported by some of the country's best-known chefs. Orchards are being replanted and farm shops, greengrocers and supermarkets countrywide are being encouraged not only to stock British cherries but also to name the varieties.

For me, nothing quite equals the crunch of the cherry's firm flesh and taut skin followed by an intense flood of sweet tangy juice. Like apples, cherries are incredibly diverse; some varieties are commonplace, such as 'Summer Sun' or 'Stella' – the equivalent of Cox's apple, say – while others are rare treats (see **Varieties to look for**). In size they range from big glossy fleshy fruits to those no bigger than a raspberry; colours range from deep inky-black to translucent scarlet and albino cream.

Most cherries on sale in the UK are the sweet dessert type, but occasionally you come across tart morello cherries, commonplace in the rest of Europe. Worth buying for their intense flavour, these are the ones to use for jam-making, bottling and liqueurs.

Cooking

Cherries are so good eaten straight from the bag that it seems a shame to do anything more with them. However, they do make gorgeous desserts. Add them to **Compôte of Dark Fruits in Spiced Syrup** (page 196) or use in a crumble with crimson-fleshed plums or in the **Cherry Clafoutis** (see opposite).

Cherries and chocolate are another unmissable sensory experience; try them instead of raspberries in **Raspberry Chocolate Tartlets** (page 222), or have a go at making Black Forest gateau, a glorious concoction of chocolate, cherries and cream, for which there are many recipes elsewhere.

Cherries also make **sensational ice cream**: purée about 650g pitted black cherries with 175g sugar and a slug of Kirsch or brandy. Fold into 250ml of organic double cream or thick yogurt. Churn and freeze in an ice cream machine, or follow the directions for still-freezing **Quince and Ginger Sorbet** (page 213).

Moving on to savoury things, cherries work well with duck, pork or any type of game. Eastern Europe, where cherries grow prolifically, is awash with recipes for **cherry sauce**; an excellent peppery one comes from Transylvania. Simmer 600g pitted cherries and 1 teaspoon of juniper berries in 450ml fruity red wine until soft. Whizz in a food processor then push through a fine sieve, pressing hard. Tip the purée back into the pan and add 4 tablespoons of hot stock or juices from the meat, 1–2 teaspoons of clear honey, $1/4$–$1/2$ teaspoon of freshly ground black pepper and a squeeze each of orange and lemon juice. Bubble for 5 minutes, stirring, until thickened. Taste and add more of anything if needed. Pour over sliced meat or serve in a jug.

UK season
• June–August.

Varieties to look for
• *'Early Rivers'*, large black fruits, tender flesh.
• *'Merton Bigarreau'*, large purple-black fruits, firm, juicy red flesh.
• *'Rainier'*, scarlet and cream fruits, crisp flesh.
• *'Reine Hortense'*, sour morello variety, rich carnelian-red fruits, yellow flesh.
• *'Stella'*, large, dark red juicy fruits.

Shopping notes
• Choose firm, plump, glossy cherries with the stalks attached.
• Don't buy any with brown spots or cracks.

Storing
• Cherries do not keep very well. Eat on the day you buy them or store in a cool place, preferably not the fridge, for 1–2 days.

Preparation
• Pitting cherries is laborious but sometimes necessary. Speed up the task with a cherry pitter or a metal garlic press with a protuberance for removing stones.

Cherry Clafoutis

Make the most of British cherries with this very simple pudding – batter poured over cherries and baked in the oven. The recipe is based on one from the classic tome *Mastering the Art of French Cooking*, through which I worked my way as a fledgling cook.

Preheat the oven to 180°C/gas 4. Lightly butter a 2-litre baking dish.

Put all the batter ingredients in a blender or food processor and whizz for 1 minute until smooth. Pour a very thin layer of batter into the prepared baking dish and place in the oven for a few minutes until set.

Spread the cherries over the batter and sprinkle with the sugar. Pour in the rest of the batter and level the surface with the back of a spoon.

Bake for 1 hour until puffy and brown, and a skewer inserted into the centre comes out clean. Sprinkle with sifted icing sugar before serving.

Variation
• For a sumptuous alcoholic version, macerate the pitted cherries in 4-5 tablespoons of Kirsch and 50g caster sugar for 1 hour. Measure the liquid and use in the batter, reducing the amount of milk accordingly. Don't add sugar to the cherries once they are in the dish.

butter for greasing
cherries 400g, pitted
sugar 50g
icing sugar for dusting

for the batter
whole milk organic, 300ml
caster sugar 4 tbsp
eggs organic 3, at room temperature
vanilla extract 1 tsp
salt a pinch
plain flour 70g, sifted

Serves 6–8

Chestnuts

Grown mainly in southern England, home-produced fresh chestnuts are occasionally found in farm shops in late autumn. Divested of their hedgehog armour, these are gleaming polished mahogany with moist crisp flesh – a far cry from dried imported specimens.

Cooking

It's hard to beat the winter ritual of roasting chestnuts over an open fire. A long-handled perforated chestnut pan comes in handy for tossing them. Slit or prick the shells first or they will explode like hand grenades. Failing access to an open fire, roast at 230°C/gas 8 for 20–25 minutes. Once roasted, the texture is mealy and crunchy at the same time – lovely dipped in sea salt, or try honey and black pepper for a change.

Peeled chestnuts (see **Preparation**) are a classic partner to Brussels sprouts, and a key ingredient in turkey stuffing – although I've never understood why, since both have a tendency to dryness. They are especially good in braises with game, however. Both are in season at the same time and the rich flavours complement each other. Add a handful to **Partridge with Braised Red Cabbage, Apples and Juniper** (page 180) or **Pigeon Casserole with Shallots, Mushrooms and Juniper** (page 194).

If peeling does not daunt you, **home-made sweetened purée** is lovely for folding into fools or ice cream, or for topping meringue. Roughly chop 500g large fresh peeled chestnuts and put in a pan with enough water to just cover. Add a split vanilla pod, or a sprig of rosemary. Bring to the boil and simmer until tender – about 30 minutes. Strain, keeping the cooking liquid but removing any added flavourings. Purée in a food processor moistening with 3–4 tablespoons of the liquid. Tip the purée back into the pan and add 225g caster sugar and another 3–4 tablespoons of liquid. Bring to the boil, then cook gently, stirring often, until thickened. Pour into warm sterilised jars and seal.

• October–November.

Shopping notes
• Select the largest plumpest nuts with glossy brown shells.
• Chestnuts should feel heavy for their size. Give them a squeeze to make sure the nut meat isn't shrivelled.

Storing
• Keep loosely wrapped in the salad drawer of the fridge, a cool larder or dry shed.

Preparation
• *Peeling chestnuts:* cut a vertical slit through the shell and put the nuts in a pan of cold water. Bring to the boil and boil for 4–5 minutes, then remove from the heat, leaving the nuts in the pan. Fish out one or two at a time and peel off the shells and brown membrane – easier when the nuts are warm.

Chicken

As the 19th-century French gastronome Brillat-Savarin rightly observed, '... fowls are to the kitchen what his canvas is to the painter', and it is certainly true that chicken gets top marks for versatility. It is a universal favourite, deeply rooted in almost every national cuisine. Brillat-Savarin also wrote something chillingly prescient: '... under the pretext of improving them... Not only do we take away their means of reproduction, but we keep them in solitary confinement, cast them into darkness and force them to eat willy-nilly.' Concerns over chicken welfare are obviously nothing new.

Given our liking for chicken, it's worth paying attention to provenance. The differences between a factory-farmed chicken and its naturally reared counterpart are striking. A bird that has been allowed to roam unrestricted in open pastures and forage for food will have a noticeably different shape and flavour. Since the bones will be better developed and the legs longer, it may even look scrawny rather than unnaturally plump. There is a difference in the flesh, too: the leg meat is darker and chewier than the breast, and the flavour speaks for itself.

In the words of food writer and campaigner Hugh Fearnley-Whittingstall, it is entirely logical that free-range chickens should be considered the norm and anything that deviates should be identified with meaningful epithets such as 'confined-space' or perhaps 'cage-bound'. Most farm shops stock humanely reared chicken as a matter of policy, but it is always worth inspecting the label to see what you're getting (see **Chicken to look for**).

Cooking

From slow-cooked **Coq au Vin** (page 78) to deep-fried chicken Kiev, chicken can be cooked in every imaginable way. That said, a **simple roast** has to be one of the most comforting and satisfying meals. I like to stuff a few lemon or lime quarters into the cavity, along with a sprig or two of rosemary. A properly reared bird has plenty of fat under the skin making it virtually self-basting, so you don't really need to bother with extra oil; just rub the skin with salt and black pepper, and perhaps some cumin seeds and dried chilli flakes as well. If you seal the cavity with a couple of skewers, the skin will crisp and puff up nicely. Start off with the breast-side down at 180°C/gas 4. Turn over after 30 minutes and cook for 20–25 minutes per 500g (including the first 30 minutes). Raise the heat to 200°C/gas 6 for the final 20 minutes. There will be enough lemony juices for a simple gravy.

The owner of a farm shop once told me the extraordinary tale of a well-healed customer who complained that chickens were too big and there was too much waste. Hard to believe, when leftovers are such an asset. Bathed in mayo or a creamy yogurt dressing, they make excellent sandwich material. Add chopped spring onion, peppers, celery, segments of apple and you have a substantial salad. Nuggets of meat are perfect for a risotto or stir-fry. Simmer the carcass and jellied juices with onion, carrot, celery and a handful of parsley, and you have stock for a lovely soup.

Chicken to look for
• *Organic:* organic-certified production methods and feed. Small flocks, slow-growing breeds, unrestricted daytime open-air access, minimum slaughter age 81 days.
• *Traditional free-range:* humanely reared, extensive daytime open-air access, low stocking density, minimum slaughter age 81 days.
• *Free-range – total freedom:* humanely reared, unrestricted daytime open-air access, minimum slaughter age 81 days.
• *Corn-fed, free-range:* yellow flesh, diet based on maize or other cereal for improved flavour.

Shopping notes
• Check that the bird is well chilled and within the 'use by' date.
• Skin should be evenly coloured and feel soft, smooth and powdery-dry to touch.
• If wrapped in plastic, check that the flesh looks plump and gives slightly when pressed.
• Don't buy chickens with reddened bruised flesh or torn skin.

Storing
• Store on the bottom shelf of the fridge so raw juices cannot drip onto cooked meat or other food.
• Remove wrapping and store in a shallow dish, loosely covered with foil, for 2–3 days depending on 'use by' date.
• Remove giblets and store separately.
• If vacuum-packed or in a rigid plastic container, leave unopened until ready to cook.

Preparation
• Check the cavity for giblets and remove before weighing.
• Wash chicken inside and out, and pat dry with paper towels.
• After handling, wash and rinse hands and utensils in hot water, disinfect sinks and surfaces.

Serving size
• Whole bird: 1.4kg serves 4; 1.8kg serves 4–5; 2kg serves 5–6.

Though a whole chicken is more economic there is a case for buying portions, particularly if you are in a hurry to get dinner on the table. Make sure the breast and leg portions come with skin and bones intact; these add flavour and help prevent the meat from shrinking and becoming dry.

Thighs and drumsticks are juicier than breasts. They are the best cuts for barbecues and slowly simmered braises such as the classic **Coq au Vin** (page 78). Cooked with care, though, **crisply fried chicken breasts** are also something to be relished. The trick is to salt the skin first, massage it with olive oil and cook skin-side down in a roomy pan. Resist the temptation to inspect the underside before it is ready; if you do so, steam will form underneath and the meat will fail to brown. After 15–20 minutes the skin should be gloriously golden and crusty. At this point you can flip the breasts over and cook the other side. Remove to a warm serving dish and deglaze the pan with lemon juice, wine or stock. Swirl in a knob of butter and any juices that have flowed from the breasts. Pour the sauce over the breasts and shower with chopped flat leaf parsley or chives.

Alternatively, skip the sauce, let the breasts cool and use them in a delectable salad. They are good shredded and mixed with matchsticks of crisp kohlrabi, carrot and cucumber, a handful of sprouted seeds or micro leaves (page 229) and a **lemon yogurt dressing** (page 278). Equally delicious are sliced chicken breasts, watercress and crunchy hazelnuts on a mound of fluffy barley or spelt, sharpened with a tangy vinaigrette dressing.

Sticky Chicken Wings

Farm shops often sell bargain packs of chicken wings from free-range flocks. They are meaty and delicious, so snap them up and store in the freezer, ready for finger-licking entertaining.

Wash the chicken wings well and pull out any stray feathers. Pat the wings dry with paper towels and put in a shallow bowl.

Combine all the marinade ingredients and pour over the wings, turning until thoroughly coated. Cover and leave in the fridge for at least 2 hours or up to 24 hours. Bring the wings to room temperature at least 1 hour before you want to cook them.

Preheat the grill. Reserving the marinade, arrange the wings in a single layer on a rack in the grill pan. Brush with rapeseed oil and place about 17cm from the heat source. Grill for 20–25 minutes, turning regularly and brushing with oil and the reserved marinade. They are ready when the flesh is no longer pink and the skin is beautifully blackened in places.

Pile in a warm serving dish, sprinkle with crumbled sea salt flakes and strew with lime wedges.

Cook's note
• When arranging the wings in the grill pan, make sure the tips point downwards to begin with. They burn very easily if too close to the heat source. Once the thickest part has started to brown it's fine if the tips point upwards.

chicken wings 12
rapeseed oil for brushing
sea salt flakes
lime wedges to garnish

for the marinade
tomato ketchup 5 tbsp
hoi sin sauce 2 tbsp
clear honey 2 tbsp
soy sauce 1 tbsp
cider vinegar 1 tbsp
Worcestershire sauce 1 tbsp
hot English mustard 1 tbsp

Serves 4–6

Coq au Vin

Made with a good chicken, dry-cured bacon and fruity Burgundy, this is as satisfying as a stew can get.

Toss the chicken thighs in seasoned flour. Heat a wide shallow casserole. Add the rapeseed oil and a knob of butter, brown the chicken in batches and move to a plate. Fry the bacon in the same casserole until crisp, then add it to the chicken. Next brown the shallots and button mushrooms, adding more oil if you need to.

Put the chicken and bacon back in the casserole with the juices that have flowed from the chicken. Add the herbs, garlic and Cognac and stir everything together to deglaze the pan. Pour in the wine and bring to the boil, pressing the chicken pieces down to submerge them as much as possible. Lower the heat and simmer, uncovered, for 15 minutes or until the wine has reduced slightly, turning the chicken halfway through. Pour in the stock, bring to the boil, then cover and simmer very gently for 30–40 minutes.

Pour the chicken and sauce into a colander set over a bowl. Strain the sauce through a fine-meshed sieve into the casserole and simmer briskly until reduced and thickened enough to coat a spoon lightly. Check the seasoning. For a smoother glossier sauce, blend the cornflour to a thin paste with some of the liquid, return to the pan and stir until thickened.

Tip the chicken and vegetables back into the sauce, discarding the bay leaves and thyme. Simmer for a few minutes to heat through. Sprinkle with the parsley when ready to serve.

Cook's notes
• For seasoned flour, mix 6 tablespoons of plain flour with 2 teaspoons each of salt and freshly ground black pepper. Tip into a roomy plastic bag, add the chicken portions and shake until evenly coated.
• The preliminary browning of the chicken, bacon and shallots is vital for the flavour of the finished dish. Don't be tempted to rush things at this stage.
• The dish is even more delicious after a day in the fridge. Once chilled, you can remove the layer of solidified fat before reheating.

chicken thighs with bones and skin, 12
seasoned flour (see **Cook's notes**)
rapeseed oil 4 tbsp
butter a knob
dry-cured streaky bacon 6 thick rashers, derinded and cut into squares
shallots 20, peeled and left whole
button mushrooms 250g, trimmed
thyme 3–4 sprigs
fresh bay leaves 2
garlic cloves 4, crushed with the flat of a knife
Cognac 4 tbsp
red wine 1 bottle Burgundy
chicken stock preferably home-made, 750ml
cornflour (optional) 1 tbsp
flat leaf parsley chopped to make 3 tbsp

Serves 6

Chillies

Chillies are fun to cook with and come in spectrum-spanning shades from acid yellow to deep green, flaming orange to vibrant red and even chocolate brown or purple. Most chillies start life as green, changing colour as they mature. They have eclectic names such as 'Rooster Spur', 'Cherry Bomb' and 'Scotch Bonnet' that offer clues to their shape and size. Some are hot and some are not, even within the same variety. It is always wise to approach chillies with caution.

There are literally thousands of chilli varieties although relatively few find their way into the shops. Fortunately for enthusiasts, an excellent choice can be found at the increasing number of chilli farms that are springing up. You can buy direct from the farm or in local farm shops and delis, as well as on-line or by mail order. The joy of buying from a specialist is that you can choose a named variety (see **Varieties to look for**) suitable for the dish you intend to cook. Like potatoes, chillies vary in texture and this in turn affects the success of the finished dish.

Cooking

Though mainly known for their heat, there is much more to chillies than *chile con carne*. Used judiciously, they add pleasing warmth to bland dishes. A small amount finely chopped is good with couscous or mildly flavoured root vegetables, or add with garlic to a simple dish of pasta dressed with olive oil and coarsely ground black pepper. Chillies also liven up white fish – chop a little into a marinade of lime juice, salt and olive oil and brush the fish with this while grilling.

For Chinese stir-fries, sizzle small whole chillies with garlic and ginger for a few seconds, then remove them from the pan. The flavour will permeate the oil, adding zesty flavours to the dish without making it unbearably hot. Provided they are unbroken, chillies make soups and casseroles glow rather than burn. Just add two or three to the pot and fish them out at the end.

If you are wary of heat, roasted chillies are another option. The flavour becomes richer and mellower, adding a less strident touch to soups (**Roasted Squash and Chilli Soup,** page 207), and dressings (**Colourful Beets with Roasted Shallot and Chilli Dressing,** page 33). Use a firm fleshy variety such as 'Jalapeño'. Place under a preheated very hot grill, or better still, on the barbecue, until the skin blisters and blackens slightly. Remove the skin and scrape out the seeds with the tip of a knife. Don't be tempted to rinse under running water or you will wash away the lovely juices. If the skin doesn't come away easily, cover with a cloth and leave for 10 minutes – the steam helps loosen the skin.

Chillies can even be added to sweet dishes or turned into a potent preserve to eat with cold meats. A **chilli-flavoured syrup** is surprisingly good with chilled slices of tropical fruit, or, for a sensational cold-hot experience, trickled over very cold ice cream. A fruity-flavoured Habanero is the best type to use. Put 140g sugar in a

UK season
• July–October.

Varieties to look for
• '*Anaheim*', elongated, green turning to red, thin-skinned, mildly hot. Ideal for stews and salsas.
• '*Cherry Bomb*', small round, bright red, tough skin, thick flesh, super-hot. Excellent roasted, peeled and stuffed.
• '*Jalapeño*', torpedo-shaped, deep grassy green turning to red, fleshy, medium heat. Good roasted or barbecued, or in breads and jam.
• '*Hungarian Hot Wax*', elongated, brilliant yellow, thin skin, medium-thick flesh, mild heat. Use in salads and stir-fries.
• '*Habanero*', puckered lantern shape, orange, thin skin and flesh, extremely hot, fruity tropical flavour. Use with care in any dish. Good in syrups, chocolate desserts and ice cream.
• '*Mulato Isleño*', heart-shaped, rich chocolate brown, tough skin, complex flavour, one of the best-tasting chillies. Excellent stuffed with meat or cheese.
• '*Scotch Bonnet*', flattened tam o'shanter shape, red when mature, thin skin and flesh, extremely hot. Prized in Caribbean cookery. Use with care in any dish.

Shopping notes
• Look for firm fresh-looking fruits with vibrant colour and smooth skin.
• Steer clear of any that look flabby or wrinkled, or have brown marks or watery bruises.
• Jalapeño chillies sometimes have white lines on the skin. This is a natural marking and nothing to worry about.

Storing
• Freshly harvested chillies can be stored in a ventilated plastic bag in the fridge for 1–2 weeks.
• For the best flavour, bring to room temperature before using.
• Once cut, the flesh soon starts to rot. Wrap in cling film and use within 24 hours.

small saucepan with 300ml water and 1 deseeded chilli. Bring to the boil, stirring to dissolve the sugar, then simmer briskly for 5 minutes. Leave to cool then fish out the chilli. The syrup will keep in a screw-top jar for up to 2 weeks in the fridge.

Hungarian Hot Wax Chillies, Tomatoes and Courgettes

Each time I make this I am bowled over by the beauty of the vibrant colours and the rich complex flavours. This dish is a real celebration of summer produce.

Remove the stem and seeds from the chillies, and slice the flesh crossways into 2-cm strips.

Heat a large frying pan over medium-high heat. Add the olive oil, then stir-fry the chillies, spring onions and courgettes for a few minutes until just starting to soften. Add the garlic and reduce the heat a little. Cover and leave for 2-3 minutes; the vegetables will cook in their own steam.

Stir in the tomatoes and their juice, then add the vinegar, sea salt flakes and plenty of freshly ground black pepper. Cook, uncovered, for 3-4 minutes more. By now the vegetables should be producing plenty of liquid. Tip the contents of the pan into a large sieve set over a bowl. Once the juices have dripped through, tip the vegetables into a warm serving dish.

Pour the juices back into the pan and simmer briskly until slightly thickened. Pour over the vegetables and sprinkle with the parsley.

Cook's note
• If you can't find 'Hungarian Hot Wax' chillies, use a long thin-fleshed sweet red pepper such as 'Romano' and add a tiny bit of finely chopped green chilli.

'Hungarian Hot Wax' chillies (see Cook's note) 350g
olive oil 2 tbsp
small purple spring onions 3-4, thinly sliced
small courgettes 350g, thinly sliced
fat 'green' garlic cloves 2, thinly sliced
plum tomatoes 450g, peeled and chopped
cider vinegar 2 tsp
sea salt flakes
freshly ground black pepper
flat leaf parsley trimmed and chopped to make 1 tbsp

Serves 2–4 as a light meal

Cobnuts

A cultivated form of hazelnut, cobnuts are the finest example of a British nut. Grown mostly in Kent, cobnut orchards, or plats as they are known, have shrunk since the first world war from 7000 to 250 acres, but it seems that a quiet revolution is taking place to save them from extinction. New trees are being planted and the nuts are increasingly available at farm shops, PYO farms and farmers' markets.

Unlike most nuts, cobnuts are sold fresh and 'green' with the soft shaggy calyx still in place, partially enclosing the shell. Inside, the nutmeat is sweet, moist and crisp – quite unlike the chewy dry flesh of filberts sold at Christmas. The season at this 'green' stage is brief, so snap them up before the calyxes turn brown.

Cooking

Cobnuts are delicious eaten raw, preferably cracked by a loved one ready for you to dip in sea salt. Add them to salads, both fruit and leafy, or chop finely and sprinkle over chilled desserts. They add subtle sweetness and crunch to a **custard tart** (see **Eggs**, page 98). You'll need 450g of nuts (about 175g when shelled); it's a labour of love to crack them but worth it for the result. Chop by hand or pulse in quick bursts in a food processor, then add to the thickened custard before baking in the oven.

Also good are roughly chopped cobnuts lightly fried in butter – take care not to burn them. They add irresistible crunch scattered over crushed roast potatoes or root vegetables (**Duck Breasts with Young Turnips, Carrots and Cobnuts,** page 96) or as a topping for a thick smooth soup.

See also **Damson and Cobnut Sweet Pickle** (page 92)

UK season
• Late August–mid-September.

Varieties to look for
• '*Kentish Cob*', traditional variety with superior flavour.

Shopping notes
• Choose nuts with a soft green pliable calyx and satiny shells.

Storing
• Treat as fresh produce and keep in a paper bag in the fridge.
• Eat within a day or two of buying, before the husks dry out.

Preparation
• Crack as needed and peel off the soft brown fibre encasing the nut.

Courgettes

Smooth dark green or yellow courgettes are the best known of the summer squash, but there are other varieties too. Worth snapping up if you see them are stylish two-tone green courgettes with heavily ridged skin – they look fantastic sliced into ovals. Keep an eye out too for flattened scallop-edged patty pan squash in green or yellow, or bulbous yellow crookneck types, or round ones the size of a billiard ball.

Farm shops are also good places to find gorgeous yellow courgette flowers. Freshly gathered and covered with dew they are culinary jewels to be pounced on for stuffing and deep-frying in batter.

Cooking

Courgettes and other summer squash need quick and simple cooking to preserve their tender flesh and muted flavour. Steaming, grilling or light sautéing are the order of the day.

Like cucumbers, courgettes suffer from water retention, particularly as they mature. The flesh easily becomes mushy when cooked, especially if finely sliced or chopped. Salting is one solution but you can also **grate them coarsely**, then wrap in a square of cheesecloth and squeeze. Once devoid of excess moisture, cook briefly in a covered pan with a generous knob of butter, finely chopped rosemary and plenty of seasoning. Serve as a side dish with fish or poultry, or toss with pasta and freshly grated Parmesan, or mix into a risotto.

A colourful mixture of finger-sized dark green courgettes and baby yellow patty pans is excellent with **Hungarian Hot Wax Chillies and Tomatoes** (page 80). Another favourite is a warm sloppy vegetable salad made with lightly steamed courgettes and carrot ribbons (see **Preparation**), tossed with walnut oil, walnuts and chives.

Alternatively, dip courgette batons into a light egg batter and deep-fry in hot oil. Stack on a serving plate and serve hot with wedges of lemon. Simpler still, steam halved small courgettes, pat dry and smear with pesto sauce. Both are delicious as a starter or with drinks.

UK season
• June–October.

Varieties to look for
• *'Costata Romanesco'*, elongated, light and dark green stripes, deeply ribbed skin, superb earthy flavour.
• *'Gold Rush'*, elongated, bright yellow, crisp texture, mild flavour redolent of mushrooms.
• *'Peter Pan'*, flattish scallop-edged patty pan type, light green, crisp texture, mild flavour.
• *'Sunburst'*, rounder patty pan type, bright yellow, crisp texture, rich flavour.
• *'Tondo di Nizza'*, spherical, mottled light green, meaty flavour.

Shopping notes
• Look for firm small fruits that feel heavy for their size. Beware of flaccid flesh and broken skin.
• Flowers should be dewy-fresh and unblemished.

Storing
• Store loosely wrapped in a paper bag in the fridge for 2–4 days.
• Use courgette flowers on the day you buy them.

Preparation
• If the skin is slightly hairy, soak in cold water to float away clinging dirt.
• Trim both ends but leave the skin intact as it adds taste, colour and texture.
• Cut into shapes according to the recipe:
Coins or ovals: slice crossways or diagonally.
Batons: cut whole courgettes into shorter lengths, then slice lengthways into quarters.
Ribbons: cut in half lengthways, then use a swivel peeler to shave each half into long wide ribbons.

Sautéed Courgettes with Lemon and Rosemary

This is such a simple dish but utterly delicious nevertheless – perfect with grilled lamb chops. You will need courgettes with firm meaty flesh – some varieties are too watery to fry crisply.

Slice the courgettes diagonally into 1-cm pieces. Heat a non-stick ridged frying pan over medium-high heat. Add the olive oil and fry the courgettes in a single layer, in batches if necessary, for 3 minutes or until the underside is lightly flecked with brown. Turn carefully with tongs, add the garlic and rosemary and fry for 2–3 minutes more, taking care that the garlic doesn't burn.

Tip into a warm serving dish and sprinkle with sea salt flakes, freshly ground black pepper and the lemon zest.

Cook's note
• Don't crowd the pan, otherwise the courgettes will steam in their own juices rather than becoming brown and crisp.

small green or **yellow courgettes** 500g
olive oil 1 tbsp
garlic cloves 1–2 large, thinly sliced
tender rosemary leaves a few, chopped
sea salt flakes
freshly ground black pepper
lemon finely grated zest of $\frac{1}{2}$

Serves 4 as a side dish

Stuffed Courgette Flowers

If you are sure the flowers haven't been sprayed, there is no need to wash them – just shake them free of insects. Otherwise dip briefly in cold water and drain on paper towels.

Carefully insert your finger and thumb into each flower and nip off the stamen. Snip off any stalk that is still attached as well as the sepals if they are prickly.

Combine all the stuffing ingredients. Insert a teaspoonful of stuffing into each flower and twist the petals round to keep the stuffing in place.

Pour the water into a shallow dish and gradually whisk in the flour, sprinkling it through a sieve to make sure there are no lumps.

Heat a medium frying pan and pour in enough groundnut oil to come to a depth of 2cm. When it is almost smoking, quickly dip a flower into the batter, swirling until thoroughly coated, and then put into the hot oil. Fry in batches for 2–3 minutes on each side, until crisp and golden. Remove with tongs, shaking to remove excess oil, and drain on paper towels. Repeat with the remaining flowers. Sprinkle with sea salt flakes and serve at once with lemon wedges.

Cook's note
• The batter should have the consistency of thin pouring cream. Add more flour or water if necessary.

courgette flowers 8–10
water 175ml
plain flour 75g
groundnut oil for deep-frying
sea salt flakes
lemon wedges to serve

for the stuffing
ricotta cheese or **fresh goat's cheese** 225g
egg organic 1, beaten
plain flour 1 tbsp
Parmesan cheese 3 tbsp, freshly grated
basil leaves chopped to make 3 tbsp
freshly ground black pepper $\frac{1}{4}$ tsp
sea salt flakes

Serves 4–5 as a starter or light meal

Cream

Traditionally, cream was simply scooped from milk that had been left to ripen, unrefrigerated, in the dairy. Nowadays milk must be chilled within seconds, and most mass-produced cream is consequently bland. Cream found in farm shops, however, is likely to come from local Jersey or Guernsey herds and is noticeably different: thick, exquisitely flavoured and rich in colour. The cream may be organic or unpasteurised (see **Milk**, page 164) – the most sublimely flavoured of all. Some farm shops also sell fermented crème fraîche and soured cream, made with milk ripened with souring cultures.

In west country farm shops you'll find clotted cream. Devastatingly thick, the cream has a grainy texture, a deep yellow crust and a unique flavour that is hard to describe – boiled milk and toffee come to mind. Cornish clotted cream has achieved PDO (Protected Designation of Origin) status awarded by the EU. This means that it is made only in the geographic area of origin and complies with stringent regulations governing the way it is produced.

Cream is classified according to the amount of butterfat it contains, with clotted cream (55 per cent) at one end of the scale and single cream (18 per cent) at the other. In between are double cream (at least 48 per cent but more if from Jersey cows) and whipping cream (35 per cent). It is the fat content that determines how cream may be used. Low fat cream curdles when heated; double and whipping cream may be heated and can also be whipped to almost twice their volume.

Cooking

Whether used as is or whipped to a billowing cloud, cream improves a significant number of dishes. A few spoonfuls swirled into a soup or stew add richness and round out harsh flavours, particularly in a curry. Similarly, if used to deglaze a pan in which meat has been cooked, cream produces a magnificently flavoured sauce. Flavoured with garlic (**garlic cream**, page 112) or left unadulterated, cream lubricates root vegetables (**Pan-Fried Celeriac with Dill and Mustard Sauce**, page 60) and pasta (**Mushrooms with Pappardelle, Pine Nuts, Cream, Garlic and Parmesan**, page 167).

In sweet dishes, whipped cream lightens mousses and soufflés, and provides ice cream with richness, smoothness and body. It is used to sandwich cake layers together, as a filling for meringues and profiteroles, and a topping for trifles and gateaux.

Clotted cream is traditionally eaten with scones and jam for afternoon tea; jam first, cream on top in Cornwall, the reverse in Devon. It's also sublime with any kind of dessert – particularly apple pie – and makes ambrosial ice cream (**Clotted Cream Ice Cream with Blackcurrants**, page 88). It's just as good in savoury dishes – stir it into fluffy mashed potatoes, or mix with horseradish as a sauce for smoked fish.

See also **Milk** (page 164)

Cream to look for
• *Clotted cream*: west country speciality made from extra-rich milk from Jersey or Guernsey cows.
• *Organic Jersey double cream*: rich yellow, smooth, heavy texture, outstanding flavour.

Shopping notes
• Make sure the cream is within the 'use by' date, and the carton is clean and properly sealed.

Storing
• Double cream and whipping cream: 4–5 days in the fridge.
• Single cream: 2–3 days in the fridge.
• Clotted cream: 1–2 weeks in the fridge.

Preparation
• Double and whipping creams can be whipped to expand the volume. Take care not to over-whip or the cream will turn to butter. Make sure it is well-chilled and, if possible, the bowl and beaters too.
• If adding sugar to whipped cream, do so at the beginning so that the granules have dissolved by the time the cream is fully whipped.

Baked Custards with Vanilla and Caramelised Honey

This is adapted from a recipe from food writer Mike Feasey's book *Eat Dorset*. Mike is a neighbour of mine and a staunch supporter of local food producers.

Preheat the oven to 170°C/gas 3. Lightly grease six ovenproof ramekins or custard cups with butter.

Combine the cream, milk, vanilla pod and honey in a saucepan and heat to a near simmer. Remove from the heat and leave to cool and infuse.

Whisk the whole eggs and the yolks in a bowl. Pick out the vanilla pod from the cream mixture. Pour half the cream mixture onto the eggs, whisk well, then add the rest. Strain through a fine sieve to remove threads or bits.

Pour the egg mixture into the prepared ramekins. Place a piece of foil over the top of each and put in a roasting tin with enough hot water to come halfway up the sides. Bake for about 30 minutes or until just set. Remove from the oven, allow to cool, then remove the foil. Cover with cling film and chill in the fridge for 2–3 hours before serving.

For the syrup, boil the honey quite fiercely in a saucepan and reduce to a thick caramel, stirring occasionally to prevent sticking and burning. Remove from the heat and leave to cool down for 5 minutes. Stir in the water and allow to cool to room temperature.

To serve, dip the base of each ramekin briefly in hot water, then turn upside-down and unmould on to a serving plate. Pour the caramelised honey over the top.

Cook's note

• Be careful not to overcook the custards. As Mike points out, the latent heat in each ramekin will continue to set the custard even after you have removed it from the oven.

unsalted butter for greasing
whipping cream organic, 400ml
whole milk organic, 200ml
vanilla pod 1, split lengthways
clear honey 5 tbsp
eggs organic, 2 medium
egg yolks organic, 3

for the syrup
clear honey 150g
water 3 tbsp

Serves 6

Clotted Cream Ice Cream with Blackcurrants

Clotted cream makes the most unctuously rich ice cream with a distinctive flavour. A swirl of blackcurrant purée adds welcome tartness.

Pour the milk into a saucepan with two-thirds of the sugar and the vanilla pod. Stir over medium heat for about 5 minutes or until steaming (80°C) but don't let the mixture boil. Remove from the heat and leave to infuse.

Beat the egg yolks with the remaining sugar until very pale and creamy – about 4 minutes. Remove the vanilla pod from the warm milk. Gradually whisk the milk into the thickened yolks.

Pour the custard back into the pan and stir over medium-low heat for 8–10 minutes until thickened (85°C). Pour into a metal bowl and cool. Stir in the clotted cream, making sure you get rid of any lumps. Cover the surface with cling film and chill in the fridge for up to 24 hours.

Meanwhile, for the purée, cook the blackcurrants very gently with the water until soft. Push through a fine sieve to get rid of the pips. Stir in the icing sugar and a squeeze of lemon juice. Pour into a small jug and chill.

Churn and freeze the cream mixture in an ice cream machine for 12–15 minutes until it reaches the soft scoop stage. Quickly swirl in the blackcurrant purée. Pack into a freezer-proof container, cover the surface with cling film, then store in the freezer to harden completely.

Cook's notes

• Take care not to let the custard boil or you will end up with scrambled eggs.
• If you don't have an ice cream machine, follow the directions for still-freezing Quince and Ginger Sorbet (page 213).
• If using an ice cream machine, take care not to over-churn. Clotted cream is high in fat and can easily turn to butter.

Variation

• For a plainer ice cream to serve with desserts such as **Spiced Roasted Quinces with Honey and Clotted Cream** (page 204), leave out the blackcurrant purée.

whole milk organic, 300ml
caster sugar 100g
vanilla pod 1/2, split
egg yolks organic, 3
clotted cream organic, 300g

for the blackcurrant purée
blackcurrants 150g
water 2 tbsp
icing sugar 1 1/2 tbsp
lemon juice a squeeze

Makes about 750ml

Cucumber

Farms or market gardens occasionally sell cucumbers that you are less likely to find elsewhere: warty-skinned picklers, spiny outdoor-grown ridge types or slender Lebanese miniatures. You may also find ordinary hot-house cucumbers picked while still small. At this stage they actually taste of cucumber – mild, for sure, but certainly not bland.

Cooking

If the cooling qualities of cucumber are to be fully appreciated, it's best to eat them raw, preferably unsalted and in slices thick enough to get your teeth into. Baking or frying simply misses the point. However, if you feel compelled to cook your cucumber, in a stir-fry or noodle dish, say, or you want to rid it of moisture for a particular type of salad, then it will need salting (see **Preparation**).

It seems to me that the UK is sadly lacking in recipes for cucumber; we put them in sandwiches and salads, and that's about it. We could usefully take a lead from the cuisines of the Middle East and India. Here, cucumbers are traditionally combined with **yogurt and mint** (page 278) to make a soothing sauce for grilled meat or to offset the heat of a spicy curry. The Turks make a refreshing **'shepherd's' salad** with chunks of baby cucumbers, cherry tomatoes, red onion, olives and crumbly goat's cheese, showered with flat leaf parsley and dressed with lemon juice and olive oil.

Also very refreshing is a tangy **cucumber, lime and mint salsa**. Peel, deseed and dice 1–2 ridge cucumbers, and salt them for 1 hour. Rinse and pat dry, then mix with the juice of $\frac{1}{2}$ a lime, 1 finely chopped garlic clove, 2 teaspoons of chopped mint and some freshly ground pepper – preferably white – and a pinch of sugar. Add 3–4 tablespoons of finely diced root vegetables, such as kohlrabi, white radish or turnip. This hits the spot with **Tandoori Turkey Tikka** (page 281).

Cucumbers complement smoked fish such as mackerel, kippers or trout. For a loose **pâté**, scoop out the seeds from a chunk of cucumber weighing about 115g. Grate the flesh coarsely, giving it a squeeze to get rid of some of the liquid. Mix with 85g each of flaked smoked fish and ricotta cheese. Add lemon juice, some chopped dill, and salt and black pepper to taste. Serve chilled.

Cucumbers are almost synonymous with East European cuisine. A traditional salad is made with peeled and salted ultra-thin slices sprinkled with dill and chopped spring onion, floating in a watery sweet-sour dressing. It works in a curious sort of way, especially with the fatty meat dishes that are commonplace in the region.

Cucumbers are also the mainstay of pickles, for which there are innumerable recipes – sour, half-sour, sweet-and-sour, dill, new green and so on. A favourite is the old-fashioned **Bread and Butter Pickle** (page 90). As the name suggests, this is good on a hefty slice of thickly buttered bread.

UK season
• July–October.

Cucumbers to look for
• *Pickling cucumbers or gherkins:* fat and dumpy, warty skin, slightly dry flesh, full flavour, sometimes bitter.
• *Ridge, outdoor type:* fat and dumpy, spiny tough skin, crisp flesh, lemony flavour.
• *Smooth-skinned, hot-house type:* slender, spineless tender skin, seedless, crisp watery flesh, slightly sweet flavour.

Shopping notes
• Choose stiff fruits that feel firm along the entire length.
• Check the cut end of cucumber portions. It should look clean and crisp rather than yellowing.
• Choose ridge and pickling cucumbers no more than 15–18cm long. The seeds become as tough as finger nails if allowed to grow bigger and the flesh can be bitter.

Storing
• Store in a cool larder or the salad drawer of the fridge for up to 1 week.
• Once cut, keep tightly wrapped in cling film, including the cut end, and use within 2–3 days.

Preparation
• Peeling smooth-skinned varieties is a matter of preference since the skin is edible. Rather than denude the cucumber completely, remove alternate strips along the length.
• Remove the peel from ridge or pickling cucumbers and scoop out the seeds if large.
• To remove their liquid, sprinkle sliced or chopped cucumbers with salt, a little sugar and a teaspoon of wine vinegar. Put in a colander with a weighted plate on top. After 30 minutes the liquid will start to flow.

Bread and Butter Pickle

Unlike many pickles this can be eaten immediately. I like it still warm and enjoyed ratatouille-style with rice.

Arrange the vegetables in layers in a wide dish, sprinkling sea salt flakes over each layer. Cover and leave in a cool place overnight. Drain off the liquid, plunge the vegetables into a large bowl of cold water, rinse and drain again.

Put the sugar, vinegar and spices in a saucepan, bring to the boil and boil for 2 minutes. Add the vegetables, bring back to the boil, and cook for 5–10 minutes, depending on how crunchy you like your pickle.

Remove from the heat, leave to cool, then store in plastic boxes in the fridge for up to a week. For long-term storage, ladle the hot pickle into warm sterilised jars. Seal and store in a cool dark place.

Cook's note
• If you can't find pickling cucumbers, use ordinary hot-house ones instead.

pickling cucumbers 750g, peeled and thickly sliced
onion 1 large, thinly sliced
red or **yellow pepper** 1, deseeded and thinly sliced
fresh red chilli $^1/_2$ –1, deseeded and thinly sliced
sea salt flakes
sugar 175g
white wine vinegar 350ml
mustard seeds $^1/_2$ tbsp
dill seeds $^1/_2$ tbsp
ground turmeric $^1/_2$ tsp

Makes about 1kg

Damsons

A wild relative of the cultivated plum, damsons are small and oval, with dark purple skin and firm yellow-green flesh. The flavour is sensational – intensely acidic yet sweet and plummy at the same time. Damsons have a brief late-summer season – blink and you'll miss it.

We should make the most of these under-appreciated gems; they are fast becoming a rarity and farm shops look like their last stronghold. Fortunately, pockets of survival exist in the southern Lake District where enthusiasts have replanted orchards and annually celebrate Damson Day in April to coincide with the stunning snow-white blossom. The Slow Food movement have added support by including Westmoreland Damsons in the Ark Project, a register of endangered foods that members are encouraged to use.

Cooking

Writing in World War II, cookbook author and farmer's wife Lucie G. Nicoll concluded, 'Although one enjoys uncooked damsons after the age of reason and before the age of discretion, the fruit is much better cooked.' I do remember as a child unwisely eating damsons plucked from a hedge, and I remember the ensuing stomach upsets. Mrs Nicoll certainly had a point.

Once cooked, damsons come into their own but need a copious amount of sugar to tame their mouth-puckering tartness. They are a natural candidate for preserves and can be transformed into the most sublime jellies, jams, chutneys and pickles, or even damson 'cheese' – a firm, intensely flavoured relish served in gleaming slabs with cold meats (**Plum Cheese** page 195). Try your hand at ruby-coloured **Damson and Cobnut Sweet Pickle** (page 92), a delicious reminder of late summer when both the fruit and the nuts are in season. The pickle needs to mature for at least 6–8 weeks. Eat it at Christmas – it's excellent with duck or goose, or any cold meat.

Teamed with less acidic orchard fruits, damsons make richly flavoured tarts, pies and crumbles. They are also tamed by dairy products and eggs, and can be whipped into lovely rose-coloured fools and ice creams. In Cumbria's Lyth Valley, home to important damson orchards, cooks make a traditional damson and apple tansy with fried apples, eggs and soured cream. The mixture is simmered until thick then sprinkled with sugar and browned under the grill.

Stunning both in flavour and colour is **damson sorbet** – a rich deep crimson with an assertive almost chocolate-like flavour. Gently stew about 650g damsons with 3–4 tablespoons of water. Once soft, push through a fine sieve, pressing hard with the back of a wooden spoon. Stir in 1 tablespoon of lemon juice and 250ml sugar syrup (made by dissolving 150g sugar in 150ml water and bringing to the boil). Leave to cool, then chill for 2 hours before freezing. Eat within a week while the flavour is at its peak.

UK season
• September.

Varieties to look for
• *'Blue Violet'*, local to southern Cumbria, oval, not overly acid, juicy, fairly rich flavour.
• *'Farleigh'*, small, round, olive green flesh, rich flavour.
• *'Merryweather'*, large, plump, sweeter than most, real damson flavour.
• *'Prune'* or *'Shropshire Damson'*, small, oval, stunning flavour.

Shopping notes
• Look for firm unblemished fruit with a powdery blue-grey bloom.
• Steer clear of any that are whizened or bruised.

Storing
• Keep not-quite-ripe damsons at room temperature for a few days.
• Once ripe, store in the fridge for up to 3 days.

Preparation
• Stones are difficult to remove – cook the fruit in a little water, then fish out the stones as they separate from the pulp.
• Push the pulp through a sieve if you want to get rid of the skin as well.

Damson and Cobnut Sweet Pickle

Damsons and cobnuts enjoy a brief season together in late summer. This recipe, inspired by one from preserve doyenne Pam Corbin (alias Pam the Jam of River Cottage HQ), celebrates both.

Combine the vinegar and spices in a saucepan with the ginger and orange zest and juice. Bring to the boil, then simmer briskly for 5 minutes. Remove from the heat, leave to cool, then strain.

While the vinegar is cooling, prick the damsons with a needle to stop them bursting. Put them in a saucepan with the strained vinegar solution. Bring slowly to simmering point, then simmer very gently for 10–15 minutes until just tender.

Using a perforated spoon, lift the damsons from the liquid and divide between four warm, sterilised jars (see **Cook's note**), interspersing them with the cobnuts.

Dissolve the sugar in the vinegar solution, stirring over medium heat. Boil for 10 minutes or until the bubbles start to look thick and syrupy. Pour into the jars, cover with waxed discs and seal. Leave in a cool dark place to mature for 6–8 weeks before eating.

cider vinegar 600ml
cinnamon stick 5-cm piece, broken
allspice berries 2 tsp
cloves 6
fresh ginger root 6 thin slices
orange finely grated zest and juice of 1
damsons 1.25kg
cobnuts 200g, shelled and roughly chopped
sugar 750g

Makes four 450ml jars

Cook's note
• Sterilise your jars just before filling. Either run them through the dishwasher, or wash with hot soapy water and dry upside-down in a low oven.

Duck

Often overlooked as a day-to-day food, duck is surprisingly versatile and makes a welcome change from chicken. Farmed duck is meaty, succulent and slightly sweet, and wild duck is on a par with other richly flavoured game birds. You'll find both in farm shops, and they are worth snapping up even if you're not planning on cooking right away – just stash the birds in the freezer.

People often tell me they are nervous about cooking duck. Perhaps the legendary amount of fat is off-putting, yet the fat is an advantage – it prevents the meat from drying out. Once drained and sieved, it can be stored for several weeks in the fridge and put to endless good uses. Also worth bearing in mind is that speciality breeds such as Barbary and Gressingham are leaner than the traditional Aylesbury duck, so go for these if you are after more meat and less fat.

A valid disadvantage to duck is the high proportion of bone and cavity space compared with the amount of meat. This means that a roast duck of average weight will serve three at the most, so you will need to buy two ducks for four people, or perhaps throw in a mysterious extra leg joint.

Cooking

There are almost limitless ways of cooking duck. Roasting springs to mind first, but duck can also be braised, stewed, stir-fried or grilled, or used in risottos and spicy curries. The carcass makes a well-flavoured stock and the liver is delicious.

Returning to roasting, the trick is to cook the duck on a rack over a roasting tin and regularly pour off the fat. Don't throw this away – it makes the best roast potatoes ever.

Grilled breasts are simple to deal with and make a tasty treat. Just brown them quickly in a frying pan, then finish in a very hot oven. Leave to rest so the juices flow evenly through the meat, then carve in thin diagonal slices. Serve either as **Warm Duck Breast Salad** (page 94) or with turnips – their slightly bitter and pungent flavour contrasts beautifully with sweet succulent duck meat (**Duck Breasts with Young Turnips, Carrots and Cobnuts**, page 96). **Roasted swede** (page 252) is another tasty accompaniment, as are steamed green and leafy turnip greens (*cima de rapa*). A dollop of chilli jam on the side is the perfect condiment.

The rich succulent meat holds its own with strongly flavoured sauces, especially fruit-based ones. Duck *à l'orange* and duck with apple sauce are well known, but equally good is **Duck with Quince**, the juices enriched with honey and ginger (page 97).

During the season, farm shops are purveyors of wild duck such as mallard or widgeon. These should be roasted and served pink so they need very little time in the oven – no more than 30 minutes at 200°C/gas 6. Blackberries, crab apples and mushrooms – all in season at same time – are excellent accompaniments.

See also **Duck Eggs** (page 98)

UK season
- *Duckling* (less than 2 months old): spring.
- *Older birds*: year round.
- *Wild duck*: 1 September–31 January (mallard), 1 October–11 February (teal and widgeon).

Breeds to look for
- *Barbary duck*: mild gamey flavour, not excessively fatty, plenty of lean breast meat.
- *Gressingham duck*: mild gamey flavour, not excessively fatty, plenty of lean breast meat, thin crispy skin.
- *Mallard*: gamey flavour, lean dark flesh.

Shopping notes
- Skin should be slightly moist but not overly greasy, with no discoloured patches.

Storing
- Store on the bottom shelf of the fridge so raw juices cannot drip onto other food.
- Remove wrapping and store in a shallow dish, loosely covered with foil, for 2–3 days depending on 'use by' date.
- Remove giblets and store separately.
- If vacuum-packed or in a rigid plastic container, leave unopened until ready to cook.

Preparation
- Wash well and pat dry with paper towels.
- *Roasting:* for crispy skin, prick all over with a fork. Put in a colander and douse with a kettleful of boiling water to encourage subcutaneous fat to flow. Dry well, then rub with sea salt before roasting.
- *Grilling breasts:* score the skin diagonally 3–4 times to allow the fat to flow, rub with sea salt and freshly ground black pepper.
- *Wild duck:* rub with butter and season to taste. There's no real need to bard the breast – the roasting time is too short for the meat to dry out.

Serving size
- Whole bird: 1.8kg serves 2; 2kg serves 3.
- Boneless breast: 200g serves 1.
- Whole wild duck: 600–700g serves 2.

Warm Duck Breast Salad with Watercress, Walnuts, Sugar Snap Peas and Bean Sprouts

Juicy duck breasts with crisp skin, peppery leaves, crunchy sugar snaps and bean sprouts make a terrific salad with mouth-watering textures and flavours.

Preheat the oven to 220°C/gas 7. Wash the duck breasts and pat dry with paper towels. Slash the skin diagonally in three or four places. Rub with crumbled sea salt flakes and freshly ground black pepper.

Heat a small non-stick ovenproof frying pan over medium-high heat. Add the duck breasts skin side down and sizzle for 3–4 minutes. Move to the oven and roast for 5 minutes, then turn and roast for 5 minutes more. Leave to rest in a warm place for at least 15 minutes.

Meanwhile, plunge the sugar snap peas into a large pan of boiling salted water. Bring back to the boil and boil for 1 minute. Drain under running water then pat dry with paper towels.

Slice the pods in half diagonally then put in a bowl with the watercress, spring onions, bean sprouts and walnut halves. Sprinkle with a little sea salt and freshly ground black pepper. Toss with enough walnut oil to barely coat the leaves, then add the merest splash of balsamic vinegar.

Divide the salad between serving plates. Thinly slice the duck diagonally and arrange on top. Sprinkle with a little more sea salt, walnut oil and balsamic vinegar, then pour over the juices that have flowed from the duck. Serve while the duck is still warm.

Cook's notes
• Don't worry if the duck looks rare when it comes out of the oven; it will continue to cook as it rests. However it will still be slightly pink when carved. Duck meat tends to toughen up and become dry if cooked for too long.

boneless duck breasts 2
sea salt flakes
freshly ground black pepper
sugar snap peas 100g
watercress 2 bunches, trimmed, thick stalks removed
spring onions 4, thinly sliced diagonally
mixed bean sprouts 2 small handfuls
walnut halves 25g
walnut oil
balsamic vinegar

Serves 2–3 as a light meal or 4 as a starter

Duck Breasts with Young Turnips, Carrots and Cobnuts

This is a great mix of flavours and textures: rich juicy duck, slightly bitter turnips, sweet carrots and crunchy fried cobnuts. If cobnuts are out of season, use hazelnuts instead.

Preheat the oven to 240°C/gas 9. Wash the duck breasts and pat dry with paper towels. Slash the skin diagonally in three or four places. Rub with crumbled sea salt flakes and freshly ground black pepper. Heat a small heavy-based frying pan over medium-high heat. Add the duck breasts skin-side down and sizzle for 3–4 minutes.

Meanwhile, steam the turnips and carrots together for 3–4 minutes until barely tender.

Put the duck breasts skin-side down in a small roasting tin. Scatter the turnips and carrots on top and pour over any fat from the frying pan. Roast for 5 minutes, then turn the duck over and roast for another 5 minutes. Remove the duck breasts to a plate and leave to rest in a warm place for 10–15 minutes.

Carry on roasting the vegetables for another 5–10 minutes or until starting to brown round the edges. Fry the cobnuts in duck fat or butter for a few minutes until just golden.

Put the roasted vegetables in a warm serving dish. Slice the duck diagonally and arrange on top of the vegetables, pouring over the juices, and scatter with the cobnuts.

Cook's notes
• Slice the vegetables fairly thickly so that they keep their shape while roasting.
• Use a roasting tin just big enough to take the duck breasts comfortably in a single layer.

boneless duck breasts 2
sea salt flakes
freshly ground black pepper
turnips 4 small, sliced into discs then halved
carrots 2, sliced diagonally
cobnuts 10–12, shelled and halved
duck fat or butter for frying

Serves 2

Roast Duck with Quince, Honey and Ginger

The distinctive rich flavour of duck marries well with quince and ginger. This dish is also good made with pears.

Quarter the duck by first removing the backbone – cut along the length either side of it with poultry shears – then open the bird out flat and cut in half lengthways down the breast bone. Cut each piece in two across the ribs. Trim off any fatty flaps of skin.

Combine all the marinade ingredients, whisking well. Put the duck quarters in a ziplock bag and pour in the marinade. Seal the bag and leave to marinate for at least 2 hours or up to a day in the fridge.

Preheat the oven to 180°C/gas 4. Quarter, core and peel the quinces (it's easiest to do it in that order), then slice lengthways into eighths. Arrange with the onion quarters in a single layer in the base of a roasting tin.

Take the duck quarters out of the bag, reserving the marinade. Pour all but 4 tablespoons of the marinade over the quinces and onions, tossing with your hands to coat. Arrange the duck skin-side up on a rack that will fit over the roasting tin. Sprinkle with crumbled sea salt flakes and freshly ground black pepper.

Roast for 40 minutes, brushing halfway through with some of the reserved marinade. Turn the duck pieces over, brush with the remaining marinade and roast for 10–15 minutes more.

Arrange the duck in a warm serving dish and surround with quinces and onion. Drain most of the fat from the roasting tin. Place over medium-high heat and briefly sizzle the remaining liquid, stirring in any sediment. Add a little water or stock if necessary. Pour over the duck and serve.

Cook's note
• Ducks sold in farm shops often come with giblets. Combine them with the backbone and surplus fatty skin to make stock for a soup or a game casserole.

free-range duck 1, weighing about 2kg (without giblets)
quinces 2
onions 2, quartered lengthways
sea salt flakes
freshly ground black pepper

for the marinade
clear honey 4 tbsp
cold-pressed sunflower oil 2 tbsp
orange zest and juice of 1
aged balsamic vinegar 2 tbsp
English mustard 1 tbsp
fresh ginger root 1 tsp, grated
cinnamon $\frac{1}{2}$ stick, broken
salt $\frac{1}{2}$ tsp
freshly ground black pepper $\frac{1}{4}$ tsp

Serves 3–4

Eggs

Eggs sold in farm shops are likely to be supplied by small producers whose output is intended purely for local sale. There may be photographs of flocks on display, or you might be able to visit them yourself. There are few sights more reassuring than stress-free hens enjoying a dust bath or roaming the fields in search of food.

If you are lucky you might come across eggs from rare breed hens, duck, goose and bantam eggs, quail's eggs and, for a limited season, game bird eggs and gull's eggs. Once sampled, you will appreciate that the egg can be a luxury item with a fabulous fresh flavour, gloriously golden yolks and dense texture – a direct result of a diet of greenery, grains and edible grubs rather than commercial feed additives.

Hen's eggs

Particularly sought after are eggs from special breeds. Maran eggs have striking brown shells the colour of builders' tea, while those from the Old Cotswold Legbar come in pretty pastel colours. They all have rich pure flavours quite unlike mass-produced eggs.

Bantam eggs come from naturally small hens and are ideal for children or those wary of too much egginess. These are a mere 5cm long, weighing 30–45g, with delicate pink-white or pale beige shells. Softly boiled for 3–4 minutes, they are lovely on top of a creamy **cauliflower curry** (page 57), sprinkled with freshly ground cumin and chopped fresh coriander.

By law, hen's eggs are graded according to weight. Small means less than 53g, medium 53–62g, large 63–72g, extra large 73g or more. Boxes of farm shop eggs may contain mixed sizes, albeit to a standard total weight. This is useful for the producer as it prevents odd sizes from being ignored and standard sizes from running out.

Duck eggs

Duck eggs are slightly larger than hen's eggs, weighing in at 70–90g. They can be used instead of hen's eggs, though they contain slightly more fat and consequently have a richer flavour. They make unctuously creamy scrambled eggs, and are superb when **deep-fried** (pages 99–100). Depending on breed, the shells are white, pale grey or green-blue. They are tough and need an extra-firm tap to break the shell. Since ducks are farmyard or pond birds living in potentially unhygienic conditions, their eggs should be thoroughly cooked to destroy any harmful bacteria.

Goose eggs

With graceful elongated curves and a chalky white shell, goose eggs have a sculptural Dalì-esque quality that makes one hesitate to crack them. At least three times the size of a hen's egg, the goose egg is rich and intensely eggy with an enormous yolk kept aloft by a viscous white. The flavour is strong on its own but goose eggs are excellent for enriching cakes, and, combined with savoury ingredients, make a tasty **fritatta** (page 104). Like ducks, geese live in potentially unhygienic conditions, and their eggs should be thoroughly cooked to destroy any harmful bacteria.

UK laying season
• *Speciality hen's eggs:* mid-February–July.
• *Goose eggs:* March–July.
• *Game bird eggs:* April–July.
• *Gull's eggs:* late April–mid-May.

Shopping notes
• Always check the 'best-before' date.
• Bear in mind how you intend to use your eggs. Recently laid eggs have a plump yolk and viscous well-defined white. These are best for poaching, shallow-frying and deep-frying as they don't spread much when cracked. Almost out-of-date eggs are ideal for meringues. They have thin whites that incorporate air more easily.
• Make sure the eggs aren't cracked. Leaking egg white will glue undamaged eggs to the box and they may break when you try to dislodge them.

Storing
• Store in the fridge with the pointed end facing down so that the yolk remains centred in the white.
• Leftover yolks or whites will keep for a few days in the fridge covered with cling film.

Preparing
• Never break eggs straight into the pan or mixture. Crack into a small bowl first to check that they are fresh.
• To test for freshness, immerse the egg in a bowl of cold water. If it is really fresh it will lie horizontally on the bottom. If it rises to the vertical and bobs on the bottom it is about two weeks old but edible. If it floats, the egg is rotten and should be thrown away.
• At room temperature, more air can be incorporated into whisked or beaten eggs and this produces a lighter fluffier mixture. Remove from the fridge an hour or so before needed. Immediately break individually into small bowls to rid them of their chill.
• Older eggs are easier to peel after boiling. The inner membrane starts to come away from the shell, creating an air space that makes it easy to separate from the white.

Quail's eggs

An erstwhile game bird, most quail are now farmed and their beautiful little eggs are widely available. Flecked with random splashes of brown, they weigh no more than 20g, and have a mild flavour similar to hen's eggs. Hard-boiled and dipped in celery salt, they make a tasty bite-sized canapé; softly boiled or poached they sit prettily in a **leafy salad** (page 100).

Guinea fowl and game bird eggs

Guinea fowl, pheasant and partridge eggs are all edible, though are only sporadically on sale as they are usually kept for breeding purposes. Guinea fowl eggs (5cm long) are slightly smaller and rounder than hen's eggs, but with a similar mild flavour. They weigh about 35g and have an all-over brown speckling and a dense shell. Pheasant eggs come in military khaki without any speckling. They are small (4.5cm long) and have a powerful flavour best tamed by hard-boiling. Dumpy little partridge eggs (4cm long) are the most exquisite with tasteful coffee-coloured speckles on a pale beige shell.

Gull's eggs

Collecting gull's eggs is restricted to two or three weeks from the end of April, depending on the weather. The short season makes them a rare treat and this is certainly reflected in the price. About 5cm long with sludge-coloured shells bearing dark splotches, the eggs have a somewhat sombre air. The flavour is exquisite, however, though slightly fishy because of the bird's diet. Peter Gordon, chef-patron of London's Providores restaurant, is a fan; he serves gull's eggs poached on warm, hot-smoked flaked salmon with browned butter and a few chopped toasted walnuts. The eggs are also delicious softly boiled and sprinkled with smoked sea salt flakes.

Cooking

Eggs can be boiled, fried, poached, scrambled, baked or made into omelettes – each producing a completely different result. They provide cakes with bounce, soufflés with height and sauces with thickness and gloss. Eggs make pasta silky, pastry shiny and they help breadcrumbs stick to food. Beaten with oil, the yolks emulsify into mayonnaise; whisked with air, the whites transmute to the miraculous foam that gives meringues and mousses their lightness. I can think of no other food so versatile and so essential as eggs.

It is interesting to experiment with different types of egg. Scrambled eggs made with duck eggs, for example, have a dense, creamy, almost chewy texture, whereas scrambled hen's eggs are smoother and lighter. Similarly, goose eggs make a hefty omelette with a much firmer texture than one made with hen's eggs.

I am not a great fan of shallow-fried eggs but **deep-fried eggs** are another matter. They are fun to make and have an appetising crunchy texture. You will need very fresh eggs that hold their shape well – duck eggs are excellent. Begin by breaking the egg into a small bowl. Heat about 10cm of groundnut oil in a small but tall saucepan over medium heat. When the temperature reaches 180°C, or when a cube of bread browns in 1 minute, tip in the egg. It will sizzle and spit at first but will quickly start to cook. Coax it into a rounded shape with the help of two dessert spoons. After 1 minute, carefully roll the egg over so that the yolk stays more or less centred in the white. Cook for another 30 seconds or up to 1½ minutes depending on how you like your eggs. Gently remove with a perforated spoon and drain on paper towels. Sprinkle with crunchy sea salt and a grinding of black pepper. Best served right away with grilled bacon, HP sauce and toast.

For a more delicate dish, try a **salad of lightly boiled quail's eggs** tumbled with watercress sprigs or radicchio, pale green frisée, purple radish sprouts and a few chopped toasted hazelnuts. Take care not to over-boil the eggs. A foolproof method is to start them off in a pan of cold water, then immediately remove from the heat once the water is boiling fast. Sluice under cold running water to stop further cooking. Peel, slice in half lengthways and arrange on the greenery. Anoint with the merest splash of hazelnut oil and a drop of wine vinegar. Season with crumbled sea salt flakes and cracked Tellicherry peppercorns and you have a stunning starter.

Eggs make delectably silky custards. Try them in a savoury version with **chillies and tomatoes**: gently fry a small onion, 2 garlic cloves and a deseeded green chilli – all finely chopped – in a tablespoon of olive oil. Purée and sieve 400g chopped tomatoes, add to the vegetables and simmer until thickened. Season and leave to cool. Lightly beat 4 eggs and mix into the cooled sauce. Pour into greased ramekins. Place in a roasting tin with enough hot water to come halfway up. Bake at 180°C/gas 4 for 35–40 minutes until set.

Moving on to sweeter things, there is nothing more tempting than a **nutmeg-flecked custard tart**. You can buy good-quality frozen pastry in farm shops, so a tart is easy to make. Just roll out the pastry and line a 19–20cm loose-based tart tin. Line with foil, weigh down with baking beans and bake blind for 15 minutes at 190°C/gas 5. For the filling, heat 284ml double cream with a vanilla pod until not quite boiling. Leave to steep for 10 minutes, then remove the pod. Whisk 3 eggs plus 1 yolk with 3 tablespoons of caster sugar. Gradually add to the hot cream, whisking all the time over gentle heat until starting to thicken. Pour the filling into the pastry case (removing the beans and foil) and sprinkle with a layer of freshly grated nutmeg. Bake at 170°C/gas 3 for 20–25 minutes until just set but still slightly wobbly. Cool and chill before serving.

Other delectable eggy classics are cream caramel, lemon meringue pie and the ghostly white angel food cake. You'll find recipes for these in most comprehensive cookbooks.

Deep-Fried Egg (page 99)

Eggs with Fried Tomato, Onion and Peppers

Based on a recipe from Claudia Roden's award-winning book *The Book of Jewish Food*, this is a delicious way of cooking eggs and makes a change from the traditional British fry-up.

Heat a medium non-stick frying pan, then add the rapeseed oil. Fry the onions over medium heat until golden. Stir in the peppers, chilli flakes, and coriander and caraway seeds, and fry until the peppers are soft.

Add the garlic and tomatoes, and season with salt and pepper. Simmer over low heat for 10 minutes, uncovered.

Crack the eggs over the surface, cover and cook for 3–4 minutes more or until the eggs are set. Sprinkle with a little more salt and pepper, and the chopped parsley. Serve with warm pitta bread.

Variations
• Add a few chunks of Cumberland sausage and/or some sliced boiled potato.
• Leave out the peppers and stir in some blanched young broad beans or sliced baby courgettes.

rapeseed oil 2 tbsp
onion 1 large, finely chopped
red peppers 2, deseeded and diced
dried chilli flakes $1/4$ tsp
coriander seeds $1/2$ tsp, crushed
caraway seeds $1/2$ tsp, crushed
garlic clove 1, finely chopped
tomatoes 4 ripe, peeled and chopped
sea salt
freshly ground black pepper
eggs, organic 4
flat leaf parsley chopped, to garnish
warm pitta bread to serve

Serve 4 as a light meal

Sweet Puffy Pancakes with Walnuts

Similar to a soufflé omelette, these pancakes are wonderfully light and puffy. With a crunchy Kirsch-spiked walnut filling they make a very special dessert.

Put half the walnuts in a food processor and whizz to a powder. Finely chop the rest. Mix both lots of nuts to a paste with $1^1/2$ tablespoons of the sugar, the cream, orange zest and Kirsch.

Preheat the grill and set the oven to a low temperature. In a large bowl, beat together the egg yolks, milk and remaining caster sugar. In another large bowl, whisk the egg whites until stiff. Using a large metal spoon, carefully fold the whites into the yolk mixture.

Melt a knob of butter in a 23–24cm non-stick crêpe pan, tilting the pan to cover the base. Once the butter is sizzling, spoon in half the egg mixture and spread out gently with the back of a wooden spoon. Cook for 2 minutes until the base is lightly browned.

Put the pan under the grill and cook for another 2 minutes or until the pancake is puffy and golden. Slide it out of the pan onto a plate and keep warm in the oven while you make the other pancake.

Spoon the walnut paste down the centre of each pancake. Roll up the pancakes around the filling and dust with caster sugar.

Cook's note
• It's best to use eggs at room temperature. They will lose their chill more quickly if you separate the yolks from the whites as soon as they come out of the fridge.

shelled walnuts 75g
caster sugar 2 tbsp, plus extra to decorate
double cream organic, 2 tbsp
small orange finely grated zest of $1/2$
Kirsch 2 tsp
eggs 3, preferably organic, yolks separated
milk 1 tbsp
unsalted butter for frying

Serves 2

Goose Egg Frittata with Potato, Piquillo Peppers and Crispy Onions

Perfect for Sunday morning brunch, this thick tortilla omelette is a special treat made with goose eggs. If you don't have any, use very fresh organic hen's eggs instead.

Heat a 25-cm non-stick frying pan, then add the rapeseed oil and half the butter. Fry the onion over medium heat until golden, seasoning with the oregano. Add the potatoes and fry for about 5 minutes until golden on all sides. Stir in the piquillo peppers and season with salt and pepper.

While the vegetables are cooking, beat the eggs well, then stir in $\frac{1}{2}$ teaspoon of salt, a generous grinding of pepper, the chilli flakes and most of the parsley.

Add the remaining butter to the pan. When it foams, quickly pour in the egg mixture, stirring with a fork to spread out the filling. Cover and cook over medium-low heat for 5–7 minutes until the eggs are almost set. Place under a hot grill for 2–3 minutes to finish cooking the top.

Garnish with the rest of the parsley, slide onto a plate and cut into wedges. Serve hot, warm or at room temperature, but not cold.

Cook's notes
• Using the right size pan is important when making a frittata. The pan should be deep and wide enough to hold a thick omelette but not so large that the egg mixture spreads out without encasing the filling. A 25-cm diameter pan is just right for this recipe.
• If you are feeling dextrous you can finish the fritatta in the pan instead of under the grill. Slide it out of the pan onto a large plate. Cover with the pan, then quickly invert back into the pan, holding the pan and plate together as you do so.

rapeseed oil 1 tbsp
butter 60g
onion 1, halved and thinly sliced
dried oregano or **thyme** $\frac{1}{2}$ tsp
boiled potatoes 3 medium, cut into 1-cm cubes
bottled piquillo peppers 4, drained and chopped
sea salt
freshly ground black pepper
goose eggs 3 or **organic hen's eggs** 9
dried chilli flakes $\frac{1}{4}$ tsp
flat leaf parsley leaves chopped to make 3 tbsp

Serves 4–6 as a light meal, or 10–12 as a shared snack

Fish

As farm shops become ever more successful, some of them now boast a dedicated wet fish counter, invariably manned by a knowledgeable and enthusiastic fishmonger only too happy to advise you on what to buy and how to cook it.

Coastal farm shops tend to have a wider choice, but inland shops within reach of the ports have good supplies too. You'll also find fresh water fish such as trout or perch, as well as delectable smoked and pickled fish products (see **Fish to look for**), many of which are produced on the premises.

A gratifying number of farm shops source their fish from sustainably managed fisheries. You can find out more about this from various web sites (see **Resources**, page 284–286). The choice may vary according to season, and weather also plays a part; there may not be any fish at all if conditions are too treacherous. With such unpredictability, it's a good idea to be flexible when you shop for fish. Rather than have a recipe in mind, go for the best fish that the fishmonger can offer and then decide what to do with it.

There are several ways of classifying fish, the two main divisions being finfish and shellfish. However, the following grouping is the most useful as far as the cook is concerned:

White fish

The fat is stored in the liver and the flesh is therefore white, delicately flavoured and almost fat-free. White fish needs careful cooking and seasoning.
Round: cod, coley, haddock, hake, ling, monkfish, pollack, red mullet, sea bass, whiting. Available whole or as steaks, fillets and cutlets depending on size.
Flat: dab, Dover sole, lemon sole, plaice. Sold whole.
Flat, large: brill, halibut, turbot. Usually sold as cutlets.

Oily fish

The fat is distributed throughout the flesh, giving it colour, flavour and succulence. Oily fish stand up to a wide range of cooking methods.
Large: salmon, swordfish, tuna. Available whole or as steaks, fillets and cutlets depending on size.
Medium: herring, mackerel, pilchard, trout. Sold whole.
Small: sardine, sprat. Sold whole.

Shellfish

This is a broad term for invertebrates with a hard outer shell, although some, like the squid, have a hard internal shell.
Cephalopods: cuttlefish, octopus, squid.
Crustacea: crab, crayfish, langoustine (scampi), lobster, prawn, shrimp.
Molluscs: clam, mussel, oyster, scallop, whelk.

Season

• Fish is at its best when not spawning. The spawning season varies depending on variety; a good fishmonger will advise you when this is. Meanwhile, try to avoid fish with roes and crustacea with eggs.

Fish to look for

• *Sustainable fish* such as black bream, gurnard, lemon sole, pilchard, pollack and sprats.
• *Arbroath smokies:* small haddock sold in pairs, hot-smoked over peat. The best type of smoked haddock.
• *Freshwater eel:* smoked or hot-smoked. Very rich and tasty.
• *Morecambe Bay potted shrimps:* tiny brown shrimps potted in butter and eaten whole. Beautiful sweet delicate flavour.
• *Undyed oak-smoked kippers*: these are smoked and salted herrings. Wonderfully tasty brown flesh. Eat raw, grilled or poached.

Cooking

With whole books devoted to fish cookery, the information here is no more than the basics to help you make the best of the fish you might find in a farm shop. It's hard to go wrong if you stick to the simple cooking methods below and learn how to recognise when fish is cooked.

Timing
The flesh of uncooked fish looks translucent; when it's cooked it becomes opaque, regardless of cooking method or type of fish. You need to inspect the thickest part by making a small incision down to the bone and pressing the flesh open. Cook for longer if necessary, but if the fish is almost done, move it to a warm place, cover with foil and wait a few minutes for the heat to spread evenly through the flesh.

Shallow-frying
This is certainly the best method for white fish. The outside becomes appetisingly crisp and the inside soft and steaming. Dust with seasoned flour, or beaten egg and breadcrumbs to protect the surface. Two rules: the fish must be dried thoroughly before coating and the pan good and hot. Start off by heating a thin layer of oil and wait until you see a slight haze before adding the fish. Resisting the urge to prod, wait until the underside has caramelised and the fish is almost cooked before you turn it over and cook the other side. Drain on crumpled paper towels before serving.
Good for: dab, plate-sized sole, red mullet, plaice and sea bass; white fish fillets, steaks and cutlets; prawns and scallops.

Grilling
Grilling under direct heat crisps the skin beautifully and keeps the flesh moist. The trick is to preheat the grill to its highest setting and cook the fish 10–12cm from the heat source, depending on thickness. Slash the flesh two or three times to allow the heat to get to the middle. Brush the fish and the rack with oil to prevent sticking.
Good for: oily fish such as sardines, plate-sized herring, mackerel and trout; thick salmon steaks; thin trout fillets; kippers; skewered prawns or meaty white fish like monkfish.

Barbecuing
It's hard to improve on barbecued fish, especially mackerel and sardines. Make sure the grill rack is clean, then brush it, and the fish, with oil to prevent sticking. The fire is ready when you can hold your hand over the coals and count slowly to four before you have to pull away; any less and the coals are too hot.
Good for: oily fish such as herring, mackerel, red mullet, sardines and trout; thick salmon steaks; skewered prawns or meaty white fish like monkfish.

Roasting and baking
This is a trouble-free way of cooking whole large fish or chunky portions, particularly if wrapped in foil to keep the fish juicy. Rub the fish with oil and lemon juice, strew with herbs if you like, and season

Shopping notes
Finfish
- Look for firm-fleshed fish with perky pink or scarlet gills and bright clear eyes that are not sunken.
- The skin should be moist, shiny and slightly slippery. A really fresh fish is almost impossible to grasp.
- Check that the tail is stiff and the scales are firmly attached to the skin.
- Ask the fishmonger to remove the guts and gills from whole fish.
- Cutlets, fillets and steaks should be firm and moist, without any discolouration. Cuts from white fish should be translucent.
- Fish should smell very faintly of the sea – very fresh and almost sweet. Leave well alone if there is a whiff of fish or ammonia.
- Smoked fish should look glossy and have a fresh smoky smell.

Shellfish
- The shells on mussels and other bivalves should be tightly closed.
- Lobster and crab should feel heavy for their size.
- Prawns and shrimps should look dry and firm, and smell faintly of salt or iodine.
- Raw prawns are grey, pre-cooked are pink. Choose raw ones if you intend to cook them; pre-cooked prawns become tough when reheated.

Storing
- Remove wrapping and wash the fish. Remove the guts if not already done (see **Preparation**, page 107).
- Store on the bottom shelf of the fridge in a shallow dish, loosely covered with foil, for 24 hours maximum. Shellfish should be eaten on the day you buy it.
- If vacuum-packed or in a rigid plastic container, leave unopened until ready to cook.

with sea salt and freshly ground black pepper. Set the oven temperature to 190°C/gas 5 if cooking in a parcel, 200°C/gas 6 if not. A whole salmon weighing 1.5–2kg will take 30–35 minutes in a parcel; plate-sized fish will need 20–25 minutes, or about 15 minutes uncovered; chunky steaks or fillets 8–10 minutes, or a minute or two longer in a parcel. These are only estimates: the time depends on your oven, the weight and thickness of fish, and its temperature at the start of cooking.

Good for: whole black bream, large salmon, sea bass and trout; large flat fish such as brill or halibut.

Steaming

Though the very term 'steamed fish' smacks of invalid food and blandness, steaming actually intensifies the flavour, so much so that you feel as if you are tasting the essence of the fish concerned. Delicately flavoured white fish come into their own cooked this way. Steaming is also handy for small pieces of any type of fish or shellfish that you want to cook quickly and plainly. Since no additional fat need be involved, it's worth trying if you want to lose weight.

Season the fish and put in a steamer basket over a pan of boiling water, or on a heat-proof plate in the base of a wok, over about 5cm of boiling water. For exquisitely aromatic steam that will flavour the flesh, add leafy herbs such as mint, basil or tarragon to the cooking water. For more robust seasoning, sprinkle the fish with slivers of chilli, fresh ginger root, garlic or spring onion. Cover tightly and steam for 5–8 minutes depending on size.

Steaming is the best way of cooking a quantity of mussels for soup or moules marinière. Throw the cleaned mussels into a large pan with a few centimetres of liquid in the bottom – fish stock, white wine, cider or just plain water. Cover tightly and cook over high heat for 5 minutes until the shells open, shaking the pan occasionally, then finish according to the recipe.

Good for: fillets, steaks and cutlets of salmon, trout and white fish; prawns and mussels.

Poaching

This is a handy technique if you plan to serve fish cold. Just cover the fish with a pre-cooked *court bouillon* made with water, white wine, carrots, celery and onions plus a few thyme, tarragon and parsley sprigs, some lemon zest and seasonings. Lower the fish into the broth, making sure it is completely submerged, then barely simmer for 20–30 minutes until done. Another method is to bring the fish to a simmer, then remove from the heat and leave to cool in the liquid.

Smoked fish such as kippers or haddock are also good poached. Submerge them in a fifty-fifty mix of milk and water, bring to the boil, then gently poach for 12–15 minutes.

Good for: large whole fish such as salmon, sea bass and sea trout; kippers and smoked haddock.

Preparation

• *Scaling:* Coarse scales from fish such as salmon, sea bass and sardines need removing. Scrape a fish scaler or large knife from tail to head in the opposite direction of the scales. The scales will fly everywhere so do this in a deep sink or roomy plastic bag that will catch the scales.

• *Gutting:* Make a slit through the underside of the belly starting at the vent. Pull out the innards and sluice the fish under cold running water. Be sure to scrape out the dark blood surrounding the spine – it can taint the flavour of the fish. Removing the head is optional, but if you leave it in place, carefully snip out the gills using sharp kitchen scissors.

• *Cleaning mussels:* Scrub to remove barnacles. Pull off the stringy beard. Tap shells that are open and discard if they do not close. Discard any with cracked or broken shells.

• *Preparing prawns:* Pull the head away from the body and carefully peel away the shell. You might want to leave the tail in place – it looks attractive and gives people something to hold when eating with the fingers. If necessary remove the dark intestinal vein as it can taste bitter. Make a small incision on the back, insert a pin under the vein and pull gently to remove it.

Serving size

• On the bone with head: 350–450g serves 1.
• On the bone without head: 250–375g serves 1.
• Steaks and fillets: 175–225g serves 1.
• Prawns in shell with heads: 175g serves 1.
• Prawns shelled: 125g serves 1.

Flour

It's hard to imagine life without flour – no pizza or pasta, no cakes, tarts or biscuits, no Yorkshire pudding or pancakes, and no bread. Given its major role in the kitchen, flour is surprisingly unappreciated, yet, like rare breed meat, the differences in flavour and texture are quite remarkable.

Fortunately, larger farm shops usually stock a selection of high-quality organic wheat flours, stone-ground in the traditional way. Farm shops also stock flours made from unusual grains (see **Flours to look for**), which open up interesting possibilities for baking enthusiasts. For example, Sharpham Park in Somerset has brought spelt flour into the limelight (see **Spelt** page 237), while Shipton Mill in Gloucestershire is pushing khorosan flour (otherwise known by the brand name 'Kamut'). Also worth seeking out is oak-smoked flour from Bacheldre Watermill in Powys, Wales. Bread made with it tastes and smells divine, reminiscent of bread baked in a wood-fired oven.

Cooking

Good bread and pastry start with good flour, and experienced bakers agree that organic stone-ground flour is the best; the flour simply has more life and this is reflected in the end product. You'll see for yourself if you try **Pizza Bianca** (see opposite) or make your own bread.

There are plenty of recipes for pastry in other cookbooks, but this one for **shortcrust pastry** unusually combines strong bread flour and self-raising flour. It makes a particularly crisp tart case which you can use in the recipe for **Tomato Tart** (page 257). Sift 125g each strong organic white flour and self-raising flour with a pinch of salt. Sift again to mix the flours thoroughly. Work in 125g diced chilled butter, rubbing it between your fingers until crumb-like. Beat 1 egg yolk with 4 tablespoons of chilled water, and stir this into the flour mixture with a fork. Once the dough starts to clump, gently knead it into a compact ball. Wrap in cling film and leave in the fridge for at least 30 minutes before rolling out.

For foolproof **egg pasta** (made in a slightly unorthodox way), lightly beat 3 very fresh room-temperature eggs in a large bowl with a pinch of salt. Gradually add 300–350g organic stone-ground plain white flour, working it into the eggs until well amalgamated into a not-too-sticky dough. Knead by pushing forward against the dough with the heel of your hand, then fold in half, give it a half turn and push forward again. Keep kneading and turning for 15 minutes until you have a silky-smooth elastic dough. The dough is now ready for rolling through a pasta machine and cutting to the shape of your choice.

Egg pasta is the one to use for creamy sauces, but **eggless pasta** is better for tomato- or oil-based sauces. For this you will need durum or khorosan flour. Both produce a slightly rough pasta that gives the sauce something to cling to. The dough takes a bit more effort to knead: mix 350g sifted durum flour, $\frac{1}{2}$ teaspoon of salt, 2 teaspoons of olive oil and 150ml warm water to a pliable dough. Knead for 15 minutes before rolling out.

Flours to look for

- *Barley:* grey-brown, low gluten, sweetish nutty flavour. Good for blinis and bannocks, best combined with wheat flour for bread.
- *Bere meal:* a rare type of barley flour from the Orkneys, low gluten, traditionally used for bannocks.
- *Durum wheat:* creamy yellow, high gluten, hard wheat, the flour to use for eggless pasta.
- *Khorosan:* creamy yellow, ancient hard wheat variety, related to durum wheat, high gluten, nutty flavour. Good for eggless pasta.
- *Rye:* grey-brown, low gluten, produces dense, moist bread. Needs wheat flour to make it rise. Ideal for sourdough or Scandinavian- and German-style breads.
- *Spelt:* ancient wheat variety, medium gluten, strong nutty flavour. Easier to digest than wheat. Ideal for breadmaking.

Shopping notes

- Buy flour little and often, and check that it's well within the 'best-before' date.

Storing

- Keep all flours in a sealed container in a dry place away from light and heat. Don't use a cupboard that is close to hot water pipes or above the fridge – both will raise the ambient temperature and the flour will suffer.
- Wholemeal flour contains more fat than plain flour. It can go rancid if the flour is kept for too long or in a warm place.
- Check the 'best-before' date from time to time and throw out flour that is past its best.

Preparation

- For baking: sift to get rid of lumps and introduce air. This makes a lighter mixture.
- Mix sifted-out bran back into the flour.
- For bread: gently warm flour in a low oven before adding yeast.

Pizza Bianca

This is a typical Roman-style pizza with a thin chewy crust and a light topping of paper-thin garlic slices, rosemary and sea salt. Its simplicity depends on top-notch ingredients: organic stone-ground flour, fresh garlic and very good olive oil, preferably estate-bottled.

To make the dough, sift the flour and salt into a large bowl. Sprinkle in the yeast, mixing well. Make a well in the centre and stir in the olive oil and water, drawing in the flour from around the edge until completely incorporated. Gather the dough into a ball and knead on a floured surface for at least 10 minutes, until it feels silky-smooth and springy. Place in a lightly oiled bowl, turning once so the surface is coated. Cover and leave to rise in a warm place for at least 2 hours or until doubled in size.

Preheat the oven to 240°C/gas 9. Roll the dough into a thin circle slightly larger than 35cm. (Lift and stretch the dough with your hands if it is resistant.) Place on a lightly greased perforated pizza pan or baking sheet. Turn in the edges and brush the entire surface with olive oil.

Slice the garlic cloves lengthways into paper-thin slices and arrange on top of the dough. Sprinkle with the rosemary and some crumbled sea salt flakes. Bake for 10–12 minutes until golden.

Cook's note
• This is best made with fresh 'green' garlic (page 112), available in early summer. The cloves are mild-flavoured and juicy, and survive the heat of the oven more easily than ordinary garlic, which tends to burn and become acrid.

Variation
• Instead of sliced garlic, cover the dough with 300g coarsely grated mozzarella cheese and 100g coarsely grated Parmesan. Sprinkle with 2 tablespoons of chopped tender rosemary leaves, crumbled sea salt and freshly ground black pepper. Bake as above, remove from the oven and arrange 3–4 small handfuls of rocket on top. The heat will slightly wilt the rocket.

extra-virgin olive oil for brushing
large 'green' garlic cloves (page 112) 16, peeled
rosemary leaves chopped to make 2 tbsp
sea salt flakes

for the dough
stone-ground strong white flour organic, 225g
salt 1 tsp
easy-blend dried yeast 1 tsp
extra-virgin olive oil 1 tbsp
tepid water 125–150ml

Makes one 35cm pizza

Garlic: Green and Wild

There is a world of difference between fresh heads of green garlic (also called wet garlic) and the garlic we use through the rest of the year. The fresh bulbs have a very short season in summer and are a treat to look for in farm shops and good greengrocers.

Earlier in the year there are also wild garlic leaves to be enjoyed. They taste similar to spring onions, although milder, but still with a hint of garlic. Sporadically on sale in farm shops, they are more easily found growing in verdant swathes under shady trees.

Unlike ordinary garlic, which is left in the ground to mature, green garlic is harvested while young and tender. With a thick white stem, bulging head and moist pliable skin, it looks rather like a fat spring onion. The pearly white cloves are mild, juicy and tender, with a skin so fine and silky that most don't need peeling. Some cloves are no more than a cluster of delicate embryos jostling for space with the plumper ones. The mild flavour leaves hardly a trace on the breath. Highly prized by cooks and chefs, this is the garlic for eating raw.

Cooking

As Dorset garlic farmer James Davey explains, 'In France they use garlic as a vegetable rather than a seasoning.' James likes to put thin slivers of the raw bulb and stem on dark pumpernickel bread. You certainly experience the essential oils on the palate, but the flavour isn't overwhelming.

Green garlic is at its best in light summery dishes that allow its subtlety to shine through. Try it in soups, egg dishes, or even raw and thinly sliced in sandwiches. Mashed with sea salt, the raw cloves are perfect in chilled gazpacho with diced cucumber, tomatoes and peppers (**Yellow Tomato Gazpacho**, page 258). They are also good sprinkled over the yolk of a fried egg with a few drops of vinegar.

The whole head can be thickly sliced or chopped without separating or peeling the cloves. Lightly fry in butter or olive oil in a summery stir-fry, or try them with colourful **Mediterranean vegetables**. Thickly slice 2 green garlic bulbs and fry in 2 tablespoons of olive oil with sliced red onions, and red and green peppers. After 5 minutes over medium-high heat, cover and cook over low heat for 15 minutes. Remove the lid, season with salt and pepper, and finish by frying over high heat to thicken the juices.

To make **garlic croûtons**, gently fry 2 or 3 thinly sliced fat garlic cloves in 4 tablespoons of olive oil until just golden. Remove with a perforated spoon, then add 100g bread cubes (made with day-old bread or ciabatta). Fry over medium heat until golden and crisp on all sides. Drain on paper towels, cool and store in an airtight container.

Garlic and parsley butter is delicious spread on toast and enjoyed with a glass of chilled rosé. Finely chop a whole green garlic head with some parsley, fold into unsalted butter and season with crunchy sea salt flakes and good-quality freshly ground black pepper.

For **garlic cream**, simmer briskly 275ml whipping cream with

UK season
• *Wild leaves*: April–May.
• *'Green' bulbs*: May–July.

Varieties to look for
• *'Early Wight'*, strong purple colour. The earliest British green garlic, harvested in May.
• *'Rose de Lautrec'*, deep purple cloves with a creamy smooth flavour. Considered a delicacy in France and the ultimate *ail de cuisine*.
• *'White Hispanic'*, massive bulbs with fat cloves. Warm rounded flavour.

Shopping notes
• Look for bulbs with a thick juicy stem and tight, slightly moist skin covering bulging cloves.

Storing
• Green garlic quickly loses freshness. Keep it in a paper bag in the salad drawer of the fridge. Once sliced or broken into, wrap heads tightly in cling film.
• Wash wild garlic leaves in several changes of water. Drain thoroughly, wrap in paper towels and keep in a sealed bag in the fridge.

Preparation
• Slice off the stem and peel away the outer layer of papery skin.
• Depending on the recipe, divide the head into individual cloves, or use the head whole or thickly sliced. If necessary, remove the membrane-like skin surrounding the cloves.

6–8 lightly crushed large garlic cloves and a sliver of lemon peel for about 5 minutes until slightly reduced. Remove from the heat and leave to steep in a warm place. Strain into a jug, then add a squeeze of lemon juice and season with salt and freshly ground black pepper. Swirl into soups or serve as a sauce with lamb or mutton.

To roast whole bulbs, score them across the top to make a cross that cuts deeply into the cloves. Either brush with oil or wrap in foil, then roast at 180°C/gas 4 for 50–60 minutes. The resulting goo that pops from the roasted cloves is wonderfully sweet and mellow – perfect for smearing on bruschetta or home-made pizza, or tossing with pasta and olive oil. It can also be whisked into salad dressings or added to gravy.

Roasted for a shorter time, the bulbs can be served as a vegetable in their own right, with roast chicken or lamb, or in a substantial salad (**Couscous Salad with Roasted Green Garlic, Tomatoes and Peppers**, page 114).

However you choose to cook green garlic, be sure to use lots of it. The flavour is surprisingly mild and becomes more so the longer it is cooked.

Wild garlic leaves

Use these in the same way as spring onions. Roughly shredded, a few leaves perk up a leafy salad. Snipped more finely, they add colour and a suggestion of garlic to fried eggs, baked potatoes or lightly cooked broad beans – the heat brings out the flavour. The uncooked leaves also make a vibrant **Wild Garlic Soup** (below) with a powerful peppery flavour.

Wild Garlic Soup

A brilliant green soup made with tender uncooked wild garlic leaves. It has a strong peppery flavour – for garlic-lovers only.

Stack the washed garlic leaves with the stalks pointing the same way. Cut off and discard the stalks, then slice the leaves into very thin ribbons. Set aside a small handful as a garnish, and slice these even more finely.

Melt the butter in a saucepan over medium heat. Add the potatoes and shallots, cover and sweat for 10 minutes, stirring now and again. Pour in the stock, bring to the boil, then simmer gently with the lid askew until the potatoes are soft.

Tip the mixture into a food processor or blender, add the sliced garlic leaves and whizz to a purée. Return to the pan, pour in the milk and season with a little sea salt and the merest soupçon of black pepper. (The flavour of the garlic is innately peppery so you won't need much.)

Reheat gently and pour into soup plates. Swirl in a little garlic cream, and sprinkle with warm croûtons and the reserved garlic leaves.

Variation

• For a milder flavour, cook whole garlic leaves in boiling water for 5 minutes while the potatoes and shallots are cooking. Drain and add to the soup before puréeing.

wild garlic leaves 2 handfuls, washed thoroughly
unsalted butter 25g
floury potatoes 2 small (about 250g), cubed
shallots 2, chopped
vegetable or **chicken stock** preferably home-made, 500ml
Jersey milk organic, 300ml
sea salt
freshly ground black pepper

to serve
garlic cream (page 112)
garlic croûtons (page 112)

Serves 4

Couscous Salad with Roasted Green Garlic, Tomatoes and Peppers

For garlic lovers only, a substantial salad based on the best of summer produce.

Preheat the oven to 230°C/gas 4. Place the peppers cut side down on a non-stick roasting tray. Roast for 15–20 minutes until the skin is blistered and blackened. Remove from the oven, cover with a clean tea towel and leave to cool. Peel away the skin and discard. Slice the flesh into small pieces.

Reduce the oven temperature to 180°C/gas 4. Using a sharp knife, remove the stem from the garlic heads slicing level with the bulb. Leave the outer skin in place. Cut a deep cross in the top of each head. Put them in a shallow baking dish and pour over 5 tablespoons of olive oil. Roast for 25–30 minutes, basting occasionally, until the cloves are tender but not mushy. Remove from the oven and leave to cool in the dish. Separate the cloves and reserve the oil. Remove the skin from the larger cloves if it seems chewy.

Measure the couscous into a large shallow bowl and pour over the hot water. Leave to soak for 30 minutes. Stir with a fork to separate the grains.

While the couscous is soaking, heat a medium-sized frying pan and add a film of oil. Fry the pine kernels until golden, taking care that they don't burn. Drain on paper towels.

Tip the couscous into a large serving dish. Using a fork, lightly stir in the lemon juice and the oil from the garlic. Season with sea salt and plenty of black pepper.

Mix in the roasted peppers, tomatoes, pine kernels and parsley. Add the garlic cloves, forking them in lightly but leaving some on the surface so people know what they are eating.

Check the seasoning, adding more sea salt, pepper and lemon juice as you think fit.

Cook's notes
• Since the vegetables need different times and temperatures for roasting, it's a good idea to cook some, or all of them, the day before. Make sure they are at room temperature before adding them to the couscous.
• The salad tastes better if left to stand at room temperature for at least an hour to allow the flavours to develop.

yellow peppers 2, halved lengthwise, cored and deseeded
plump green garlic 2 heads, stems removed
extra-virgin olive oil
roasted tomatoes (page 256) 5, roughly chopped
couscous 250g
water 600ml, almost boiled
pine kernels 50g
lemon juice of $\frac{1}{2}$
flat leaf parsley leaves sliced to make 6 tbsp
sea salt flakes
coarsely ground black pepper

Serves 6 as a side dish

Globe Artichokes

These magnificent vegetables are the flower heads of big edible thistles. They are made up of a central hairy choke surrounded by spine-tipped leaves. You can sometimes find small home-grown globes in farm shops, as well as the interesting varieties that are commonplace in Italy.

Globe artichokes have a wonderful nutty flavour, similar to the Jerusalem artichoke (page 145). In the UK, they are not as popular as they might be, perhaps because people are unsure of how to cook and eat them. This is how it's done: boil the heads (see **Preparation**), detach the leaves one-by-one and dip into an appropriate sauce – perhaps a lemony vinaigrette or home-made mayonnaise if serving cold, or Hollandaise sauce or just melted butter if serving hot. Suitably anointed, pass each leaf decorously between the teeth and scrape off the meaty portion. Make a tidy pile of discarded leaves at the side of your plate.

Once you've dealt with the leaves, there remains the *fond* or base – a tender and intensely flavoured delicacy in its own right. Cut it up and eat using a knife and fork. Artichoke bottoms are so prized that they are sometimes served alone, either tossed in oil and lemon, or used as a rather pretentious garnish for roast meat.

Cooking

Large globes are usually boiled or, for a more intense flavour, steamed. To boil, submerge the prepared globes in a large saucepan of boiling water acidulated with lemon juice. Use a non-reactive pan (stainless steel or glass) otherwise the globes will discolour. Cover with a heatproof plate to stop them bobbing up above the water level. Simmer briskly for 30–40 minutes until tender and an outer leaf pulls out easily. Leave upside-down on a plate to drain. Boiled artichokes are best served at room temperature. Once cooked and cooled, they can be wrapped in cling film and kept in the fridge for a day or two, but give them time to lose their chill before serving.

Globes can also be **stuffed and braised**, Roman-style, in olive oil and white wine. Stuff the centre of each prepared globe (and between the leaves if not too tightly packed) with about 1 teaspoon of finely chopped mint mixed with a little chopped garlic, lemon zest, salt and black pepper. Place cut-side down in a saucepan with a good layer of olive oil in the bottom. Add enough wine, or wine and water, to come halfway up. Cover and cook over medium heat for about 40 minutes until tender. Eat warm or at room temperature with the pan juices poured over.

Small globes are tender enough to be **deep-fried**, either whole or cut into wedges. The outer leaves become beautifully crisp, enclosing a soft tasty heart. Plunge into very hot oil and deep-fry for about 5 minutes, covering the pan so they cook in a mixture of steam and oil. Lift into a bowl using tongs, add a sprinkling of lemon juice, sea salt flakes and coarsely ground black pepper, and shower with chopped flat leaf parsley. Eat right away while still hot and crisp.

UK season
• May–November.

Varieties to look for
• *'Green Globe'*, large-headed, pale green round globes. Succulent fleshy leaves.
• *'Spinosi'*, viciously thorny lime-green leaves tipped with gold. Rich meaty flavour, slightly sweet, redolent of parsnips.
• *'Violetta'*, small-headed, purple-green elongated globes, tender enough to cook whole. Strong earthy flavour.

Shopping notes
• Choose heads with firm tightly packed leaves and a vibrant fresh colour.
• Steer clear of any with brown or slack-looking leaves.

Storing
• Preferably eat on the day of purchase. Otherwise, wrap large single heads tightly in cling film and store in the fridge for 2–3 days.

Preparation
Boiling and steaming:
• Use kitchen scissors to snip off the tips of the outer leaves just above the fleshy part.
• Working round the head, remove the tips of the leaves higher up until you are left with a central cone of thinner leaves.
• Use a very sharp knife to slice the tip off the central cone.
• Rub all cut surfaces with a lemon half as you work, to stop blackening.
• If the stem is attached and you want to cook it (it's as delicious as the leaves), pare away the tough outer green skin.
• Scoop out the hairy inner choke with a teaspoon after cooking – easier to do when warm.
Frying baby artichokes whole:
• Discard 10–12 of the outer leaves.
• Slice off the top 2cm of the remaining leaves.
• Leave the hairy choke in place if it is very small. Otherwise, force a pointed coffee spoon into the centre, rotate it and scoop out the innermost leaves and choke.

115

Baby Artichoke Salad with Olives and Rocket

As the name suggests, the small 'Violetta' artichoke is deeply tinged with purple. It looks beautiful with the purple-black olives.

Heat a large saucepan of water acidulated with lemon juice. Trim the artichoke stalks at the base. Pull off some of the outer leaves until the visible leaves are mostly green and purple. Slice the top 2cm off the remaining leaves. Rub the cut surfaces with the squeezed lemon half to prevent blackening.

Once the water is boiling, plunge the artichokes into it. Cook for about 35 minutes or until just tender, then drain. When cool enough to handle, slice in half lengthways and scoop out the small hairy chokes.

Arrange some rocket leaves on a serving plate and place the artichoke halves on top, cut-side up. Add the olives and trickle over the olive oil. Sprinkle with sea salt flakes, cracked black pepper and a few shavings of Parmesan.

Cook's note
• If you can't find 'Violetta' artichokes, any small ones will do as long as they are no more than 6–8cm in diameter.

lemon juice of $1/2$, plus extra for acidulating water
small artichokes such as 'Violetta', 4
rocket a good handful
kalamata olives 4–5, pitted and halved
extra-virgin olive oil $1^1/2$ tbsp
sea salt flakes
cracked black pepper
Parmesan shavings

Serves 4

Goat

British cooks seem reluctant to use goat meat although it is much appreciated in other parts of the world. I have enjoyed spicy goat curries in Jamaica, superb spit roasts and kebabs in the Middle East, and succulent cutlets cooked over a wood fire in Italy. In Greece and Portugal, goat is often the meat of choice for important celebrations.

I suppose we are put off by the unmistakable goatiness; goat-based dairy products, particularly yogurt and milk, have a distinctive flavour that is not to everyone's taste. The meat, however, is another matter. It is deep-red, rich and gamey but not that different from lamb, mutton or beef. Meat from the kid (a young male between 6 weeks and 3 months old) is paler and sweeter. Goat meat is certainly nutritious; unlike most red meat, it is low in cholesterol and saturated fat – an ideal food if you are a committed carnivore but are concerned about health.

In the UK, there are an encouraging number of goat flocks and the meat is beginning to show up on restaurant menus and receive regular mentions in the food media. Increasingly, goat meat and products are on sale in farm shops, but rarely, if ever, the supermarkets. Sausages made with goat meat are excellent (page 232), as is goat liver (page 162).

Cooking

Because it contains very little internal fat, goat meat quickly dries and becomes tough if you cook it too fast, at too high a temperature or without enough moisture. The cut of the meat determines the best cooking method. The leg, ribs, loin and breast are tender enough for direct heat such as roasting, grilling or gentle frying, though they benefit from a leisurely marinade in oil, vinegar, herbs and seasoning before cooking, and the addition of a little liquid during cooking. Less tender are the shoulder and shanks – these need slow moist treatment such as stewing, braising or pot roasting.

Goat meat lends itself to assertive or acidic flavours such as citrus juices, tomato, mint, red wine, vinegar, pungent spices and chilli. These cut the innate richness and help tenderise the meat. Most recipes for mutton and venison can be used for goat. Kid meat can be cooked like lamb or veal. It is generally more tender than goat and has a milder flavour.

UK season
• *Kid:* mid-March–May.
• *Goat:* year-round.

Shopping notes
• The meat is usually sold vacuum-packed and conveniently cut-up into joints and chops, diced for casseroling or minced for burgers.
• Choose the cut according to your intended cooking method (see **Cooking**).
• The flesh should look moist and deep-red, and any fat should be creamy-white.

Storing
• Store on the bottom shelf of the fridge so the raw juices cannot drip onto cooked meat or other items of food.
• Remove wrapping and store in a shallow dish, loosely covered with foil.
• If vacuum-packed, leave unopened until ready to cook.

Preparation
• Wash well and pat dry with paper towels.

Serving size
• Off the bone: 175g serves 1.
• On the bone: 225–350g serves 1.

Pepperpot Kid

This is real fusion food. I have combined Italian hunter's-style (*cacciatore*) seasonings – lemon zest, white wine and herbs – with zesty chillies and spices from the traditional Jamaican pepperpot. The result is a fresh-tasting but richly flavoured stew that is not overly goaty. This is easy to make, so don't feel daunted by the long list of ingredients.

Combine all the spice rub ingredients and pound to a paste using a mortar and pestle. Stir in the cider vinegar. Put the meat in a non-reactive bowl and add the spice rub, tossing the meat with your hands until well coated. Cover and store in the fridge for at least 4 hours or up to 3 days.

Heat a wide heavy-based saucepan or casserole over high heat. Add the rapeseed oil and sugar. Stir until very hot, then add the meat and any spice rub left in the bowl. Fry for 15–20 minutes, stirring often until the liquid from the meat starts to thicken and evaporate.

When the meat seems about to start sticking to the pan, pour in the wine and cook for a minute or two. Add the thyme sprigs and stock, bring back to the boil, then reduce the heat to medium-low. Cover with the lid slightly askew and simmer for 1½–2 hours or until the meat is very tender.

Strain the meat, reserving the liquid, and put in a warm serving dish. Cover and keep warm. Pour the liquid back into the pan. Blot off the fat with several sheets of paper towels. Bring to the boil and boil hard for 6–8 minutes until slightly thickened and reduced. Pour over the meat and scatter with the lemon zest and coriander just before serving. Serve with baked sweet potatoes or plainly boiled rice.

Cook's note
• This tastes better the next day after the flavours have had a chance to meld and mature. Don't add the lemon zest and coriander until you are ready to serve.

cider vinegar 2 tbsp
goat meat 1.2kg, cubed
rapeseed oil 2 tbsp
soft brown sugar 1 tbsp
white wine 150ml
thyme sprigs 2–3
meat stock 600ml, preferably homemade
lemon coarsely grated zest of 1
coriander leaves trimmed and chopped to makes 4 tbsp
baked sweet potatoes or **plainly boiled rice** to serve

for the spice rub:
ground cloves ⅛ tsp
ground cinnamon ½ tsp
freshly grated nutmeg ¼ tsp
thyme leaves 1 tsp
black peppercorns 1 tsp
salt 1 tsp
allspice berries 1 tsp
fat garlic cloves 2, sliced
onion 1, grated
fresh red chilli ½–1, deseeded and chopped

Serve 4 as a main course

Butterflied Leg of Goat

Grilled or barbecued, goat tastes very similar to lamb – rich, juicy and meaty, and excellent with simple accompaniments such as peppery salad leaves, grilled cherry tomatoes and crushed new potatoes.

Using a sharp knife remove the leg bone. Make a few shallow slashes in the thickest part of the meat and open it out to a rough rectangle about 4cm thick. Trim and discard any excess fat.

For the marinade, pound the garlic, bay leaves, mint, salt and peppercorns to a paste using a mortar and pestle. Mix in the lemon juice and olive oil.

Keeping the meat flat, slide it into a large leak-proof plastic bag. Pour in the marinade and seal the bag. Place it in a shallow dish and leave in the fridge for up to 3 days, turning occasionally. Allow to return to room temperature for an hour or so before you are ready to cook.

Preheat the oven to 230°C/gas 8 and preheat the grill to very hot. Remove the meat from the bag and scrape off the solid bits from the marinade. Strain the liquid into a small bowl or jug.

Place the meat on a rack in a grill pan, shaping it into a rough rectangle. Grill for 5 minutes on each side, basting with the marinade. Move the pan to the oven and continue cooking for 20–25 minutes, turning once and basting frequently.

Place the meat in a shallow dish, tent with foil and leave to rest in a warm place for at least 15 minutes.

Carve into thick slices and pour over the tasty juices that have flowed from the meat while resting. Serve with cherry tomatoes, rocket and crushed new potatoes.

Cook's notes
• For the best results, allow enough time for the meat to marinade for 3 days. If you don't have time, 2–3 hours is better than nothing.
• The meat can also be cooked on a barbecue. Prepare as above and grill close to the heat for 5 minutes on each side. Raise the rack a little and cook more gently for 10–15 minutes a side, basting regularly. The meat should still be pink inside when cooked. Leave to rest as above.

goat leg $\frac{1}{2}$, weighing about 1.2kg

for the marinade
fat garlic cloves 2, finely sliced
fresh bay leaves 2, crumbled
mint leaves chopped to make 3 tbsp
salt 1 tsp
black peppercorns 2 tsp
lemons juice of 2
olive oil 6 tbsp

to serve
roasted cherry tomatoes on the vine
rocket or **watercress**
crushed new potatoes

Serves 4

Goose

I look on geese as poultry with attitude. I love the way they strut about in gangs, defending their territory and refusing to succumb to intensive farming. They persist in laying eggs only in spring so it will be September before you can buy a goose of reasonable size (hence the association with Michaelmas). They also like to graze on grass, so they are reared mainly in the open and are free to roam at will.

Once considered something of a speciality, geese are currently experiencing a renaissance in the UK, doubtless fuelled by concerns about provenance. Geese tick all the correct boxes – they have a healthy outdoor lifestyle, a natural diet of grass and grain, and easy traceability. They are mainly available direct from the farm or a traditional butcher, and are also sold increasingly through the internet or by mail order. Geese are not cheap – expect to pay upwards of £50 for a goose to feed four, though if you buy from a farm shop the price may well be lower.

Like duck, the goose has a broad rib cage and a consequently high proportion of bone to meat. However, a little goes a long way. The meat is rich and sumptuous – all that grass gives it massive depth of flavour. Though the meat is very lean, the goose is well-endowed with subcutaneous fat, and this is part of the appeal. Not only does the fat help prevent the meat from becoming dry, it also contains a high proportion of the more desirable mono-unsaturated fatty acids. In practical terms, this means it is closer to olive oil in structure, so you can use it for making irresistible roast potatoes without worrying unduly about health and safety.

Cooking

Roasting is the usual way with goose, really no more complicated than roasting a chicken except that you must regularly pour off the fat. The trick is to cook it on a rack over a roasting tin and get someone to hold the goose in place while you tilt the tin. Strain the fat into a jar and store in the fridge for up to 3 months. It is superb for frying, roasting and even making pastry.

If you have an oven fitted with a rotisserie, try **Spit-Roasted Goose** (page 122) – it makes an adventurous change from conventional roasting. The rotary movement of the spit allows juices and fat to trickle continuously over and through the bird, bathing it in unctuous goo. Meanwhile, the fat drips on to potatoes and slivers of onion browning in the drip pan below. The result is magnificent – unlike any goose I've tasted.

There is no reason why goose cannot be jointed, the breasts and legs cooked in different dishes and the carcass turned into richly flavoured soup or stock. Especially delicious are **barbecued goose breasts** – use a young Michaelmas goose unless you are a fan of winter barbecues. Slash the breasts in several places through the skin and fat (but not the flesh). Wrap separately in foil, season with salt and black pepper, and add thyme sprigs and a slice or two of quince or apple if

UK season
• *Gosling, green goose*: late September.
• *Mature goose*: December.
• *Frozen goose*: all year-round.

Breeds to look for
• *Legarth*: top-selling breed, good meat yield.
• *Roman*: small, chubby, good meat-to-bone ratio.
• *SuperStow*: large, greater meat-to-bone ratio.

Shopping notes
Unplucked goose:
• Look for a plump breast, downy feathers round the legs, and soft pliable webs and underbill. An older bird will reflect its age with harder feet and bill.

Plucked goose:
• The bird should smell clean and fresh, have unblemished skin, a plump breast and a good layer of fat.

Frozen goose:
• Check that the packaging and the skin are undamaged.

Storing
• Store on the bottom shelf of the fridge so raw juices cannot drip onto other food.
• Remove wrapping and store in a shallow dish, loosely covered with foil, for 2–3 days depending on 'use by' date.
• Remove giblets and store separately.
• Thaw a frozen goose thoroughly, preferably in the fridge. Follow the pack instructions but allow about 48 hours.

Preparation
• Remove cavity fat and reserve for frying.
• For crisp skin, prick all over with a fork. Put bird in a colander and douse with boiling water. Dry well, then rub all over with sea salt before roasting.

Serving size
• Whole bird: 4kg serves 4–5; 5kg serves 5–7; 6kg serves 8–12.

you like. Cook for 15 minutes then open the foil, carefully reserving the liquid. Arrange the breasts skin-side down on the grill and cook over a not-too-fierce fire for about 10 minutes. Turn and cook for another 2 minutes. Leave to rest in a warm dish, then carve into elegant slices and serve with the reserved juices.

The legs make **succulent goose confit** that will keep for months, ready for when you next fancy a bit of goose. Divide into drumsticks and thighs, and place in a roasting tin with thyme and bay leaves. Season well and spoon over enough goose fat to cover (use the fat from the cavity or buy an extra jar). Roast at 150°C/gas 2 for 2 hours, turning now and then if not completely submerged in fat. Leave to cool in the fat, then store in a Kilner jar or sealed plastic container with enough fat to cover. When ready to use, just scrape off the fat. Use in a hearty casserole, or roast at 220°C/gas 7 for about 15 minutes until heated through and crisp. Wonderful with lentils and Savoy cabbage.

People often complain that there isn't enough meat on goose. While it's true you will not be ploughing through endless leftovers, there will still be plenty of tasty nuggets to enjoy. Strip the meat after roasting and use the bones and skin to make a rich stock. Kept in the freezer, this will give you the makings of superb soups and goosey risottos for weeks to come.

The meat is good in sandwiches of course, perhaps anointed with **Horseradish and Beetroot Relish** (page 142) or **Damson and Cobnut Sweet Pickle** (page 92). However, after heavy-duty Christmas fare a **goose salad with celery, apple and citrus fruit** makes a palate-cleansing change. For four people you'll need 2 sliced crisp red apples (unpeeled for cheery colour), halved segments from 2 clementines and 5 tender celery stalks sliced diagonally. Combine these in a bowl with about 225g cooked goose meat cut into bite-sized chunks. Toss with a dressing made with 1 teaspoon each of Dijon mustard, redcurrant jelly, lemon juice and wine vinegar, the grated zest of $\frac{1}{2}$ an orange, 5 tablespoons of extra-virgin olive oil, and salt and pepper. Throw in a few chopped nuts if you like, and garnish with chopped celery leaves.

Spit-Roasted Goose

The size limitation of the average domestic rotisserie means that the goose must be cooked in two sections. Some people might feel that the presentation is not as impressive as a whole bird. Nevertheless, a platter of golden crisp goose pieces, suitably garnished, has its own majesty.

Preheat the oven according to the manufacturer's instructions. Pour some water into a drip pan and add the onion quarters, potato and thyme sprigs. Place the pan on the floor of the oven.

Cut the goose in half across the carcass just in front of the thigh joint. Remove the wing tips and discard, or use in stock. Prick the skin all over with a fork, put both sections in a roomy colander or on a rack set over the sink, and douse with boiling water. Drain and pat dry thoroughly. Massage the skin with a generous amount of sea salt and black pepper. Tie the wings and thighs securely to stop them flopping while they rotate on the spit.

Secure the rear end on the spit by inserting the rod underneath one thigh, through the body and out above the other thigh. (The above-and-below technique helps keep the bird in position.) Spit-roast for about 1 hour 15 minutes (see **Cook's notes**) or until the juices run clear. Slide off the spit and put on a warm platter. Loosely tent with foil and leave to rest in a warm place, ideally a second oven, while you cook the wing section. Assemble this on the spit using the above-and-below technique as before. Roast for 50–60 minutes or until the juices run clear. Remove from the spit.

Cut both sections into neat joints and arrange on a serving platter, along with the onions and potato from the drip tray. Garnish with watercress sprigs.

Pour the excess fat from the drip pan. Place the pan over medium-high heat and deglaze using stock, wine or a mixture, scraping up the crusty bits. Strain into a small saucepan, adding any juices that have flowed from the meat. Simmer briskly until slightly reduced. Check the seasoning and stir in some redcurrant jelly if you think it needs it.

Cook's notes
• It's best to follow the manufacturer's instructions for spit-roasting times. I usually allow 35 minutes per kilo.
• The rear section of the goose should still be warm enough after you have cooked the front section. If necessary, give it a quick blast in a hot oven just before serving.

onions 2, quartered
potato 1, quartered
thyme 2–3 sprigs
goose 1 small, weighing about 4.5–5kg
sea salt flakes
freshly ground black pepper
watercress sprigs to garnish
poultry stock home-made, 350–400ml
redcurrant jelly (optional) 1 tbsp

Serves 4–6

Gooseberries

There is something quintessentially English about gooseberries. They remain one of our few truly seasonal fruits, enjoying their heyday in the early 1800s when the industrial north was a hotbed of working men's gooseberry clubs. As the late garden writer Edward Bunyard stated somewhat snootily in *The Anatomy of Dessert*, 'The plebian origin of the Gooseberry has been, I fear, a handicap to its appreciation at cultured tables.' He goes on to say, quite rightly, that if the flavour were found in a tropical fruit, it 'would be exalted in the most fervent language'.

Gooseberries often get a bad press, but they are not necessarily green or sour or bristling with hairs. Some are as smooth and taut as an inflated balloon, others are soft and downy. Some are a strange milky white, others look like lemon drops, and there are those that are a deep exotic red.

Like apples and plums, gooseberries are classified as cooking or dessert, though the boundaries are somewhat blurred. Cooking gooseberries are the first on the scene, signalling, as they do, the possibility of summer. Dessert gooseberries are harvested later; they may be a dedicated variety, or a cooking variety left longer on the bush to sweeten. They are larger and softer, irresistibly juicy and sweet, with an almost translucent skin.

There is a good chance of finding interesting varieties if you buy from a PYO farm. If vicious thorns deter you from picking, bear in mind there are thorn-free varieties that are painless to harvest.

Cooking

With their tart grassy flavour, gooseberries need plenty of sugar to help them along. They are natural candidates for jams and jellies, pickles and chutneys, and they also make excellent ice cream. They are tamed by elderflower and the comforting blandness of pastry or oats, as in the recipe for **Gooseberry and Elderflower Brose** (page 124).

Sweet gooseberries are very good **roasted with honey, orange and star anise**. Put 600g topped and tailed gooseberries in a small roasting tin, drizzle with 4 tablespoons of clear honey and dot with butter. Add 3 decent-sized strips of thinly pared orange peel and 5 star anise pods, roughly broken up. (Star anise has a delicate flavour that goes well with gooseberries in the same way as elderflower.) Roast at 200°C/gas 6 for 20 minutes, stirring halfway through. By then the berries should be bubbling away and appetisingly browned in places. Serve hot or warm with whipped Jersey cream or very cold ice cream. You could also turn this into a lovely sweet crumble using the topping for greengages (page 129).

Gooseberries make a pleasantly sharp **sauce for fatty fish** such as mackerel or salmon. Top and tail 250g gooseberries and put in a small saucepan with 1 tablespoon of sugar and a knob of butter. Cover and cook over medium heat until the juices start to flow. Remove the lid and boil for a few minutes to get rid of most of the liquid. Push through a fine sieve if you want to get rid of the pips, otherwise mash to a rough purée. Stir in 100ml whipping cream and a pinch of salt. Add a little more sugar if you like, but remember the sauce is intended to be on the sharp side. Round out the flavour with 1–2 tablespoons of juice from the cooked fish.

UK season
- *Cooking:* late May–mid-July.
- *Dessert:* July–August.

Varieties to look for
- *'Captivator'*, red-skinned, sweet and juicy.
- *'Golden Drop'*, thin-skinned, greenish-yellow, sweet.
- *'Invicta'*, plump, pale green, very sweet but very thorny.
- *'Langley Gage'*, small, smooth pale green, incredibly sweet.
- *'Leveller'*, large, golden-green, great flavour cooked or raw.
- *'Pax'*, deep red, very sweet, few thorns.
- *'Whinhams Industry'*, dark red, hairy, very sweet cooked or raw, makes great jam.

Shopping notes
- Look for firm undamaged gooseberries with fresh-looking brown tips.
- Don't bother with very squashy gooseberries even if they are a dessert variety.

Storing
- Store unwashed in a paper bag in the fridge.
- Cooking gooseberries will keep for 4–5 days.
- Dessert gooseberries will keep for 2–3 days.

Preparation
- Top and tail with scissors or sharp fingernails. There is obviously no need to do so if the fruit is to be cooked and sieved.
- Cook in very little water – the berries produce plenty of liquid once the skins burst.

Red Gooseberries with Orange and Bay Syrup

Plump red dessert gooseberries have their own special flavour and they look stunning. Allow time for the berries to macerate in the hot fragrant syrup.

Top and tail the gooseberries and put them in a serving bowl – white china looks best.

To make the syrup, put the sugar in a saucepan with the remaining ingredients. Stir over medium heat until the sugar has dissolved, then boil for 7–10 minutes until syrupy.

Pour the hot syrup over the gooseberries and leave to cool. Serve at room temperature.

Cook's note
• You can strain the syrup if you like, but I think the bay leaves and orange peel look beautiful with the ruby-red gooseberries.

red dessert gooseberries 450g
sugar 200g
water 300ml
fresh bay leaves 2–3
orange peel 1 thinly pared strip
orange juice 1 tbsp

Serves 3–4

Gooseberry and Elderflower Brose

A traditional dish from Scotland, adapted from Catherine Brown's fascinating book *From Broth to Bannocks*. Brose is an oat-based meal-in-a-bowl of which there are many versions, both sweet and savoury. This one makes a lovely sustaining breakfast as long as you remember to soak the oats in time.

Put the oats in a dry frying pan and toast over medium heat for about 3 minutes or until pale golden. Tip into a bowl and stir in the cream. Leave to soak for at least 1 hour or overnight.

Put the gooseberries and sugar in a small saucepan with the merest splash of water. Cover, bring to the boil and simmer for 2–3 minutes until just soft. Leave to cool, then stir in the elderflower cordial.

Squash the gooseberries to a chunky purée and swirl into the cream-soaked oats. Add more sugar to taste. Divide between serving bowls and trickle a thin swirl of honey over each.

Variation
• This is lovely made in early summer when fresh creamy elderflowers are in season. Leave out the cordial and instead cook two or three elderflower heads with the gooseberries. Remove once the mixture has cooled.

See also **Oats** (page 170)

rolled oats 4 rounded tbsp
single cream organic, 150ml
gooseberries 250g, topped and tailed
sugar 1 tbsp, plus extra to taste
elderflower cordial 2 tsp
clear honey to serve

Serves 2–3

Green Beans

Green beans are a rather ill-defined group made up of beans with edible fleshy pods, rather than those that need shelling. There are two basic types: the quintessentially British runner bean with its long, flat, coarse-textured pods, and the more elegant French bean with short, round fleshy pods. French beans include the slim *haricot vert*, the fatter snap or bobby beans, and the yellow wax bean.

Despite the name, green beans are not necessarily green; some are yellow and others are purple. All are delicious and farm shops are good places to find them, green or otherwise, freshly picked on a daily basis.

Cooking

Young green beans benefit from a light touch. Steaming, rather than boiling, intensifies the subtle flavour and allows purple varieties to keep some of their otherwise water-soluble colour. Steam for 5–10 minutes depending on variety and your preferred degree of doneness; otherwise drop them into a large pan of boiling salted water and cook for 3–10 minutes. Drain thoroughly and sizzle in olive oil or melted butter just before serving. If you like, add a few wisps of lemon zest, chopped fresh coriander or garlic chives. Very finely chopped raw tomato and wafer-thin slivers of garlic are also good additions.

Later in the season as the pods become more fibrous, green beans are better in curries and vegetable stews. One of the best-ever combinations is a simple Middle Eastern dish of blanched **French beans fried with onion, thinly sliced garlic and chopped tomatoes**. Season with salt, black pepper and lemon zest and serve warm or at room temperature with plenty of pitta bread to mop up the juices.

Another favourite is to sizzle blanched chopped **runner beans with Indian spices** – ground turmeric, mustard seeds, garam masala and dry-fried cumin and coriander seeds. Add a little sugar and salt, some chopped green chilli, and simmer with a cupful of chopped tomatoes. Sharpen with a squeeze of lime juice and sprinkle with chopped fresh coriander just before serving.

A mixture of lightly cooked green, yellow and purple beans looks and tastes stunning in a **Warm Bean Salad** (page 126). Beans are also good ballast for pickles and chutneys.

UK season
- *French beans:* June–September.
- *Runner beans:* July–early October.

Varieties to look for
French beans:
- *'Blue Lake'*, small fleshy green pods, a long-standing favourite.
- *'Mercana'*, dark green, super-thin pods, great flavour.
- *'Orinoco'*, golden pods, excellent flavour.
- *'Purple Teepee'*, dark purple, stringless pods, good beany flavour.

Runner beans:
- *'Lady Di'*, stringless variety, clean flavour.
- *'Scarlet Emperor'*, old variety, one of the best flavoured.

Shopping notes
- Look for French beans with crisp pods with a satiny sheen. Avoid any that look wizened or discoloured.
- Choose Runner beans with tender flat pods, 25–30cm long; they can be tough if longer. Steer clear of flabby specimens; the pods should snap crisply when bent.

Storing
- Keep in a paper bag in the salad drawer of the fridge for 3–4 days.

Preparation
French beans:
- Snap both ends off bobby or snap beans, pulling them back along the length of the pod to remove the strings.
- Line up stringless beans and chop off the tips. Tender tips of thin *haricots verts* can be left intact.
- Leave whole if slim and tender, otherwise chop into shorter lengths.

Runner beans:
- Remove strings with a swivel peeler and slice thinly diagonally. Otherwise push through a bean slicer to make spaghetti-like strands.

Warm Bean Salad with Sheep's Cheese, New Potatoes and Lemon Thyme Vinaigrette

For an attractive presentation use a mixture of beans – yellow, green or purple, flat or round. Look for semi-hard sheep's cheese such as Lord of the Hundreds or Swaledale.

Whisk together the dressing ingredients, then leave to stand so that the flavour develops.

Boil the potatoes for 7–10 minutes or until they are just tender. Drain and leave to cool a little. Steam the beans for 5 minutes or until just tender but still brilliantly coloured and crunchy.

While the vegetables are still slightly warm, divide the frisée between four plates. Arrange the beans and potatoes attractively on top. Add the crumbled cheese and garnish with a sprig of lemon thyme. Whisk the dressing again and spoon over the salad.

Cook's note
• Serve the beans slightly warm to appreciate the subtle flavour. If you have to cook them ahead of time, keep at room temperature rather than in the fridge.

small waxy new potatoes such as 'Ratte' or 'Pink Fir Apple', 12
tender green, yellow or purple beans 280g, stalks trimmed
frisée or **Batavia lettuce** 4 handfuls, cut into bite-sized pieces
sheep's cheese 25g, crumbled
lemon thyme sprigs to garnish

for the dressing
lemon juice 1½ tsp
Dijon mustard ½ tsp
lemon thyme leaves chopped to make 2 tsp
sea salt flakes
freshly ground black pepper
extra-virgin olive oil 6 tbsp

Serves 4 as a starter

Green Bean and Dill Pickle

This is good for stashing away in late summer when farm shops are awash with beans. Serve as part of a mixed antipasti or use to perk up cold meat or chicken.

Plunge the beans into a large pan of boiling water. Bring back to the boil, cook for 3 minutes, then drain. Pack vertically into four clean 600ml jars. Add the onion slices, garlic cloves and dill sprigs, tucking them between the beans.

Heat the vinegar, sugar, salt and dill seeds in a saucepan, stirring until the sugar has dissolved. Bring to the boil briefly, remove from the heat and leave to cool for a few minutes. Pour into the jars, making sure the liquid comes right to the top. Seal and leave to cool completely.

Store in a cool place for at least a week before eating. Once open, keep in the fridge.

Cook's notes
• Distilled vinegar is colourless and the best for showing off brightly coloured vegetables such as these.
• The easiest way of packing beans vertically is to place a quarter of them parallel on a board, lining up the ends. Grasp them in your palm and push into the jar all at once.
• If necessary, add extra vinegar to cover the beans.

green beans 850g, stalks removed
onion 1 large, halved and thinly sliced
large garlic cloves 4, peeled
dill 8 sprigs
distilled vinegar 1.25 litres
sugar 280g
salt 2½ tsp
dill seeds 2½ tsp

Makes four 600ml jars

Green Bean and Dill Pickle

Greengages

Greengages are a superior kind of plum – smaller and sweeter with a lovely fresh green colour and youthful bloom. In France they are known as 'Reine Claude' and are classified as plums; it is a peculiarly British convention to differentiate them.

The flavour is unique – rich and honeyed with a very faint hint of pear drops. When very ripe and sweet a bead of moisture drips from the base of the stalk, as if the fruit was about to explode with sweetness and juice.

Sadly, greengages are becoming a rarity, like damsons, but farm shops are not generally concerned with continuity or size of supply, and will happily stock them when available.

Cooking

Greengages are best enjoyed straight from the fruit bowl. However, if you have some to spare, they make a lovely **sparkling green jelly** for spreading on warm croissants or toast. Simmer 1 kg of halved greengages in a little water until soft. Strain the pulp through a scalded jelly bag. Let this take its course – if you squeeze the bag you'll end up with a cloudy jelly. Measure the juice and pour into a saucepan. Bring to the boil, and only then add 450g sugar for every 600ml of juice. Boil for 5–15 minutes until set. Remove any scum and pour into clean jars.

I am not a great fan of crumbles but they are another matter made with **greengages and a crunchy oat topping** as in the recipe opposite. Greengages are also good in a shallow French-style tart, with the thinly sliced segments of fruit facing upwards so the edges catch the heat.

Gardener/cook Sarah Raven makes an intense greengage sorbet with 675g of baked greengages puréed with the juice of 1 lemon and sugar syrup made with 150ml each of sugar and water. Whiz together, chill and freeze. That's it.

I think greengages are too precious to be drowned in pickles and chutney, as we do with a glut of plums. But they are certainly worth bottling on their own or preserving in syrup to enjoy as a winter dessert.

UK season
• August–September.

Varieties to look for
• *'Coe's Golden Drop'*, golden melting flesh, luscious rich flavour.
• *'Dennistons Superb'*, fantastic flavour.
• *'Old English'*, outstanding flavour, succulent and sweet.
• *'Reine Claude'*, ancient variety, rich sweet flavour.

Shopping notes
• Choose undamaged greengages with a powdery bloom – a sign that they have not been handled too much.
• For home ripening, choose slightly firm (but not hard) fruit.
• Don't bother with any that look wizened or bruised.

Storing
• Store ripe greengages at room temperature and eat within 24 hours.
• Unripe fruit will continue to ripen if left at room temperature for a few days.

Preparation
• To remove the stone, slice round the indentation and twist the two halves in opposite directions to separate them. Scoop out the stone with a pointed teaspoon.

Greengage and Cobnut Crumble

Enjoying a brief season together, greengages and cobnuts make a lovely late summer crumble. Here I have used oats and chopped cobnuts to make the topping crisper. I have also pre-cooked it like a giant biscuit, so it keeps its crunch and needs only a short time cooking on top of the fruit.

Remove the stones from the greengages (see **Preparation**). Slice each section in half again to make quarters. Spread them out in a single layer in a 1.4-litre baking dish.

Put the sugar, water and orange peel in a small saucepan, and stir over medium heat until the sugar has dissolved. Raise the heat and boil rapidly for 5 minutes or until the bubbles start to look syrupy. Pour the syrup over the greengages and set aside.

Preheat the oven to 190°C/gas 5. Line a baking sheet with parchment.

Combine the topping ingredients, except the chopped cobnuts, in a food processor. Pulse in short bursts until the mixture starts to form a ball. Alternatively mix by hand, rubbing the butter into the flour first then adding the rest of the ingredients. Press the cobnuts evenly into to the dough then spread the mixture in a thin layer on the parchment, flattening it with your fingers. Bake for 20 minutes or until golden. Remove from the oven and leave to cool – it will become crisp as it does so.

Once the topping is cool enough to handle, break it into rough pieces and use to cover the fruit. Bake for 10–15 minutes or until the juices are bubbling.

Variation
• Use pistachios if you don't have any cobnuts.
• Try a richly coloured mixture of crimson-fleshed plums and cherries instead of greengages.

greengages 600g
sugar 75g
water 150ml
orange peel 2–3 thinly pared strips

for the topping
rolled oats 75g
plain flour 100g
butter 100g
sugar 125g
vanilla extract 2 tsp
salt a pinch
shelled cobnuts 4 tbsp, chopped

Serves 4–6

Grouse

There is something undeniably special about grouse. Not only is there the razzmatazz of the Glorious Twelfth, but the bird itself has a particularly striking appearance with its curiously feathered ankles and quizzical red brow. With a diet consisting almost entirely of heather, grouse has a flavour that sets it apart from other game birds. Perhaps faintly redolent of wood smoke or jasmine tea, it lingers in the memory long after the season is over.

When preparing an oven-ready bird don't be alarmed if you find claws and feathery ankles misleadingly tucked inside the cavity but still attached to the drumsticks. Being claw-phobic I was horrified the first time I discovered them – I was expecting an empty cavity. I have since learned that this is a deliberately upfront way of doing things; if the claws are there you can check the age of the bird by the pliability of the spur.

Cooking

If you have not eaten grouse before, try it plainly roasted before embarking on cheffy titivations. That said, a handful of blackberries stuffed into the bird does no harm; they complement rather than detract.

Quickly seared breasts are superb in a warm salad. Use them instead of duck breasts in the recipe on page 94, or pigeon on page 194. Older birds are best braised or casseroled (**Casserole of Grouse with Juniper and Gin**, opposite). Again, keep it simple and don't add too many competing ingredients.

Potted grouse is an efficient way of using up every last scrap, as you will undoubtedly want to do. Use the carcasses of four roasted grouse, or four from which you have removed the breasts. Put in a saucepan with a few chunks of onion, celery and carrot, and a handful of parsley stalks. Season with a bay leaf and a few black peppercorns, but no salt at this stage. Add water to cover, bring to the boil and remove the scum. Reduce the heat and simmer for 30 minutes until the meat is very tender. Drain, saving the liquid, and pull the meat from the bones. Pour the liquid back into the pan, add the bones and vegetables, and boil hard for 30 minutes until reduced. Strain through a sieve and discard the bones and vegetables. Put the meat in a food processor and moisten with 3 tablespoons of the liquid (use the rest as stock). Add 25g butter, a pinch of cayenne pepper, salt and freshly ground black pepper, and blend until smooth. Spoon into ramekins, level the surface and cover with a layer of melted butter before chilling or freezing.

UK season
• *Open shooting*: 12 August–10 December.

Varieties to look for
• *Scottish red grouse*: heather-based diet gives it a unique flavour.

Shopping notes
• Choose plump oven-ready birds with undamaged skin.
• Avoid birds with dark bloody patches – a possible sign of embedded shot.

Storing
• Store on the bottom shelf of the fridge so raw juices cannot drip onto other food.
• Remove wrapping and store in a shallow dish, loosely covered with foil, for 2–3 days depending on 'use by' date.
• Remove claws and giblets. Store giblets separately.

Preparation
• Cut off the claws just below the ankle.
• Pull out any stray quills.
• Check the flesh for shot – the pellets can break a tooth.
• Rinse under running water and pat dry thoroughly.
Jointing:
• Cut out the backbone and press the bird flat, skin-side up. Slice down the length of the breast cutting through the bone. Slice crossways into four joints, cutting behind the wing joint and in front of the thighs.
Roasting:
• Cover the breasts with buttered paper to prevent drying (don't use bacon).

Serving size
• Whole bird: 280–350g, serves 1.

Casserole of Grouse with Juniper and Gin

This is a good way of cooking an older bird. It becomes meltingly tender and produces a richly flavoured sauce.

Heat a medium frying pan, add 3 tablespoons of rapeseed oil and fry the lardons for 5 minutes. Add the shallots and carrot, fry until soft, then add the garlic, bay leaves and juniper berries. Fry until the vegetables are beginning to brown, then stir in the tomato purée. Tip everything into a casserole and set aside.

Season the grouse joints with salt and black pepper. Heat a large frying pan over medium-high heat, add 3 tablespoons of oil and fry the grouse skin-side down until brown all over. Add the legs to the casserole with the vegetables and set the breasts aside.

Deglaze the grouse pan with the gin, stirring with a wooden spoon to scrape up any sediment. Tip into the casserole along with the stock. Bring to the boil, simmer gently with the lid on for 30 minutes. Add the breasts and cook for 15 minutes more.

Meanwhile, heat a large frying pan over medium-high heat, add 3 tablespoons of oil and fry the bread cubes, turning occasionally, until crisp and golden.

Tip the grouse and vegetables into a warm serving dish and scatter with the bread cubes, parsley and lemon zest.

rapeseed oil for frying

pancetta lardons 100g

shallots 4, chopped

carrot 1, chopped

garlic cloves 4, sliced

fresh bay leaves 3

juniper berries 10, lightly crushed

tomato purée 1 tbsp

grouse 2, jointed (see **Preparation**)

salt

freshly ground black pepper

gin 5–6 tbsp

game stock or **strong chicken stock** preferably home-made, 500ml

wholemeal bread 3 thick slices, cubed

flat leaf parsley leaves chopped to make 3 tbsp

lemon finely grated zest of 1

Serves 2–3

Roast Grouse with Blackberries

Blackberries are in season at the same time as grouse and make a natural partner. Their juice enriches the sauce. The bird is roasted on a grouse-sized slice of bread that becomes beautifully crisp round the edges while the centre soaks up the flavoursome juice.

Preheat the oven to 220°C/gas 7. Season the grouse inside and out with salt and freshly ground black pepper. Stuff the cavities with blackberries and a knob of butter. Smear the breasts with more butter and cover with a piece of baking parchment.

Butter the bread on one side and place buttered-side up in a small roasting tin. Sit the grouse on top and roast for 20–30 minutes. Remove the grouse on their rafts of bread and leave to rest in a warm place.

Pour off most of the fat from the roasting tin. Sprinkle in the flour and stir with a wooden spoon over medium heat until slightly brown. Deglaze for a few minutes with the wine, then pour in the stock. Add the thyme sprigs and bring to the boil. Simmer for 15 minutes, skimming off the creamy scum that gathers round the edge. Once the sauce has reduced by about half, pour in any juices that have flowed from the grouse. Check the seasoning and strain the sauce into a jug.

Place the grouse on warmed serving plates, garnish with watercress sprigs and serve with the sauce.

Cook's notes
• The bread slices should be the same size and shape as the grouse. Trim off the edges if you don't have the correct size.
• Roasting for 25 minutes produces meat on the rare side but not excessively bloody. Increase the roasting time to 35–40 minutes if you prefer grouse well-done, but bear in mind that the birds will continue to cook during the resting period.

oven-ready grouse 2
salt
freshly ground black pepper
blackberries 20
unsalted butter
good bread 2 oval slices, 1cm thick
plain flour 2 tsp
white wine 100ml
game stock or strong chicken stock preferably home-made, 600ml
thyme 2 sprigs
watercress sprigs to garnish

Serves 2

Guinea Fowl

With their speckled black and white plumage, guinea fowl are a delight to watch. They wander around pecking for insects, and at night they like to roost high in a tree rather than tucked up in a coop. They are acutely aware of predators and cackle noisily at the slightest provocation.

Sometimes misleadingly classified as game, guinea fowl are available for most of the year and, unlike game birds, are not shot. Most are intensively farmed but if you buy from a farm shop or direct from the producer you stand a good chance of finding a properly free-range bird or, better still, an organic one.

Cooking

Recognizable by black scaly legs and dark breast meat, guinea fowl have a flavour midway between pheasant and a free-range chicken. The flesh tends to be dry when roasted or grilled, so it's a good idea to lubricate it with plenty of seasoned butter pushed under the skin, as in the recipe opposite. Alternatively bard the breasts with bacon – if you don't mind bacon-flavoured guinea fowl, that is.

Guinea fowl is good instead of goose in a **salad with celery, apple and citrus fruit** (page 121), though you will probably have to roast a bird especially, instead of using leftovers.

Older birds are best in a slowly cooked **casserole with Puy lentils**. Fry some pancetta cubes with a chopped onion and 3–4 diced celery stalks. Brown two jointed guinea fowl in a separate pan, and add to the vegetables along with the deglazed pan juices. Season with thinly sliced garlic, a couple of rosemary sprigs, a bay leaf and plenty of freshly ground black pepper. Add 350g Puy lentils and 1.5 litres home-made chicken or game stock. Cover, bring to the boil, then simmer very gently for about an hour until the guinea fowl is tender, the lentils plump and the juices thickened. I like to brighten the flavour with the finely grated zest of 1 lemon mixed with 6 tablespoons of chopped flat leaf parsley. Add this just before serving.

See also **Guinea fowl eggs** (page 99)

Guinea fowl to look for
• *Free-range:* humanely reared, continuous daytime access to open-air runs or perchery, minimum slaughter age 82 days.

Shopping notes
• Check that the bird is well chilled and within the 'use by' date.
• Look for undamaged yellow skin that is very slightly moist.

Storing
• Store on the bottom shelf of the fridge so raw juices cannot drip onto other food.
• Remove wrapping and store in a shallow dish, loosely covered with foil, for 2–3 days depending on 'use by' date.
• If vacuum-packed or in a rigid plastic container, leave unopened until ready to cook.

Preparation
• Wash the bird well and pat dry with paper towels.
• After handling, wash and rinse hands and utensils in hot water, disinfect sinks and surfaces.
• For moist flesh and crisp skin, push plenty of seasoned butter under the skin before grilling or roasting.

Serving size
• Whole bird: average weight 1.3kg serves 2–3.

Grilled Spatchcocked Guinea Fowl with Green Peppercorn Butter

Pushing a tasty mix of peppery butter, garlic and lemon zest under the skin keeps the flesh juicy and the skin crisp.

Remove the backbone from the guinea fowl by cutting either side with kitchen scissors. Also remove the wing tips and any stray feathers. Open out the bird and place it skin-side up on a board. Press sharply with the heel of your hand to flatten the breastbone.

Loosen the skin over the legs, thighs and breasts by working your fingers underneath and detaching the membrane separating the skin from the flesh. Try not to tear the skin.

Mash together the butter, peppercorns, lemon zest, garlic and sea salt flakes. Insert most of the flavoured butter under the loosened skin, pushing it in as far as possible and smoothing it to the shape of the bird. Smear the rest over the outside of the skin. Cover and leave in the fridge for at least 2 hours or up to 24 hours. Remove from the fridge at least 1 hour before you want to cook.

Preheat the grill until very hot. Place the guinea fowl skin-side up on a board. Position the drum sticks so that they are bent at the joint with the thigh turned inwards and pushed up towards the wings, and the leg nestling close to the rib cage. Insert a metal skewer through one bent drumstick and the lower rib cage and out through the drumstick on the other side. Take a second skewer and insert it through the wing, upper rib cage and out the other side.

Place the guinea fowl skin-side down on a rack in a clean grill pan, positioning the pan 15cm from the heat source. Brush the upper surface of the bird with oil. Grill for 15 minutes, then turn over and grill for another 15 minutes. Turn once more and grill for another 10 minutes until the juices are no longer pink when you pierce the thickest part of the thigh.

Pull out the skewers. Using poultry shears or clean kitchen scissors, cut the bird into sections – breasts, thighs and drumsticks. Pile them up in a warm serving dish. Pour the buttery juices over, scraping up the sticky tasty sediment from the bottom of the pan. Scatter with parsley and lemon wedges.

Cook's note
• Spatchcocking is an easy technique that involves cutting out the backbone of the bird and pressing the carcass flat. This makes a flat compact shape that grills evenly and quickly. Skewers keep the bird rigid when you turn it and help conduct heat through the thickest part of the thighs.

guinea fowl 1, weighing about 1.3kg
unsalted butter 100g, at room temperature
dried green peppercorns 1 tbsp, lightly crushed
lemon finely grated zest and juice of 1/2
garlic clove 1 large, crushed
sea salt flakes generous pinch
oil for brushing
flat leaf parsley chopped, to garnish
lemon wedges to serve

Serves 2–3 as a main course

Ham

Farm shops take pride in their home-cooked hams and with good reason. The meat is likely to have been cured to a traditional local recipe, so you will find hams with distinctive flavours that vary from region to region (see **Hams to look for**). A proper ham will not contain any added water to boost the weight; the texture therefore tends to be relatively dry and dense.

Air-dried hams for eating raw are another find. On a par with Parma ham or the Spanish Iberico, excellent air-dried hams are emerging from various regions in the UK. Though the curing and drying techniques are inspired by those from mainland Europe, British air-dried ham has a character all of its own. There are infinite nuances in texture and flavour influenced by the breed of pig, the way it is raised and even the quality of the wind and air in which the meat hangs to dry.

Another long-lost British speciality is mutton ham, a centuries-old method of preserving sheep meat over the winter. The ham is dry-cured in spiced salt, then cold-smoked over wood before it is air-dried. Now enjoying a revival, mutton ham is produced in Cumbria and parts of Wales and Scotland.

Cooking

Thickly carved cooked ham with fat chips and a fried egg is one of my favourite pub lunches. And I never tire of ham during the days after Christmas when meals seem to lose their normal pattern. Ham is equally welcome in summer, too, when appetites flag in unaccustomed heat. I love the simplicity of a few slices of ham with watercress and buttery new potatoes.

Bite-sized chunks of cooked ham are handy for adding to all sorts of things: a savoury tart or a frittata perhaps, or a dish of warm earthy Puy lentils. Then there is hash – raggedy nuggets of ham fried with mashed potatoes until pleasingly crisp round the edges. Leftover ham is also great in **Ham and Root Soup** (page 138).

Air-dried ham needs no cooking unless you want to fry little bits of it for sprinkling over pasta shapes or steamed Savoy cabbage. Otherwise, enjoy it with peppered figs, perhaps, or shaved celery or fennel, or wrapped around grissini sticks, or on sourdough bread thickly spread with unsalted butter.

See also **Bacon and Gammon** (page 21)

Hams to look for
Cooked:
- *Bradenham:* unmistakable treacle-cured black skin, unique sweet flavour.
- *Cumberland:* dry-salted, unsmoked, slightly spicy complex flavour, dense texture.
- *Suffolk:* oak-smoked, cured in beer or cider, superb sweet flavour.
- *York:* oak-smoked, pronounced pork flavour, salty, dry texture.

Air-dried:
- *Cumbria:* unsmoked, deep translucent red flesh, intense salty flavour, slightly sweet.
- *Denhay:* lightly smoked, brownish-pink flesh, quite salty.
- *Mutton ham:* smoked, dark red-brown flesh streaked with creamy gold fat. Gamey flavour, redolent of herbs and smoke.

Shopping notes
Cooked:
- Buy in one piece or freshly sliced.
- Look for a high proportion of meat to fat.
- Meat should be pink and moist without any dry shredded areas.

Air-dried:
- If vacuum-packed check that it is well within the 'use-by' date.

Storing
- Whole ham or large portions will keep in the fridge for up to 7 days loosely wrapped in foil.
- Vacuum-packed sliced ham should be used within 2–3 days of opening.

Preparation
- Remove packaging from air-dried ham, separate the slices and allow to breathe at room temperature for 30 minutes before serving.

Glazed Ham with Membrillo and Mustard

Make your own home-cooked ham from a gammon joint. Membrillo (quince paste) and hot English mustard make a sweet and pungent glaze.

Soak the gammon in water for 12–24 hours, changing the water once or twice. Drain, put in a large saucepan and cover with fresh water. Bring to the boil, skimming off the scum, and simmer for 30 minutes. Taste the cooking water and if it is very salty, discard it. Cover the meat with fresh water and start again, subtracting 30 minutes from the total cooking time.

Add the onion, carrots, celery, bay leaves, parsley and peppercorns. Simmer very gently, partially-covered, for 2 hours. Remove from the heat and leave to cool in the liquid for at least 30 minutes. Preheat the oven to 200°C/gas 6.

When cool enough to handle, lift the meat out of the liquid and place in a small roasting tin lined with foil. Carefully remove the string. Peel away the skin and discard, leaving a thick layer of fat. Score the fat in a diamond pattern.

Melt the glaze ingredients in a saucepan and simmer for a minute or two until syrupy. Brush evenly over the meat making sure it gets into all the crevices. Roast for 25–30 minutes, brushing with the glaze every 10 minutes, until sticky and slightly blackened. Leave the meat to rest in a warm place for 30 minutes before carving.

Cook's notes
• Make sure the gammon has a thick layer of fat covering the meat.
• Keep the cooking liquid (discard the vegetables) and use it to make **Ham and Root Soup** (page 138), or freeze to use as stock.
• If you don't have any membrillo, use good quality marmalade instead.

boneless gammon joint 2.3–2.5kg, rolled and tied
onion 1, halved
carrots 2
celery stalks 2, halved
fresh bay leaves 2
flat leaf parsley handful with stalks
black peppercorns $\frac{1}{2}$ tsp

for the glaze
membrillo (quince paste) 200g
hot English mustard 1 tbsp
lemon juice 3 tbsp
rapeseed oil 3 tbsp

Serves 6–8

Ham and Root Soup

A befitting end to the Christmas ham and lovely for a winter weekend lunch when you have a houseful of guests.

Heat a large saucepan over medium heat. Add the rapeseed oil with the bay leaf and rosemary and let them warm through. Sizzle the bits of ham until beginning to crisp around the edge. Scoop out with a perforated spoon and set aside.

Add all the vegetables, cover and cook for about 15 minutes or until nicely soft. Give them a stir now and again. Pour in the stock and bring to the boil. Reduce the heat and simmer, partially covered, for 30 minutes.

Purée about half the mixture in a food processor – the amount depends on how much solid matter you want left in your soup. Pour the purée back into the pan and stir in the reserved ham. Stir in the wine vinegar. Season with plenty of freshly ground black pepper and a little salt, remembering the saltiness of the ham and stock. Cook gently until heated through. Sprinkle with greenery before serving.

Cook's note
• Use a mixture of whatever roots you happen to have – parsnips, celeriac, swede, carrot and potatoes are all fine.

rapeseed oil 2 tbsp
fresh bay leaf 1, shredded
rosemary leaves chopped to make 1 tsp
home-cooked ham 200g, diced
onion 1 large, finely chopped
celery stalks 2, halved lengthways and diced
root vegetables peeled and trimmed, 800g, diced
ham or **chicken stock** 1 litre
white wine vinegar 2 tsp
freshly ground black pepper
salt
celery leaves or **flat leaf parsley** to garnish

Serves 6

Hare

One of the truly wild creatures, hare are regarded by connoisseurs as top-of-the-range game. They are elusive and shooting is restricted to the open season. Hare may not be sold between March and July, though you may find one tucked away in the farm shop freezer.

Though hare can often be used in the same dishes as wild rabbit, it's worth bearing in mind that it is much larger and longer-limbed, running at speeds of up to 45 miles an hour if pushed. As a result, the muscles are more hardworking and the meat has a much stronger flavour. The flesh is a deep mahogany-red, rich and earthy with a strong gamey flavour.

Hares are hung head down for 2–3 days, and the blood is collected in a bag. The blood is a key ingredient in a number of dishes, but you will probably have to put in a request for it if you need it specifically.

Cooking

The robustly flavoured meat needs equally robust seasonings – port, Cognac and hearty red wine spring to mind, as do pungent ingredients such as mustard and cracked black pepper.

The best meat comes from the saddle and hind legs – use the other bits in a stew or for stock. A real delicacy is **seared and roasted fillet**. Brush with olive oil and season well with crushed black peppercorns and sea salt. Heat 1 tablespoon of olive oil in a large frying pan over medium-high heat, quickly brown the fillets all over, then roast for 4 minutes at 220°C/gas 7. Transfer to a board, cover with foil and leave to rest in a warm place for 8–10 minutes before carving.

Another option is to roast the whole **saddle with mustard, onions and bacon**. Smear the saddle with Dijon or English mustard and put in a roasting tin with 3–4 tablespoons of olive oil. Scatter with 2 coarsely chopped onions and 100g diced streaky bacon. Add a couple of thyme sprigs and season with sea salt and freshly ground black pepper. Roast at 200°C/gas 6 for 30 minutes, moistening with a splash of boiling water from time to time. Lower the temperature to 180°C/gas 4, stir in 100ml double cream and roast for 10 minutes more. Transfer the saddle to a warm serving dish, cover and leave to rest in a warm place. Strain the cooking juices and pour back into the tin. Place over medium heat, scraping up any sediment, and stir in 1 tablespoon of plain flour. Add a further 150ml double cream and simmer gently for a few minutes, stirring all the time. Carve the meat and pour over the sauce.

Meat from older hares is better braised as it can be tough. Leftover meat can be pulled from the bone and used to enrich a risotto or pasta dish. An iconic dish is jugged hare for which there are numerous recipes. As the name suggests, the hare is cooked in a jug, standing in a container of simmering water. This is an all-day job that needs planning and requires blood from the hare to thicken the cooking liquid.

Less ambitious but equally good is an **Italian-style baked casserole** (see **Rabbit**, page 216) or try using hare instead of chicken in the recipe for **Coq au Vin** (page 78).

UK season
- Open shooting 1 August–29 February.
- Best eaten between October and January.

Breeds to look for
- English Brown hare: larger, superior flavour to Scottish Blue or Mountain Hare.
- Young female hares are more tender.

Shopping notes
- Choose a hare suitable for the dish you intend to cook:
Roasting: leverets 2–4 months old, weighing about 1.5kg
Braising, stewing, jugging: 1-year old hare, 2.5–3kg.
Terrines: older hare, 4–6kg.
- Ask the butcher to skin the hare and save the blood.

Storing
- Store on the bottom shelf of the fridge so raw juices cannot drip onto other food.
- Wash well, pat dry and store in a shallow dish, loosely covered with foil, for 1–2 days.
- Remove the liver and store separately.

Preparation
- Remove any shot pellets and damaged meat before cooking.
- Soak in wine vinegar or lemon juice for several hours to tenderise the meat.
- For extra flavour and tenderness, marinate in full-bodied red wine, robust herbs such as thyme, rosemary and bay leaves, olive oil, garlic, crushed juniper berries and plenty of freshly ground black pepper.

Serving size
- Whole young hare weighing 1.5kg serves 4.
- Hare fillet: 100g serves 1.

Herbs

I like the way farm shops sell loose herbs kept fresh in homely jugs of water. You just take what you need and have it weighed – far more amenable than a plastic packet that isn't the right size. Whether you want an armful or a few sprigs, you can usually be confident that the herbs will be freshly harvested and have not spent hours on a plane.

Some farms sell whatever herbs they happen to grow for their own use – the selection may be limited or it may contain some fragrant gems (see **Herbs to look for**). Specialist herb farms are another matter. Here you are likely to find twenty kinds of mint or basil, or rarities like lovage and hyssop.

Cooking

Culinary herbs bring exquisite flavours to any dish, either sweet or savoury. Aromatic *fines herbes*, such as rosemary and thyme, are so robust they are used only in small amounts. Some of the leafier varieties are less potent and can be used with greater abandon. Orache, nasturtium and purslane, for example, are almost vegetables in their own right, contributing body, texture and colour as well as flavour. Look out for them in the interesting salad bags found in the better farm shops.

Mediterranean cooks are adept at making simple but superb salads of leafy herbs. To the Greeks, a green salad is often a single variety such as purslane. In the Middle East, huge quantities of mint and flat leaf parsley are key ingredients in a proper tabbouleh.

Leafy herbs also make potent sauces and dressings. A good handful of basil, for example, pureed with olive oil or light stock, is perfect with fish or a warm vegetable salad. Add parsley, gherkins and anchovies to make piquant *salsa verde* (**Pig's Trotters with Salsa Verde**, page 192), or Parmesan and pine nuts for pesto sauce.

When using leafy herbs in cooked dishes, remember that prolonged exposure to heat tends to destroy the flavour, so add them just before serving. Robust herbs such as rosemary and thyme can be added earlier on.

See also:
Broad Bean Bruschetta with Summer Savory and Goat's Cheese (page 48)
Celery and Dill Soup with Spelt (page 63)
Gammon Steaks with Parsley Sauce (page 23)
Green Bean and Dill Pickle (page 126)
Herb-Crusted Barbecued Fillet of Beef (page 30)
Porchetta with Fennel, Lemon and Rosemary Stuffing (page 201)
Red Gooseberries with Orange and Bay Syrup (page 124)
Strawberry Compôte with Tarragon and Orange Zest (page 251)

UK season
• *Tender annuals:* May–September.
• *Hardy perennials:* year round.

Herbs to look for
• *Chervil:* tender fronds, mild anise flavour, use in salads or as a garnish.
• *Hyssop:* tiny pointed leaves, strong flavour, use like thyme with pasta or lamb.
• *Lovage*: deeply toothed leaves, strong meaty flavour, use sparingly.
• *Myrtle*: thick glossy pointed leaves, lemony flavour, use like bay leaves.
• *Nasturtium:* vivid orange-red or yellow flowers, saucer-shaped grass-green leaves, peppery flavour.
• *Orache* (mountain spinach): triangular purple, gold or green leaves, lemony flavour.
• *Purslane:* succulent round stems, green or gold spatula-shaped leaves, peppery flavour.
• *Savory* (summer and winter): small pointed leaves, aromatic, good with broad beans.
• *Sorrel* (buckler-leaved): brittle light-green leaves, startling lemony flavour.

Shopping notes
• Look for dewy-fresh herbs. Don't bother with any that look dry, limp or have rotting leaves or stems.

Storing
• Use on the day of purchase if possible.
• Otherwise wrap small bunches loosely in damp paper towels, unwashed, and store in a sealed plastic bag in the salad drawer of the fridge for 1–2 days .
• Keep large bunches of leafy herbs in a jug of water loosely covered with a plastic bag.

Preparation
• Strip the leaves from coarse stems if necessary (keep stems for stock or soup).
• Dunk leaves in cold water, drain and dry in a salad spinner. Blot with paper towels.
• Pound, chop or slice according to the recipe, but wait until needed.
• Use a very sharp blade, otherwise you will bruise the herbs rather than cutting them cleanly.

Horseradish

The most pungent of edible roots, horseradish has long been a favourite in Scandinavia and Eastern Europe. There it shows up in a number of sauces and dressings, but in the UK we tend to limit our enjoyment to a dollop of commercially bottled sauce served with roast beef.

Much more exciting is the fresh root, though its appearance belies the power-packed flavour. An undistinguished beige, it is usually tightly encased in plastic and easily overlooked. Unbroken, the root has no smell but once the flesh is exposed, beware – eyes will stream and sinuses clear. The flavour, though intense, is not unpleasant – clean and fresh but also mustardy and slightly bitter, similar to swede or turnip. A little goes a long way, so it's worth looking for horseradish in farm shops where it is often sold in sensible-sized chunks rather than whole roots.

Cooking

Prolonged heat diminishes horseradish's fiery bite, so it's best to use it raw or add it to a dish at the very end of cooking.

Horseradish is stunning in a **palate-tingling ice cream** served in melon ball-sized scoops with roast beef or smoked salmon. Make a custard in the usual way with 250ml each whole milk and whipping cream, and 3 egg yolks, but only a modest amount of sugar – about 2 tablespoons. Once thickened, add 4–5 tablespoons of freshly grated horseradish and a good pinch of salt. Leave until completely cold, then chill for at least 2 hours. Push through a fine sieve to get rid of horseradish shreds, then churn and freeze in an ice cream machine.

For **horseradish and apple sauce** (lovely with roast pork), peel, core and slice 2 cooking apples and put in a saucepan with a splash of water. Cover and cook for about 7 minutes, shaking the pan occasionally to prevent sticking. Beat until smooth, then push through a sieve. Stir in a knob of butter, 3 tablespoons of freshly grated horseradish and a pinch each of salt, sugar and freshly ground black pepper. As a variation, stir in 3 tablespoons of mayonnaise and use as a dressing for smoked fish or herring, or to perk up grated celeriac or cold chicken.

For a **creamy horseradish dressing**, ideal for a robust beef salad, soak a finely grated 5-cm piece of root in 2 tablespoons each of stock and water. Leave for 10 minutes to soften, then mix with 3 tablespoons of lemon juice, a pinch of sugar, and salt and black pepper to taste. Whizz in a blender with 100ml extra-virgin olive oil, followed by 4 tablespoons of whipping cream.

Tangy horseradish cream makes an excellent dip for chips or for mixing into a potato salad. Combine 3 tablespoons of freshly grated horseradish with 6 tablespoons of organic double cream and 2 tablespoons of Greek yogurt. Stir in the finely grated zest of $\frac{1}{2}$ a lemon, 1 tablespoon of lemon juice, 1 teaspoon of Dijon mustard, a pinch of sea salt flakes and some freshly ground black pepper. Leave to stand at room temperature for 30 minutes to allow the flavours to develop.

UK season
• June–September.

Shopping notes
• Look for fat hard roots, without any bruising, soft spots or signs of sprouting.

Storing
• Store in the fridge, tightly wrapped in cling film, for up to 2 weeks.

Preparation
• Prepare just before needed as the root quickly discolours and loses pungency.
• Remove the skin and grate the flesh by hand, or cut into small chunks and whizz in a food processor.

Crushed Red Potatoes with Horseradish, Fried Onions and Soured Cream

This is an absolute winner, destined to partner barbecued **Cumberland sausages** (page 234) or thick slices of home-cooked ham.

Put the potatoes in a large saucepan with enough salted water to cover. Bring to the boil, then reduce the heat and simmer for 20 minutes. Drain, then return to the pan and cover with a folded tea towel and a lid. Leave to dry for 5 minutes.

While the potatoes are boiling, heat a heavy-based frying pan over medium heat. Add the oil and fry the onion for 7 minutes or until beginning to brown. Add the garlic and continue frying until the onions are golden.

Roughly crush the potatoes, leaving visible chunks, and stir in the onion and garlic. Combine the remaining ingredients and stir into the potatoes. Serve hot or warm.

red-skinned salad potatoes 1kg, unpeeled
rapeseed oil 2 tbsp
onion 1, chopped
garlic cloves 3, finely chopped
soured cream 150ml
fresh horseradish 2-cm piece, peeled and coarsely grated
sea salt flakes 1 tsp
freshly ground black pepper $1/4$ tsp
flat leaf parsley leaves trimmed and chopped to make 2 tbsp

Serves 4–6

Cook's notes
• If you don't have fresh horseradish, use bottled grated horseradish but it won't taste quite the same.
• Take the soured cream out of the fridge before you start to cook. It should be at room temperature when mixed with the potatoes.
• Make sure the potatoes are a similar size so that they cook evenly.

Horseradish and Beetroot Relish (*Chrain*)

These two under-appreciated vegetables make a memorable fuchsia-red relish from Eastern Europe – a perfect balance of hot, sweet and sour. It's easy to make and so good with cold meats and smoked fish. It will keep for a week or two in the fridge. After that it will still be tasty it will gradually lose its zest.

Peel the horseradish and grate it, using the finest blade of a food processor, then add the rest of the ingredients. Whizz to a purée, scraping down the sides of the bowl every so often until everything is well blended.

Scrape into a bowl and leave at room temperature for at least an hour to let the flavours develop. Decant into a screw-top jar and store in the fridge until required.

fresh horseradish 6-cm piece from the fat end of the root
beetroot 2–3 small, peeled and grated
water 3 tbsp
cider vinegar 2 tbsp
caster sugar 2 tsp
salt

Makes 250g

Cook's note
• The trick with *chrain* is to keep tasting, adding more beetroot, vinegar or sugar as you think fit.

Horseradish and Beetroot Relish

Pan-Fried Jerusalem Artichokes (page 146)

Jerusalem Artichokes

These knobbly little tubers look more like fresh ginger rather than their namesake, the globe artichoke. The flavour is similar but the two are unrelated. Jerusalem artichokes are relatives of the sunflower, as implied by the name. This comes from the Italian *girasole* meaning sunflower (and has nothing to do with Jerusalem). Western growers have renamed the tubers 'sunchoke' which is perhaps more apt.

The tubers are the size of a small elongated potato, the skin an undistinguished beige, though some are a more striking reddish-pink. Some varieties are intensely gnarled and crevice-ridden, and therefore tedious to peel; others are smoother and more elongated.

Farmers love Jerusalem artichokes – they are reliable croppers, especially prolific after a wet summer, and happily impervious to major pests and diseases. Cooks love them for their versatility and unique flavour. That said, there's no denying that Jerusalem artichokes cause flatulence. Though various tips exist for reducing wind-power, I have not found anything particularly effective. Go easy the first time you try them, and remember that any temporary discomfort is a small price to pay for the enjoyment of their sweet nutty flavour.

Cooking

Jerusalem artichokes are wonderfully adaptable. They are delicious hot or cold, with or without the skin, steamed or boiled, fried or roasted, and they marry well with sweetish mildly flavoured ingredients such as potato, hazelnuts, scallops or prawns.

For a simple side dish, boil or steam the tubers for 7–12 minutes depending on size. But be vigilant – they can disintegrate in seconds. Serve with melted butter, a soupçon of freshly grated nutmeg and a sprinkling of snipped chives. Another option is to stir-fry thickly sliced Jerusalem artichokes with meaty field mushrooms, garlic, parsley and plenty of sage – an excellent dish for the autumn.

The French have a real knack with Jerusalem artichokes, putting them to good use in soufflés, gratins and daubes. A classic is **Escoffier's Palestine Soup**, a rich velvety purée made especially delicious by hazelnuts. Chop 1kg tubers (peeled or unpeeled) and sweat in a covered pan with a large knob of butter. After 10 minutes, add a few toasted crushed hazelnuts and 500ml light chicken stock. Simmer until tender, purée in a food processor and push through a sieve. Mix 150ml milk with 1 tablespoon of potato flour (or arrow-root) and add this to the soup. Season with salt and black pepper and reheat gently, adding a little more stock or milk if you find the soup too thick. Swirl in a knob of butter just before serving. For crispness and crunch, serve with **garlic croûtons** (page 112).

Lightly steamed and thickly sliced, Jerusalem artichokes make a great **winter salad**. Toss them with robust well-flavoured leaves such as chicory, frisée and lambs' lettuce. Add some juicy prawns or crisp nuggets of bacon, then anoint with a thick mustardy dressing.

UK season
- October–March.

Varieties to look for
- *'Fuseau'*, beige, smooth-skinned, elongated.
- *'Gerard'*, purple-red, smooth-skinned, round.

Shopping notes
- Choose the smoothest tubers you can find.
- Don't bother with any that are flabby, broken or starting to sprout.

Storing
- Store in a paper bag in the salad drawer of the fridge for up to 2 weeks.

Preparation
- Scrub well under running water. Cut off stringy bits and dark tips.
- The skin is edible so need not be peeled except for aesthetic reasons.
- If you do peel or slice them, drop into acidulated water to stop cut surfaces turning brown.

Pan-Fried Jerusalem Artichokes

Frying adds welcome texture and colour to an otherwise soft beige vegetable. Crisp hazelnuts and a shower of parsley make it a feast.

Peel the artichokes, dropping them into water acidulated with lemon juice. Slice in half if they are large. Place in a steamer basket set over boiling water and steam for 5 minutes (they won't be tender at this stage – the aim is to keep them crisp). Let them cool for a few minutes, then slice fairly thickly.

Heat a large non-stick frying pan, then add the sunflower oil and butter. Once the butter starts to sizzle, add the artichoke slices in a single layer, in batches if necessary. Fry for 3 minutes until coloured on one side, then turn with tongs and fry the other side for 2–3 minutes. Drain on paper towels and keep warm.

Pour the fat into a smaller pan and sizzle the hazelnuts for 1 minute or until golden, taking care not to let them burn.

Tip the artichokes into a warm serving dish and season with sea salt and plenty of freshly ground black pepper. Strew with the parsley and hazelnuts.

Cook's note
• Peeled Jerusalem artichokes quickly turn an unappetising shade of grey. Dunking in acidulated water will keep them creamy-white.

Jersualem artichokes 500g
lemon juice
extra-virgin sunflower oil 3 tbsp
butter a good knob
shelled hazelnuts 30g, roughly chopped
sea salt
freshly ground black pepper
flat leaf parsley leaves trimmed and sliced to make 2 tbsp

Serves 4 as a side dish

Gratin of Jerusalem Artichokes with Cobnuts, Bacon and Garlic Cream

A many-textured dish of soft creamy artichokes, crunchy nuts, succulent bacon and crisp golden breadcrumbs. This is rich and filling stuff – a simple green salad or a steamed leafy vegetable are all that's needed as a side dish.

Preheat the oven to 190°C/gas 5. Peel the artichokes, dropping them into water acidulated with lemon juice. Slice in half if they are large. Place in a steamer basket set over boiling water and steam for 8–10 minutes until just tender at the edges. Let them cool a bit, then slice fairly thickly.

While the artichokes are cooking, grill the bacon on a rack until slightly crisp. Snip into bite-sized pieces.

Grease a 2-litre baking dish with some of the butter. Arrange half the artichoke slices in the base and season with sea salt and freshly ground pepper. Sprinkle with the bacon and chopped nuts, then top with the rest of the artichokes and a little more seasoning.

Pour in the warm Garlic Cream, sprinkle with the breadcrumbs and dot with the remaining butter. Bake for 30–35 minutes until the artichokes are tender and the topping is golden and bubbling.

Cook's notes
• The first of the Jerusalem artichokes coincide with the brief cobnut season. These crisp sweet nuts are particularly good with artichokes, but you could use hazelnuts instead.
• It's fine to use whipping cream if you don't have any Garlic Cream. Just add a bit more salt and pepper.

Jerusalem artichokes 650g
lemon juice
dry-cured back bacon 3 thick rashers
butter a generous knob
sea salt
freshly ground black pepper
shelled cobnuts 3 tbsp, roughly chopped
Garlic Cream (page 112) warm, 250ml
breadcrumbs (from a day-old loaf), 40g

Serves 4

Kale

Classified as a 'superfood', kale truly deserves the accolade. It is one of the most nutritionally rich vegetables, packed with health-promoting stuff like phytochemicals, carotenoids and vitamins. Not only is kale good for you, it actually tastes good too. It has a satisfyingly rich and earthy flavour with a hint of sweetness. Many people find it more appetising than cabbage.

Kale is also beautiful. It sports graceful leaves that are deeply toothed or flamboyantly frilled, puckered or flat. Some varieties have dazzling purple stems that contrast with luminous blue-green leaves; others are a green so deep it could almost be black.

Historically, kale is one of the oldest members of the brassica family and a major UK crop. Farm shops can be relied on to have a good choice of varieties and a continuing supply from autumn to spring. Kale is one of the few green vegetables that is abundant and flavourful during a lean time of year.

Cooking

Kale is best cooked simply, either boiled or steamed, or quickly sautéed in olive oil with a little onion or garlic, a splash of wine vinegar and a pinch of chilli flakes. Tender baby leaves can be used raw in a salad, dressed with a little walnut oil, or lightly cooked in a stir-fry with ginger, garlic and soy sauce.

I like lightly steamed kale tossed in butter with lemon zest, freshly ground white pepper and a generous sprinkling of chopped fresh coriander. The clean flavours of lemon and coriander, and the punch of the pepper are just right with the rich earthy flavour. For some reason, kale seems to go cold very quickly so serve it right away, ideally on warm plates.

Kale can be put to good use **in a soup**, provided it isn't allowed to dominate. The Portuguese have a hearty classic called *caldo verde* (green soup): simmer 750g floury potatoes until tender, then purée. Reheat with enough water to give a thin-to-medium consistency. Roll 450g trimmed kale leaves into a wad and shred very finely with a sharp knife. Add to the potato along with a finely chopped onion. Season well and simmer for 10–15 minutes, uncovered, until the kale is tender-crisp. The Portuguese add slices of garlic sausage. Pour into bowls as soon as the kale is cooked, and top with a slick of fruity olive oil.

Kale is also very good in a slow braise with bacon, onion, stock and a handful of pearled spelt or barley stirred in.

UK season
• October–April.

Varieties to look for
• *'Red Russian'* (also called *'Ragged Jack'* and *'Red Winter'*), smooth serrated blue-green leaves, soft texture, superb flavour.
• *'Nero di Toscano'* (also called *'Black Kale'* and *'Laccinato Blue'*), long dark green heavily puckered leaves.
• *'Dwarf Green Curled'*, deeply curled tender green leaves.

Shopping notes
• Look for bouncy leaves with an almost luminous colour and no sign of yellowing.

Storing
• Store washed and trimmed leaves in damp paper towels in a roomy plastic bag in the salad drawer of the fridge. Use within 1–2 days.

Preparation
• Dunk in several changes of water to remove grit.
• Strip tough stems and central vein from larger leaves by folding the leaf in half so the upper surfaces touch, then grasp the stem and pull firmly towards tip.

Kale, Pork and Bean One-Pot (page 150)

Kale, Pork and Bean One-Pot

This is a fortifying main-meal soup based on the classic combination of pork, beans and greens found in most cuisines. Lime juice, coriander and avocado give this a New Mexican twist. Don't be put off by the long list of ingredients – they are there to build the flavour.

Heat a large saucepan over medium-high heat. Add the groundnut oil and pork, and fry until lightly browned. Remove with a perforated spoon and set aside.

Lower the heat and add the onions, cumin and oregano, stirring to coat them in the fat. Cover and cook gently for 25–30 minutes until very soft, stirring occasionally to prevent sticking. Add a splash of stock if necessary. Add the garlic, chillies and tomatoes and cook for 10 minutes more.

Next, add the pork, beans, stock, salt and black pepper. Bring to the boil, then lower the heat again and simmer gently with the lid askew for 45 minutes or until the meat is tender.

Just before you're ready to serve, raise the heat and stir in the kale. Simmer briskly, uncovered, for 5–7 minutes or until the kale is tender but still brightly coloured. Stir in the coriander and lime juice. Pour into bowls and serve with the garnishes.

Cook's note

• You can use canned borlotti beans, thoroughly drained and rinsed, but soaked and freshly cooked dried beans will taste better. You'll need 175g beans before soaking. Cook them until tender but not too soft, before adding them to the soup.

groundnut oil 4 tbsp
lean boneless pork 500g, cut into bite-sized pieces
white onions 2, thinly sliced
cumin seeds 1 tsp, crushed
dried oregano $\frac{1}{2}$ tsp
chicken stock preferably home-made, 1 litre
garlic cloves 2 large, thinly sliced
green chillies 1–3, deseeded and finely chopped
tomatoes 3, peeled and chopped
cooked borlotti beans or **butter beans** 350g
salt $\frac{1}{2}$ tsp
black peppercorns $\frac{1}{2}$ tsp, crushed
kale trimmed and shredded, 150g
coriander leaves trimmed and chopped to make 5 tbsp
lime juice of 1

to garnish
white onion cut into slivers
avocado diced and tossed with lime juice
lime wedges

Serves 6

Kidney

Let's face it – the kidney's job is to filter urine, and the thought always persists. However, having eaten extremely fresh kidney from a farm shop with an immaculate butchery, I have finally come around to it after lifelong resistance. I am still slightly wary of massive multi-lobed veal and ox kidneys, but lamb and pig kidneys are single-lobed and pleasingly small. Kidneys from younger animals are milder and the ones to go for if you are not used to the flavour. Freshness is key. Bacteria soon get to work even on chilled kidney, and while it may still be edible, it will certainly develop an 'off' flavour.

Cooking

What won me over were delicate little **lamb's kidney kebabs** with bacon and bay leaves. They are more like calf's liver and not in the least bitter or chewy. Allow 2 or 3 kidneys per person, slice them lengthways and cut out the gristly white core. Put in a bowl with the juice of $\frac{1}{2}$ a lemon, $\frac{1}{2}$ teaspoon of mustard powder, 2 tablespoons of chopped red onion, a crushed garlic clove and 1 tablespoon of extra-virgin olive oil. Marinate for 30 minutes, then thread onto skewers, alternating with fresh bay leaves and squares of thick de-rinded bacon. Season with sea salt flakes and coarsely ground black pepper. Barbecue or grill for 4–5 minutes each side. If you like, bubble down the marinade with a few spoonfuls of stock to make a sauce.

Lamb's kidneys are also good sliced and fried, perhaps with a splash of balsamic vinegar, but be careful not to over-cook or they will become tough.

Stronger-tasting ox and pig kidneys are best mixed with other ingredients and used in slow-cooked dishes such as **Steak and Kidney Pie** (page 153).

Shopping notes
• Look for plump, deep red-brown, glossy kidneys with no dryness round the edges.
• They should smell scrupulously clean and fresh.

Storing
• Store on the bottom shelf of the fridge so raw juices cannot drip onto other food.
• Remove any wrapping and store in a shallow dish, loosely covered with foil, for 24 hours maximum.

Preparation
• Separate multi-lobed kidneys into single pieces.
• Remove any white fat and coarse membrane.
• Slice in half and cut out the gristly white core.
• For a milder flavour, soak ox and pig kidneys in milk, or water and lemon juice, for 30 minutes before cooking.

Steak and Kidney Pie

Probably the most iconic pie in the land with many variations. I have omitted the traditional oysters; they are put to better use elsewhere.

Combine the flour, salt and black pepper, and spread out on a tray. Toss the beef and kidneys in the seasoned flour, turning with your hands until evenly coated.

Heat a large heavy-based frying pan over medium-high heat. Add 2 tablespoons of rapeseed oil and fry the beef and kidneys, a few handfuls at a time. Transfer to a large casserole as each batch gets fried. Add a bit more oil if the pan starts to get dry. When all the meat and kidneys are in the casserole, deglaze the pan with the balsamic vinegar and 4 tablespoons of the stock. Heat until bubbling, scraping up all the tasty sediment with a wooden spoon, and add to the casserole.

Heat a little more oil in the frying pan and gently fry the shallots until they are soft but not coloured. Add these to the casserole along with the tomato purée, bay leaves, thyme sprigs and cloves. Pour in enough stock to barely cover the meat. Bring to the boil, then reduce the heat and simmer gently, with the lid askew, for 1½ hours until the meat is just tender. Check the seasoning, then add the Worcestershire sauce. Remove from the heat, pour into a bowl and leave until completely cold.

Meanwhile, fry the mushrooms in some more oil, just long enough for them to give up their juices. Season with crumbled sea salt flakes and freshly ground black pepper, and set aside.

Preheat the oven to 200°C/gas 6. Put a baking tray in to heat. Drain the meat mixture, reserving the liquid, and tip into a deep 1.5-litre pie dish with a flat rim. Mix in the fried mushrooms. Pour in enough of the liquid to not quite cover the filling.

Make sure the pastry is 2.5cm wider than the rim of the pie dish – roll it out a bit more if necessary. Cut a 1-cm strip and press it onto the dampened rim. Brush the strip with egg yolk, then carefully place the pastry on top. Trim with a knife, then crimp the edges with your finger and thumb, so that the pastry sticks to the rim. Make four X-shaped slashes at opposite ends of the pie to allow the steam to escape. Use the trimmings to make artistic decorations and glue these in place with a dab of egg yolk. Finally, brush the whole surface with egg yolk.

Put the pie on the baking tray (to catch any overflowing juices) and bake for 15 minutes. Reduce the oven temperature to 180°C/gas 4 and bake for 45–55 minutes more, or until the pastry is golden and risen, and the filling piping hot.

Cook's notes
• Kidneys are slithery little things – easier to core if you grasp one between your fingers and do the snipping with scissors.
• Take care not to overcrowd the pan when frying the beef and kidneys, otherwise they won't brown.
• Speed up cooling the filling by dividing it between two or three smaller containers. Stand them in a washing-up bowl of cold water or ice cubes.
• The filling can be cooked well ahead of time, then chilled or frozen.

plain flour 5 tbsp
salt 1 tsp
freshly ground black pepper ½ tsp
stewing beef 900g, cut into bite-sized chunks
pig or **ox kidneys** 350g, split and cored
rapeseed oil for frying
balsamic vinegar 2 tbsp
meat stock preferably home-made, 500–600ml
banana shallots 2, chopped
tomato purée 1 tbsp
fresh bay leaves 2, shredded
thyme 2 sprigs
cloves 2
Worcestershire sauce 1 tbsp
flat portabello mushrooms 250g, cut into quarters or eighths
sea salt flakes
ready-made puff pastry 375g
egg yolk beaten, for glazing

Serves 4–5

Kohlrabi

With a youthful bloom to its green or purple skin, kohlrabi not only looks good, it tastes good too. The greenish-white flesh has a crisp crunchy texture and a mildly cabbage-like flavour with a clean hint of mint. Inexplicably, greengrocers like to remove the graceful upward-growing stems, leaving the vegetable with a rather bad haircut. You have a better chance of finding stems intact if you buy kohlrabi from a farm shop.

Despite its exotic appearance, kohlrabi is in fact a member of the common brassica family, as are Brussels sprouts and broccoli. It is often thought of as a root vegetable but is actually a swollen stem, like fennel, which grows on top of the soil.

Cooking

The crisp, juicy flesh is best eaten raw to appreciate the delicate flavour. Cut into matchsticks and add to coleslaw tossed in a **Lemon Yogurt Dressing** (page 278).

The crisp flesh is dense enough to remain intact even when very thinly sliced in a colourful **carpaccio of kohlrabi, carrot and radishes.** Slice 3 small kohlrabi, 1 fat carrot and 4 large radishes horizontally into paper-thin circles (use a mandolin). Arrange in a shallow dish and pour over a dressing made with 2 teaspoons each of orange and lime juice, 3 tablespoons of extra-virgin olive oil, 1 tablespoon of walnut oil, and salt and black pepper. Leave at room temperature for an hour or so, then strew with 1 tablespoon of snipped chives and a handful of coarsely chopped 'wet' walnuts.

More unusually, **kohlrabi** goes well with **lemon** and **lovage** – a neglected but flavoursome herb. Cut 4 tennis ball-sized kohlrabi into small cubes and mix with the finely grated zest of 1½ lemons and 3 tablespoons of chopped lovage (or a mixture of flat leaf parsley and celery leaves). Sprinkle with 1 teaspoon of white wine vinegar and 4 tablespoons of extra-virgin olive oil, and season to taste with sea salt flakes and freshly ground black pepper. This salad is lovely with cold poached salmon.

Older kohlrabi is best cooked but it still needs a gentle touch to preserve the flavour and texture. Don't overpower it with too many other ingredients. Try it cut into cubes or thin semi-circles, then steam or blanch briefly until only just tender. Serve tossed with melted butter or a blob of soured cream and a few chopped dill fronds or chives.

For an Asian touch, cut the flesh into matchsticks and stir-fry with shredded leafy greens, a sliver or two of fresh ginger root, and a splash of soy sauce and toasted sesame oil.

UK season
• June–November.

Varieties to look for
• *'Eder'*, green-skinned, full-flavoured, minty with juicy texture.
• *'White Superschmelz'*, large but not fibrous.

Shopping notes
• Buy tennis ball-sized bulbs with a powdery bloom and sprightly fresh leaves.
• Don't bother with larger bulbs that feel light for their weight. The texture will be fibrous and the flavour insipid.
• Avoid wrinkled or discoloured bulbs, particularly those with deep scars – a sign of age.

Storing
• Store loosely wrapped in a paper bag in the salad drawer of the fridge, for 1–2 weeks.

Preparation
• Cut away stems and leaves, keeping if young and fresh. Chop stems and cook with main bulb. Cook leaves like cabbage.
• Remove peel unless exceptionally young and tender.
• Older specimens may have a fibrous layer under the skin that must also be removed.
• Grate or slice the flesh according to the recipe.

Kohlrabi, Apple and Watercress Salad with Walnuts

Delicious early autumn produce – crisp apples and new season walnuts – combine beautifully with kohlrabi in an appetising salad. The fresh mild flavour goes well with peppery watercress and sweet, slightly acidic apples.

Quarter the kohlrabi vertically, trim the ends and remove the skin. Slice each quarter crossways into very thin segments. Put in a salad bowl and toss with the lemon juice.

Quarter and core the apples but do not peel. Slice lengthways in half again to make eighths, then slice each piece crossways into four chunks. Mix with the kohlrabi in the bowl.

Add the walnuts and watercress, sprinkle with sea salt flakes and toss well.

Combine all the dressing ingredients and whisk until smooth. Pour over the salad and toss again.

See also **Apples** (page 14)

kohlrabi 2, small
lemon juice of 1
red-skinned apples 2, such as 'Cox's Orange Pippin', 'Rubens' or 'Ingrid Marie'
shelled 'wet' walnuts 40g, roughly chopped
watercress 1 bunch, trimmed
sea salt flakes

for the dressing
lemon juice 1 tbsp
sugar $\frac{1}{2}$ tsp
freshly ground black pepper $\frac{1}{4}$ tsp
celery salt $\frac{1}{4}$ tsp
extra-virgin olive oil 3 tbsp
walnut oil 1 tbsp

Serves 4–5 as a starter or light meal

Lamb and Mutton

All kinds of factors contribute to the quality of lamb and mutton: breed, rearing, grazing and the way the animal is slaughtered. Farm shops increasingly sell naturally reared meat, some of it from minority and rare breeds that graze on herbs, berries, lichens, wild flowers and even seaweed, all of which give it an unrivalled flavour.

A spring-born British lamb is at its sweetest and most tender in May and June; towards autumn, after a summer of grazing on lush grass, it develops a fuller and richer flavour that some people prefer. A lamb in its second spring or summer is known as a hogget, though it is usually sold as lamb. By now the animal will also have enjoyed a diet of winter roots that mellow the flavour even more.

In the third spring or summer, a lamb graduates to mutton status. Out of favour for years, mutton is now enjoying a renaissance thanks to a campaign initiated by HRH The Prince of Wales. Mutton is on the menu in some of the country's best restaurants, it is lauded by food writers and is available all year round. Even so, it is still surprisingly difficult to find in supermarkets or even butchers; your best bet is a farm shop or farmers' market, or online.

Cooking

Whether a juicy chop or steak, or a whole shoulder or leg, it's hard to better spring lamb cooked as simply as you can manage. The meat has a succulence and flavour that needs no detraction, except possibly a nice fat wedge of lemon for appearances sake. I particularly relish the rack – a special cut that makes the most of the cutlets (**Roast Rack of Lamb**, page 158).

As the season wears on and special breeds from hills and mountains come on the market, simple roasting or stewing are the best ways to appreciate their individual flavours. Some of the gamier breeds, particularly salt marsh lamb, benefit from ingredients that echo their seasidy diet. A stuffing of laverbread, onion, oatmeal and lemon zest is perfect in a boned and rolled shoulder of Welsh lamb.

Of the cheaper cuts, lamb shanks anointed with honey, cracked black pepper and thyme are a winner. Moistened with stock, and gently roasted with stubby carrots, small potatoes and chunks of parsnip, the meat caramelises and falls from the bone while the juices turn into a rich and unctuous goo.

Though it doesn't compare with lamb for sweetness and tenderness, mutton comes into its own when braised or casseroled. Mutton with caper sauce is a classic (**Poached Leg of Mutton with Caramelised Onions and Caper Sauce**, opposite) but the meat also lends itself to spiced dishes like tagines and curries, or full-flavoured soups and stews. Try it in chunks simmered very, very slowly with peeled garlic cloves – a whole bulb at least. With the pot tightly covered, you won't need to add any liquid; the meat produces its own juices and fat. After about 1 hour, throw in some chopped mixed herbs – rosemary, thyme and oregano – and continue simmering until the meat is very tender.

UK season
• *Lamb:* May–November.
• *Mutton:* year-round, best October–March.

Breeds to look for
• *Blackface:* from Scotland and the Borders, lean, tender, sweet flavour.
• *Herdwick:* from the Lake District, lean, dark, gamey flavour.
• *North Ronaldsay:* lean, dark, exceptional rich flavour from seaweed-based diet. Possibly the rarest meat in the UK.
• *Shetland:* tender, fine-grained, mild gamey flavour.
• *Welsh Salt Marsh:* dark, tender, distinctive long-lasting sweet flavour.

Shopping notes
• Look for bright, moist, flesh: rosy-pink in younger animals, brownish-pink to dark red in older animals. Mutton should be dark brownish-red; avoid if grey.
• Fat should be firm and creamy white. Yellow crumbly fat is a sign of age.
• Choose a cut suitable for the dish:
Slow cooking and stewing: scrag end of neck, breast, shanks, shoulder.
Grilling, frying: chops, steaks, fillet.
Roasting: leg, shoulder, cushion, saddle, best end of neck (rack).

Storing
• Store on the bottom shelf of the fridge so raw juices cannot drip onto other food.
• Remove wrapping and store in a shallow dish, loosely covered with foil. Large joints will keep for 5 days; chops, steaks and small joints 2–3 days; small chops 1–2 days. Mince should be eaten within 24 hours.
• If vacuum-packed or in a rigid plastic container, leave unopened until ready to cook.

Preparation
• Trim excess fat from chops and joints.

Serving size
• Boneless joints: 100–175g per person.
• Bone-in joints: 225–350g per person.

Poached Leg of Mutton with Caramelised Onions and Caper Sauce

This is based on a recipe by Henry Harris, chef-patron of Racine restaurant in London. It is one of the classic ways to cook mutton. The gentle poaching encourages the meat to reach optimum tenderness, and the sharp-flavoured capers cut the richness of meat, cream and buttery onions.

Put the meat in a large heavy-based casserole in which it fits snugly, and bury it in the sliced onions. Tie the bay leaves, cinnamon stick and orange zest in a piece of muslin and add to the pan with the salt and peppercorns.

Pour in the chicken stock and half the wine. Bring to a gentle simmer, spooning off any scum that forms on the surface. Cover, leaving the lid slightly askew, and simmer gently for about 2 hours or until the mutton is tender.

After 1 hour, heat a large high-sided frying pan over medium-low heat. Add half the butter and, when melted, the shallots and capers. Fry gently until soft, then raise the heat to lightly brown the shallots. Add the rest of the wine and cook briskly for about 10 minutes or until the wine has reduced by half.

Scoop up a couple of jugs of cooking liquid from the casserole – don't worry if you scoop up onions as well. Strain through a sieve placed over a measuring jug. Once you have enough liquid to make 850ml, tip the onions back into the casserole and leave the mutton to carry on simmering.

Pour the strained liquid into the pan with the capers and shallots. Bring to the boil, then simmer briskly for about 20 minutes or until reduced to 500ml. Next, pour in the cream and continue to simmer until reduced and thickened further – about 20 minutes. Check the seasoning, then pour into a jug and keep warm.

When the mutton is ready, lift it onto a warm serving dish, tent with foil and keep warm. Strain and discard the poaching liquid from the onions and fish out the muslin bag.

Wipe out the frying pan and place over medium-high heat. Add the remaining butter and, when sizzling, the drained onions. Fry briskly for 10–12 minutes or until they turn golden and start to caramelise. Drain in a sieve.

Slice the mutton elegantly, strew with the caramelised onions and pour over the caper sauce.

Cook's note
• Don't waste the strained cooking liquid. Leave to cool, then chill thoroughly and remove the layer of fat. Freeze for use as stock or in a muttony broth.

---

leg of mutton bone-in, 1.7kg
sweet onions such as Vidalia, 4, sliced
fresh bay leaves 4
cinnamon stick $\frac{1}{4}$
orange zest 3 strips
salt 2 tsp
black peppercorns 2 tsp
light chicken stock home-made, 1.7 litres
dry white wine 600ml
unsalted butter 250g
shallots 2 small
capers drained, 3 tbsp
double cream organic, 300ml

Serves 6

Roast Rack of Lamb

A little treat for two – expensive but worth every penny. The roast can be on the table in less than 30 minutes. You will need a French-cut chined rack (see **Cook's notes**).

Preheat the oven to 200°C/gas 6. Put the meat in a small roasting tin, skin-side up. Lift the flap of fat where it meets the exposed bones and tuck in a few tiny sprigs of rosemary along the entire length. Massage the meat with olive oil, crumbled sea salt flakes and plenty of freshly ground black pepper. Sprinkle with the lemon juice and splash a bit of stock or water in the base of the tin.

Roast for 20 minutes if you like your lamb rare, or 23–25 minutes for medium-rare. Remove from the oven, tent with foil and leave to rest for 5 minutes. Transfer to a warm serving platter and serve the pan juices in a small jug.

Cook's notes
• In a French-cut rack of lamb the thin layer of meat between the long bones is removed, exposing and separating the bones (making it easier to eat with your fingers).
• Chining refers to removing the bone running along the backbone so you can carve down between the cutlets.

Variation
• This is just as delicious cooked on the barbecue and served with **Camping Potatoes** (page 205).

6-cutlet rack of lamb chined
rosemary a few sprigs
extra-virgin olive oil
sea salt flakes
freshly ground black pepper
lemon juice of ½
meat stock or **water** a splash

Serves 2

Leeks

Ranging from pencil-slim babies to fat-shanked monsters, leeks are one of autumn's gems. They are cheap, versatile and delicious and, unlike their cousin the onion, do not cause tears once sliced. The downside, if there is one, is that leeks need a thorough clean before cooking. Grown deep in the ground, grit and soil invariably infiltrate the close-layered white shaft. And they come topped with a muddy tangle of leaves that are usually left intact in farm shops. That said, leeks are a stalwart staple, sweeter and milder than onions, and tasty enough to stand alone or provide background support to other ingredients.

Cooking

Leeks need a gentle touch to appreciate their fine flavour. Simple boiling or steaming are best, though young tender leeks are delicious **roasted until slightly caramelised**. Halved lengthways, they need no more than a lick of olive oil, a sprinkle of sea salt and black pepper, and a 15-minute blast at 240°C/gas 9. Wonderful with roast lamb.

I also like them thickly sliced and shaken for a few minutes in a covered pan with a dab of butter and a shower of chopped flat leaf parsley. Shredded into matchsticks and lightly cooked, they add fresh green colour to a stir-fry, perhaps with prawns or strips of tender chicken breast.

Leeks are a definite asset in soups. Indeed, they are the key ingredient in national ones such as Cock-a-Leekie from Scotland, and **Cawl** (opposite) from Wales, land of the leek. They also go into the deliciously velvety French *vichysoisse*, served chilled and topped with snipped chives.

Combined with bacon snippets and mild cheese, leeks make a satisfying tart or even a pizza. If the leeks are young and sliced thinly enough, the edges will catch the heat in a most appetising way and will not need any pre-cooking. Tender leeks are also very good raw – paper-thin slices add definite pep to a tomato salad with black olives and chunks of hard-boiled egg.

UK season
• September–March.

Varieties to look for
• *'King Richard'*, thin, long-stemmed, pleasant mild flavour, excellent for early summer eating.
• *'Musselburgh'*, old-fashioned variety, fat short stems, good solid flavour.

Shopping notes
• Buy firm fresh-looking leeks with plenty of white shaft.
• Small or medium-sized are best; large ones are likely to have a woody core.
• Avoid any with bulbous roots – they will be past their prime.
• Don't buy any with yellowing tops or slimy outer leaves.

Storing
• Store unwashed, in a sealed plastic bag in the salad drawer of the fridge for up to 1 week.
• Trim the tops if they are very long.

Preparation
• Remove any damaged or limp outer leaves. Trim the roots and cut off about two-thirds of the green top (use in stock or slice very thinly and add to a casserole).
• To remove trapped soil, make a lengthways cross cut down the middle of the leek, stopping short of the white part. Fan out the leaves and immerse upside-down in a bowl of water for 15 minutes. If not using whole, slice into thick rings and swish in water until the soil floats out.

Cawl

The leek and other roots are the stars of this hearty Welsh soup, traditionally served in china pudding bowls and eaten with a wooden spoon. The soup is thickened with oatmeal, which gives it a comforting porridge-like flavour.

Put the prepared vegetables in a large bowl, sprinkle with the oatmeal and toss until coated.

Melt the butter in a large heavy-based saucepan and add the bacon cubes. Fry gently over medium heat, stirring frequently until nicely browned. Add the vegetables, giving them a good stir to coat with fat. Cover and sweat over low heat for 10 minutes, stirring now and again, until they start to soften.

Pour in the stock and bring to the boil. Simmer gently with the lid askew for about 40 minutes, or until the vegetables are soft but just about holding their shape.

Stir in the parsley and season with salt and freshly ground black pepper, bearing in mind the saltiness of the bacon.

Cook's notes
• The vegetables need cutting into similar-sized chunks so that they cook evenly.
• If you don't have medium oatmeal, use 2 tablespoons of rolled oats instead.

leeks 4 medium, halved lengthways and thickly sliced
new potatoes 350g, unpeeled, quartered
carrots 2, sliced
parsnip 1, cut into small chunks
swede 1 small, cut into small chunks
medium oatmeal 1 tbsp
butter a large knob
smoked bacon 350g in one piece, derinded and cut into 2-cm cubes
chicken stock preferably home-made, 1.7 litres
curly parsley trimmed and chopped to make 3 tbsp
salt
freshly ground black pepper

Serves 6

Liver

Given that the liver's main job is to process and disperse toxins in the body, it is well worth seeking out a farm shop or dedicated butcher whose supply of liver, and other offal, is scrupulously fresh. It should be sourced from humanely reared stock, unsullied by growth promoters, antibiotics and other additives.

Farm shops are the place to look for calves' liver from UK-reared rose veal calves rather than Dutch veal calves, (see **Veal**, page 263). Also worth seeking out (and, in my opinion, the only ones to buy) are livers from top-quality traditional free-range or organic chicken. Not only are they larger and meatier, they are also free from the cocktail of contaminants fed to intensely raised birds.

You'll also find more esoteric liver in farm shops. Goat and ostrich livers are surprisingly tasty, as are those from rabbit and hare. You might come across duck or geese livers too, though more often than not they are tucked into the bird's cavity and included in the overall weight. As yet, the UK doesn't produce birds for *foie gras*, so the livers are small rather than grossly fattened.

Cooking

Liver is one of the easiest of organ meats to cook. Cut into thin slices, calves' liver is delectable flash-fried for a few minutes, perhaps with some sage, until the outside is appetisingly browned and slightly crisp and the inside pink and soft. Chicken livers are cooked in the same way. **Caramelised onions** (page 172) are the perfect accompaniment, although grilled field mushrooms are also tempting.

Alternatively try it **Albanian-style, tossed in flour and paprika** before briefly frying in oil. Drain on kitchen paper and put in a warm dish with a large sliced and crisply fried onion. Spoon over some thick Greek yogurt – a small pot will do – then dribble with olive oil and dust with a little paprika. Top with sizzled sage or mint leaves if you like. Serve at room temperature as a starter or part of a mixed meze.

Because of its soft texture, liver naturally makes rich smooth pâté, sometimes with other meats added for body. Try the recipe for **Goat Liver Pâté** (opposite) – you can use chicken livers if you prefer.

Large ox liver can be good, too, provided it comes from top-notch grass-fed beef. An overnight soak in milk or lightly salted water will tenderise it and help tame the flavour. The liver can then be slowly braised or casseroled, either on its own, or with beef. Try it instead of kidney in **Steak and Kidney Pie** (page 153).

Buying
- Look for glossy brownish pink or deep red flesh, depending on animal and age.
- Flesh should smell clean and fresh.
- Don't bother with liver that looks dull, dry or mushy.

Storing
- Store on the bottom shelf of the fridge so raw juices cannot drip onto other food.
- Remove any wrapping and store in a shallow dish, loosely covered with foil, for no more than 24 hours.
- Poultry livers can be frozen for up to 3 months.

Preparation
- Rinse well in cold water, drain and pat dry with paper towels.
- Remove and membrane, tubes, connective tissue and discoloured flesh.

Warm Chicken Liver, Bacon and Watercress Salad

This salad is filling but the peppery watercress cuts the richness.

Fry the bacon strips in a non-stick frying pan, in their own fat, until crisp. Drain on paper towels, put in a dish and keep warm. Fry the Garlic Croûtons and keep these warm in a separate bowl.

Wipe out the pan, then heat 1 tablespoon of olive oil over medium heat. Gently fry the shallot until soft but not coloured. Add the garlic and fry for a few seconds more.

Raise the heat to medium-high and fry the livers for about 3 minutes or until cooked through, adding a little more oil if necessary. Season with sea salt flakes and freshly ground black pepper, then add to the warm bacon in the dish.

Deglaze the pan with the balsamic vinegar and stock, stirring to scrape up any tasty sediment.

Arrange a bed of watercress on serving plates, add the liver and bacon mixture, and scatter with the croûtons. Sprinkle with a little parsley and pour the pan juices over the top.

dry-cured streaky bacon 6 rashers, cut into 7-cm pieces
Garlic Croûtons (page 112)
olive oil for frying
shallot 1, finely chopped
garlic clove 1, finely chopped
chicken livers 225g, cleaned and sliced into bite-sized chunks
sea salt flakes
freshly ground black pepper
balsamic vinegar 1 tbsp
chicken stock 3–4 tbsp
watercress 2 bunches, trimmed
flat leaf parsley coarsely chopped, to garnish

Serves 2–3 as a light meal

Goat Liver Pâté

Goat liver is surprisingly mild and fresh-smelling – not in the least redolent of goat. It makes excellent pâté.

Heat a frying pan over medium heat. Add about one-third of the butter and fry the onion until soft but not starting to brown. Stir in the garlic and gently fry for another 3 minutes.

Add the liver and cook, stirring, for 2 minutes. Sprinkle in the bay leaf, thyme and balsamic vinegar. Season with crumbled sea salt flakes and black pepper. Once the liver is no longer pink inside, remove the pan from the heat and allow to cool slightly.

Purée the mixture in a food processor along with the rest of the butter and the cider brandy if you are using it.

Spoon into ramekins or one larger bowl, pressing down well and smoothing the surface. Cover and chill for 2 hours before serving.

butter 75g
onion 1, finely chopped
garlic cloves 2, chopped
goat liver 225g, sliced into thin strips
fresh bay leaf 1, shredded
thyme leaves from 2 sprigs
balsamic vinegar 2 tsp
sea salt flakes a large pinch
freshly ground black pepper
Somerset cider brandy (optional) 1 tbsp

Serves 4–6 as a snack

Cook's note
• If you are not going to eat the pâté on the day you make it, it's a good idea to seal the surface with a layer of melted butter. That way it will keep in the fridge for 5–6 days.

See also **Goat** (page 117)

Milk

Milk found in farm shops is likely to come from local dairy herds and will have a noticeably different flavour and colour to mass-produced milk. The breed of cow, its feed, the season, and where it was raised, all have an effect on the finished product. For example, milk from Jersey cows contains nearly one-third more fat than Friesian milk, giving it a richer, creamier flavour. The type of feed is influential too: organic pasture is not treated with chemical fertilisers and herbicides, and the resulting variety of plants contributes a wide spectrum of subtle flavours. The difference between spring and autumn grass also has an effect, as do winter feed supplements.

Farm shops sometimes sell unpasteurised 'raw' milk, recognisable by the green top. The herds must be certified as brucellosis-free and the milk produced according to stringent hygienic procedures. Raw milk tastes richer, sweeter and creamier than ordinary milk – an altogether different experience. Some farms also sell goat's and sheep's milk which many people find more digestible than cow's milk.

Cooking

Milk goes into a substantial range of dishes: soups and sauces, batters and cakes, milky puddings and custard tarts. We whizz it into shakes and smoothies, pour it over breakfast cereal and stir it into porridge. It's worth paying attention to the quality of such a fundamental food. As with wine, it can affect the flavour of the finished dish.

Handy to have under your culinary belt is **béchamel**, a classic milk-based sauce that lubricates a number of popular dishes. Scald 300ml organic whole milk, then leave to infuse for 15 minutes with some thin slivers of onion, freshly grated nutmeg, a fresh bay leaf and 2 or 3 crushed black peppercorns. Strain into a jug, discarding the bits and pieces. Next, melt 50g butter and stir in 3 tablespoons of plain flour. Stir vigorously over medium-low heat for a minute or two to cook the flour, then whisk in half the milk. Keep whisking until thickened and creamy, then add the rest of the milk. Bring to the boil and simmer for a few minutes, then proceed according to the recipe.

Together with eggs, milk is a key ingredient in **French toast**, or eggy bread as it is sometimes called. It's excellent with warmed strawberries (page 248) or any kind of soft fruit. Whisk 1 egg with 150ml organic whole milk, $1/2$ teaspoon of sugar, $1/4$ teaspoon of vanilla extract and a pinch of salt. Quickly dunk slices of slightly stale crust-free bread in the mixture. Fry in butter until brown on both sides.

Milk is also fun to play around with and learn some basic kitchen chemistry at the same time. For example, enzymes such as rennet or acids like lemon juice will split the proteins in milk, changing the texture in the process (**West Country Junket** and **Indian Paneer**, opposite). Prolonged simmering will evaporate the watery whey and reduce the solids to a wonderfully rich sticky cream that can be used in indulgent desserts such as *kulfi* – a very rich Indian ice cream – or a toffee-making session with the kids.

Shopping notes
- Make sure milk is properly chilled and within its 'use by' date.
- Check that the container is clean and the seal unbroken.

Storing
- Keep unopened milk in the fridge for 5–7 days depending on 'use by' date. Once opened, use within 2–3 days or before the 'use by' date.
- Always keep cartons sealed, otherwise milk can pick up flavours from other food in the fridge.

West Country Junket

Junket is one of those old-fashioned milk puddings that appear to be enjoying a renaissance. It is really easy to make, and looks and tastes rather like white blancmange with a hint of sharpness, similar to soured cream. Served chilled, it slips down the throat in the most deliciously soothing way.

Heat the milk in a saucepan with the bay leaves until it reaches blood heat (38°C) – just warm on the inner side of the wrist.

In a large bowl, dissolve the sugar in the cider brandy, stirring to mix, then pour in the warm milk. Stir in the rennet and leave the mixture to set undisturbed at room temperature. Cover and chill for an hour or two. Sprinkle with nutmeg when ready to serve.

Cook's notes
• Rennet is an enzyme from the cow's stomach and a key ingredient in cheese-making. It is sold in small glass bottles that you'll find in larger supermarkets rather than farm shops.
• If you don't have unpasteurised milk, you'll need slightly more rennet to make ordinary milk thicken and set. Follow the directions on the bottle.

unpasteurised 'raw' milk 600ml
fresh bay leaves 2
caster sugar 1 tbsp
Somerset cider brandy 1½ tbsp
rennet ½ tbsp
freshly grated nutmeg or
ground cinnamon for sprinkling

Serves 3–4

Indian Paneer

Curdled milk is the basis for this Indian home-made soft cheese, vaguely reminiscent of ricotta but with a more lemony flavour. It is surprisingly simple to make – children will enjoy lending a hand.

Heat the milk until it foams and starts to rise in the pan. Add the yogurt, lemon juice and salt. Let it boil for 5 minutes – the milk will separate into watery whey with a coagulated flotsam of cheese floating on top. Remove from the heat and leave for a minute or two to finish coagulating.

Strain the mixture through a sieve lined with two or three large squares of damp muslin. Tie up the corners loosely and hang the bundle over a bowl for 10 minutes to let excess liquid drain. Shape the paneer into a thin block, still in the cloth, and place on an upturned plate with a heavy weight on top. After a few hours the liquid will have drained away and the cheese solidified enough to be cut into crumbly slices.

Cook's notes
• To serve as a snack, cut the solidified paneer into chunks, coat with a little seasoned flour and turmeric, and lightly fry in oil. Sprinkle with crushed cumin seeds or a pinch of chilli powder and serve with lemon wedges. It is also good in a spicy curry with peas (**Peas and Paneer**, page 187).
• Paneer will keep in a sealed container in the fridge for up to 1 week.

Jersey whole milk organic, 600ml
Greek-style live yogurt 200ml
lemon juice 2 tbsp
salt a pinch

Makes about 200g

Mushrooms

There was a time when the only mushrooms to be found in the shops were characterless white button mushrooms. Nowadays there is an exciting choice of both cultivated and wild varieties with names that reflect their rich meaty flavours: beefsteak, oyster or chicken of the woods, for example.

Cultivated mushrooms are available all year round. Farm shops usually sell top-quality varieties grown in small quantities by specialist producers. The ones to look for are the brown chestnut mushrooms – they have more flavour than white ones.

Some farm shops also sell limited supplies of locally gathered wild mushrooms, particularly in early autumn. The most sought-after is the 'penny bun' or 'cep', with its bulging spongy cap and fat stalk. Also to be relished is the 'morel' – a spring variety rather than an autumnal one – instantly recognisable by its crevice-ridden cone-shaped cap.

Cooking

Cultivated or wild, mushrooms add savoury meatiness to risottos, stir-fries, soups, stews and omelettes. They add bulk to pies (**Steak and Kidney Pie**, page 153) and pâtés (**Watercress and Mushroom Pâté**, page 274), and are equally good as a pizza topping or pasta sauce (**Mushrooms with Pappardelle, Pine Nuts, Cream, Garlic and Parmesan**, opposite). They are also delicious in their own right; mushrooms on toast or a giant portabello mushroom burger are treats not to be missed.

Depending on variety, mushrooms are good fried, grilled or roasted. The only slight problem is dealing with the amount of liquid that some exude when fried. They may seem dry at first, but after a few minutes the juices start to flow and the pan will be awash with liquid. You can either pour this off (save it for a soup or risotto) or wait for it to evaporate. I usually take the latter option. Once the pan is drier I add thinly sliced garlic or shallots, chopped flat leaf parsley, a wisp of lemon zest, seasonings and perhaps a bit more oil or butter if necessary.

Dense-fleshed small mushrooms or chunks of meaty portabellos are excellent **grilled or barbecued on skewers**. Trim the stems, then toss in olive oil, lemon juice and a sprinkling of sea salt, freshly ground black pepper and thyme or oregano. Thread onto skewers with a fresh bay leaf or two, and grill for 10–12 minutes, turning regularly until tender.

Roasting is another option for large mushrooms. Toss in plenty of olive oil and place skin-side down on a roasting tray. Season with salt and black pepper and splash with soy sauce if you like – this helps produce flavoursome gravy. Roast on the bottom shelf at 220°C/gas 7 for 12–15 minutes, pressing occasionally with a spatula to encourage juices to flow. Turn and roast for 5 minutes more until brown and tender. Serve on crisp squares of grilled polenta, or as a side dish with roast beef or lamb.

UK season
• *Cultivated:* year-round
• *Wild:* May–November depending on variety.

Varieties to look for
• *Buna shimeji:* cultivated in clumps, tiny round heads, long edible stems, firm crunchy texture, nutty flavour.
• *Cep, penny bun, porcino*: firm succulent flesh, immensely savoury.
• *Chanterelle*: Highly prized, striking orange flesh, strong nutty/fruity flavour.
• *Chestnut:* medium-sized, brown skin, nutty flavour.
• *Cremini:* miniature portabello, intense flavour.
• *Enoki:* cultivated in clumps, tiny round heads, long thin edible stems, delicate flavour.
• *Giant puffball:* football-sized, dense cheese-like flesh, delicate flavour.
• *Morel:* rare, first to appear in spring. Open porous texture, mild flavour.
• *Oyster:* delicate flavour, springy texture. Best cooked briefly, otherwise becomes tough.
• *Portabello:* large, flat, dense flesh, meaty texture and flavour.

Shopping notes
• Choose soft downy mushrooms that feel slightly damp but not slimy.
• Avoid those with broken caps, bruising or wrinkled dry patches.

Storing
• Keep loosely wrapped in a paper bag in the salad drawer of the fridge for up to 2 days.

Preparation
• Contrary to myth, whole mushrooms absorb very little water and can be washed before slicing. Dunk briefly and scrub lightly with a vegetable brush. Drain and blot dry with paper towels.
• Trim and discard the base from clusters of buna shimeji and enoki. Separate into individual mushrooms. Leave stems intact.

Mushrooms with Pappardelle, Pine Nuts, Cream, Garlic and Parmesan

A rich and creamy sauce that clings unctuously to broad ribbons of pasta. You can use one type of mushroom, or, for different textures and flavours, try a mixture.

Bring a large saucepan of salted water to the boil for the pasta. While the water is heating, fry the shallots in the olive oil and butter for about 2 minutes or until softened. Add the garlic and fry for another minute.

Add the mushrooms and thyme to the pan, and cook, stirring, for about 5 minutes or until the mushrooms start to give up their liquid. Sprinkle with the lemon zest and season with sea salt flakes and freshly ground black papper. Cook for another minute or two or until the liquid has evaporated.

Meanwhile, cook the pasta until *al dente*. Add the pine nuts, cream and Parmesan to the mushroom pan and stir until heated through. Check the seasoning.

Drain the pasta and tip into a large warm serving dish. Pour the mushroom mixture over the top and sprinkle with the parsley. Serve with extra Parmesan.

Cook's notes
• Make sure you cut the mushrooms into more-or-less even-sized pieces so they take the same time to cook.
• You will need a broad flat ribbon pasta to carry the sauce. If you don't have pappardelle use tagliatelle instead, or large shells such as conchiglie.

shallots 2, finely chopped
olive oil 2 tbsp
butter 25g
garlic cloves 2 large, very thinly sliced
mushrooms 450g, thickly sliced, cut into segments, left whole if small
thyme leaves 1 tsp
lemon zest of $\frac{1}{2}$
sea salt flakes
freshly ground black pepper
pappardelle 450g
pine nuts 75g, toasted
Jersey whipping cream organic, 300ml
Parmesan cheese 6 tbsp, freshly grated, plus extra to serve
flat leaf parsley leaves chopped to make 2 tbsp

Serves 4

New Zealand Spinach

As the name suggests, this distinctive vegetable is native to New Zealand though it is now cultivated in other temperate regions, including the UK. Market gardeners value it for its resistance to bad weather and cooks love it for the rich full flavour. Completely unrelated to ordinary spinach, it is recognisable by bright green triangular leaves and crisp round stalks. The leaves are slightly abrasive, smaller than ordinary spinach, and do not reduce much in bulk when cooked. You will find it in farm shops rather than supermarkets, often mixed with other tasty leaves in a salad bag.

Cooking

Young tender leaves can be eaten raw, but only in small amounts since the flavour is somewhat acidic. It's best to mix them with sweeter-tasting leaves to offset the sharpness.

The leaves are tasty when cooked until lightly wilted. They go well with assertively flavoured ingredients such as beetroot (**Colourful Beets with Roasted Shallot and Chilli Dressing**, page 33) and they match the richness of eggs as in the recipe opposite.

New Zealand spinach is also good in a **curry with potatoes**. Heat some curry spices and finely diced fresh ginger root in a little oil, then add chopped potatoes, onion and a little finely diced fresh chilli. When lightly browned, add 2 chopped tomatoes and a handful of New Zealand spinach leaves, and stir until wilted. Pour in enough water or stock to just cover the potatoes, then cover and cook for about 20 minutes. Excellent with mango chutney, poppadums and cooling **Yogurt and Cucumber Sauce** (page 278).

UK season
- Year-round.

Shopping notes
- Leaves should be bright green and crisp with no signs of wilting or bruising.

Storing
- Store unwashed and untrimmed, wrapped in damp paper towels in a roomy plastic bag in the salad drawer of the fridge.
- Use within 2–3 days.

Preparation
- Trim any tough stalks.
- Wash the leaves just before use.

Wilted New Zealand Spinach Salad with Bacon and Bantam Eggs

This is lovely for a leisurely Sunday brunch. Bantam eggs are a rare treat but you can use quail's eggs instead, or even hen's eggs as long as they are absolutely fresh and come from organic or free-range flocks.

Grill the bacon on a rack for 7–8 minutes, turning once, until crisp. Set aside and keep warm.

Heat a large frying pan over low heat. Add the olive oil and fry the garlic very gently for 2–3 minutes, or until just beginning to colour.

Raise the heat to medium. Throw in the spinach leaves, season with chilli flakes, sea salt and black pepper and stir for 2–3 minutes until just wilted. Splash with the balsamic vinegar and stir briefly.

Divide between two warm plates, and pour over the pan juices. Top with the bacon, a few warm Garlic Croûtons if you like, and the hard-boiled egg halves.

Cook's notes

• Try not to over-boil the eggs. The yolks should be just firm, or even slightly runny in the middle.
• Use ordinary spinach if New Zealand spinach is not available. You will need an extra handful to compensate for the reduction in bulk when cooked.

Variation

• Instead of hard-boiled eggs, top with a **deep-fried duck egg** or hen's egg (pages 99–100). They are fun to make and have an appetising crispy texture that goes well with the soft spinach.

dry-cured streaky bacon 4 rashers
extra-virgin olive oil 3 tbsp
garlic cloves 2, preferably 'wet', thinly sliced
New Zealand spinach fibrous stalks removed, 150g
dried chilli flakes $\frac{1}{4}$ tsp
sea salt
freshly ground black pepper
balsamic vinegar 1 tsp
warm Garlic Croûtons (page 112) (optional)
bantam's eggs 3 or **quail's eggs** 6, hard-boiled, halved

Serves 2 as a light meal

Oats

Justifiably hailed as a 'superfood', oats are packed with cholesterol-lowering soluble fibre, slow-release carbohydrate, protein, vitamins and minerals. They actually taste good too – nutty, creamy and deeply comforting.

A rugged grain that thrives in rugged conditions, oats are said to have their spiritual home in Scotland, though Ireland lays claim to them too. Oats were vitally important during the Irish potato famine and were long valued for their keeping qualities. That said, the Scots have been the most inventive, not only with their variety of oat-based dishes but also with oat grades and products. The range is impressive and demonstrates the high value placed on the grain.

Cooking

Given the nutritional credentials, it's worth expanding one's oat repertoire. Try sprinkling oatmeal over sautéed kale or cabbage, or use instead of breadcrumbs as a crisp topping for cauliflower cheese and other gratins. In Scotland, a favourite dish is skirlie – a fried mixture of oatmeal and onions – served with meat or as a stuffing. Herring fillets dipped in oatmeal and fried in butter are also very good.

Best-known is **porridge**, preferably made with oatmeal rather than porridge oats (don't even think about instant oatmeal). The resulting mush is beautifully soft and smooth with just a touch of crunch from the oatmeal. For one serving allow 50g medium oatmeal. Start by gently warming it with a knob of butter in a small heavy-based saucepan. When you smell the oaty fragrance, slowly mix in 300ml water and a pinch of salt. Stir over medium-low heat until boiling, then keep stirring for 5 minutes or more until creamy. Once cooked, swirl in milk or cream and a sweetener – brown sugar, honey or golden syrup are all delicious. Some people make porridge with milk instead of water, but they miss out on the pleasure of adding ice-cold milk to piping hot porridge once it is cooked.

Oats are the main ingredient in **muesli**. There are some excellent mixes on the market, but it's fun and much cheaper to make your own. My favourite is 350g jumbo oats mixed with 50g each toasted, coarsely chopped hazelnuts and almonds, and 75g toasted coconut ribbons. Throw in a handful each of barley and rye flakes, 100g raisins and some chopped dried apple rings or other dried fruit. If you don't like milk, soak the required amount of muesli overnight in watered-down apple juice.

Oats add texture to crumble toppings (**Greengage and Cobnut Crumble**, page 129). They also make wonderfully crisp biscuits, chewy flapjacks and, mixed with cream and a slug of whisky, the most heavenly desserts.

Types of oats

Groats: the whole grain from which the husk has been removed. Need lengthy soaking and cooking to make them palatable.

Steel-cut oats: groats that have been mechanically cut into two or three pieces to produce a very coarse meal. Need lengthy soaking and cooking.

Pinhead oats: the Scottish term for steel-cut oats.

Rolled oats, porridge oats, jumbo oats: pinhead or whole groats steamed and flattened to speed up cooking.

Oatmeal: ground groats in three basic grades: coarse, medium and fine. There are also rough and superfine grades at either end of the scale.

Oat bran: the thin outer layer of fibre enclosing the grain. Sprinkle on breakfast cereal to increase fibre intake, or add to cakes and biscuits.

Oat germ: the nutritious seed or embryo at the heart of the grain. Use in the same way as bran.

Shopping notes

• Buy packaged oats that are well within the 'best before' date.

• If buying loose oats, buy in quantities that you will use within a few months.

Storing

• Oats have a long shelf-life but eventually deteriorate once their natural oils become rancid.

• Keep in an airtight container in a cool dark cupboard or in the fridge.

• Never mix a new batch with an old one.

Preparation

• Dry-fry for a few minutes over gentle heat to bring out the nutty flavour.

Raspberry Cranachan

This irresistible concoction of raspberries, toasted oats and whisky-flavoured cream was traditionally served in Scotland to celebrate the end of the annual harvest.

Spread the oatmeal on a baking tray and toast under a preheated grill for 6–8 minutes, shaking the tray every 30 seconds to prevent burning. When the oatmeal is golden, tip it into a dish and leave to cool.

Combine the two creams in a large bowl, mixing well. Stir in the whisky and 2 tablespoons of the honey. Fold in the cold oatmeal, stirring until evenly mixed.

Set aside some of the best raspberries as a decoration, then fold the rest into the cream mixture. Cover and chill for at least 1 hour.

Spoon the mixture into serving dishes (glass or plain white look best). Decorate with the reserved raspberries and trickle over the remaining honey before serving.

Cook's notes
• Instead of raspberries, you can use loganberries, blackberries or even mulberries if you are lucky enough to find any.
• See also **Gooseberry and Elderflower Brose** (page 124)

coarse oatmeal 75g
double cream organic, 425ml
single cream organic, 150ml
whisky 2 tbsp
clear honey 3–4 tbsp
raspberries 350g

Serves 6

Onions

Apart from salt and pepper, the onion must be the world's most widely used ingredient. Belonging to the same family as leeks and garlic, onions come in a wildly varying range of colours, shapes and sizes, from bulging yellow bruisers to pencil-thin spring onions. Depending on variety, soil and sun, the flavour when raw may be mildly pungent or searingly hot, though it becomes innocuously mellow when cooked.

Cooking

It's important to choose the right kind of onion for your chosen dish. Juicy varieties such as Spanish, or large white or red onions, make excellent **deep-fried onion rings**. Dip the rings in flour, then in a spicy batter made with 300ml water and 125g self-raising flour seasoned with plenty of ground black peppercorns, sea salt and cumin seeds. Deep-fry in hot oil a few at a time, then drain on paper towels.

Equally irresistible are **caramelised onions**. They cook down to a delicious mahogany-coloured mass, which is wonderful to have on tap to serve with sausages or liver, or as a topping for mashed potatoes or rice. Slice 3 medium-to-large red onions, or 2 Spanish onions fairly thickly. Separate the rings and put in a large bowl with 4 tablespoons of rapeseed oil, 1 tablespoon of sugar, and some sea salt flakes and freshly ground black pepper. Toss with your hands until thoroughly coated. Spread out on a large roasting tray. Bake at 190°C/gas 5 for 20–30 minutes, stirring every 10 minutes. Once golden, mix in 1 tablespoon of balsamic vinegar, spread out again and roast for another 5–8 minutes until caramelised.

Smallish yellow onions can be baked whole alongside a juicy roast. They will caramelise beautifully, adding flavour and rich colour to the juices. Pickling onions are good in a rich braise such as **Coq au Vin** (page 78) or the Greek *stifado*. They are useful for kebabs; with their dense flesh they are unlikely to disintegrate. Unless they are very small, slice them in half lengthways before threading onto skewers.

Red onions are delicious sliced into the thinnest of crescents and scattered over salads; or dice them very finely and add to a tangy salsa with tomato, chilli, lime juice, salt and chopped coriander – perfect with grilled fish.

Finely chopped spring or salad onions add bite to sliced tomatoes or a potato salad. They also tolerate light cooking. Add to stir-fries, or try them French-style seethed in butter with peas, or in the **Irish staple 'champ'**. Roughly chop spring onions and simmer briefly in milk, then stir into hot mashed potatoes. Pile up on plates, make an indentation in the top and fill with a generous knob of butter. This will melt into a buttery puddle to be carefully swirled into the mash.

See also **Garlic** (page 112), **Leeks** (page 160), **Shallots** (page 235)

Onions to look for

Yellow: hot, tear-provoking, dense-fleshed. All-purpose cooking variety.
White: crisp and sharp. More watery than the yellow onion. Initial sweet flavour before pungency kicks in. Use raw or cooked.
Red: crisp flesh, slightly sweet but pungent. Use raw or cooked.
Spanish: very large with brown skin. Crisp, juicy, with mild flavour. Use raw or cooked.
Pickling onion, pearl onion: small versions of the yellow onion. Sweet flavour with a sharp bite. Use whole in stews or roasted.
Spring onion: the immature shoots of the bulb onion, with long green tops and a slender white base. Fresh pungent flavour, crisp texture. Use raw or lightly cooked.
Salad onion: similar to spring onions but with a more swollen base.

UK season

• *Main crop:* August–September, cold storage until following July.
• *Pickling onions:* June–August.

Shopping notes

• Choose plump solid onions with tight skins and no sign of mould, bruising or sprouting.
• Look for spring and salad onions with firm bulbs and sprightly stems. Don't bother with any that look limp, dry or slimy.

Storing

• Yellow onions will keep for several weeks in a cool airy place such as a shed, preferably tied on a string or raffia onion rope. Otherwise store in a paper bag in a vegetable rack or ventilated drawer for 7–10 days.
• White, red and Spanish onions tend to rot and will keep for 1 week at the most.
• Store spring and salad onions in the salad drawer of the fridge for up to 1 week.

Preparation

• Plunge pickling onions in boiling water before peeling. This softens the skins and they slip off more easily.

Sweet-and-Sour Baby Onions (page 174)

Sweet-and-Sour Baby Onions

These are wonderful with roast pork or gammon, or fatty poultry such as duck or goose. The juices are deliciously rich and sticky, tasting almost like treacle.

Leaving the tips and peel intact, trim the roots from the onions as close to the base as possible. Drop the onions into a large pan of boiling water. Bring back to the boil, blanch for 2 minutes, then drain. Remove the outer layer of skin without trimming the tips (this will stop the onions disintegrating later on).

Heat a heavy-based frying pan large enough to take the onions in a single layer. Add the rapeseed oil, butter, bay leaves and cloves. When the butter foams, add the onions, swirling them round the pan to coat. Gently fry for a few minutes until lightly browned.

Add the vinegar and simmer until reduced and sticky. Stir in the sugar, 150ml of the stock, and season with salt and black pepper. Cook over low heat for 1 hour, stirring and turning the onions regularly, or until the juices are syrupy and the onions soft. Add more stock if the pan starts to look dry. Add the raisins 15 minutes before the end of cooking. Season with extra pepper just before serving.

Cook's note
• Take care not to let the pan dry out when reducing the vinegar. Moisten with a spoonful of stock if necessary.

small onions 500g
rapeseed oil 1 tbsp
butter a knob
fresh bay leaves 2, shredded
cloves 3
balsamic vinegar 3 tbsp
sugar 1 tsp
chicken stock 150–200ml
salt
freshly ground black pepper
raisins 1 tbsp

Serves 4 as a side dish

Oxtail

Farm shop butchers are likely to sell all parts of the animal, not just steaks and chops but extremities like tails and trotters. These may not be mainstream meat, but they are every bit as tasty and a bargain in times of thrift.

Oxtail is probably the most familiar of these undervalued cuts. It is a bony protuberance made up of much sinew and fat, and seemingly very little meat. The meat is richly flavoured, however, and there is plenty of it tucked away in the crevices. With patient cooking, it falls from the bones in delectable nuggets, and unpromising-looking gristle melts into glorious gelatinous juices.

Cooking

Oxtail depends on really slow moist cooking. Gently simmered in a casserole for several hours with wine and plenty of herbs, the meat will fall from the bones and be bathed in a delectable glossy sauce. Starchy ingredients such as root vegetables or haricot beans are good additions; they soak up the flavour in a most appetising way. Oxtail is also perfect for hearty mixed meat stews such as the Italian *bollito misto* or the Brazilian national dish *feijoda completa*.

Cooked oxtail can also be used to bulk up a terrine or a **Steak and Kidney Pie** (page 153). Or add it to a masculine salad with waxy new potatoes, gherkins, slivers of red onion and a strong mustard dressing. The thinner bits from the tip of the tail are handy for soups and stock.

Shopping notes
• Oxtail is usually sold skinned and chopped crossways into thick chunks.
• If intended for a casserole, make sure there are plenty of big pieces from higher up the tail.

Storing
• Store on the bottom shelf of the fridge so raw juices cannot drip onto other food.
• Remove wrapping and store in a shallow dish, loosely covered with foil, for 2–3 days.
• If vacuum-packed, leave unopened until ready to cook.

Preparation
• Trim any thick chunks of fat.
• Soak in salted water for 1–2 hours before cooking. Drain and wipe dry.

Serving size
• 1.4–1.5kg serves 4.

Casserole of Oxtail with Turnip, Celeriac and Carrots

Given a few hours gentle simmering, nuggets of unpromising-looking meat and sinew melt into a deeply satisfying stew.

Trim any thick chunks of fat from the oxtail. Dredge the meat in the seasoned flour. Heat a heavy-based casserole over medium-high heat, add the rapeseed oil and brown the oxtail a few pieces at a time. Remove from the pan and set aside.

Reduce the heat to medium. Add the diced vegetables and fry for about 10 minutes until beginning to soften. Add the garlic and herbs, and cook for another 5 minutes. Stir in the tomato purée and cook for a minute. Pour in 300ml of the wine, bring to the boil and then simmer for 3–4 minutes.

Put the oxtail pieces back in the pan, mixing them in with the vegetables. Season generously with sea salt flakes and black pepper, then pour in the stock. Bring to the boil, cover and leave to simmer over the lowest possible heat for at least 3 hours or until the meat pulls easily from the bone. Leave to cool completely, then chill, overnight if necessary, until the fat solidifies into a layer.

Discard the layer of fat and pick out the oxtail. Scrape the solid bits and jellied sauce sticking to the oxtail back into the casserole. Set aside the oxtail and gently reheat the sauce enough to make it runny again. Tip into a food processor and whizz to a purée. Push through a sieve and return to the casserole. Add the oxtail pieces and orange strips, and reheat gently.

While the oxtail is reheating quickly blanch or steam the uncooked vegetables together for 5 minutes until barely tender. Add them to the casserole along with the remaining 100ml of wine. Bring to the boil, then simmer over medium heat for 30–40 minutes until the vegetables are tender. Check the seasoning and sprinkle with parsley before serving.

Cook's notes

• Start the day before so you have time to chill the partially cooked dish and remove the layer of solidified fat. If you don't have time for this, blot up the liquid fat with wads of paper towels.
• Some recipes suggest discarding the bones before reheating, but I prefer to leave them in place.

oxtail 1 weighing 1.4–1.5kg, cut into 5-cm pieces
rapeseed oil 2 tbsp
onions 2, diced
carrots 2, diced
celeriac 1/2, diced
garlic cloves 2, finely chopped
thyme 2–3 sprigs
fresh bay leaf 1, shredded
rosemary 1 small sprig
tomato purée 2 tbsp
sea salt flakes
freshly ground black pepper
red wine 400ml
beef stock preferably home-made, 800ml–1 litre
orange zest 2–3 thinly pared strips
flat leaf parsley chopped, to garnish

for the seasoned flour
plain flour 3 tbsp
salt 1 1/2 tsp
freshly ground black pepper 1/2 tsp
mustard powder 1/2 tsp

vegetables to finish
celeriac 1/2 small, cut into 2-cm chunks
carrots 3, thickly sliced diagonally
celery stalks 3, destringed and thickly sliced diagonally
turnip 1, cut into 2-cm chunks

Serves 4

Parsnips

The parsnip is one of those quietly understated vegetables that has always had staunch fans in Britain but is sniffed at by our European neighbours. Here we turn them into chips and crisps, we mash them and roast them and whizz them into tasty soups; elsewhere they are fed to the pigs.

Bizarrely, we import parsnips from as far away as Tasmania even though they grow on home turf for much of the year. Don't bother with pallid imported specimens; buy your parsnips from a farm shop, caked in mud and freshly dug. They really do taste better. Snap one in half and you immediately get a heavenly whiff of clean fresh sweetness that heralds the flavour to come.

Cooking

Parsnips lend themselves to all kinds of dishes – soups, gratins, soufflés – but are at their best roasted. The sugars caramelise beautifully, transforming the ivory root into beautiful golden batons. Cut them into even-sized pieces, or leave whole if small, and chuck them in with the roast potatoes after about 15 minutes (they cook more quickly).

Also delectable are crispy **parsnip wisps** for sprinkling on soup or winter salads. Peel 2 small parsnips and slice into very thin matchstick strips. Heat 4 tablespoons of rapeseed oil in a small frying pan until shimmering. Stir in the parsnips and keep stirring for 2–3 minutes until golden. Remove immediately and drain on paper towels.

For a lovely colour and flavour combination, serve thickly sliced parsnips with carrots – be careful to cut the carrots a bit smaller so they cook at the same time.

Cut into matchsticks and lightly steamed, young parsnips make a lovely salad with grilled smoked mackerel and slightly bitter leaves. Sliced paper-thin, they can even be eaten raw in a **wintery white salad**. Mix them with finely sliced kohlrabi, celeriac and black or white radishes. Dress with a **Lemon Yogurt Dressing** (page 278) and sprinkle with a shower of snipped chives or flat leaf parsley for colour.

UK season
• September–April.

Varieties to look for
• *'White King'*, medium-sized, stump-ended roots, exceptionally good flavour.
• *'Tender and True'*, long tapering roots, wide shoulder, tender, very sweet flesh.

Shopping notes
• Choose medium-sized or small parsnips – they are likely to be less fibrous.
• Don't bother with any that are bruised, slimy or flabby.

Storing
• Keep in a paper bag in the salad drawer of the fridge for up to 1 week.

Preparation
• Trim both ends and remove the peel. Slice or chop according to recipe.
• For roasting, separate the tapered end from the wide top. Slice the top in half lengthways.
• Cut out the fibrous central core of large parsnips by cutting a V-shaped channel down the centre.

Roasted Parsnip and Cumin Soup

Roasting the parsnips before adding them to the soup really does concentrate the flavour and brings out earthy sweetness. A garnish of Parsnip Wisps adds appetising crunch to this rich and silky soup.

Preheat the oven to 190°C/gas 5. Halve the parsnips crossways, then quarter each piece lengthways. Put in a bowl with the rapeseed oil, 1 teaspoon of the cumin seeds, the sugar, some sea salt flakes and plenty of freshly ground black pepper. Toss with your hands until well coated, then spread out in a single layer on a roasting tray. Sprinkle with 4 tablespoons of the stock. Roast for 25–30 minutes, turning every so often, until golden and browned at the edges.

Meanwhile, melt the butter in a large saucepan and gently fry the onion and potato with the rest of the cumin seeds. Cover and leave to sweat, shaking the pan occasionally to prevent sticking. Pour in the rest of the stock, bring to the boil, then simmer with the lid slightly askew until the parsnips are cooked.

Tip the roasted parsnips into a food processor. Add a jugful of soup from the saucepan and purée until smooth. Tip the purée into the saucepan and stir until well blended. Season with more salt and black pepper to taste. Bring back to the boil and simmer for 5 minutes.

Pour into bowls and sprinkle with parsley and a few Parsnip Wisps.

parsnips 5
rapeseed oil 3 tbsp
cumin seeds 1½ tsp, crushed
sugar ½ tsp
sea salt flakes
freshly ground black pepper
chicken stock preferably home-made, 1.2 litres
butter 40g
onion 1, finely chopped
floury potato 1 large, diced
flat leaf parsley chopped, to garnish
Parsnip Wisps (page 177), to serve

Serves 6

Partridge

There was a time when partridge and other feathered game could be sold only through licensed game dealers during the open shooting season. Now the laws have been relaxed, game birds are increasingly on sale in farm shops and are available all year round, albeit frozen outside the season. For partridges, the season starts a month early to give them extra growing time. Those reared on farms are normally released into the wild for shooting when they are under one year old; birds raised completely in the wild are likely to be older.

Of the two types, the English grey-legged partridge is sadly on the verge of becoming an endangered species and should probably be conserved rather than consumed. The red-legged or French partridge is much more common.

Cooking

Partridges are just the job if you are not too sure about daunting gamey flavours. They are milder and relatively small – a single bird will serve one. Cook them in the same way as pheasant but for a shorter time. They are also very good with blackberries as in **Roast Grouse with Blackberries** (page 133). The same rules hold good for the cooking method: grilling or roasting for young birds, moist slow braising for older ones.

See also **Pheasant** (page 188)

UK season
• Open shooting 1 September–1 February.

Partridge to look for
• *English grey-legged:* prized for succulence and superior flavour.

Shopping notes
• Choose a bird suitable for the dish you intend to cook:
Young birds: pliable feet and breastbone, softly rounded spurs. Suitable for roasting, grilling and pan-frying.
Mature birds: long sharp spurs, hard scaly feet. Suitable for braising and stewing.
• Regardless of age, choose plump smooth birds not visibly damaged by shot.

Storing
• Store oven-ready birds on the bottom shelf of the fridge so raw juices cannot drip onto other food.
• Remove wrapping and store in a shallow dish, loosely covered with foil, for up to 3 days.

Preparation
• Tie legs and wings in place with string.
• Bard with thin slices of pork back fat to prevent breast meat from drying.

Serving size
• Whole bird: 280–350g, serves 1.

Partridge with Braised Red Cabbage, Apples and Juniper

A celebration of the best of autumn produce, ideal for a weekend dinner or a festive Christmas meal.

Preheat the oven to 220°C/gas 7. Wash the partridges under cold running water and pull out any stray feathers. Pat dry with paper towels. Push the thyme sprigs into the cavity of each partridge and season with sea salt and freshly ground black pepper. Place the streaky bacon slices over the breast of each bird and tie with string.

Measure the rapeseed oil into a small roasting tin and place it on top of the stove over medium-high heat. Add the partridges and keep turning them until slightly browned. Lay them on their sides and roast in the oven for 8 minutes, then turn them over and roast on the other side for another 8 minutes. Remove from the oven and leave to rest.

While the partridges are roasting, bring a large saucepan of water to the boil. Add the cabbage, bring back to the boil and blanch for 3 minutes (it will turn an alarming shade of blue – don't worry). Drain and set aside.

Melt the goose fat in a large casserole. Add the green bacon and fry over medium heat for 5 minutes, stirring. Add the onions and apples and fry until just beginning to colour. Next add the garlic, juniper berries, peppercorns and a little salt. Reduce the heat to low, and stir in the cabbage, honey and vinegar (which will revert the cabbage to a reassuring red). Cover and cook for 5 minutes.

Reduce the oven temperature to 180°C/gas 4. Place the partridges on the cabbage mixture breast-side up, pressing them down so that they are partly submerged. Pour in the stock and bring to the boil. Cover and cook in the oven for 20 minutes.

Lift the partridges onto a plate. Remove the string but leave the bacon in place. Leave to rest in a warm place for 10 minutes.

Drain the cabbage mixture into a dish, reserving the liquid, and keep warm. Pour the liquid back into the casserole and boil hard for about 10 minutes to reduce. Stir in any juices that have flowed from the partridges.

Divide the cabbage between four large warmed serving plates. Place the partridges on top of the cabbage and pour over the reduced juices. Serve with small baked potatoes and a spoonful of redcurrant jelly.

oven-ready partridges 4
thyme 4 sprigs
sea salt
freshly ground black pepper
dry-cured streaky bacon or **pancetta** 4 thin rashers
rapeseed oil 2 tbsp
red cabbage 2 small, finely shredded, tough stalks discarded (about 450g shredded)
goose fat or **butter** 100g
green bacon 150g, cut into strips
onions 2, finely chopped
dessert apples 3, quartered, cored, peeled and thickly sliced
garlic cloves 2, crushed
juniper berries $1/2$ tsp, lightly crushed
black peppercorns $1/2$ tsp, lightly crushed
clear honey 2 tbsp
cider vinegar 4 tbsp
game stock or **chicken stock** preferably home-made, 300ml

to serve
small baked potatoes
redcurrant jelly

Serves 4

Pears

A perfect pear is a uniquely pleasurable fruit. The flavour is subtle, almost fleeting, but at the same time uniquely pear-like. The texture is meltingly soft, either smooth or grainy, but certainly not crisp. As the late Edward Bunyard commented in his poetic *Anatomy of Dessert*, 'a pear should have such a texture as leads to silent consumption'.

Though they are a welcome autumn treat, pears have never quite had the mass appeal of apples. For one thing, they must be picked before they are ripe, so they arrive in the shops after a long spell in cold storage which does nothing for the flavour. They may also be disappointingly rock-hard or mushy in the middle. Your best bet is to look out for local varieties in a farm shop or PYO fruit farm. There'll be a more interesting selection and the pears are unlikely to have suffered the rigours of prolonged cold storage.

Cooking

Like apples, pears are classified as dessert or culinary, but many of the so-called dessert pears are suitable for cooking as long as the flesh is reasonably firm.

One of the simplest and loveliest dishes is **poached pears**. Make a light syrup with 160g sugar and 600ml water. Let the syrup boil for about 5 minutes, then add 4 quartered, cored and peeled pears. Gently simmer for about 10 minutes or until the pears are translucent and tender. Serve warm or at room temperature.

Also very good are **sautéed pears with honey**, perhaps with some finely chopped stem ginger. You'll need a firm-fleshed pear such as 'Forelle'. Prepare as above, then slice each quarter lengthways into thin segments. Sizzle in foaming butter for 5–7 minutes until golden. Add 3 tablespoons of clear honey, and a chopped knob of stem ginger if you like. Stir carefully until the bubbling dies down, then pour into a serving dish, adding all the sticky sediment from the pan.

Pears and pepper are a good combination. Mash some unsalted butter with a few crushed dried green peppercorns (not brine-cured) and some finely grated orange zest. Put a knob of the peppery butter in the cavity of halved, cored and peeled pears. Arrange cut-side up in a shallow baking dish and sprinkle the edges with sugar. Place under a very hot grill for 10–12 minutes until blackened and bubbling.

Pears are good in savoury dishes too. I love them sliced, **topped with goat's cheese** and a dribble of olive oil on toasted sourdough bread. Flash under the grill until the cheese melts. Grind over plenty of black pepper and serve with sprightly sprigs of watercress. Pears are equally delicious in salads, especially with walnuts and slightly bitter leaves as in **Roasted Peppered Pear Salad with Sheep's Cheese, Honey and Walnuts** (page 183); or try them with celery and blue cheese (**Celery, Pear and Walnut Salad with Blue Vinny Cheese**, page 63).

UK season
• September–January.

Varieties to look for
• *'Calebasse Bosc'*, smooth juicy flesh, superb sweet flavour.
• *'Double de Guerre'*, large firm-fleshed cooking variety. Flesh and syrup become rose-red when cooked.
• *'Nectarine'*, soft grainy flesh, strongly perfumed long-lasting flavour.
• *'Norman no.1'*, smooth succulent flesh, outstanding buttery flavour.
• *'Président Heron'*, soft melting flesh, strong pear-drop flavour.

Shopping notes
• Check for ripeness by pressing the stem end gently. If the flesh yields the pear is ripe.
• Avoid pears that are shrivelled at the stem end or soft at the base.
• Handle with care to prevent bruising.

Storing
• Pears need air – store in the fruit bowl rather than a sealed plastic bag.
• Eat right away if ripe. Otherwise leave at room temperature for a day or two to speed up ripening.

Preparation
• If serving halved pears, use a melon baller to remove the core neatly, then draw the baller from the cavity to the top of the pear to remove the interior stem.
• Sprinkle flesh with lemon juice to prevent browning.

Roasted Peppered Pear Salad with Sheep's Cheese, Honey and Walnuts

This is a simple but impressive starter that relies on top-notch ingredients (see **Cook's notes**)

Preheat the oven to 200°C/gas 6. Slice the pears in half lengthways and remove the cores, interior stems and peel. Place cut-side up in a small roasting tin.

Combine the sea salt flakes and peppercorns and lightly crush using a mortar and pestle. Sprinkle the mixture into the cavities of the pears, then spoon the honey over the top. Drizzle with the olive oil and lemon juice. Pour the water into the base of the tin.

Roast for 20–25 minutes or until the pears are beginning to brown at the edges. Move to a plate and leave to cool slightly.

Divide the chard leaves between four serving plates. Place a warm pear half on top with a few slices of sheep's cheese to one side. Sprinkle with the walnuts. Drizzle with more honey, crumbled sea salt flakes and a dribble of sticky aged balsamic vinegar.

Cook's notes
• You need good-quality peppercorns for this, preferably organic. Farm shops are a likely source of single estate varieties that have a much better flavour than ordinary kitchen pepper.
• Use a delicately flavoured honey such as acacia or orange blossom.
• Lord of the Hundreds, Herriot Farmhouse and Swaledale are good-quality hard sheep's cheeses. If you can't find them, use a white cow's milk cheese such as Caerphilly.
• Aged or traditional balsamic vinegar is sweet-sour and syrupy with a rich complex flavour. You could use manufactured Balsamic Glaze instead, but ordinary balsamic vinegar isn't a good substitute.

pears 2
sea salt flakes $^1/_2$ tsp, plus extra for sprinkling
black peppercorns such as Wynad or Tellicherry, $^1/_2$ tsp
clear honey 2 tsp, plus extra for drizzling
extra-virgin olive oil 1 tsp
lemon juice of $^1/_4$
water 6 tbsp
baby chard leaves or **beet leaves** 4 small handfuls
hard sheep's cheese 100g, thinly sliced
shelled walnuts preferably 'wet', 30g
aged balsamic vinegar

Serves 4 as a starter

Peas

Farm shops and PYO farms are good places to find the perfect pea, newly harvested and squeaky fresh. They remind one that summer might possibly be on its way. Once bought, however, don't let them sit around; the natural sugars quickly turn to starch, and both flavour and texture start to deteriorate.

Also to be relished are UK-grown peas with edible pods – flat mangetouts, also called snow peas, and the rounder sugar snap peas. Freshly picked, they are startlingly different from the dreary imported specimens sold all year round.

Look out for tender pea shoots too. Leaves, stems and tendrils are all edible and can be eaten raw or lightly cooked. They have an exquisite quintessentially pea-like flavour.

Cooking

Peas are incredibly versatile, enhancing so many different types of dishes. The Chinese add them to stir-fries, noodles and soups, Indians use them in curries and samosas, or fry them with paneer cheese (**Peas and Paneer**, opposite), and the Italians like them in a soupy rice dish called *risi e bisi*, as well as in pasta dishes with snippets of ham and lots of cream.

I am fond of a mint-flavoured soup made with equal quantities of peas and sweetcorn, 2 or 3 small potatoes and a young courgette or two. All are in season at the same time and go very well together.

Peas are an iconic accompaniment to the Christmas turkey, the Sunday roast and classic fish dishes such as grilled Dover sole. When calculating quantities, remember to allow for about 50 per cent wastage; for 2–3 servings you need at least 450g peas before shelling.

Mangetouts and sugar snaps are at their best in stir-fries, adding texture and brilliant colour. They are also good blanched briefly and added to an oriental-style salad with a mix of peppery Chinese leaves, mizuna, crisp-fried nuggets of chicken, shredded spring onions and slivered almonds, tossed with soy sauce and sesame oil.

Pea shoots need tender treatment. Enjoy them raw in a salad, sprinkled with a few drops of lemon juice and extra-virgin sunflower oil, or float them in a clear oriental soup to show off the beautiful tendrils, or use them to crown the **four-pea stir-fry of shelling peas, sugar snap peas and mangetout** (opposite).

When cooking any type of pea, keep it quick; the fresh flavour and colour vanish in minutes and the texture soon becomes mealy. Some cooks opt for a small amount of water, others a large panful, some prefer to steam them. I cook young peas in a very small amount of boiling water until barely tender, then toss them in melted butter and sometimes a delicately flavoured herb such as chervil or lemon balm, or the traditional mint. Slightly older peas are good lightly braised in butter and a little stock.

See also **Salad Greens and Micro Leaves** (page 229)

UK season
• May–September.

Varieties to look for
Shelling peas:
• '*Lincoln*', one of the sweetest varieties.
• '*Waverex*', small-seeded petit pois variety, sweet, tender, delicious raw.

Mangetout:
• '*Dwarf Sweet Green*', flat short pods, very sweet when young.
• '*Oregon Sugar Pod*', broad flat pods, extremely sweet.

Sugar snap:
• '*Sugar Ann*', sweet fleshy pods, stringless when young.

Shopping notes
• Look for shelling peas with plump, bright green pods.
• Choose crisp flat mangetout. Don't buy any that are bumpy, broken or limp.
• Sugar snap peas should be crisp and fresh with unblemished pods.
• Pea shoot tendrils should look sprightly yet tender.

Storing
• Unpodded peas will keep in a paper bag in the salad drawer of the fridge for 1–2 days.
• Pea shoots will keep in a plastic box lined with damp paper towels in the fridge for 1 day.

Preparation
• Remove the pods from shelling peas no more than an hour before cooking.
• To remove strings from mangetout and sugar snap peas, break off each end and pull down the sides of the pod.
• Slice mangetout diagonally for stir-fries. Sugar snaps are best left whole.
• Discard any excessively large leaves and tough stems from pea shoots.

Four-Pea Stir-Fry with Spring Onions and Sprouted Seeds

This really shows off what the simple pea has to offer – pods, shoots and seeds all with subtly different textures and flavours. Pea shoots (the tender growing tips and tendrils) are usually found in the chiller section near the sprouted beans and seeds.

Heat a wok or roomy frying pan over medium-high heat. Add the groundnut oil and butter, and stir-fry the salad onions for 1 minute. Throw in the three types of pea and stir-fry for another 2–3 minutes. Moisten with the stock and a squeeze of lemon juice, then add sugar, sea salt flakes and freshly ground black pepper to taste. Stir in the sunflower sprouts and mint, and stir-fry for a few seconds until just heated through.

Tip the contents of the pan into a warm serving dish. Scatter the pea shoots over the top – they will wilt in the heat from the rest of the vegetables.

Cook's notes
• Make sure the pea shoots are no more than 4cm long. Larger ones tend to be rather chewy.
• If you can't find sunflower sprouts, use mung bean or chick pea sprouts. You need large crunchy sprouts rather than delicate ones.

groundnut oil 2 tbsp
butter a knob
salad onions 6, thickly sliced diagonally, including some of the green part
mangetout 100g, sliced diagonally
sugar snap peas 100g, trimmed
peas 100g, shelled weight (225g in pods)
chicken or **vegetable stock** 3 tbsp
lemon juice a squeeze
sugar a pinch
sea salt flakes
freshly ground black pepper
sunflower sprouts 50g
mint stalks discarded, leaves sliced to make 5 tbsp
pea shoots 50g

Serves 4 as a side dish

Peas and Paneer

A popular combination in India, fresh green peas, tomatoes and tangy paneer make a spicy supper. Paneer is a home-made cheese that is fun to make (see **Milk**, page 164). It is also produced commercially by Long Clawson Dairy in Leicestershire and is sold in larger farm shops.

Heat a medium frying pan. Add the rapeseed oil and sizzle the cumin seeds. Once they start to pop, stir in the onion, ginger, turmeric and chilli powder. Gently fry for a few minutes until the onion is soft.

Add the chopped tomatoes, peas and salt. Cover and cook over medium-low heat for 5 minutes. Add a splash of water if the mixture looks dry.

Stir in the crumbled paneer and gently fry until heated through. Sprinkle with garam masala and coriander just before serving.

rapeseed oil 2 tbsp
cumin seeds $\frac{1}{2}$ tsp
onion 1, finely chopped
fresh ginger root 1-cm piece, finely chopped
ground turmeric $\frac{1}{2}$ tsp
chilli powder $\frac{1}{2}$ tsp
tomatoes 5, diced
peas 100g, shelled weight (225g in pods)
salt $\frac{1}{2}$ tsp
paneer 150g, crumbled
garam masala $\frac{1}{2}$ tsp
coriander leaves, chopped to make 3 tbsp

Serves 2–3 as a light meal

Pheasant

Thanks to more relaxed game licensing regulations, pheasant and other feathered game are increasingly on sale in farm shops rather than through licensed game dealers. The actual shooting of game, however, remains restricted to the open season, though it is now permissible to sell the birds all year round, albeit frozen. Those reared on farms are normally released into the wild for shooting when they are still young (under one year); birds raised completely in the wild are likely to be older.

Cooking

Young pheasant are tender enough for **roasting**. Season inside and out, and bard with bacon or pork back fat. Place in a small roasting tin with a splash of water or stock, and roast at 200°C/gas 6 for 40–50 minutes, basting often. Remove from the pan, discard the bacon and keep warm. Sprinkle a teaspoon of plain flour over the pan juices. Sizzle on the hob for a few seconds, stirring with a wooden spoon. Add 1 tablespoon of ruby port, 1 teaspoon of redcurrant jelly and any juices that have flowed from the pheasant. Boil for a minute or two, stirring. Check and adjust the seasoning, then strain the sauce into a jug. Serve with game chips and bread sauce or crisp fried breadcrumbs.

Older birds are better cooked in a moist braise in the same way as chicken – try the recipe for **Coq au Vin** (page 78). It is delicious served with Puy lentils and celeriac, or teamed with red cabbage, juniper and a slug of best gin.

If you have used the breasts in a separate dish, use up the legs and carcass in a hearty **pheasant and barley soup**. Brown the meat and chopped bones with some diced streaky bacon in a large saucepan. Add a couple of sliced leeks, chopped celery stalks and carrots. When soft, stir in a 400g can chopped tomatoes, a large glass of good red wine and 1.25 litres home-made chicken or game stock. Season with a fresh bay leaf, a thyme sprig, and salt and black pepper. Bring to the boil, then simmer slowly for 30 minutes, skimming off any scum. Add about 175g rinsed pearled barley and simmer for another 30–40 minutes, adding more stock if necessary. Fish out the bones, strip the meat and return it to the pan. Serve garnished with chopped flat leaf parsley.

UK season
• Open shooting 1 October–1 February.

Pheasant to look for
• Hen birds prized for succulence and superior flavour.

Shopping notes
• Choose a bird suitable for the dish you intend to cook:
Young birds: pliable feet and breastbone, softly rounded spurs. Suitable for roasting, grilling and pan-frying.
Mature birds: long sharp spurs, hard scaly feet. Suitable for braising and stewing.
• Regardless of age, choose plump smooth birds not visibly damaged by shot.

Storing
• Store oven-ready birds on the bottom shelf of the fridge so raw juices cannot drip onto other food.
• Remove wrapping and store in a shallow dish, loosely covered with foil, for up to 3 days.

Preparation
• Tie legs and wings in place with string.
• Bard with thin slices of pork back fat to prevent breast meat from drying.

Serving size
• Young bird: 800g–1kg, roasted, serves 2.
• Mature bird: 1–1.3kg, casseroled, serves 4.

Warm Salad of Pheasant Breasts with Wet Walnuts and Bacon

Perfect for autumn dining, this classy salad makes the most of good seasonal produce – young pheasant, robust salad leaves and the first-of-the-season walnuts.

Cut away the breasts from the pheasant, cutting as close to the bone as possible. Discard the carcass or use for game stock. Freeze the legs for future use.

Remove the skin from the breasts and, if they are large, slice neatly in two. Place in a bowl with the marinade ingredients and turn to coat. Cover and leave in the fridge for at least 1 hour or up to 2 days.

Reserving the marinade, remove the breasts, scraping off any solids. Sprinkle with crumbled sea salt flakes and freshly ground black pepper. Strain the marinade – there will be only a tablespoon or so – and set aside.

Heat a heavy-based pan over medium-high heat, then add the rapeseed oil. Fry the breasts for 2 minutes, then turn them over and cook for another minute. Immediately remove from the pan and put on a plate. Leave to rest in a low oven with the door slightly ajar for 10 minutes; the breasts will continue to cook so don't worry if they seem very rare to begin with.

Wipe the pan clean with paper towels. Fry the bacon snippets over medium heat until crisp. Remove, drain on paper towels and keep warm in the oven.

Add the walnuts to the pan with the reserved marinade, the stock, balsamic vinegar and any juices from the breasts. Stir with a wooden spoon, scraping up any sediment, and bubble for a few minutes until the walnuts are warmed through and the liquid slightly reduced. Taste and add more black pepper and more sea salt if necessary.

Arrange the salad leaves and herbs on serving plates. Carve the pheasant breasts into 1-cm diagonal slices and arrange on top of the greenery. Strew with bacon snippets, then pour the sauce and walnuts over the top.

Cook's note

• Salad bags sold in farm shops often contain a tasty mix of hand-picked leaves and whole leafy herbs with delicious flavours.

young oven-ready pheasant 1, weighing 800-900g
sea salt flakes
freshly ground black pepper
rapeseed oil or olive oil 2 tbsp
thick-cut green streaky bacon 2–3 rashers, cut into snippets
'wet' walnuts 6, freshly shelled, halved
chicken or game stock preferably home-made, 6 tbsp
aged balsamic vinegar 1 tsp
salad leaves and leafy herbs preferably organic, 2 good handfuls

for the marinade
walnut oil 5 tbsp
lemon juice of $\frac{1}{2}$
fresh bay leaf 1, shredded
fat garlic clove 1, crushed
sea salt flakes
freshly ground black pepper

Serves 4 as a starter or 2 as a light meal

Braised Pheasant with Apples and Somerset Cider Brandy

This is based on the classic French dish from Normandy, *Faisan à la Normande,* where apples, cream and apple brandy are a feature of the cuisine.

Preheat the oven to 180°C/gas 4. Heat a roomy frying pan over medium-high heat. Add half the butter and when it sizzles, add the apple slices and bacon, and shunt them around the pan until the apples are just beginning to brown but are still firm. Sprinkle with salt and black pepper. Remove from the pan with a perforated spoon and arrange in a layer in the base of a casserole. Pour over about one-third of the cream.

Wipe out the pan, then heat the rapeseed oil and the remaining butter. Brown the pheasants over medium heat for 7–10 minutes, turning often. Place them breast-side down on top of the apples and season with a little more black pepper and salt. Cover and cook in the oven for 1–1¼ hours until tender.

Lift the pheasants onto a board and carve into neat joints, discarding the backbone and rib cage. Arrange the joints in a warm serving dish with the apples around the edge. Leave to rest in a warm place while you finish the sauce.

Pour the casserole juices through a fine sieve into a small frying pan. Bring to the boil, then add the cider brandy. Allow to warm through, then ignite. Once the flames have died down, pour in the remaining cream and bubble until slightly thickened. Check the seasoning, then pour the sauce over the pheasant joints and apples. Strew with parsley and serve.

Cook's note

• You need a sweet dessert apple that holds its shape when cooked. The French would probably use 'Reinette'. Good alternatives would be 'Claygate Pearmain' or a true 'Cox's Orange Pippin'.

unsalted butter or **goose fat** 50g
crisp dessert apples 6, peeled, cored and thickly sliced (see **Cook's note**)
green bacon 85g, diced
salt
freshly ground black pepper
double cream organic, 250ml
rapeseed oil 1 tbsp
oven-ready pheasants 2, weighing about 800g each
Somerset cider brandy or **Calvados** 120ml
flat leaf parsley coarsely chopped, to garnish

Serves 4–6

Pig's Trotters

Farm shop butchers are good places to find animal extremities like tails and trotters, especially in South Lancashire where cooks are reluctant to discard any part of an animal that can be used for food. Charmingly known as 'crubeens' in Ireland and pig's 'petitoes' in other regions, they may not be mainstream but they are tasty and cheap.

Cooking

Though trotters may look unpromising, they produce protein-rich jelly and tasty nuggets of meat. Use them to enrich home-made stock – it will set to a richly flavoured wobbly mass once cold, handy for moistening a terrine or filling a raised pie.

Trotters are usually brined or soaked (see **Preparation**) before gently poaching in stock for 2 or 3 hours. They may be served whole or the meat can be removed and coated with seasoned flour or batter and fried. The Irish roll the meat in beaten eggs mixed with mustard before coating with breadcrumbs and frying in hot bacon fat until crisp. In Lancashire the meat is served with parsley sauce made from the liquid in which the trotters were cooked. A tangy herb sauce as in **Pig's Trotters with Salsa Verde** (page 192) is another tasty accompaniment.

Shopping notes
• Look for large meaty trotters, preferably with some of the knuckle attached.
• If bristly, ask the butcher to scorch off the hairs (or do it yourself with a razor).

Storing
• Remove wrapping and store in a shallow dish, loosely covered with foil, in the fridge for up to 2 days.

Preparation
• *For adding to stock*: scrub under cold running water.
• *For cooking*: wash and put in a large pan, cover with water and bring to the boil, skimming off the scum. Cook for 5 minutes, then drain and proceed with the recipe.
• *Brining*: wash, then soak for 12–24 hours in a brine solution made up of 3.25 litres water, 350g salt, 350g soft brown sugar, 1 tsp black peppercorns and 4 cloves.

Serving size
• 1 large trotter serves 1.

Pig's Trotters with Salsa Verde

A classic dish that could be straight from the menu of a traditional French brasserie. The tangy bright green sauce is the perfect condiment.

Wrap the prepared trotters in muslin bandages or tie with string in several places to keep their shape. Put in a large saucepan with the vinegar, onion, carrots, celery, a little salt and enough water to cover. Bring to the boil, then partially cover and simmer very gently for 3 hours, removing the scum from time to time. Leave the trotters to cool in the cooking liquid for 30 minutes.

Make the salsa verde while the trotters are cooling. Using a hefty mortar and pestle, bash the anchovies and garlic to a cream with a good pinch of sea salt flakes. Add the egg yolks, gherkin, mustard, black pepper, parsley and basil, and grind to a paste. (Transfer to a bowl at this point if your mortar is on the small side.) Mix in the vinegar and then the breadcrumbs. Finally, thoroughly whisk in the olive oil until it forms a thick emulsion with the rest of the ingredients.

Lift the trotters from the cooking liquid and remove the string or muslin. Carefully peel away the skin, keeping the trotter shape as far as possible. Arrange on warm serving plates and spoon over the salsa verde.

Cook's notes
• If you don't have time to brine the trotters, just boil them briefly (see **Preparation**).
• Salsa verde can be whizzed up in a blender, but I prefer the chunkier texture of a hand-mixed sauce.
• Salsa verde can be made in advance and stored in a screw top jar in the fridge for up to a week. Bring it to room temperature and give it a thorough whisk before using.

Variation
• Try **Parsley Sauce** (page 23) or **Grilled Tomato Sauce** (page 257) instead of the Salsa Verde.

pig's trotters 4 large, preferably brined (see **Preparation** and **Cook's notes**)
white wine vinegar 175ml
onion 1, halved
carrots 2, cut into chunks
celery stalks 2, cut into chunks
salt

for the salsa verde
oil-cured anchovies 4, drained and rinsed
garlic clove 1
sea salt flakes
hard-boiled egg yolks 2, chopped
gherkin 1, finely chopped
mustard powder $1/2$ tsp
freshly ground black pepper
flat leaf parsley stalks discarded, leaves finely chopped to make 4 tbsp
basil stalks discarded, leaves finely chopped to make 4 tbsp
red wine vinegar $1^1/2$ tbsp
stale breadcrumbs 3 tbsp
extra-virgin olive oil 150 ml

Serves 4

Pigeon

The wood pigeons you find in farm shops and traditional butchers are a far cry from the emaciated birds doing battle for scraps in the city. The country cousins are plump and well fed on grains and peas to which they freely help themselves, much to the annoyance of farmers. Since pigeons are looked on as vermin rather than game, shooting isn't restricted to a closed season as it is for pheasant and partridge, for example. Though available all year round, pigeon is at its best in late summer and every bit as tasty as the posher birds.

Cooking

Pigeon needs careful cooking if it is not to become dry and tough. A young bird can be **roasted** – bard the breasts well with thin slices of pork back fat to prevent drying. Cook breast-side down at 180°C/gas 4 for 15 minutes, then turn over and roast for another 15 minutes. Leave to rest for 10 minutes to allow the juices to settle.

Another option is to remove the breasts and cook them separately. Sear them quickly and serve slightly rare; the meat develops a bitter livery taste if over-cooked. They can be used instead of pheasant breasts in the salad on page 189 but are particularly good with **salsify, chicory and wet walnuts** – lovely to eat in the autumn. Peel four thick salsify, slice into 10-cm lengths and boil for 20 minutes until just tender. Meanwhile, season four pigeon breasts and fry in olive oil for 6 minutes, turning once. Keep warm on a plate. Drain the salsify, fry until lightly coloured, season and set aside. Add a splash more oil to the pan and fry two large lightly crushed garlic cloves with three heads of chicory, quartered lengthways. Season with sea salt flakes, freshly ground black pepper, a little sugar and lemon juice. When the chicory begins to colour, throw in a handful of walnuts and warm through. Stir in any juices from the pigeon and some chopped flat leaf parsley. Divide between warm serving plates and serve with the pigeon breasts.

The legs, or whole older birds, are excellent in **Pigeon Casserole with Shallots, Mushrooms and Juniper** (page 194), or in the partridge or pheasant casseroles on pages 179 and 190. The rich gamey meat needs assertive ingredients to match its strength. Gin and port, mushrooms, red cabbage and walnuts, balsamic vinegar and black pepper are the order of the day.

UK season
• Year-round.

Shopping notes
• Choose a bird suitable for the dish you intend to cook:
Young birds: pliable breastbone, plump rounded breast, smooth slightly pink skin. Suitable for roasting and searing.
Mature birds: hard breastbone, prominent breast, greyish skin, very dark dry meat. Suitable for stews, soups and stock.
• Regardless of age, choose birds not visibly damaged by shot.

Storing
• Store oven-ready birds on the bottom shelf of the fridge so raw juices cannot drip onto cooked meat or other food.
• Remove wrapping and store in a shallow dish, loosely covered with foil, for 2–3 days.

Preparation
• If roasting whole, tie legs and wings in place with string.
• Bard with thin slices of back fat to prevent breast meat from drying.
• If cooking the breasts separately, remove them by cutting the meat as close to the bone as possible with a small sharp knife. If very thick, cut them in half horizontally.

Serving size
• Whole bird, 280g–350g, serves 1.

Pigeon Casserole with Shallots, Mushrooms and Juniper

This is a classic recipe dating back to the 50s – rich autumn fare and perfect for a weekend dinner.

Season the pigeons inside and out with salt and plenty of freshly ground black pepper. Insert a sage sprig, a bay leaf and a slice of pancetta into each cavity.

Heat a large frying pan, then add the olive oil and butter. Dust the pigeons with flour and immediately fry over medium-high heat for about 10 minutes, turning two or three times until all sides are browned. Place breast-side down in a casserole large enough to take them in a single layer. Set aside while you cook the vegetables.

Add the shallots, carrot, celery and mushrooms to the frying pan and cook over medium heat for 10–15 minutes until soft. Add the juniper berries and season with salt and pepper. Pour in the wine and bubble for a few minutes.

Tip the vegetables and liquid over the pigeons. Pour in the stock, bring to the boil, then cover and simmer over gentle heat for 30 minutes. Turn the pigeons breast-side up and simmer for another 20 minutes. Remove the lid and cook for 10 minutes more.

Remove the pigeons with a slotted spoon and place in a warm serving dish.

Blot up any fat with a sheet of paper towel laid over the surface of the liquid. Raise the heat and boil for a minute or two until slightly reduced. Pour over the pigeons and sprinkle with a little chopped parsley.

pigeons 4

salt

freshly ground black pepper

sage 4 small sprigs

bay leaves 4

pancetta 4 thin slices

olive oil 4 tbsp

butter a knob

flour for dusting

shallots 3 finely chopped

carrot 1, preferably organic, thinly sliced

celery 1 stalk, halved lengthways and diced

baby button mushrooms such as crimini, 225g

juniper berries 1 tbsp, crushed

red wine 125ml

game stock or **chicken stock** preferably homemade, 600ml

flat leaf parsley chopped, to garnish

Serves 4

Plums

British plums come in a magnificent range of sizes, shapes, colours and flavours. There are some splendid vintage varieties on sale at farm shops, PYO fruit farms and the more enlightened supermarkets. Snaffle them up – the season is brief and supplies can be sporadic.

Cooking

Plums are classified as dessert or cooking, but many can be cooked as well as eaten raw. Best-known of the dessert plums is the prolific 'Victoria' but there are plenty of others (see **Varieties**).

Though plums are wonderful eaten fresh, they also make superb tarts and pies, jams, liqueurs and, best of all, **fruit cheese** – a thick intensely flavoured preserve to eat with cold meats or real cheese. Simmer about 650g plums with a little water until very soft. Push through a sieve, pressing hard. Weigh and put in a wide heavy-based saucepan with 350g sugar for every 450g pulp. Heat gently, stirring, until the sugar has dissolved. Increase the heat and boil, stirring often, until you can see the bottom of the pan when you pass a wooden spoon through the mixture. Pour into ramekins and cover the surface with waxed paper. Once cool, wrap in cling film or foil and store in a cool dark place.

I particularly like a **plum and blackcurrant tart** made with ready-made pre-rolled 25 x 32-cm oblong of puff pastry weighing about 375g. Place on a baking tray and score a border 1cm from the edge – this will puff up into a parapet once cooked. Sprinkle the base with 1 tablespoon each of plain flour and sugar. Halve and stone 10–12 plums and arrange them on top, cut-side up. Fill the gaps with blackcurrants, then sprinkle with 3 tablespoons of demerara sugar, 2–3 good pinches of ground cinnamon and dot with 25g butter. Bake at 200°C/gas 6 for 25 minutes until the pastry is golden and the fruit sticky and bubbling.

Plums make excellent ice cream and sorbets (**Damson Sorbet**, page 91), and they are also good poached or stewed. Try them **barbecued** too: wrap in thick foil with a knob of butter, a spoonful of demerara sugar and a pinch of ground cinnamon. The juices turn into a lovely buttery syrup for pouring over the fruit.

Plums are equally delicious in savoury dishes. Spiced stewed plums go well with gammon, cold meats and terrines, and they can also be turned into a **thick and jammy sweet-sour sauce** for serving with duck or pork or as a dip for spring rolls. Simmer 8 quartered and stoned plums for 20 minutes or so with a splash of water, 150g muscovado sugar, grated 5cm chunk of fresh ginger root, 2 tablespoons of cider vinegar, 1 tablespoon each of soy sauce and tomato purée, $1/2$ teaspoon of Chinese five-spice powder, and salt and black pepper to taste. Leave to cool slightly, then whizz in a food processor and push through a sieve. Reheat the purée for a few minutes to thicken it

See also **Damsons** (page 91), **Greengages** (page 128)

UK season
• July–September.

Varieties to look for
• '*Ariel*', dessert plum, orange skin and flesh, good flavour.
• '*Early Laxton*', round cooking/dessert plum, reddish skin, golden flesh, sweet and juicy.
• '*Golden Mirabelle*', small round wild plum. Bitter skin, sweet juicy flesh, good in jams, sauces and tarts. Also used for plum *eau-de-vie* called Mirabelle.
• '*Late Muscatelle*', round dessert plum, purple skin, golden flesh, sweet rich flavour.
• '*Reeves*', large round cooking/dessert plum, purple-red skin, pale yellow flesh, opulently juicy and sweet.
• '*Zwetschen*' or '*Quetsch*', small purple German-style plum, green-gold flesh, excellent for cooking and preserving.

Shopping notes
• Choose undamaged plums with a powdery bloom – a sign that they have not been overly handled.
• Flesh should be plump with some 'give', but not squashy.
• Steer clear of plums that are wizened or bruised.

Storing
• Store ripe plums at room temperature and eat within 24 hours.
• Unripe fruit will continue to ripen if left at room temperature for a few days.

Preparation
• To remove the stone, slice round the indentation and twist the two halves in opposite directions to separate them. Then scoop out the stone.
• To remove the skin, make a small cross-cut at the base end, then cover with boiling water for 10 seconds. Drain and slip off the skins.

Compôte of Dark Fruits in Spiced Syrup

A dramatic compôte with an enigmatic flavour. The redcurrants look like tiny gleaming jewels scattered over the rich dark purples and reds of the plums and berries.

Cut each plum in half through the indentation. Twist the halves in opposite directions to loosen the stone, then scoop it out. Slice the flesh lengthways into segments, then cut each segment in half crossways. Remove the cherry stones. Put the plums and cherries in a serving bowl.

Put all the syrup ingredients in a small saucepan. Stir over gentle heat until the sugar has dissolved. Raise the heat and boil for 7–10 minutes until the bubbles look syrupy. Remove from the heat and leave to cool slightly. Strain, then pour the syrup over the fruit in the bowl and leave until completely cold.

When ready to serve, scatter the soft fruit and redcurrants over the top.

Cook's note
• Serve at room temperature to appreciate the warm spicy flavours.

dark-skinned dessert plums 400g
cherries 250g
mixed dark soft fruit such as blueberries, mulberries, raspberries 250g
redcurrants 75g

for the spiced syrup
water 300ml
sugar 100g
orange peel small strip, thinly pared
rosemary 2 sprigs
fresh ginger root 2 thin slices
black peppercorns $^{1}/_{4}$ tsp, crushed
coriander seeds $^{1}/_{4}$ tsp, crushed
cinnamon stick 2.5cm

Serves 6

Pork

Outdoor-reared or free-range pork bought from a farm is a real treat, especially if it is from a rare breed. The meat from animals given the freedom to roam and forage for wild food is noticeably tastier than mass-produced pork, and noticeably pricier too. Pig-feed prices have rocketed in the past year and farmers face a bleak future as they struggle to meet the demand for cheap food and compete with low-cost imported pork. Some have abandoned pig farming altogether and there is a real danger of a domestic shortage. Buying from a farm shop or farmers' market will help keep the tradition alive since your money goes straight to the farmer.

A good butcher will sell thrifty cuts from the entire carcass, not just prime cuts like chops and loin. You should also be able to find pork belly and ribs, cheeks and knuckles, and the thick back fat that is so useful for lubricating game birds. My butcher also sells ears, left and right displayed in separate bowls – delicious boiled, crumbed and fried until crunchy.

Cooking

Cooks around the world have created the most inventive dishes using every part of the pig. The Chinese are famous for their sweet and sour ribs, the French for their terrines (**Pork and Herb Terrine**, opposite) and sausages, and the Italians for their *porchetta* (**Porchetta with Fennel, Lemon and Rosemary Stuffing**, page 201). The Germans make magnificent pot roasts and knuckle stews, while the Brazilians work miracles on trotters and tails in *feijoada*, their national dish of pork and black beans.

People are often wary of pork, believing that it is dry and not very appetising, or might contain a parasite. If the pork is thoroughly cooked it will be safe to eat, and if the pig has been outdoor-reared, the meat will have a marbling of fat that keeps it succulent and tender.

Because pork meat is young, most cuts can be roasted, grilled or fried. The hunky leg or loin joints are the best cuts for roasting but the slightly fattier shoulder is good too. It takes longer to cook but produces moist and tender meat.

Chops are delicious for a midweek supper. Marinate them in oil, lemon juice and garlic for an hour, then fry over medium heat rather than very high heat which can make them tough. Once both sides are seared, cover the pan to keep the steam in and the chops juicy.

Cut into thin strips, the tender fillet is ideal for **pork stroganoff**. Season with salt and freshly ground black pepper and quickly fry, then add some finely chopped mushrooms and onion. Once softened and amalgamated, swirl in soured cream and heat through. Sprinkle with a dusting of brick-red paprika and some chopped fresh dill, and serve with steamed greens and plainly boiled white rice.

Thick strips of fatty pork belly add richness to bean-based casseroles, such as the French *cassoulet* or Boston baked beans, but this cheap and cheerful cut really comes into its own when grilled or

UK season
- Year-round.
- *Suckling pig:* spring.

Pork to look for
- *Outdoor-reared:* first three months spent outside with the mother before moving to an open-sided shed.
- *Free-range:* whole life spent outside with the mother, protective shelter provided.
- *Organic:* responsibly produced to highest animal welfare standards.
- *Rare breeds:*
'*Berkshire*', deep pink, fine-grained lean flesh.
'*Gloucester Old Spot*', used for bacon as well as fresh pork. Deep pink, well-marbled flesh, excellent flavour.
'*Middle White*', dark, well-marbled flesh, tender and juicy.
'*Tamworth*', used for bacon as well as pork. Fine-grained succulent flesh.

Shopping notes
- Meat should look moist and pink rather than grey, with a fine marbling of internal fat. External fat should be firm, creamy white and dry.
- Choose a cut suitable for the dish you intend to cook:
Slow cooking and stewing: neck meat, diced leg, hocks, ears.
Grilling and frying: chops, belly pork, tenderloin, leg steaks.
Roasting: leg joints, hand or shoulder, spare rib, loin.

Storing
- Store on the bottom shelf of the fridge so raw juices cannot drip onto other food.
- Remove wrapping and store in a shallow dish, loosely covered with foil. Large joints will keep for 2–4 days; chops, steaks and small joints 2–3 days; small chops 1–2 days. Mince should be eaten within 24 hours.
- If vacuum-packed or in a rigid plastic container, leave unopened until ready to cook.

roasted at a high temperature. I like to rub crushed fennel seeds and black peppercorns into the flesh before it goes into the oven, then anoint with a syrupy glaze of melted quince paste (**Membrillo**, page 212), lemon juice and olive oil halfway through cooking.

Spiked with grated lemon zest, crushed garlic, freshly ground black pepper and finely chopped rosemary, minced pork makes **fabulous burgers**. Add a beaten egg, $^1/_2$ a small grated onion and a tablespoon of olive oil to the mixture before moulding and frying. Stuff into pitta bread with plenty of crisp shredded lettuce, tomato wedges, slivers of red onion and a spoonful of **Yogurt and Cucumber Sauce** (page 278).

See also **Bacon and Gammon** (page 21), **Black Pudding** (page 40), **Ham** (page 136), **Pig's Trotters** (page 191), **Sausages** (page 232), **Wild Boar** (page 275).

Preparation

• *For crisp crackling:* Score the fat but not through to the meat, at 5-mm intervals (a Stanley knife is a good tool for this). Put the meat on a rack over the sink and douse with boiling water. Drain and allow to dry. Rub the skin with a generous amount of sea salt, pushing it into the slits.
• *Cooking chops:* Snip the fat at intervals to stop it shrinking and curling.

Serving size

• Leg, loin, shoulder: boneless 250g per person, bone-in 375–500g per person.
• Belly: 125–175g per person.

Pork and Herb Terrine

This is a coarse-textured garlicky terrine strongly flavoured with herbs. It's wonderful in thick crumbly slices on sourdough toast. It makes good use of the pig: liver, belly, bacon and back fat.

Sweat the onions in the butter in a saucepan until soft but not coloured, then set aside. Chop the gammon, liver and pork belly into nuggets. Put through a mincer using the coarsest blade, or use a food processor and pulse briefly in batches. Take care when doing so; you need a bit of texture rather than a homogenous sludge.

Tip the pork mixture into a large bowl and stir in the onions. Lightly beat the eggs with the garlic, herbs, lemon zest and seasonings. Pour this liquid into the bowl and mix thoroughly with your hands.

Preheat the oven to 170°C/gas 3. Grease a 1.3-litre oblong terrine and line the bottom with myrtle leaves. Remove the rind from the bacon and stretch the rashers with a rolling pin. Place one in the base of the terrine on top of the leaves. Spoon in half the pork mixture, pressing it down well. Place another bacon rasher on top, then the rest of the pork mixture. Level the surface and top with the last two rashers, laying them end-to-end to cover the surface.

Cover the terrine with foil and put it in a roasting tin. Add enough boiling water to come halfway up the sides. Bake for $1^1/_2$ hours, removing the foil for the last 15 minutes.

Pour off any excess liquid, then invert into a shallow oblong dish. Turn out and leave to cool. Chill before serving.

Cook's notes

• Use a mixture of robust herbs such as oregano, thyme, rosemary, sage, hyssop and savory.
• *Quatre-épices* is a spice blend made up of white pepper, nutmeg, ginger and cloves. As an alternative, just use more black pepper.

onions 2, finely chopped
butter 50g
gammon 350g, in one piece
pig's liver 225g
pork belly 750g
eggs preferably organic, 2
garlic cloves 4, crushed
herbs chopped to make 6 tbsp (see **Cook's notes**)
lemon zest of $^1/_2$
salt $^1/_2$ tsp
freshly ground black pepper $^1/_2$ tsp
quatre-épices $^1/_2$ tsp (see **Cook's notes**)
myrtle leaves or fresh bay leaves
smoked bacon 4 thick long rashers, weighing about 175g in total

Serves 8–10

Porchetta with Fennel, Lemon and Rosemary Stuffing

This is the way roast pork is cooked in Tuscany and Umbria; it's sold from massive vans in open-air food markets and always tastes divine. The crackling crackles, the meat is moist and the flavour is superb. Make sure the meat has a thick layer of back fat.

Using a sharp knife, score the skin of the meat all over in deep lines about 7mm apart. With skin-side facing down, position the knife just beyond the inner side of the rounded 'eye'. Cut down through the flesh to within 2cm of the fat. Then cut parallel with the fat, between the eye and the fat, but don't cut all the way through – the meat should remain in one piece. Open out the meat to create a large rectangular surface.

Next make the stuffing. Bash the sea salt flakes, peppercorns, fennel seeds and garlic to a paste using a hefty mortar and pestle. Smear the paste over the cut surface of the meat. Strew with the lemon zest and chopped rosemary. Roll up the meat, forming it into a log and tie tightly with string (see **Cook's notes**). Insert the rosemary sprigs into the slits. Put the meat in a dish, tent loosely with foil and marinate in the fridge for 6–24 hours.

Preheat the oven to 230°C/gas 8. Blot the meat dry and massage the skin with olive oil and plenty of sea salt flakes. Place in a roasting tin with the skin uppermost, sitting it on the bones if you have kept them. Roast for 30–40 minutes or until the skin starts to uniformly blister.

Lower the oven temperature to 170°C/gas 3 and roast for another 45 minutes or until the meat reaches an internal temperature of 70°C or the juices run clear. Transfer to a warm serving platter and leave in a warm place to rest for at least 30 minutes.

Carve into thin slices so that everyone gets a piece of crackling. Serve with the defatted pan juices and any juices that flow from the meat while it rests.

Cook's notes
• If you bone the meat yourself, use the backbone and ribs as a flavoursome trivet to sit the loin on while it roasts.
• Use a continuous length of string, rather than separate pieces, to tie the meat in a log shape; it will keep its shape better. Tie a knot at one end, then coil the string tightly round the meat diagonally, so that it doesn't sink into the score marks.
• Take the marinated meat out of the fridge 2 hours before cooking. It must be at room temperature by the time it goes into the oven.

loin of pork boned, weighing about 2.8–3kg
rosemary 12–15 small sprigs
olive oil
sea salt flakes

for the stuffing
sea salt flakes 1 tbsp
black peppercorns 1 tbsp
fennel seeds 2 tbsp
garlic cloves preferably 'green', 8–10
lemon grated zest of 3
rosemary leaves chopped to make 3 tbsp

Serves 8

Potatoes

Given that the potato is probably the one vegetable that most people eat every day, it's surprising how most of us are potato-ignorant. There are literally hundreds of different types ranging from monster bakers to dainty 'Jersey Royals'. Farm shops provide an opportunity to enjoy some of the fine-tasting specimens that may be difficult to find elsewhere (see **Varieties**). Earth-encrusted and freshly dug, many are worthy old-fashioned varieties with real potato flavour.

Cooking

It's important to use the right kind of potato for the dish you intend to cook. At one end of the scale are the waxy types. They remain intact after cooking and are perfect for salads or serving plainly boiled. At the other end are the floury types that tend to disintegrate when boiled, but are suitable for mashing and baking in their jackets. In-between are the all-purpose types that are used for chips, sautés and roasting.

Their accommodating nature makes potatoes the perfect match for strident ingredients such as chillies, potent spices and strongly flavoured cheeses. Try them with piquillo peppers and crisp-fried onions in **Goose Egg Frittata with Potato, Piquillo Peppers and Crispy Onions** (page 104) or thickly sliced in *tartiflette* – a bubbling mass of potatoes, bacon, onion and creamy brie cheese.

Also good are numbingly hot **Bombay hash browns**. Grate some potatoes and blot dry before frying in oil with cumin, fresh ginger root, black pepper, salt and as many chopped chillies as you like. Add crushed cashews, the grated zest and juice of a lime, and a lump of creamed coconut. Toss until brown and crisp. Shower with chopped coriander before serving.

A favourite dish is **bashed potatoes**, especially when made with red-skinned 'Duke of York'. The texture of the yellow buttery flesh is superb. Cut the potatoes into even-sized chunks but don't peel them. Boil until tender, drain and tip back into the pan. Cover with a clean folded cloth and a lid for a few minutes to dry the potatoes. Preheat the oven to 220°C/gas 7 and tip the potatoes into a roomy roasting tray. Crush with a potato masher, enough to crack each potato and create broken craggy edges. Splash generously with oil and season with sea salt and freshly ground black pepper. If serving with pork, I add crushed fennel or caraway seeds, and cumin seeds with lamb. Blast in the oven for 15–20 minutes until the edges are browned and crisp.

I also love a colourful **Peruvian-style potato and egg salad** made with waxy 'Pink Fir Apple' potatoes and the dramatic purple-fleshed 'Black Congo' for contrast. Steam an equal amount of each in their skins for 10–15 minutes until tender but not disintegrating. When cool enough to handle, peel away the skin and slice the flesh crossways into thick discs. Arrange some crimson radicchio leaves on plates, with the potatoes and quartered hard-boiled eggs on top. Scatter with slivers of red onion, fresh red chilli, and some black olives, then add a dollop of good mayonnaise and sprinkle with snipped chives.

UK season
• May–December.

Varieties to look for
• *'Edzell Blue'*, blue-purple skin, luminous white flesh, complex flavour. Good for mash, slightly too dry for baking,
• *'Kennebec'*, brown skin, white flesh, great flavour, fluffy texture. Good for baking.
• *'Kerr's Pink'*, pink skin, creamy flesh, rich buttery flavour. Floury texture.
• *'Belle de Fontenay'*, long oval tubers, fine-grained yellow flesh, strong potato flavour. Waxy texture.
• *'Pink Fir Apple'*, knobbly tubers, pink skin, delicious earthy flavour. Waxy texture
• *'Ratte'*, long oval tubers, firm waxy texture, fantastic nutty flavour.
• *'Black Congo'*, purple skin and flesh, earthy flavour. Very Versatile.
• *'Duke of York'*, red skin, yellow flesh, outstanding flavour. Perfect for mash or roasting.
• *'Roseval'*, pink skin, yellow flesh, mild flavour. Very versatile.

Shopping notes
• Buy unwashed potatoes (soil acts as a protective barrier) preferably in a sealed paper sack.
• Don't buy potatoes that are spongy, sprouting or have green patches.

Storing
• Potatoes can be stored for several months in a dry airy shed, or up to 1 week in a dark well-ventilated drawer.
• Never store in a plastic bag – condensation can cause rotting.
• Do not store in the fridge – the low temperature makes potatoes sweet.

Preparation
• Scrub well, especially if cooking in their skins, and remove any eyes.
• Cut away small green patches but discard any with an overall greenish tinge.
• Lightly scrub new potatoes but don't peel unless for aesthetic reasons.

Provençal Garlic Potatoes, page 204

Provençal Garlic Potatoes

Crisp-fried potato slices with golden onions, garlic and fragrant herbs are pure perfection with any kind of grilled or roasted meat. They are especially good with **Roast Rack of Lamb** (page 158).

Put the potatoes in a saucepan with enough salted water to cover. Bring to the boil, then simmer for 5 minutes until barely tender. Drain, and when cool enough to handle, remove the skin and slice the flesh into fairly thick rounds.

While the potatoes are cooling, heat a large non-stick frying pan over medium-high heat. Fry the onions in 1 tablespoon of the olive oil and half the butter, stirring, until they begin to colour. Add the garlic and fry until just coloured. Tip the whole lot into a bowl and mix with 1 tablespoon of the parsley, half the mixed herbs and a sprinkling of sea salt flakes and black pepper. Keep warm while you cook the potatoes.

Heat the remaining oil and butter in the same pan until sizzling hot. Fry the potatoes in batches, turning with tongs, until golden brown. Drain each batch on paper towels.

When the final batch is cooked, lower the heat and tip the rest of the potatoes back into the pan along with the onion mixture and the remaining herbs. Stir together carefully, check the seasoning and cook until warmed through.

medium-sized potatoes 1kg, scrubbed but unpeeled
onions 2, halved and thinly sliced
olive oil 4–5 tbsp
butter 25g
large garlic cloves 4, thinly sliced
flat leaf parsley leaves chopped to make 3 tbsp
mixed herbs such as rosemary, thyme and sage, finely chopped to make 1 tbsp
sea salt flakes
coarsely ground black pepper

Serves 4 as a side dish

Camping Potatoes

So-called because this is the way I cooked potatoes on camping holidays many years ago. The fragrance of hot potatoes and herbs as you open the packet is pure bliss.

Scrub the potatoes but do not peel them. Cut into 3-mm slices. Plunge into a large bowl of water to wash off the starch, then drain and blot dry on a paper towel-lined tray.

Take an enormous sheet of heavyweight foil and smear butter over an area in the middle, measuring about 30 x 20cm. Arrange a single layer of potatoes on the greased area. Sprinkle with herbs, season with sea salt flakes and black pepper, and dot generously with butter. Repeat until all the potato slices are used up – there should be two or three layers. Fold over the foil to make a flat packet, sealing and crimping the edges well. Wrap the packet in another big piece of foil, and for safety, a third piece. The aim is to have a well-sealed flat packet with enough layers of foil to prevent the potatoes from burning.

Place the packet on the barbecue, and cook for 45 minutes, turning every 10 minutes, or until the potatoes are tender. Serve straight from the packet.

Cook's note
• If it's not convenient to barbecue, cook the potato packet in the oven at 220°C/gas 7.

Variation
• Add other thinly sliced vegetables to the packet, such as carrots, parsnips or slivers of onion.

medium-sized potatoes 650g
unsalted butter about 175g
rosemary or thyme leaves chopped to make
2 tbsp
sea salt flakes
coarsely ground black pepper

Serves 4–6 as a side dish

Pumpkin and Winter Squash

Most farm shops sell a glorious cornucopia of pumpkins and winter squash often piled in a glowing heap outside the shop. There is an amazing choice, ranging from chubby palm-sized babies to monsters so heavy they leave an impression in the soil. Some look like spinning tops, some are torpedo-shaped, others have graceful swan-like necks. The colours are stunning – fluorescent oranges, deep forest greens and paint box yellows. You may not always find the familiar butternut squash, however – it doesn't do well in the northern European climate.

To clear up potential confusion over names, the round flat-bottomed smooth varieties with orange skin are usually thought of as pumpkins; everything else is a winter squash. They have a seed-filled cavity and tough inedible skin, whereas summer squash – courgettes, for example – have tender edible skin and no cavity.

Cooking

Pumpkins and winter squash are wonderfully user-friendly. They can be baked, roasted, stuffed, puréed or fried, used in cakes and tarts, and served either as an accompaniment or a main dish.

The appropriate cooking method depends on texture and flavour (see **Varieties**). Pumpkins tend to be watery and disintegrate easily; squash are firmer. They may be smooth or stringy, moist or dry, and the flavour may be savoury, bland or overwhelmingly sweet.

My favourite way with squash is to roast chunky segments with olive oil, thyme sprigs and plenty of black pepper – delicious with roast pork or turkey. Also immensely pleasing are baby pumpkins stuffed with couscous, chopped onion, broad beans and walnuts, and baked until softly steaming and fragrant.

Dense-fleshed varieties are good in casseroles and stir-fries. West Indian cooks make a hefty stew with squash, beans, chillies and sweetcorn, while the Japanese dip wedges into tempura batter and fry them. Also good are cubes fried in olive oil until slightly brown. Add thinly sliced garlic, a pinch of dried chilli flakes and toss for a few seconds before showering with fresh coriander.

The puréed flesh of 'Crown Prince' or 'Onion Squash' makes an excellent filling for ravioli; or work it into yeast dough for the most deliciously moist and colourful bread.

See also **Courgettes** (page 83)

UK season
• September–November.

Varieties to look for
• *'Baby Bear'*, medium-sized orange pumpkin, recognisable by dark green stalk. Moist, slightly stringy flesh, excellent for pumpkin pie and cakes. 'Hull-less' seeds are good sprinkled over salad or soup.
• *'Crown Prince'*, large, round, slightly flattened. Blue-grey skin, deep yellow flesh, very sweet and smooth. Good roasted or puréed. Use as a filling for ravioli.
• *'Delicata'*, elongated, striped ivory green skin, honey-flavoured moist flesh. Excellent for pumpkin pie and cakes.
• *'Jack Be Little'*, small, round, orange skin, sweet sticky flesh. Lovely stuffed, baked and served whole.
• *'Kabocha Green'*, large, round, dark green skin. Lovely chestnut flavour. Dense dry flesh. Use for stir-fries and casseroles.
• *'Onion Squash'* or *'Uchiku Kuri'*, medium-sized onion-shaped, bright orange skin, smooth moist flesh. All-purpose, good for sweet or savoury dishes.

Shopping notes
• Choose hard pumpkins and squash with undamaged skin that feel heavy for their size.

Storing
• Will keep for 2–6 months in a dry airy shed, or 2–3 weeks at room temperature.

Preparation
• Slice into large segments and scoop out the seeds and fibre.
• Remove skin if using in a stir-fry, soup or casserole.
• If baking or roasting large segments, leave skin in place and remove after cooking.

Roasted Squash and Chilli Soup

Roasting rather than frying the vegetables really intensifies the flavours. The garnishes bring the soup to life, adding texture, colour and yet more complex flavours.

Preheat the oven to 200°C/gas 6. Cut the prepared squash into large evenly sized chunks. Arrange in a large roasting tin and brush with rapeseed oil. Add the potato to the tin. Roast for 45 minutes, turning now and again, until the squash is beginning to brown at the edges.

Put the garlic and chilli in a small roasting tin and put in the oven after the squash has been roasting for 30 minutes. Roast until the garlic is soft and the chilli is starting to blacken and blister. Remove the skin from the garlic and the skin and seeds from the chilli.

Put two-thirds of the roasted squash in a food processor. Peel the potato and add the flesh, along with the garlic, chilli and about 300ml of the stock. Blend to a purée.

Tip the purée into a saucepan and stir in the rest of the stock. Chop the whole pieces of squash into bite-sized bits and add them too. Season with salt and black pepper and reheat gently.

Ladle into bowls, sprinkle with the garnishes and finish with a swirl of pumpkin seed oil if you are using it.

Cook's note

• Rich dark amber pumpkin seed oil is occasionally found in farm shops that stock deli-style ingredients. If you can't find any, use extra-virgin olive oil instead.

butternut or **onion squash** 2, peeled and deseeded
rapeseed oil
baking potato 1 large
garlic cloves 2, unpeeled
fresh red chilli 1
chicken stock preferably home-made, 700ml
salt
coarsely ground black pepper

for the garnish
pumpkin seeds 3 tbsp, dry-fried
tomatoes 3, peeled, deseeded and diced
hard crumbly cheese such as Wensleydale or Caerphilly, 50g
pumpkin seed oil for drizzling (optional)

Serves 4

Peppery Squash Cake

This is adapted from a recipe by Italian food writer Valentina Harris. It makes a great dessert served with organic Jersey cream. I have spiced the cake with pepper, which gives it a beautifully warm flavour.

Put the sultanas and liqueur in a bowl and soak for at least 20 minutes until the sultanas are plump. Preheat the oven to 180°C/gas 4. Grease and line a shallow 22–23-cm round cake tin.

Put the cubed squash in a saucepan with the butter. Cover and cook over medium heat for about 15 minutes until soft. Add a pinch of salt, then tip the mixture into a large bowl and beat until smooth. Stir in the sugar, almonds, candied orange peel, lemon zest and black pepper. Add the sultanas and any remaining liqueur, mixing thoroughly.

Sift the flour and baking powder together, then gradually add to the squash mixture, beating well with each addition.

Beat the egg yolks until pale and thick, then fold into the squash mixture. Whisk the egg whites in a separate bowl until stiff, then fold in carefully using a large metal spoon.

Spoon the mixture into the prepared cake tin and bake for 1–1$\frac{1}{4}$ hours or until a skewer inserted into the middle comes out clean. If the cake is browning too much, cover the top with a sheet of foil. Turn out onto a wire rack to cool. Dust with sifted icing sugar before serving.

Cook's notes

• Use a dense-fleshed squash such as dark green 'Kabocha' or bright orange 'Onion Squash'. Butternut squash are fine too.
• You will need about 425g squash after peeling and deseeding.
• Farm shops often stock good quality peppercorns, such as Wynad single estate or Tellicherry. These have real flavour and are a far cry from ordinary kitchen pepper.

sultanas 50g
Galliano liqueur or grappa 100ml
squash (see Cook's notes) 600g, peeled, deseeded and cubed
unsalted butter 150g
salt a pinch
sugar 150g
whole almonds 50g, finely chopped
candied orange peel or citron peel 50g, finely chopped
lemon grated zest of 1
black peppercorns (see Cook's notes) 1 tbsp, coarsely ground
plain flour 85g
baking powder 1 heaped tsp
eggs organic, 2
icing sugar for dusting

Serves 8–10

Quail

Although quail are thought of as game, naturally reared in the wild, the truth is that wild quail are a protected species and, as such, cannot be shot for the table. Most quail are as intensively reared as battery chickens, and are killed in slaughterhouses rather than shot. The good news is that a few small specialist farms are starting to produce humanely reared quail, with access to outdoor aviaries that allow them to stretch their wings and fly.

Cooking

Though they are small, there is a surprising amount of meat on a quail. It is juicy and tender if cooked carefully, and more forgiving than pigeon or other game birds if overcooked. Quail can be cooked in a simple casserole, but I think the direct heat of roasting or grilling is a better way to preserve the delicate flavour. They are particularly delicious roasted and served on toasted sourdough bread or a slab of grilled polenta to soak up the juices.

Quail are also sensational cooked on a barbecue, spatchcocked (see **Preparation**) and threaded onto skewers. They will be ready in 20–25 minutes, providing crisp succulent meat that begs to be eaten with the fingers; it is simply too frustrating to use a knife and fork to cut the meat off such a small bird. Ring the changes with different marinades or rubs. I have used Spanish pimentón in the recipe opposite but equally delicious is an Asian-style mixture of sesame oil, soy sauce, wine vinegar, brown sugar, crushed fresh ginger root and garlic. The skin becomes wonderfully crisp and sticky.

It's always worth cooking a few extra birds. Served with a dab of home-made chutney, cold quail is a satisfying snack to have in the fridge. Alternatively, strip the meat from the bones and add it to a salad of bitter and peppery greens such as frisée, radicchio and watercress.

UK season
• Year-round.

Quail to look for
• Free-range, free-to-fly.

Shopping notes
• Choose plump birds with pink unbroken skin.

Storing
• Store on the bottom shelf of the fridge so raw juices cannot drip onto other food.
• Remove wrapping and store in a shallow dish, loosely covered with foil, for 2–3 days, depending on 'use by' date.

Preparation
• Spatchcocking is a handy technique for grilling quail and other poultry. The bird is split lengthways and opened out flat to make a compact shape of more-or-less uniform thickness that will cook more evenly than a whole round bird. First remove the backbone by cutting either side with kitchen scissors. Remove the wing tips and any stray feathers. Open out the bird and place it skin-side up on a board. Press sharply with the heel of your hand to flatten the breastbone.

Serving size
• 1–2 quail serves 1.

Grilled Spatchcocked Quail with Smoked Paprika, Garlic, Cayenne and Cumin

Plump little quails are rubbed with fragrant brick-red smoked paprika (pimentón) and a pungent mix of garlic, cayenne and cumin. You should be able to find the spices in larger farm shops – especially those that sell the Bart Spices Delicatessen range.

Put the prepared quails in a large dish. Combine all the marinade ingredients, mixing well. Pour the mixture over the quails, rubbing it in with your fingers, until evenly coated. Cover and marinate in the fridge for up to 2 days, but for at least 2 hours (see **Cook's notes**).

Preheat the grill or light the barbecue. Place the quails skin-side up on a board. Position the drum sticks so that they are bent at the joint with the thigh turned inwards and pushed up towards the wings, and the leg nestling close to the rib cage. Insert a metal skewer through one bent drumstick and the lower rib cage and out through the drumstick on the other side. Take a second skewer and insert it through the wing, upper rib cage and out the other side. Skewer a second bird on the same pair of skewers. Repeat with the remaining birds, positioning two birds on each pair of skewers.

Place the quails skin-side down in a grill pan about 17cm from the heat source or on a rack over hot coals. Grill for 10 minutes, then turn skin-side up and grill for another 10 minutes. Turn again and grill for 5 minutes more or until the flesh of the inner thigh is no longer pink.

Pull out the skewers and arrange the quail in a warm serving dish. Sprinkle with parsley and garnish with lemon wedges. Serve with the sauce and warm pitta bread.

Cook's note
• Quails should be at room temperature when you grill them. If they have spent time in the fridge, allow at least an hour for them to lose their chill before you start to cook.

quail 8, spatchcocked (see **Preparation**)
flat leaf parsley roughly chopped, to garnish
lemon wedges to garnish
Yogurt and Cucumber Sauce (page 278)
warm pitta bread

for the marinade
rapeseed oil 4 tbsp
smoked Spanish pimentón 1 tbsp
garlic cloves 2 large, crushed
cayenne pepper $^1/_2$ tsp
cumin seeds 1 tsp, crushed
dried oregano or dried herbes de Provence $^1/_2$ tsp
salt a good pinch

Serves 4

Quinces

There is something magical about quinces – the way they hang in a tree like golden orbs long after the leaves have fallen, and the way a bowl of them can perfume a room with the most exquisite fragrance, redolent of Turkish Delight and guavas. That said, the quince is a somewhat austere and forbidding fruit. The skin is covered in mouse-coloured fluff, although this often rubs off during transportation and handling. The ivory-coloured flesh is hard and grainy, turns brown the minute it is exposed to the air and is so astringent that it cannot be eaten raw.

Preparation is a chore but, once cooked, quinces are sublime. A plus point is that the peelings and cores need not be wasted. They can be turned into a sparkling rosy syrup (see below) that makes a delicious glaze for fruit tarts, or a sauce to trickle over ices and chilled desserts.

Cooking

If you have not eaten quinces before, a good way to get acquainted with them is to slice one into segments and add to an apple or pear compôte. If you like the flavour, you can then experiment with dishes made entirely of quinces.

For **quince compôte**, peel about 500g quinces (keep the peel and cores) and slice lengthways into segments. Simmer gently with 1 litre water, 150g sugar and a split vanilla pod. After about $1\frac{1}{2}$ hours the fruit will have turned a deep rosy pink and the vanilla pod will have produced a trail of contrasting black seeds. Leave to cool in the pan. Strain the liquid (reserving the quinces), pour it back into the pan and add the reserved peel and cores. Boil for 20–30 minutes until syrupy. Strain into a jug, leave to cool, then pour over the quinces.

Alternatively, segments of cooked quince can be used in a crisp tart. Spoon a billowing layer of whipped organic Jersey cream into a cooked pastry case, arrange quince segments in concentric circles on top and glaze with the syrup made as above.

Membrillo is a gorgeous quince paste, popular in Spain where it is served in thin slices with sheep's cheese and slivers of gherkin. It is easy to make and will keep in the fridge for months. You need ripe fragrant quinces – 1–2kg will be fine. There's no need to peel or core them, just roughly chop and put in a saucepan with just enough water to barely cover. Cook for an hour or so or until soft, then leave in the pan overnight. Push through a sieve, weigh the resulting pulp and tip back into the pan. Add an equal weight of sugar and stir over gentle heat until dissolved. Simmer gently for an hour or more until you can see the bottom of the pan when you pass a wooden spoon through the mixture. Pour into shallow plastic containers and leave to cool. Cover the surface with greaseproof paper, then seal and store in the fridge.

The quince is a traditional ingredient in the subtly spiced stews of the Middle East – the fruit's ancestral home. A classic dish is quinces with lamb, onions and split peas seasoned with turmeric. They are also excellent roasted as in **Roast Duck with Quince, Honey and Ginger** (page 97).

UK season
• October–November.

Varieties to look for
• '*Vranja*', large, pale yellow-green skin, good flavour.

Shopping notes
• Look for quinces that smell fragrant.
• Don't buy any that are bruised or have brown patches on the skin.

Storing
• Unripe quinces (with green skins) can be left to ripen at room temperature.
• Once ripe, store in the fridge or a cool dark place for several days.

Preparation
• Rinse under running water to remove any grey fuzz on the skin.
• Quarter, peel and cut out the core, reserving the trimmings. Chop or slice the flesh according to the recipe.
• Immerse in water acidulated with lemon juice if you want to prevent the cut fruit from turning brown.

Quince and Ginger Sorbet

This divinely pretty pale pink sorbet is studded with nuggets of stem ginger. The warm flavour of the ginger brings out the best in quinces.

Quarter and core the quinces, then slice lengthways into eighths. Remove the peel and chop the flesh into three chunks. Put in a saucepan with 700ml of the water and the vanilla pod. Bring to the boil, then cover and simmer over medium-low heat for 50 minutes or until the quinces are very soft.

Meanwhile, pour the remaining 400ml of water into a separate saucepan. Add the sugar and dissolve over medium heat. Bring to the boil and boil hard for 5 minutes until the bubbles look syrupy.

Drain the quinces, discarding the liquid. Purée the quince flesh in a food processor until very smooth. Scrape into a bowl and stir in the syrup – there should be about 700ml in total. Add some more water if necessary. Mix thoroughly, then push through a fine sieve to get rid of the gritty texture.

Stir in the lemon juice, stem ginger and ginger syrup. Leave until completely cold, then chill in the fridge for at least 1 hour.

Freeze in an ice cream machine following the manufacturer's instructions. Pack the sorbet into a freezer-proof container, cover the surface closely with cling film, seal and freeze.

Cook's notes
• If you don't have an ice cream machine, still-freeze the mixture in a shallow, freezer-proof container for several hours, until it begins to harden around the edges. Transfer to a deep bowl and whisk until smooth. Return to the container, freeze again, then repeat the whisking process once more before the final freeze.
• The sorbet is best eaten within a few days of making, before the delicate flavour starts to fade.

quinces 2–3, weighing about 600g in total
water 1.1 litres
vanilla pod 1, split lengthways
sugar 400g
lemons juice of 2
stem ginger 2 pieces, very finely chopped
ginger syrup 2 tbsp from the stem ginger jar

Makes about 1.2 litres

Spiced Roasted Quinces with Honey and Clotted Cream

This is one of the best ways of cooking quinces – roasted in fragrant buttery syrup until beginning to caramelise round the edges. If serving hot, try this with **Clotted Cream Ice Cream** (page 88). At room temperature, the quinces are better with clotted cream rather than ice cream.

Quarter and core the quinces, reserving the cores and pips. Cut the quarters in half lengthways, then remove and reserve the peel. Place the quinces cored-side up in a single layer in a 2-litre baking dish. Preheat the oven to 180°C/gas 4.

Put the cores, pips and peel into a saucepan with the 100g sugar, the cinnamon and mace. Pour in the water and bring to the boil. Simmer briskly for 20 minutes until syrupy. Strain through a sieve and pour the liquid over the quinces.

Dot with the butter, then sprinkle with the tablespoon of sugar and a pinch of salt. Place in the oven and bake for 1 hour or more, until the quinces are soft and blackened round the edges. Stir after 30 minutes to keep the quinces bathed in syrup. Stir again once they start to blacken.

Serve hot, warm or at room temperature with the juices, a dollop of clotted cream and a trickle of honey.

Cook's note
• If you don't have any mace blades use $1/4$ teaspoon of freshly grated nutmeg instead.

quinces 3, about 250g each
sugar 100g, plus 1 tbsp
cinnamon sticks 2
mace blades 2
water 600ml
butter 25g
salt a pinch

to serve
organic clotted cream
clear honey

Serves 4

Rabbit

The rabbit has always been the poor relative of the hare, the latter classified as top-notch game and the rabbit as vermin. While it is true that rabbits breed prolifically and help themselves to anything that's growing, they are a versatile and tasty food and, unlike the hare, are available all year round.

Feasting as rabbits do on vegetables and tender shoots, their meat is sweet and nutty, though all that scampering to escape the farmer's gun can make it tough. Wild rabbit, as opposed to farmed, is what you are likely to find in farm shops. The meat is darker and full-bodied, while farmed rabbit is pale, dry and comparatively flavourless – the equivalent of a battery chicken. Rabbits are usually sold skinned, minus the head, and with the liver intact. Don't throw this out – it's delicious fried and tossed in a salad or used in a pâté (**Chicken livers**, page 162).

Cooking

It is usually more practical to joint a rabbit (see **Preparation**) as the various parts need different cooking times. Meatiest and most tender is the saddle or loin, which can be fried as in **Balsamic-Glazed Saddle of Rabbit with Shallots, Mushrooms and Bitter Leaves** (page 218). It is also good roasted, as are the hind legs. Set the oven temperature to 200°C/gas 6, and toss the meat in plenty of oil and seasonings. Roast the loin for 7–8 minutes and the legs for 12–15 minutes, then leave to rest for 10 minutes before serving.

Provided they come from a young rabbit, the hind legs are wonderful **barbecued** – real campfire stuff and so much better than chicken drumsticks. Just slash the thickest part, rub with olive oil, lemon juice, herbs and black pepper, and cook for 6–8 minutes a side. The front legs are not very meaty but are fine to add to a casserole or use in soups and stock.

A classic French bistro dish is rabbit cooked with a mustard cream sauce, for which there are numerous recipes. I prefer it in an **Italian-style baked casserole**. Use a whole jointed rabbit in this case, or all the legs from 2 rabbits if the saddles have been used in another dish. Cut the joints into smaller chunks and brown in olive oil in a large frying pan. While the rabbit is browning, blanch 500g thickly sliced waxy potatoes in boiling salted water for 3–4 minutes. Pour 3 tablespoons of olive oil into a wide shallow casserole or a roasting tin with a lid. Add the rabbit joints, drained potatoes, a thickly sliced onion, 400g can chopped tomatoes, 3 crushed garlic cloves and plenty of sea salt and freshly ground black pepper. Sprinkle with the leaves from 2 thyme sprigs, and tuck in sage leaves and a fresh bay leaf or two. Give everything a good stir, then trickle a little more oil over the top. Cover and bake in a preheated oven at 200°C/gas 6 for 30 minutes. Stir once more, adding some stock if the mixture is getting too dry, and bake for another 30 minutes or until the rabbit is tender.

Rabbit is equally delicious with **pasta** or in a **risotto**; it's a good way of using a whole rabbit, particularly an older one. Soak it overnight

UK season
• Year-round, but best August–February.

Shopping notes
• Wild rabbit has brownish-pink flesh; farmed rabbit is greyish-white.
• Look for a plump young rabbit, 3–4 months old, weighing 1–1.25kg. Older, heavier rabbits are likely to be tough.

Storing
• Store on the bottom shelf of the fridge so raw juices cannot drip onto other food.
• Wash well, pat dry and store in a shallow dish, loosely covered with foil, for 1–2 days.
• Remove the liver, heart and kidneys, and store separately.

Preparation
• Remove any shot pellets and damaged flesh before cooking.
• Soak in salted water for several hours to take away any bitterness.
• To joint a rabbit: trim and discard the tips of the feet. Place belly-side down and slice around the hindquarters where they join the pelvis. Turn over and cut round the ball-and-socket joint on the insides of the legs. Sever the ligaments and remove the legs. Slice under the shoulder blades and remove the front legs. Remove any excess bone or thin flaps of skin from the saddle. Depending on size, the saddle may be cut crossways into two or three pieces.

Serving size
• Jointed rabbit weighing 1kg will serve 3.

(see **Preparation**), then drain and simmer in fresh water for an hour or until the meat is practically falling from the bone. Remove from the pan and leave to cool. Strip the meat, put it in a bowl, season, then cover with olive oil. As long as it is completely covered with oil to exclude air, it can be left in the fridge for up to 2 weeks.

To make a **sauce for pasta**, heat a large knob of butter and 2 tablespoons of olive oil in a roomy pan. Gently fry a finely chopped carrot, celery stalk, small onion and 2 garlic cloves with 4 rashers of chopped streaky bacon, a sprig of marjoram or thyme and 2 fresh bay leaves. Season with sea salt and freshly ground black pepper. Once soft, pour in half a glass of dry white wine and let it evaporate for a few minutes. Add 200g finely chopped mushrooms and 350g picked rabbit meat, and cook for another 10 minutes. Serve with broad ribbon pasta such as tagliatelle, and plenty of freshly grated Parmesan.

For risotto, follow a standard recipe or the one for **Spinach and Lemon Risotto with Scallops** (page 240). Leave out the spinach and stir in 350g picked rabbit meat once the rice is almost cooked.

See also **Hare** (page 139)

Balsamic-Glazed Saddle of Rabbit with Shallots, Mushrooms and Bitter Leaves

This recipe is based on a Tuscan dish in which the sturdy leaves are an integral part rather than a garnish. Their slight bitterness is balanced by the sweetness of balsamic vinegar.

Put the rabbit loins in a frying pan large enough to take them in a single layer. Pour in the vinegar and simmer over medium-high heat, turning several times, for about 15 minutes or until the vinegar is stickily coating the rabbit (the pan will be quite dry by then). Remove the rabbit from the pan and set aside.

Heat the butter and olive oil in the same pan. When the butter is foaming, add the shallots and mushrooms, then add 5–6 tablespoons of the stock. Stir everything around so that the vegetables are coated with the sticky residue. Add the garlic, cook for a minute, then pour in a little more stock to moisten.

Put the rabbit back in the pan and pour in about 300ml of the stock. Add the thyme and season with sea salt and freshly ground black pepper. Cover and leave to cook gently for 25–30 minutes or until the rabbit and shallots are tender. Sprinkle with the parsley, then check the seasoning.

Arrange the leaves on a large serving platter. Place the rabbit, shallots and mushrooms on top, and garnish with the croûtons.

Add the remaining stock to the pan and bubble down the juices over high heat. Pour over the rabbit and vegetables and serve at once.

Cook's notes
• Use the loins from 2 or 3 rabbits, and keep the rest for a casserole.
• When choosing leaves, look for batavia, radicchio or beautiful red-spotted chicory, or use a mixture. Make sure the leaves are dry.

rabbit loin portions 1.3kg (see **Cook's notes**)
balsamic vinegar 150ml (see **Ingredients**, page 12)
butter 25g
extra-virgin olive oil 2 tbsp
small shallots 450g, peeled and left whole
chestnut mushrooms 150g, sliced
chicken or **meat stock** preferably home-made, 600ml
garlic cloves 3, finely chopped
thyme leaves chopped to make 1 tbsp
sea salt flakes
freshly ground black pepper
flat leaf parsley chopped to make 2 tbsp
bitter leaves (see **Cook's notes**) 6–8 good handfuls
Garlic Croûtons (page 112) to garnish

Serves 6–8

Radishes

In the UK we play safe with radishes, preferring the small-rooted red-skinned type rather than more interesting varieties popular in the rest of Europe, the Middle East and Asia. The rough-and-ready black-skinned radish, for example, is the size of a fat carrot and intensely peppery, as are giant-sized red ones so exuberant they practically push themselves out of the ground. Then there are the exotic types with luminous green or raspberry-red flesh. They are dense but juicy with a pleasantly pungent flavour – they look stunning sliced on a plate in a salad (see below). The more familiar long white radish, known as mooli, is milder. The lesser-known varieties all grow perfectly well in the UK and can often be found at farms specialising in salad vegetables.

Cooking

With their crisp peppery flesh, milder radishes are best eaten raw – reserve the fiery ones for cooked dishes. For an appetising snack, or even breakfast, it's hard to beat a plate of glowing red-skinned radishes with a dish of sea salt flakes for dipping. They are also good with elegant triangles of thinly sliced brown bread and butter.

Sliced wafer-thin, mildly flavoured mooli is delicious floated in a clear Japanese-style noodle soup, or try it grated and dressed with a little soy sauce as a relish, or add it to coleslaw. It's also good in a colourful **radish and carrot salad with a hot sesame dressing**. Arrange paper-thin discs of white mooli, green- and red-fleshed radishes, red-skinned radishes and organic carrot on a serving plate – or use just red-skinned radishes and mooli if you can't find the exotic ones. Sprinkle lightly with sea salt flakes. Heat some sesame seeds and extra-virgin sunflower oil in a small saucepan. As soon as the seeds start to pop, pour the sizzling mixture over the radishes and sprinkle with a few drops of toasted sesame oil. Serve right away while the dressing is still warm.

Returning to the fierier dense-fleshed types, peeled and grated **black radish mixed with mayonnaise** makes a palate-tingling accompaniment to cold meats or smoked fish. Use the **celeriac rémoulade** recipe on page 59, but add a little cream and go easy on the mustard.

Also worth trying is a zesty stir-fry of diced red or green radishes tossed quickly in hot oil with mustard seeds, chopped fresh chilli, sea salt flakes and a good handful of shredded mint. Alternatively, cut a selection of large radishes into cubes and add to pickles and curries along with other vegetables.

UK season

May–January.

Varieties to look for

• *'French Breakfast'*, small, elongated, rosy roots, white tips. Mild crisp white flesh.
• *'Mantanghong'*, large, round, green skin. Exquisite dark-pink flesh.
• *'Misato Green'*, large, elongated, green skin and flesh at the top, white on the lower end. Crisp juicy flesh, slightly sweet.
• *'Black Spanish Round'*, large, round, rough black skin. Pungent though slightly sweet.

Shopping notes

• Buy with leaves and roots attached, preferably covered in soil.
• Don't bother with radishes that look spongy or limp.

Storing

• Discard the leaves but leave a short length of stalk attached.
• Wrap in damp paper towels, unwashed, and store in a plastic bag in the salad drawer of the fridge.

Preparation

• Trim and wash when ready to serve.
• Grate, chop or slice according to the recipe.

Raspberries

Plump, sun-warmed and as soft as velvet, raspberries are one of the quintessential summer fruits. The season is agreeably long, starting in June and carrying on well into autumn. Some of the best are grown in Scotland, where fairly dry summers and long daylight hours in midsummer help produce the most delicious berries. Raspberries are at their best when freshly picked and minimally packaged – farm shops and PYO farms are the places to find them.

Cooking

The first raspberries of summer need nothing more than a dusting of caster sugar and perhaps a lick of softly whipped organic Jersey cream. However, as the season wears on, you might want to experiment with other ways of preparing them.

Raspberries are the key ingredient in **summer pudding**. Use them in a ratio of 4:2:1:1 – four parts raspberries, two parts redcurrants, one part blackcurrants and one part cherries. Stew the fruit very lightly with caster sugar and then pack into a basin lined with good-quality white bread. Pour over all the juice so that the bread is well soaked. Cover the surface with more bread, cutting it to fit, then put a weighted plate on top. Leave in the fridge for several hours before turning out. If the bread is not a uniform raspberry red, moisten the paler parts with dilute blackcurrant juice.

Raspberry Chocolate Tartlets (page 222) never fail to please, and raspberry sorbet is always fantastic – vividly pink and packed with intense flavour. Use the recipe for **redcurrant sorbet** (page 225). Alternatively, fork crushed raspberries instead of blackcurrants into **Clotted Cream Ice Cream** (page 88) at the soft scoop stage.

Raspberries can also be quickly whizzed up into a **vibrant sauce** that really hits the spot with sliced peaches or nectarines. Purée 250g raspberries, push through a fine sieve to get rid of the pips, then stir in 1 teaspoon of lemon juice and 1 tablespoon of icing sugar, or to taste.

A large amount of raspberries – 1kg or more – can be put to good use in an easily made **luscious jam**. Put an equal weight of sugar and raspberries into separate roomy ovenproof bowls. Heat slowly at 150°C/gas 2 for 20–30 minutes, or until both are warm all the way through. Carefully stir the sugar into the raspberries, breaking up the fruit as little as possible. Spoon into warm, sterilised jars and cover with a disc of waxed paper dipped in brandy. Seal and store in a cool dark place. Once opened, keep in the fridge and use within 2 weeks.

UK season
• June–October.

Varieties to look for
• *'Autumn Bliss'*, late summer/early autumn variety, large delicious berries.
• *'Glen Ample'*, mid-season, large fleshy bright red berries, excellent flavour.
• *'Glen Prosen'*, early variety, top-quality berries.
• *'Tulameen'*, late variety, medium-to-large berries, aromatic and juicy.

Shopping notes
• Look for plump dry berries with a uniform colour and no signs of mould or bruising.
• Avoid berries with the hulls still in place – they will probably be hard and under-ripe.
• Don't buy punnets with seepage on the base – a sign of mushy fruit.

Storing
• Raspberries are fragile, highly perishable and best eaten on the day you buy them.
• If necessary, they will last for another day if kept in a cool dry place.
• Avoid storing in the fridge – the chill dulls the flavour.

Preparation
• Raspberries grow high off the ground and usually don't need washing. If necessary, briefly dunk in cold water to get rid of insects.
• Drain carefully, then place hollow-end down on paper towels to dry.

Raspberry Chocolate Tartlets (page 222)

Raspberry Chocolate Tartlets

These tartlets are sheer indulgence but only worth making with very tasty sun-warmed raspberries, preferably picked that day.

Put all the pastry ingredients in a food processor and pulse briefly until the dough starts to clump together. Wrap in cling film and chill for 30 minutes.

To make the ganache, break the chocolate into pea-sized pieces and put in a bowl. Heat the cream until almost boiling, then pour over the chocolate and beat until melted and smooth. Leave to cool, then chill.

Preheat the oven to 180°C/gas 4. Lightly oil six metal fluted tartlet tins (10cm diameter). Divide the dough into six equal pieces and form into balls. Roll out on a floured surface into 12-cm circles. Carefully lower into the prepared tins, pressing the dough well into the edges with the side of your forefinger. Pass a rolling pin over the top to trim off surplus dough. Press the dough into the edge again, to raise it slightly above the rim. Line the base with foil and weigh down with baking beans. Bake blind for 10 minutes, then remove the foil and beans, and bake for another 7–8 minutes or until the pastry is crisp. Remove from the oven and leave to cool. Turn out by inverting the tins and tapping gently on the base.

Whip the chilled ganache until just thickened. Spoon into the pastry cases. Arrange the raspberries on top and dust with icing sugar. Serve with a dollop of softly whipped Jersey cream.

Cook's note
• Take care not to over-whip the ganache, otherwise the chocolate will go grainy.

raspberries 400g
icing sugar for dusting
whipped Jersey cream organic, to serve

for the pastry
plain flour 125g
caster sugar 3 tbsp
unsalted butter chilled, 85g
unsweetened cocoa powder $2\frac{1}{2}$ tbsp
whipping cream organic, 3 tbsp

for the chocolate ganache
plain chocolate (at least 70% cocoa solids), 100g
Jersey double cream organic, 225ml

Makes 6

Redcurrants

Like the gooseberry, there is something quintessentially 'northern' about redcurrants. The glistening scarlet fruits give the initial impression of southern sun-warmed provenance but the actual flavour is somewhat austere – sweet for sure, but with a kick of acidity and perhaps a fleeting bitterness.

The currants grow well in the cool climates of Scandinavia, Germany and the UK, but are rarely found further south. They have a brief midsummer season, though there are somewhat flavourless specimens imported year-round from the Netherlands. To appreciate redcurrants at their peak, buy them from a farm shop, freshly picked and minimally packaged, or better still from a PYO farm.

Cooking

As long as they are very ripe and sprinkled with plenty of sugar, redcurrants are lovely to eat on their own. Mixed with other soft fruit, they add balancing bite and glistening colour. They are essential for **summer pudding** (see **Raspberries**, page 220) – without their mouth-puckering juice the pudding would be cloyingly sweet. A handful added to **Compôte of Dark Fruits in Spiced Syrup** (page 196) is also good. I love to decorate ices and jellies with perfect strings of redcurrants, sometimes frosted with egg white and sugar.

Redcurrants are also good partners for creamy chilled desserts, the dairy element toning down their acidity, and the scarlet juice adding much-needed colour. For a simple **syrup** or **compôte** to spoon over ice cream or cheesecake, cook 500g redcurrants with 150g caster sugar until soft. Drain and put the currants in a bowl. Pour the syrup back into the pan and cook until slightly thickened. Pour over the currants and add more sugar to taste. Once cool, the compôte is also good mixed with beaten curd cheese or cream cheese.

On a savoury note, redcurrants add a welcome tartness and rich colour to **gravy for serving with fatty roasts** such as lamb, pork or duck. Pour off excess fat from the roasting tin, and sprinkle the meat juices with 1 tablespoon of flour. Stir briskly over medium heat until the flour is incorporated, then deglaze the pan with about 500ml stock, scraping up any tasty sticky sediment. Stir in a small punnet of redcurrants and simmer for 5 minutes, squashing the currants with the back of a wooden spoon. If you like, stir in a spoonful of redcurrant jelly to sweeten and mellow the flavour. Season with salt and freshly ground black pepper.

UK season
• June–August.

Varieties to look for
• *'Jonkheer van Tets'*, early variety with large berries.
• *'Red Lake'*, mid-season variety with outstandingly long strings.

Shopping notes
• Look for plump gleaming sprays of currants attached to the strings.
• Check for mouldy or bruised fruit.
• Don't buy punnets with seepage on the base – a sign of mushy fruit.

Storing
• Redcurrants last longer if attached to their strings.
• They are best eaten on the day you buy them. If necessary, they will last for another day if kept in a cool dry place.
• Avoid storing in the fridge – the chill dulls the flavour.

Preparation
• Remove the strings by pulling them through the tines of a fork.
• Briefly dunk in cold water to get rid of dust and insects. Drain and dry thoroughly on paper towels.

Redcurrant Sorbet

Capture the essence of redcurrants in this intensely flavoured sorbet – at its best within a few days of making.

Put the sugar and water in a saucepan. Stir over medium heat until the sugar has dissolved. Bring to the boil briefly, then remove from the heat and leave to cool.

Purée the redcurrants in a food processor or blender, then push through a fine sieve to get rid of the pips, extracting as much juice as possible. Mix with the cold syrup, cover and chill for 2 hours.

Churn and freeze in an ice cream machine. Once thickened, store in the freezer to harden.

Put in the fridge to soften about 30 minutes before serving. Scoop into tall serving glasses and decorate with sprigs of redcurrants and borage flowers if you have any.

Cook's note
• If you don't have an ice cream machine, follow the directions for still-freezing Quince and Ginger Sorbet (page 213).

sugar 200g
water 300ml
redcurrants 450g, rinsed and stringed (see Preparation, page 223)
redcurrant sprigs to decorate
borage flowers to decorate (optional)

Makes 750ml

Rhubarb

Rhubarb suffers from an old-fashioned image, causing many to shudder at best-forgotten memories of school meals or hospital food. That said, the past few years have seen a rhubarb renaissance as people have rediscovered its clean refreshing flavour and become aware of the health benefits.

Particularly welcome is the early forced variety with slim shocking-pink stems and tiny lime green leaves. Grown in mysterious candle-lit forcing sheds in the 'rhubarb triangle' of West Yorkshire, forced rhubarb is the only fresh home-grown fruit to be found in late winter.

Outdoor-grown rhubarb arrives in spring. The stems are thicker and the colour a deep red tinged with green. As the season progresses, the stems become increasingly thick and coarse, and the flavour changes from merely sour to excessively so.

Cooking

Stewed and served with custard, rhubarb has long been a homely staple, but with its glorious colour and powerful tart flavour, it has far greater culinary potential. It makes beautiful pink-tinged ice creams and sorbets that are especially delicious flavoured with herbs such as angelica or sweet cicely (**Rhubarb and Angelica Sorbet**, page 228). It also goes well with the subtle aniseed flavour of Pernod as in **Rhubarb and Orange Tart with Pernod** (opposite).

Carefully cooked so the stems don't disintegrate, rhubarb makes a pretty pink **compôte**. You will need about 450g, trimmed and cut into 2.5cm diagonal slices. Make a light syrup by boiling 75g sugar with 450ml water for 5 minutes. Drop in the rhubarb and boil for 30 seconds exactly. It will look barely cooked, but if you leave it for one second too long you'll end up with a stringy soup. Quickly drain into a bowl. Put the rhubarb in a serving bowl and the syrup back in the pan. Boil hard for 5 minutes, then pour over the rhubarb and leave to cool. Should the rhubarb collapse, you can improve matters by adding 2 thinly sliced bananas to give the dish some substance.

Later in summer, fat stems of main-crop rhubarb come in handy for a tasty **rhubarb and cranberry chutney**. Chop 450g trimmed rhubarb and put in a stainless steel saucepan with a sliced lemon (peel and pith removed). Add 150g dried cranberries, 450g soft brown sugar, 300ml cider vinegar, 2.5-cm piece thinly sliced fresh ginger root, 1 tablespoon of salt and a sliver of fresh red chilli. Lightly crush 5 allspice berries, 5 cloves and $\frac{1}{4}$ teaspoon of black peppercorns, and add to the pan. Stir over gentle heat until the sugar has dissolved. Bring to the boil, stirring, then simmer briskly for 50–60 minutes or until you can see the base of the pan when you draw a wooden spoon through the mixture. Stir constantly during the last 5 minutes of cooking. Pour into sterilised jars, cover with wax discs and seal.

- *Forced*: January–February.
- *Early outdoor-grown*: March–May.
- *Main-crop*: May–September.

Varieties to look for
- *'Early Champagne'*, early variety, less acidic than the thicker main-crop variety.
- *'Fulton's Strawberry Surprise'*, superb flavour.

Shopping notes
- Look for sprightly stems that are not excessively large.
- Steer clear of stems that are limp, split or bruised.

Storing
- Keep loosely wrapped in the fridge for 2–3 days. Rhubarb soon becomes limp.

Preparation
- The leaves are poisonous and should always be removed.
- Trim the root end and peel away any strings from large stems.
- Slice the stem with a very sharp knife according to the recipe.

Rhubarb and Orange Tart with Pernod

This is very little trouble to make using good-quality ready-made pastry. For a beautiful shocking pink colour, use forced rhubarb with slender stems.

Cut the rhubarb into 2.5-cm diagonal slices and put in a non-reactive dish. Combine the cornflour, caster sugar, Pernod and orange zest in a small bowl. Mix with the rhubarb, tossing until well coated. Leave to stand for about 30 minutes, stirring occasionally, until the juices are flowing from the rhubarb.

Preheat the oven to 170°C/gas 3. Lightly grease a 23-cm loose-bottomed tart tin. Form the pastry into a thick disk, then roll out very thinly and use to line the tin. Pass a rolling pin over the top to trim off excess dough. Using the side of your forefinger, press the dough into the edge of the tin to raise it slightly above the rim. Line the base with foil and weigh down with baking beans, making sure they go all the way to the edge.

Bake blind for 10 minutes, then remove the foil and baking beans, and bake for 5 minutes more. Remove from the oven and raise the temperature to 190°C/gas 5.

Spoon the rhubarb mixture into the pastry case. Bake for 45 minutes or until the edges of the rhubarb begin to blacken slightly. Sprinkle with extra caster sugar and the sweet cicely seeds and leaves if you are using them. Serve hot or warm but not cold.

Cook's note
• The green unripe seeds from the flower heads of sweet cicely have a similar flavour to Pernod and look beautiful scattered over the pink rhubarb.

young pink rhubarb trimmed, 300g
cornflour 2 tsp
caster sugar 75g, plus extra for sprinkling
Pernod 1 tbsp
orange finely grated zest of 1
ready-made sweet shortcrust pastry 200g
sweet cicely seeds and tiny leaves (optional) 2 tsp

Serves 4–6

Rhubarb and Angelica Sorbet

Rhubarb and angelica go together remarkably well. You will need the fresh herb rather than the crystallised stems used in baking. It grows like a giant celery plant and has a huge flower head. A specialist herb farm would be a good place to find it.

Slice the rhubarb into 2.5-cm pieces. Leave the angelica stems in longer lengths so you can remove them later. Put the rhubarb and angelica in a saucepan with the sugar and water. Stir over gentle heat until the sugar has dissolved. Bring to the boil, then simmer briskly for 5–7 minutes or until the rhubarb collapses. Remove from the heat and leave until cold, then fish out the angelica stems.

Purée the rhubarb mixture in a food processor then stir in the lemon juice. Taste and add a little more sugar if necessary. Chill for at least 2 hours, then churn and freeze in an ice cream machine. Once thickened, store in the freezer to harden.

Cook's notes
• Make this in early summer while rhubarb is still young and pink, and angelica has not yet gone to seed.
• Eat within 24 hours while the delicate flavour is at its best.
• If you don't have an ice cream machine, follow the directions for still-freezing Quince and Ginger Sorbet (page 213).

young rhubarb trimmed, 450g
angelica stems 100g
caster sugar 300g, plus extra to taste
water 300ml
lemon juice of $^1/_2$

Makes about 750ml

Salad and Micro-Leaves

If you enjoy creating salads, farm shops are the place to buy inspiring leaves that haven't been washed in chlorine or incarcerated in a pillow pack. Here you are likely to find plump and robust lettuces that remain in good condition even if stored for several days. There will also be capacious bags of mixed leaves containing more varieties than you knew existed – New Zealand spinach, sorrel and beautiful red-spotted chicory, as well as tender young kale, beet and chard leaves. If you are lucky, fragrant leafy herbs and edible flower petals will be mixed in too, adding delicious flavours and bright colours. In autumn and winter you might find a range of oriental leaves such as tatsoi, mizuna, mitsuba and peppery mustard greens. Many of these leaves can only be found in farm shops; they don't travel well, nor do they survive well in supermarket pillow packs.

Micro-leaves are miniature versions of salad leaves and herbs harvested at the seedling stage. They look a bit like mustard and cress and come in little punnets with their roots embedded in a growing medium. Despite their minuscule size micro leaves are intensely flavoured, seeming to encapsulate the essence of the full-grown plant.

Cooking

When putting together a mixed leaf salad, it's best to use a variety of colours, textures and flavours. To give your salad sparkle, contrast light and dark, tender and robust, bitter and sweet. Peppery leaves such as nasturtium and rocket add dimension to a salad, whereas soft buttery lettuces add substance.

Choose the dressing according to the type of leaf. Those with a hot mustardy flavour are sometimes better with nut or seed oil rather than olive oil. Extra-virgin sunflower oil is pleasantly nutty and combines well with oriental leaves. Micro-leaves need a dressing so light it's barely there.

Some of the more robust leaves are unexpectedly versatile. They add an earthy note to a salad, but if they seem too strongly flavoured or chewy when raw, they can be quickly tamed by wilting them in a little oil over medium heat.

In moderation, bitter-tasting chicories are superb in salads but they can also be grilled, oven-baked, sautéed, braised or added to risottos and pasta dishes. They are an excellent foil to rich meaty dishes such as **Balsamic-Glazed Saddle of Rabbit with Shallots, Mushrooms and Bitter Leaves** (page 218).

Power-packed micro-leaves have a myriad uses. They make a striking garnish, adding hot-spots of flavour and colour to a host of different dishes. Try them scattered over a cucumber salad or one made with thinly sliced juicy roots such as radishes or kohlrabi. Use them in sandwiches or sprinkle generously over soups, rice dishes, omelettes, grilled or fried fish and stir-fries. Heat dulls the flavour – add them at the last minute so they remain more or less raw.

UK season
- *Chicory and endive:* October–March.
- *Lettuce:* May–October.
- *Micro-leaves:* year-round.
- *Oriental leaves:* July–November.
- *Rocket:* April–December.

Salad leaves to look for
- *Mizuna:* long thin leaves with serrated edges. Slightly peppery, sweet but not hot.
- *Mustard:* red-tinted or green leaves. Punchy flavour, use sparingly.
- *Radicchio:* 'Tardivo di Treviso', elongated white-veined burgundy-red leaves. Robust texture and flavour.
- *Tatsoi:* oval flat dark green leaves with fleshy white stalk. Lots of body, mild flavour.
- *Wild rocket:* deeply-toothed leaves. Peppery flavour, best when young.

Micro-leaves to look for
- *Mustard:* green-red leaves, pleasant mustardy flavour.
- *Pea shoots:* round pea-green leaves and tendrils, concentrated pea flavour.
- *Sakura:* thick rich green leaves, strong onion flavour.
- *Shiso (red perilla):* deep purple spiky leaves, mild aniseed flavour.
- *Thai basil:* delicate lance-shaped leaves, cinnamon flavour.

Shopping notes
- Loose salad greens and micro leaves should look dewy fresh.
- Don't buy radicchio or with brown patches along the leaf edges.

Storing
- *Whole lettuces*: store unwashed in a roomy plastic bag in the salad drawer of the fridge for up to 1 week.
- *Loose salad greens*: wash, dry and blot on paper towels. Roll up loosely in the paper towel and store in a large unsealed plastic bag in the salad drawer of the fridge for up to 1 week.
- *Micro leaves*: store in the punnet in the salad drawer of the fridge for 1–2 days.

Salsify and Scorzonera

To put the record straight, the thin black root usually sold as salsify is not salsify at all but the more common scorzonera. The two are easy to distinguish once you know which is which. Salsify tapers to a point and has thin light brown skin sprouting a tangle of long whiskers; scorzonera is a uniform thickness along its length and has a bark-like sepia skin and just a smattering of whiskers. The name comes from the Italian *scorza* (bark) and *nera* (black).

This muddled identity is of little consequence once the roots are cooked. They are virtually indistinguishable, although, if pushed, one could say that salsify tastes midly of oyster, giving credence to the 'oyster plant' nickname. Both share the irritating habit of bleeding milky latex when cut, making hands and pans difficult to clean, and both have the same wind-inducing capacity as the Jerusalem artichoke, to which they are related.

You might find the roots on sale at a farm shop, perhaps with the leaves still attached. Don't discard these – they are juicy with a pleasing bitter-sweet flavour and excellent tossed in a tomato salad.

Cooking

Salsify and scorzonera have a rich but subtle flavour, something akin to artichokes or even asparagus, but not quite like any of these.

They are best either boiled or steamed, and finished with a quick sizzle in melted butter and a little lemon juice (**Buttered Scorzonera with Green Peppercorns and Lemon**, opposite). They are tasty served cold (but not chilled), dressed with good olive oil, lemon juice and chopped flat leaf parsley. Scorzonera also make excellent chips – irresistible with horseradish cream (page 141).

Traditional recipes advocate preserving the milky colour by cooking the roots in 'a rather questionable sludge of water, flour, vinegar and lemon juice', as chef Rowley Leigh puts it. I have found this unnecessary, although cooking them in a 2:1 solution of milk and water produces a richer flavour and softer texture. Another culinary myth is that the roots must be cooked for up to an hour. This is simply not true; depending on thickness, 12–20 minutes is long enough.

The roots go well with mild-flavoured ingredients such as scallops, prawns or mushrooms. They are also good with cheese sauce in a bubbling gratin, or try them with cream and Parmesan instead of butter and lemon juice.

Shopping notes
• Avoid roots that are broken, flabby or wizened.
• Choose salsify that is as whisker-free as possible.

Storing
• Store roots unwashed and loosely wrapped in a paper bag in the salad drawer of the fridge, for up to 1 week.
• The roots will keep for several weeks in a dry shed or outhouse.

Preparation
• Scrub well when ready to use.
• Wear rubber gloves to prevent staining.
• Scorzonera may be cooked unpeeled and the skin removed afterwards. Otherwise, peel and drop into water acidulated with lemon juice.

Buttered Scorzonera with Green Peppercorns and Lemon

This is one of the simplest and best methods of serving scorzonera or salsify. It's especially delicious with grilled Dover sole or sautéed chicken breasts.

Put the scorzonera in a large saucepan of salted water to which you have added half the lemon juice. Bring to the boil, then reduce the heat slightly and simmer briskly for 15–20 minutes until the roots are just tender. Drain and slice diagonally into finger-length pieces.

Heat a heavy-based frying pan over medium heat. Add the butter and green peppercorns. Swirl for a few seconds until sizzling, then add the scorzonera and season with crumbled sea salt flakes. When starting to colour, increase the heat and stir in the parsley and the rest of the lemon juice.

Cook's note
• Use dried green peppercorns rather than brine-cured. Best for colour and flavour are Bart Spices biodynamic green peppercorns from Kerala in southwest India. They are easy to find in large farm shops.

scorzonera 750g, scrubbed and peeled
lemon juice of 1
unsalted butter 50g
dried green peppercorns $^3/_4$ tsp, lightly crushed
sea salt flakes
flat leaf parsley leaves chopped to make 1 tbsp

Serves 4–6 as a side dish

Sausages

A good sausage is a thing of beauty – plump, clean-smelling and moist with a slightly shiny natural casing. When cooked, the smell and the sizzle, let alone the taste, are irresistible. There are no explosions, shrinkage or leaking of dubious liquid – just a nice fat glossy brown banger. Fortunately there are a growing band of farms that pride themselves on hand-produced bangers. Made with organic, rare breed or properly reared free-range meat, these are a million miles from mass-produced sausages.

The majority of sausages are made with pork but there are also lamb, beef, venison and wild boar sausages. My local farm shop even sells goat meat sausages. These meats are more strongly flavoured than pork and the texture can be denser.

Worth looking out for are regional sausages each with their own special seasoning. Some, like the Cumberland are well-known and sold nationwide; others are found only in their particular region (see **Sausages to look for**).

Cooking

Sausages may be cooked in a number of ways: fried, grilled, barbecued or baked in the oven. Regardless of method, the rule of thumb is to cook them slowly so they brown evenly and the skins don't burst. The skins are there to trap moisture and keep the sausage succulent; it cannot do so if punctured. To avoid the risk, cook them in a non-stick pan and use tongs for turning.

To fry: cook for 20 minutes over medium-low heat, turning three or four times. Another way is to fry them very slowly over the lowest possible heat, waiting for about 10 minutes until each side is brown and sticky before turning. This method can take up to an hour, but you will end up with a beautifully cooked sausage.

To grill: place in a grill pan under a medium-hot heat for 10–15 minutes, turning occasionally.

To barbecue: position well above the coals and wait until the fire has mellowed, otherwise you'll end up with burnt skins and raw insides. (**Barbecued Cumberland Sausage Coil Sandwiches**, page 234)

To bake: place in a shallow non-stick roasting tray and cook in a preheated oven at 180°C/gas 4 for 35–45 minutes depending on size. Turn two or three times and baste with the juices or a little extra oil to prevent drying.

Sausages have traditional accompaniments: egg, chips, baked beans, ketchup or HP sauce are all possibilities. I love them with **caramelised onions** (page 172) and **bashed potatoes** (page 202). They are also good with **celeriac rémoulade** (page 59) or added to a potato salad. Spicy sausages are delicious cut into chunks and added to risotto or pasta, or used as a topping for **Eggs with Fried Tomato, Onion and Peppers** (page 103).

See also **Black pudding** (page 40)

Sausages to look for
- *Cumberland:* coarse-textured, made in a continuous coil. Distinctive peppery flavour.
- *Gloster:* large fat and stubby, made from Gloucester Old Spot pork. Rich herbal flavour.
- *Lincolnshire:* mottled pink, flecked with green herbs. Punchy sage flavour.
- *Newmarket:* brownish-pink, flecked with herbs. Spicy flavour.
- *Oxford:* short and fat, pale pink, flecked with herbs. Lemony herbal flavour.

Shopping notes
- Look for plump sausages with slightly shiny skins and no air bubbles.
- The meat content should be at least 70%.
- The label on packaged sausages should clearly state that the meat is British or bear the Quality Standard or Little Red Tractor marks.

Storing
- Store covered in the fridge for 2–3 days depending on 'use by' date.

Preparation
- Do not prick sausages before cooking – good ones don't need it.
- Cut the links cleanly with a sharp knife or scissors.

Barbecued Cumberland Sausage Coil Sandwiches (page 234)

Barbecued Cumberland Sausage Coil Sandwiches

Craggy toasted bread, good olive oil, spicy sausages and mustard –
this must be one of the most appetising sandwiches ever.

Brush the sausage coils with olive oil on both sides and place on the
barbecue (see **Cook's note**). Keep moving and turning them to begin
with, to stop any flare-ups. Once the coils have started to brown, push
a wad of rosemary sprigs underneath each one – this adds a wonderful
fragrance and protects the coils from the heat. Grill for about 15 minutes
until cooked through and slightly charred.

Toast the bread on the barbecue with the sausage coils. When it is
browned on both sides, remove from the grill and rub one side of each
slice with the crushed garlic. Put on a platter, garlic-side up, and
sprinkle with a little olive oil.

Place a sausage coil on two of the slices. Add your chosen
condiment, place the other slices on top, slice in half with a sharp
bread knife and tuck in.

Cook's note
• You will need a medium-hot barbecue for this. The fire is at the
perfect temperature when you can hold your hand close to the coals for
6–8 seconds (count slowly) before it gets too hot.

Cumberland sausage coils 2, weighing
about 250g each
extra-virgin olive oil
rosemary sprigs
good crusty bread 4 large slices, about
1–1.5cm thick
large garlic clove 1, peeled and very lightly
crushed
mustard and **relishes** to serve

Serves 2–4 as a substantial snack

Sausage Toad with Caramelised Onions

This is real comfort food – fortifying and filling, with lovely sticky
onions. Wonderful with buttered steamed cabbage and mashed
potatoes.

First make the batter: whisk all the ingredients together and leave to
rest while you cook the sausages.

Heat a non-stick frying pan over low heat. Add the sausages (don't prick
them) and fry gently for 30 minutes until brown and sticky. The longer
and more slowly you fry them, the better they will be.

Preheat the oven to 220°C/gas 7. Put the lard in a small roasting tin
and heat in the oven for 2–3 minutes until the fat is almost smoking.
Pour in the batter, arrange the sausages on top and scatter with the
caramelised onions. Bake for 30–35 minutes or until well-risen and
golden. Serve right away.

Cook's notes
• If you don't have any caramelised onions to hand, make up a batch
while the sausages are frying. They'll be ready at more or less the same
time.
• Reduce the oven temperature to 200°C/gas 6 after 20 minutes if the
batter looks too brown.

meaty pork sausages 8
lard or **groundnut oil** 2 tbsp
Caramelised Onions (page 172) 6 tbsp

for the batter
plain flour 125g
eggs organic 2, lightly beaten
whole milk organic, 150ml
water 150ml

Serves 3–4

Shallots

A member of the onion family, shallots have their own distinctive flavour – fresh, sweet and piquant, and, since they are less watery than onions, more full-bodied. Though it is possible to use both vegetables interchangeably, there are many dishes in which the mellower nature of the shallot is preferable. There are two types: the large single-bulb torpedo-shaped variety, sometimes called a banana shallot, and the smaller round ones that divide into two fat cloves.

Cooking

When chopped and cooked, shallots melt down to a well-flavoured purée that forms the foundation of many classic French dishes. They are a key ingredient in *mirepoix* – diced carrot, celery and shallots – used as a bed for braised meats or as a flavouring for sauces. They also go into *duxelles* – a mixture of sautéed mushrooms and shallots that adds bulk and flavour to a number of dishes. They add balancing sweetness and depth of flavour to *beurre blanc* (white butter sauce) used for anointing white fish, and the traditional caper sauce served with mutton (**Poached Leg of Mutton with Caramelised Onions and Caper Sauce**, page 157).

Although shallots are usually associated with French cooking, they are equally indispensable in Southeast Asian cuisine. Here they are sliced and deep-fried and used as a golden garnish for salads and rice dishes. They are also pounded with lemongrass, chillies, coriander and other seasonings to make a fragrant paste for curries.

The larger torpedo-shaped banana shallots are delicious roasted whole until caramelised as in the recipe opposite – perfect with roast beef or lamb. They will also add tremendous body to **Colourful Beets with Roasted Shallot and Chilli Dressing** (page 33).

UK season
December–March.

Varieties to look for
• *Banana shallot*, large torpedo-shaped bulbs with thin pink skin.
• *'Echalotte grise'*, round dark bulbs, the shallot of choice for French chefs, exceptional flavour.
• *'Red Sun'*, deep red-brown skin, excellent flavour.

Shopping notes
• Look for plump solid bulbs with tight skin.
• Reject shallots that are soft, mouldy or sprouting.

Storing
• If stored in a cool airy place away from light, small round shallots will keep for a couple of months.
• Banana shallots deteriorate more easily – they will keep for up to 2 weeks in a cool dark place.

Preparation
• To make peeling small shallots easier, blanch in boiling water for 1 minute to loosen the skin, then drain and run under cold water.

Roasted Banana Shallots with Sage, Parmesan and Crisp Breadcrumbs

These large torpedo-shaped shallots are mild, and sweet, so don't be daunted by the idea of eating a whole one.

Preheat the oven to 220°C/gas 7. Peel the shallots and halve them lengthways. Arrange in a single layer in a roasting tin. Brush generously with rapeseed oil and sprinkle with the breadcrumbs, sage, sea salt flakes and black pepper. Roast for 30–35 minutes until the shallots are soft and the crumbs golden and crisp.

Using a swivel peeler, shave thin flakes from the Parmesan and sprinkle over the shallots.

banana shallots 9 large
rapeseed oil for brushing
fresh breadcrumbs (preferably made from a stale sourdough loaf) 50g
sage leaves chopped to make 1 tbsp
sea salt flakes
coarsely ground black pepper
Parmesan cheese 85g

Serves 5–6 as a side dish or 3 as a vegetarian main course

Spelt

Currently a must-have ingredient, spelt is an ancient form of wheat believed to be a staple food of the Romans, which probably accounts for its spread from the Middle East to northern Europe. Though an important crop from ancient times up to the Middle Ages, spelt gradually fell out of use. It is now making a comeback, spearheaded by organic farms such as Sharpham Park in Somerset and Doves Farm Foods in Berkshire.

Like barley, spelt is a nutritional super-star, rich in protein and cholesterol-lowering soluble fibre, and packed with useful vitamins and minerals. It also tastes good – rich and nutty with a pleasantly creamy texture but still with some bite. Many people with a wheat intolerance find it more digestible, though there is no scientific evidence as to why this should be. As a result, however, spelt bread and flour are increasingly available.

Cooking

Pearled spelt is cooked just like rice and can be used in a risotto as in **Spelt with Asparagus** (page 238). The grains become creamy like risotto rice but, being not quite as absorbent, they keep some of their texture. Use it in place of barley in **Barley with Celery, Preserved Lemon and Spices** (page 25) or to add body to soups as in **Celery and Dill Soup with Spelt** (page 63).

Combined with robust greenery, morsels of chicken or game and a light dressing, spelt makes a mouthwatering and satisfying salad. Try it with shredded treviso and grilled sliced duck breasts or saddle of rabbit, or in **Warm Salad of Pheasant Breasts with Wet Walnuts and Bacon** (page 189). The trick is to use just enough spelt to make its presence felt but not so much that it overwhelms other ingredients.

Types of spelt
Wholegrain: beige-coloured grains minimally processed to remove the inedible husk. Needs lengthy soaking and cooking.
Pearled or semi-pearled spelt: whole grains polished to a creamy colour. Needs no soaking. Can be cooked like rice or pearled barley.
Spelt flakes: whole grain or pearled spelt that has been steam-rolled and dried. Add to muesli or use in baking.

Shopping notes
• Buy packaged spelt that is well within the 'use by' date.
• If buying loose spelt, buy in quantities that you will use within a few months.

Storing
• Keep in an airtight container in a cool dark cupboard or in the fridge.
• Never mix a new batch with an old one.

Preparation
• Rinse in several changes of water to get rid of dust.
• Soak wholegrain spelt overnight before cooking.

Spelt with Asparagus

This is loosely based on rice supremo Gabriele Ferron's risotto recipe, which I learned to make at his cooking school near Modena, Italy. I have used pearled spelt instead of rice, which gives the dish a slightly different texture.

Snap the woody ends from the asparagus and set aside to use in the broth. Steam the spears over boiling water for 6 minutes. Remove from the heat and pour the cooking liquid into a measuring jug. Remove the tips, then chop the stalks into small pieces and reserve both.

Next make the broth. Heat the rapeseed oil in a small saucepan over medium heat. Add the herbs, diced asparagus trimmings, vegetables and black peppercorns. Stir for a minute or so, then cover and cook for 10 minutes, stirring occasionally to prevent sticking. Add enough water to the asparagus cooking liquid to make 1 litre, and add this to the herbs and vegetables. Bring to the boil, then reduce the heat and simmer, covered, for 30 minutes. Strain (there should be 700ml) and pour the broth back into the pan. Keep warm over low heat.

Heat a large non-stick frying pan over medium heat. Add the rapeseed oil and half the butter, and fry the shallots until soft but not coloured. Stir in the spelt and keep stirring until the grains are heated through and shiny. Sprinkle in the wine, stir until the liquid is absorbed, then add a ladleful of broth. Keep stirring and adding small amounts of broth until it is all used up.

Add the reserved asparagus and season with salt and freshly ground black pepper. Lightly stir in the Parmesan and remaining butter. Remove from the heat, cover and leave to stand for 3 minutes. Transfer to a warm serving dish and sprinkle with chopped parsley.

asparagus 400g
rapeseed oil 2 tbsp
butter 50g
shallots 2, finely chopped
pearled spelt 350g, rinsed
white wine 100ml
salt
freshly ground black pepper
Parmesan cheese 40g, grated
flat leaf parsley chopped, to garnish

for the broth
rapeseed oil 1 tbsp
thyme 1 sprig
fresh bay leaf 1, torn
flat leaf parsley small handful
asparagus trimmings diced
carrot 1, diced
onion 1, diced
celery stalk 1, diced
black peppercorns $1/4$ tsp

Serves 4

Spinach

Love it or hate it, spinach is one of the most versatile and delicious vegetables. Eaten raw, the juicy but brittle green leaves have a delectable meaty flavour, slightly salty even, with an astringent but not unpleasant aftertaste. When cooked, the flavour becomes rich and buttery, the texture silky smooth – deeply satisfying in every way. Farm shops are good places to buy it freshly picked and immersed in a bucket of water rather than imprisoned in a pillow pack.

Cooking

Spinach is best cooked simply, either by boiling or steaming, or lightly sautéed. Composed mostly of water, the leaves dramatically reduce in bulk once cooked.

For **plainly boiled spinach**, stuff the leaves into a saucepan without adding any extra water – there will be enough from washing. Sprinkle with salt, clap on the lid and cook over medium-low heat, stirring after about 5 minutes. Uncover and cook over higher heat until just tender, then drain in a colander pressing with the back of a wooden spoon. Return to the pan and reheat gently. Season generously with sea salt and freshly ground black pepper. Freshly grated nutmeg, dried chilli flakes or wisps of grated lemon zest are all good additions.

To **sauté spinach** for serving with pasta, for instance, heat about 8 tablespoons of olive oil in a large frying pan over medium-high heat. Slice the spinach into broad ribbons and add to the pan with some finely chopped shallot. Cover and cook for a minute or two until wilted. Uncover and toss until barely tender. Add seasonings as suggested for boiled spinach above, and toss with cooked pasta shapes. Sprinkle with toasted breadcrumbs and freshly grated Parmesan cheese.

Spinach is also very good in a simple risotto as in **Spinach and Lemon Risotto with Scallops** (page 240). There is no need to pre-cook the leaves – the heat from the rice will be enough to wilt them and their juice will flavour the rice in turn.

Spinach has a special affinity with dairy products and eggs; both seem to tame any tendency to mouth-puckering sharpness. Classic is **Eggs Florentine**. Sit a softly poached egg on a mound of well-seasoned wilted spinach, top with creamy cheese sauce and bake in a hot oven (about 220°C/gas 7) until golden and bubbling. This hits the spot for Sunday brunch or a meat-free supper.

For a **spicy spinach and yogurt sauce** to go with omelettes or kebabs, fry a large chopped onion in oil in a spacious pan. When soft, stir in $1/4$ teaspoon each of turmeric and crushed cumin seeds. Cook for a few seconds, then add 500g spinach, trimmed, washed and chopped. Season with salt and freshly ground black pepper, then stir over medium-high heat for about 5 minutes until wilted. Drain off any excess liquid, then leave to cool. Mix with 175ml thick Greek-style organic yogurt, and add more salt and black pepper as necessary.

UK season
• April–October.

Varieties to look for
• *'Bordeaux Red'*, striking red stems and star-shaped leaves. Buttery nutty flavour, melt-in-the-mouth texture. Superb balance of acidity, bitterness and sweetness.
• *'Mediana'*, green stems, juicy tender leaves. Pleasantly earthy flavour, astringent aftertaste.
• *'Scenic'*, soft, downy, melt-in-the-mouth leaves, earthy, slightly bitter flavour, well balanced by sweetness and acidity.

Shopping notes
• Look for dewy-fresh bright green leaves, avoiding any that are bruised or yellowing.
• If buying packaged spinach, make sure the leaves aren't bruised or slimy.

Storing
• Wash and dry as below, then spread out in single layers on paper towels. Roll up loosely and store in a roomy, unsealed plastic bag in the salad drawer of the fridge for up to 2 days.

Preparation
• Trim off any tough stalks.
• Wash in several changes of water allowing the leaves to soak each time so that dirt and grit sink to the bottom of the bowl. Drain and dry in a salad spinner, then blot on paper towels.

Spinach and Lemon Risotto with Scallops

This is a simple fresh-tasting risotto which makes a good backdrop to the delicately flavoured scallops. I particularly like the way the liquid from the spinach helps cook the risotto, making it wonderfully tasty, creamy and moist.

Heat a wide heavy-based saucepan or high-sided frying pan over medium heat. Add 2 tablespoons of rapeseed oil and half the butter, and fry the shallots until soft but not coloured. Stir in the rice, and keep stirring until the grains are heated through and shiny. Pour in the wine, stir until the liquid is absorbed, then add a ladleful of stock. Keep stirring and adding small amounts of stock for about 15 minutes until the rice is just *al dente* – tender but slightly firm in the middle.

Stir the spinach and lemon zest through the rice. Season with crumbled sea salt flakes and plenty of freshly ground black pepper. Lightly stir in the Parmesan and remaining butter. Remove from the heat, cover and leave to stand for 5 minutes.

While the risotto is resting, brush the scored scallops with oil, then season with sea salt and black pepper. Heat a non-stick frying pan until very hot. Fry the scallops for 3–4 minutes on one side until the cut edges begin to brown, resisting the urge to turn them too soon. Cook the other side for 2 minutes or until the flesh is dense white.

Tip the risotto into a warm serving dish and serve with the scallops on top.

Cook's note
• The rice should be slightly on the dry side when you add the spinach; the leaves will give off plenty of liquid in addition to the stock. The rice will gradually absorb it and will continue to do so during the 5-minute standing period.

rapeseed oil 2 tbsp, plus extra for brushing
butter 50g
shallots 2, finely chopped
risotto rice such as Carnaroli, 375g
white wine 100ml
hot chicken or **vegetable stock** 600–700ml
baby spinach 200g, roughly sliced
lemon zest grated to make 2 tsp
sea salt flakes
freshly ground black pepper
Parmesan cheese 40g, grated
large scallops 12, scored with a criss-cross pattern

Serves 4

Sprouting Broccoli

The arrival of the first sprouting broccoli is a high point in the culinary calendar. It's a sign that winter is on its way out and better things are in store for the cook.

Sprouting broccoli bears little resemblance to its flabby cousin calabrese, or 'broccoli' as it is erroneously called. Its branching stems sprout verdant leaves and are tipped with bite-sized clusters of tightly packed purple or creamy-white flower heads. The leaves are delicious and can be cooked along with the flower heads and stems.

Cooking

Like most green vegetables, sprouting broccoli is agreeably adaptable. It goes well with assertive ingredients such as chilli, garlic, anchovies and Parmesan as in **Sautéed Sprouting Broccoli with Chillies and Garlic** (page 242). It is also good baked in a golden bubbling gratin with a rich blue cheese sauce, or, to really deepen the flavour, try it tossed in oil and sea salt flakes and roasted at 220°C/gas 7 until tender.

Sprouting broccoli spears can be treated like asparagus, although, unlike the Italians, we tend not to award it that status. In terms of texture and flavour the two are similar. Try lightly cooked spears with typical asparagus accompaniments such as melted butter, hollandaise sauce or soft-cooked eggs.

For serving *al dente*, either as above or dressed with extra-virgin olive oil and lemon juice, the spears are better steamed rather than boiled – they ship less water and remain crunchy. However, if destined for a gratin or frittata, for example, boiling is a better option. The spears will be softer and looser, and integrate better with other ingredients.

It's a good idea to keep the pan uncovered if you are boiling sprouting broccoli, otherwise the acids in the steam will gather under the lid and drip onto the spears. This, in turn, will change the colour to an unappetising khaki. If you are steaming the spears, you will of course need a lid, but it's a good idea to lift it every so often to allow the acid-laden steam to escape.

Chopped into bite-sized pieces, the spears give substance to a **frittata**. Mix 275g blanched chopped spears with 8 beaten eggs, 75g grated cheese such as Wensleydale or Caerphilly, 4 tablespoons of toasted pine nuts, and sea salt and black pepper to taste. Using a 25-cm non-stick pan, fry 4 chopped spring onions (include the green parts) in a knob of butter and 1 tablespoon of vegetable oil. When soft, pour in the egg mixture, stirring to distribute the broccoli. Cover and cook over a gentle heat for about 10 minutes, then brown the top under a preheated grill.

UK season
• Mid–February–early May.

Varieties to look for
• *'Early White Sprouting'*, creamy-white heads.
• *'Early Purple Sprouting'*, award-winning variety.
• *'Late Purple Sprouting'*, award-winning variety.
• *'White Star'*, creamy-white heads.

Shopping notes
• Use within a day or two of buying before the flavour deteriorates.
• Avoid limp or yellowing spears, or any that are dry or cracked at the cut end.

Storing
• Keep loosely wrapped in a paper bag in the fridge for 1–2 days.
• Alternatively, wash and prepare as below, wrap in damp paper towels and store in a sealed plastic bags.

Preparation
• Trim the tough end from the main stem. Peel the stem if fibrous and halve lengthways if thick. Cut off flower heads with about 8cm of stem and surrounding tender leaves attached.
• Don't throw out the larger leaves – they are tasty and nutritious. Strip them from the stem, chop off tough stalks and slice into ribbons.

Sautéed Sprouting Broccoli with Chillies and Garlic

Sprouting broccoli has a big meaty flavour that goes well with grilled lamb chops or steak. This is also good stirred into pasta shapes.

Strip the leaves from the sprouting stems. Chop off any tough stalks and the base of the stems. Remove the florets just below the flowering tip and slice in half if they are large. Slice the leaves and stems crossways into 2-cm pieces.

Put the florets, leaves and stems in a steamer basket over a pan of boiling water. Steam very briefly for a minute or two, then remove from the heat and set aside. Reserve the water in the pan.

Heat a large frying pan over medium-low heat. Add the olive oil and gently fry the shallots, chilli and garlic for 10 minutes to flavour the oil gently. Once the garlic starts to colour and the shallots are soft, increase the heat to medium and tip in the broccoli. Season with crumbled sea salt flakes and a grinding of black pepper, then add about 4 tablespoons of the broccoli cooking water to moisten the pan. Stir everything around and cook for $1\frac{1}{2}$ –2 minutes depending on how you like your broccoli. It should still be bright green and tender-crisp.

Cook's notes
• Steaming helps tenderise the broccoli before frying (boiling makes it too soggy). The leaves are also conveniently dry after steaming so they don't splatter when added to the hot oil.
• If you don't have a steamer, just fry the broccoli in the pan but increase the water to 6–8 tablespoons and cook for 3–4 minutes longer.
• If serving with pasta shapes, add extra olive oil to coat the pasta, and sprinkle with plenty of shaved Parmesan.

Variations
• Add three or four salted anchovy fillets, rinsed and chopped, along with the chilli and garlic.
• Fry some thinly sliced chopped pancetta and scatter over the finished dish.

purple sprouting broccoli 450g (about 14 spears)
extra-virgin olive oil 3 tbsp
shallots 2, thinly sliced
fresh red chilli $\frac{1}{2}$ –1, deseeded and finely chopped
garlic cloves 2, thinly sliced
sea salt flakes
freshly ground black pepper
cooking water 3–4 tbsp

Serves 2 with pasta as a main course, or 4 as an accompaniment to meat

Sprouting Seeds and Beans

Not to be confused with Brussels sprouts or sprouting broccoli, these power-packed shoots have a flavour so intense that feel you are eating the very essence of the seeds or beans from which they sprout. They are remarkable foods – growing in any climate at any time of year and needing neither soil nor sunshine. Cooked in minutes or eaten raw, sprouts are brimful of essential nutrients and free from preservatives and pesticide residues.

Not so long ago choice was limited to mung bean or wispy alfalfa sprouts, usually found in healthfood shops. Nowadays sprouts are a must-have superfood and the range on offer is exciting (see **Varieties to look for**). Larger farm shops with a rapid turnover are good places to find the more unusual varieties.

Cooking

Sprouts are wonderfully user-friendly and will liven up a surprising number of dishes. Sprinkle them lavishly over soups, rice dishes, stir-fries and grilled fish or chicken, adding them at the last minute so that they keep some of their juicy crispness. I love them in egg-based dishes such as omelettes and vegetable tarts, and in home-baked breads and savoury muffins. For moister and fresher-tasting meat loaves or burgers, mix in a handful of sprouts before cooking.

Raw sprouts are great for livening up salads, adding concentrated bursts of freshness, crispness and intense flavour. In general, the more robust types sprouted from pulses are best for heartier salads with a creamy yogurt or mayonnaise dressing, and the more delicate sprouted seeds are better in leafy salads with a light dressing, as in **Radish Sprout Salad with Watercress and Prink Grapefruit** (page 244) or in **Warm Duck Breast Salad with Watercress, Walnuts, Sugar Snap Peas and Bean Sprouts** (page 94).

Sprouts also make fantastic sandwich fillings. They stay beautifully moist and blend well with cream cheese, hard-boiled eggs, peanut butter or flaked tuna. They are also good stuffed into fajitas, wraps and pitta bread.

UK season
Year-round.

Varieties to look for
Aduki bean: attractive dark red leaves and shoots. Nutty and sweet, redolent of peas. Ideal for vegetarian pâté, stir-fries and casseroles.
Alfalfa: highly nutritious, small delicate shoots. Mild nutty flavour. Delicious in sandwiches and salads.
Chickpea: juicy crisp shoots with green leaves. Use in falafel or bean-based salads.
Fenugreek: dark green leaves, pungent spicy flavour. Sprinkle over rice or curry.
Mung bean: long fat crisp shoots, yellow leaves, sweet nutty flavour. Good in stir-fries.
Sango radish: stunning good looks – small purple leaves, pink shoots. Juicy and peppery with distinct after-burn. Superb for livening up leafy salads, fruit salads and sandwiches.
Sunflower: oval emerald-green leaves, rich buttery flavour. Delicious in sandwiches, salads and stir-fries.

Shopping notes
• Check the use-by date.
• Look for fresh looking sprightly sprouts.
• Don't buy sprouts that are starting to go brown or look slimy.

Storing
• Rinse and dry as below. Keep in a sealed plastic bag in the fridge for 2–5 days, depending on type.

Preparation
• Immerse sprouts in cold water for 5 minutes. If you want to remove seed hulls, stir gently. The hulls will float to the top and can be skimmed off with your hand.
• Drain and dry in a salad spinner, then blot on paper towels.

Radish Sprout Salad with Watercress and Pink Grapefruit

A colourful and pungent salad made with power-packed ingredients.

Slice the radishes lengthways to make ovals. Divide the watercress into sprigs. Slice the onions thickly diagonally.

Place the grapefruit cut-side down on a board. Remove the peel and white pith with a small sharp knife, following the contours of the fruit. Slice between the flesh and membrane of each segment and ease out the flesh.

Arrange the watercress in a shallow dish or on individual plates. Top with the radish slices, spring onions and grapefruit segments. Scatter the radish sprouts over the top. Sprinkle with crumbled sea salt flakes, black pepper and a dribble of olive oil.

Cook's note

• As an alternative to olive oil, dress the salad with **Lemon Yogurt Dressing** (page 278). The creaminess tames the heat of the radishes and onions.

fat radishes 1 bunch, trimmed
organic watercress 1 bunch, tough stalks removed
purple spring onions 8
pink grapefruit $\frac{1}{2}$
radish sprouts 2 small handfuls
sea salt flakes
coarsely ground black pepper
extra-virgin olive oil

Serves 2–3 as a starter

Squirrel

'Eat a grey and save a red' is the motto in Northumberland where squirrel meat flies off the shelves; local farm shops and game dealers just can't get enough of it. The reason for this culinary phenomenon is the direct result of attempts by voluntary groups to reverse the long-standing demise of Britain's native red squirrel for which its American cousin, the grey, is justifiably blamed. Not only do grey squirrels breed more prolifically, about 60 per cent of them also carry a lethal virus that has wiped out most of the reds. Greys are greedier too – they gobble up anything edible, stripping trees of nuts before they are ripe, and often leaving the hesitant red squirrel with insufficient sustenance. Thanks to the work of campaigners, however, and the buoyant demand for squirrel meat, pockets of land in Northumberland have been cleared of greys and the reds are making a comeback.

Cooking

It can't be denied that squirrels are scrawny creatures and, as such, there is not a huge amount of meat on them. That said, what it lacks in quantity is certainly made up in quality. Squirrels live mainly on berries and nuts so the meat is exquisitely sweet and nutty and not in the least bit gamey or overpowering.

I like my squirrel **barbecued**. It's the best way to appreciate the sweet juicy meat but is perhaps not for the dentally challenged; a certain amount of gnawing is involved. Allow two squirrels per person and use the hind legs only. Wrap in double-thickness foil parcels – 2 legs per parcel – with plenty of butter, thyme sprigs, sea salt and freshly ground black pepper. Cover with a large domed lid and cook for 10 minutes, then turn and cook for another 5 minutes. Open the parcels carefully and serve the meat with the fragrant buttery juices.

Leftover joints and bones are best gently stewed and the resulting meat used for **potted squirrel**. Follow the recipe for potted grouse (page 130) using the front legs and ribs from 4 squirrels and any other bits and pieces you happen to have.

Squirrel confit is perhaps the most successful cooking method as it keeps the meat moist and well lubricated. The meat is roasted in a deep layer of goose fat and, once cooked, will keep for a few weeks in the fridge ready for when you next fancy a bit of squirrel. Follow the recipe for goose confit (page 121) using the saddles and jointed hind legs from 4 squirrels. You will need about 600g goose fat, which is widely available and sold in cans or jars.

Squirrel is an important feature of the menu at Matfen Hall Hotel in Northumberland. Head chef Phil Hall likes it best in a textured terrine made with the haunch meat from squirrel confit, chopped chestnuts, smooth potted squirrel sweetened with onion marmalade, and the lightly fried liver. He serves the terrine with pickled walnuts and quince jelly, although as he says, anything fruity or nutty will do.

UK season
• Year-round, but best September–March.

Shopping notes
• The meat should be deep brownish-pink and smell clean and fresh.

Storing
• Store on the bottom shelf of the fridge so raw juices cannot drip onto other food.
• Wash well, pat dry and store in a shallow dish, loosely covered with foil, for 1–2 days.
• Remove the liver, heart and kidneys, and store separately.

Preparation
• Nip off the claws and divide into joints: front legs, saddle and hind legs.

Serving size
• 3 squirrels, weighing about 300g each, serves 2.

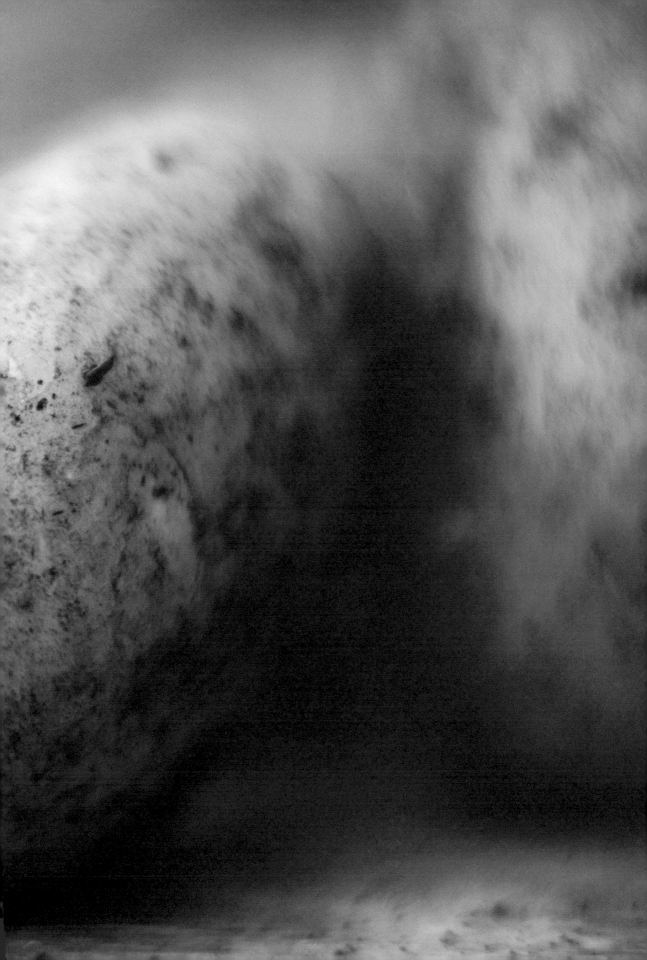

Strawberries

With their intense colour and glossy dimpled sheen, strawberries never fail to allure and for most of us they symbolise summer despite year-round availability. There are literally hundreds of varieties, shapes, sizes, and degrees of hairiness and pip, but shelf-life and shipping criteria mean that the best are rarely seen in supermarkets. Farm shops and PYO farms, however, not being overly concerned with such matters, stock a wider range of great-tasting varieties, grown in season, picked when fully ripe and at the peak of flavour.

If you are lucky you might come across much-coveted jewel-like alpine strawberries, normally found in expensive London food halls with a price tag to match. They will probably be more reasonably priced in farm shops, so snap them up while you can.

Cooking

Good strawberries are so delicious they hardly need any adornment apart from Wimbledon-style accompaniments. Make sure the cream is the best – organic and unpasteurised, preferably from Jersey cows.

Eton mess and summer pudding are strawberry classics, as are little shortcrust tarts brushed with redcurrant glaze. Another way is to serve the berries in a compôte flavoured with the aniseed-like notes of tarragon or basil, or even highly perfumed eau-de-cologne mint (**Strawberry Compôte with Tarragon and Orange Zest**, page 251). Alternatively, try them macerated in a little sugar, freshly ground black pepper and a dash of aged balsamic vinegar – the sweet syrupy kind rather than the more acidic thin variety. A mysterious alchemy takes place as the flavours mellow and meld, resulting in strawberries that taste intensely of themselves with just a hint of something else.

Strawberry ice cream is another winner, as is **Fresh and Dried Strawberry Sorbet** (opposite). Made with 'Gariguette' (see **Varieties**), a few perfumed alpines and a smattering of miniature dried strawberries, the flavour and texture are magnificent.

As the season wears on you might want to experiment with other ideas. **Warmed strawberries with French toast** are a wonderful combination. For two people, slice 350g strawberries in half lengthways, sprinkle with the merest dusting of caster sugar and leave to macerate for 20 minutes. Make the **French toast** (see **Milk**, page 164) and keep warm. Heat a small knob of butter and 1 teaspoon of caster sugar in a heavy-based frying pan. Stir over fairly brisk heat until the sugar starts to look pale golden. Add the strawberries and carefully shunt them round the pan until warmed through. Sprinkle with a squeeze of lemon juice and serve with the toast.

UK season
• June–September.

Varieties to look for
• *'Gariguette'*, elongated scarlet berries. Prized variety in France, exceptionally sweet, very soft.
• *'Jubilee'*, heart-shaped pillar-box red berries. Melt-in-the-mouth texture. Well-balanced flavour, sweet and aromatic.
• *'Mara des Bois'*, elongated brick-red berries. Firm juicy flesh, exceptional sweet wild strawberry flavour.
• *'Marshmello'*, conical deep-red berries. Well-balanced flavour.
• *'Perfection'*, chubby orange-red berries. Luscious and sweet.
• *'Royal Sovereign'*, smallish heart-shaped scarlet berries. Superb flavour.

Shopping notes
• Look for plump glossy fruits with bright green hulls.
• If buying in punnets, check the fruit underneath for signs of mould or bruising.
• Avoid punnets wrapped in cling film. It squashes the fruit and causes bruising.
• Don't buy punnets with seepage on the base – a sign of mushy fruit.

Storing
• Strawberries are best eaten on the day you buy them.
• Avoid storing in the fridge – the chill dulls the flavour. Strawberries will last for a day or two if kept away from heat and moisture.
• If you must store strawberries in the fridge, resuscitate them in a sunny spot so the warmth gets deep inside the fruit.

Preparation
• Do not wash until ready to serve. Dunk briefly in water before hulling, otherwise the berries will ship water at the stem end.
• Drain thoroughly and blot dry in a single layer on paper towels.
• Bring out the flavour by marinating in a little sugar and lemon juice for 15–30 minutes.

Fresh and Dried Strawberry Sorbet

Farm shops sometimes stock really good dried strawberries and other fruit made by Swiss Alps. They are utterly delicious, adding a lovely texture to the sorbet as well as intense nuggets of flavour. If you are lucky enough to find fresh alpine strawberries on sale, use these instead of ordinary strawberries, or add a few as a decoration.

Put the sugar and water in a saucepan. Stir over medium heat until the sugar has dissolved. Bring to the boil briefly, then remove from the heat and leave until completely cold.

Hull the strawberries and slice if they are large. Purée in a food processor or blender, then push through a sieve to get rid of the pips. Mix with the lemon juice, then stir into the cold syrup. Cover and chill for 2 hours.

Churn and freeze in an ice cream machine following the manufacturer's instructions. Once the mixture starts to thicken, add the dried strawberries and continue to churn. Once completely thickened, store in the freezer to harden.

Cook's note
• If you don't have an ice cream machine, follow the directions for still-freezing Quince and Ginger Sorbet (page 213).

sugar 225g
water 225ml
strawberries 400g
lemons juice of 2, strained
dried strawberries 50g
alpine strawberries (optional) to decorate

Makes 700ml

Strawberry Compôte with Tarragon and Orange Zest

A good solution for strawberries that aren't as sweet as they might be. Orange-impregnated sugar cubes really boost the flavour, while the tarragon adds an interesting touch.

Slice the strawberries if they are very large and put them in a good-looking bowl.

Rub the sugar cubes over the orange until they are impregnated with the oil from the peel. Crumble over the strawberries and mix carefully.

Scatter with tarragon sprigs, cover the bowl with cling film and leave to stand at room temperature for an hour or two to allow the flavours to mingle.

Cook's note
• Use unwaxed oranges if possible. Otherwise wash them under warm running water and scrub with a vegetable brush.

Variation
• Instead of tarragon, try basil or eau-de-cologne mint. I rarely use this mint in cooking as the flavour is faintly reminiscent of the toilet water, as the name suggests. However, it seems fine here.

strawberries 450g
sugar cubes 3–4
orange 1
tarragon a few small sprigs

Serves 4

Swede

Despite well-intentioned publicity from chefs and food writers, the swede still suffers from an image problem. At one time swedes were grown purely as animal fodder and, as a result, are treated with a certain amount of disdain. And with their dirt-encrusted roots and stout bulbs they certainly cannot be described as stylish.

On the plus side, farmers love swedes for their hardiness and the fact that they survive in the ground until needed. During the lean winter months there will always be a few in the farm shops and they are worth buying just for their freshness. Unlike cling-wrapped swede from the supermarket, newly dug roots actually smell of something – beautifully clean and earthy with a sinus-pricking whiff of horseradish.

Cooking

Swede offers plenty of possibilities to the creative cook. The usual way is to boil and mash it with butter and nutmeg. This is nice enough but a bit namby-pamby for such a robust vegetable. I prefer **roasted swede** – the sugars caramelize and the flavour intensifies, producing golden nuggets that are bliss with a juicy joint of beef or even roast duck. Peel 2–3 medium-sized swedes, quarter and cut into wedges, then boil in salted water for 5 minutes. Drain and toss with olive oil, sea salt flakes and freshly ground black pepper. Spread out on a roomy roasting tray and roast at 190°C/gas 5 for 40–45 minutes until golden and beginning to blacken round the edges. The wedges will be lovely and chewy on the outside, and soft and bright orange within.

Cut into thin strips and lightly blanched, swede is surprisingly good in a colourful stir-fry with an equally robust leafy vegetable such as baby kale or shredded Savoy cabbage. Alternatively, cut into thin slices and cook in a parcel either alone or mixed with potatoes as in **Camping Potatoes** (page 205).

Provided it is not too fibrous, swede can be eaten raw. Coarsely grated, it adds pep and colour to a **winter root vegetable salad**. Mix it with grated celeriac and carrot, finely chopped red onion, and toss with plenty of flat leaf parsley or chives and a mustardy vinaigrette.

For a spectacular **grilled swede salad**, toss thin slices of swede in olive oil and sea salt and cook on a ridged stove-top grill pan. Once appetisingly striped with brown, arrange on a springy mound of rocket or micro-leaves and dress with **creamy horseradish dressing** (page 141). Add some flaked smoked mackerel fillets if you like; the combination of swede, smoked fish and a pungent creamy dressing is a good one.

UK season
• July–May.

Varieties to look for
• *'Brora'*, two-tone purple and yellow skin, tender yellow flesh. Outstanding flavour and texture. Good for grating and eating raw.
• *'Marian'*, two-tone purple and yellow skin. Mild flavour, excellent roasted or mashed.

Shopping notes
• Choose small or medium-sized swedes, as these are likely to be less fibrous.
• They should be firm without any cracks or bruises.
• Don't bother with those that feel spongy.

Storing
• Store in a paper bag in a cool dry place or the salad drawer of the fridge for up to 1 week.

Preparation
• Using a sturdy sharp knife, trim the ends, then slice lengthways into quarters. Peel and cut into smaller chunks as necessary.

Sweetcorn

With our unpredictable summers, sweetcorn can take up to four months to ripen, but it's well worth the wait just for the sheer pleasure of biting into a juicy golden cob dripping with butter.

Like peas and asparagus, sweetcorn tastes best eaten within hours of harvesting. Once picked, the sugars turn to starch and the flavour starts to deteriorate. Farm shops, or better still, PYO farms are the places to go if you want to enjoy it at the peak of freshness.

There are two basic types of sweetcorn: the super-sweets, laden with several times the normal amount of sugar, and the normal sugary types that have a good old-fashioned corn flavour. Super-sweets are designed to remain that way after harvest but they are not to everyone's taste nor suitable for every dish (see **Varieties**).

Cooking

Sweetcorn is symbolic of homely North American cooking. There, it is served on the cob, in soups and chowders, relishes and pickles, custards, puddings, fritters and breads. In the UK we tend to stick to no-fuss boiling or grilling. Why bother with anything else when it's hard to better a just-boiled cob **rolled in melted butter**, sprinkled with sea salt and chopped mint or chives.

Unlike most other vegetables, sweetcorn toughens if overcooked. Depending on type and freshness, tender young cobs usually need no more than 2 or 3 minutes in rapidly boiling unsalted water; 5 minutes is about right if they are older. Use a very large saucepan and don't overcrowd the cobs. Alternatively, slice them into two or three chunks and steam over boiling water, cut-side down.

Barbecued sweetcorn is another treat. It's best to grill the cobs in their husks rather than blackening the kernels directly over the coals. The kernels will be steamily moist and tender, blissfully infused both with the aroma of the barbecue and the husk.

Try forgoing the butter for a change and serve your **barbecued sweetcorn Mexican-style**, sprinkled with lime juice, sea salt and coriander. Place the corn cobs in their husks over hot coals for about 10 minutes, turning occasionally. Slit the husks and silks lengthways and pull apart to expose the kernels. Squeeze over some lime juice and sprinkle with chopped coriander, dried chilli flakes and sea salt. Forget about corn holders – sweetcorn is an in-your-face-job. Eat straight from the husk and suck on it until every last kernel has been devoured.

Once you've had your fill of boiling and barbecuing, you may wish to consider other ideas. For a deliciously creamy soup, try **Sweetcorn and Chilli Chowder** (page 254). Sweetcorn has a real affinity with dairy products and chillies; dairy products seem to reinforce the creaminess, while chillies provide the perfect contrast to sweetness.

UK season
• July–October.

Varieties to look for
• *'Jubilee'*, organic, ordinary sweet variety. Traditional creamy texture and typical corn flavour. Good for soups and cornbreads.
• *'Sweet Nugget'*, super-sweet variety, long cobs. Crisp crunchy texture, fantastic flavour.
• *'Sweetie F1'*, super-sweet variety, extra-large golden kernels.

Shopping notes
• Look for cobs with fresh-looking green husks that tightly enclose the kernels.
• Avoid cobs with pale silks – a sign that the corn was picked too soon.
• The stem end should be pale green and moist rather than woody.
• Rub your fingers over the husk to check that the kernels are plump and tightly packed.
• Steer clear of any with hard or shrunken kernels.

Storing
• Preferably eat on the day you buy, though super-sweet varieties can be kept for a little longer.
• If necessary, wrap in damp paper towels, husks still in place, and store in a roomy plastic bag in the salad drawer of the fridge for 24 hours.

Preparation
• *To remove the husk and silks:* slice off about 2cm from the base rather than the tip. Loosen the husk a little at the bottom, then grasp the ends firmly and strip it back from bottom to tip. The silks should come away at the same time.
• *To remove the kernels:* slice the dehusked cob in half crossways. Stand the pieces upright with the narrow end at the top and shave away the kernels with a small sharp knife. Break up any clumps with your fingers.

Sweetcorn and Chilli Chowder

Tasting mildly of chillies and made with freshly harvested sweetcorn, this soup is sublime. Serve with warm bread and crumbly white cheese such as feta or Caerphilly.

Preheat the grill to high. Place the sweetcorn cobs in their husks and the green pepper in a pan under the grill. Grill for 5 minutes, turning the corn occasionally. Add the chilli and grill for another 10 minutes until the corn husks are browned and the pepper and chilli are beginning to blacken and blister.

Peel away the husks and silks from the corn and slice the kernels from the cobs (see **Preparation**). Peel the pepper and chilli, remove the seeds from the chilli, and chop the flesh of both into small dice. Purée half the corn with the milk in a food processor until fairly smooth.

Heat the rapeseed oil in a saucepan and gently fry the onion with the thyme and bay leaf until the onion is translucent. Add the chopped pepper, chilli, potatoes, puréed corn and the stock. Bring to the boil, then reduce the heat and simmer gently for 15 minutes. Add the remaining corn kernels and simmer for another 5 minutes.

Fish out the herbs and season to taste with sea salt flakes and freshly ground black pepper. Purée half the mixture, then return this to the soup in the pan. Reheat gently and stir in the coriander.

sweetcorn cobs with husks 4
green pepper 1, halved and deseeded
fleshy green chilli 1 small
whole milk organic, 400ml
rapeseed oil 1 tbsp
onion 1 small, diced
thyme 2–3 sprigs
fresh bay leaf 1
potatoes 2–3 small, diced
chicken stock preferably home-made, 600ml
sea salt flakes
freshly ground black pepper
coriander chopped to make 3 tbsp

Serves 4–6 as a light meal

Tomatoes

Tomatoes come in beautiful shapes, sizes and colours. They can be round or pear-shaped; smooth or convoluted; some scarcely bigger than a grape and others weighing in at a kilo or more. Colours range from jelly yellow to vermillion orange and deep ruby red; some come in chocolate brown or vivid shades of lime green.

The majority of varieties rarely make it to the supermarket shelves though you'll certainly see tomatoes that are 'vine-ripened' or 'grown for flavour'. Most will be imported, however, and, because of shelf-life and shipping criteria, choice is usually limited to a very few cherry, round or beefsteak varieties.

Luckily, farm shops have a different agenda. Choice may still be limited and imports might slip through in winter, but you're more likely to find different varieties, locally grown and allowed to ripen longer so they are harvested at their peak. Bear in mind that tomatoes are weather-dependent – they need the warmth of the sun and lots of light to develop that finely tuned balance of sweet and sour that is their quintessential flavour. In a poor summer, even farm shops may have depleted stocks or need to rely on imports.

Types of tomatoes

Cherry and baby plum: intensely flavoured bite-sized tomatoes for eating as a snack or in salads. Lightly crushed and warmed through in a little olive oil they make a colourful pizza topping or accompaniment to grilled meat or fish.

Slicing tomatoes: the most common type available, varying in size according to variety and maturity. Some are the size of ping pong balls, others are bulging beefsteaks. They have plenty of juice and skins that are not too thick, so are excellent for cooking or eating raw.

Vine-ripened tomatoes: these are the same as other tomatoes but are still attached to the stalk or vine. This gives them a strong tomato aroma, which comes mostly from the leaf and stalk rather than the tomato itself.

Plum tomatoes: elongated plum-shaped fruits sometimes with a pointed tip. They have thick meaty flesh, a thick core, and less juice and seeds than round varieties. They are the best for drying, roasting and processing into sauces and pastes. They are also good fried or baked, but are not great for eating raw because of the lack of juice.

Cooking

The number of tomato-based dishes is truly astonishing – salads, soups, sauces, pizzas, pasta dishes, risottos and curries as well as tarts, sandwiches and sorbets. Without them, an unbelievable number of everyday staples would be wiped off the culinary map.

In most tomato dishes the key to success is simplicity. A salad may be nothing more than thickly sliced tomatoes – preferably sun-warmed and freshly picked – dressed with a dribble of best olive oil and a little crumbled sea salt. A more spectacular salad can be made with an

UK season
• July–October.

Varieties to look for
Cherry and mini-plum tomatoes:
• *'Gardener's Delight'*, red, exceptional meaty sweet flavour.
• *'Snowberry'*, brilliant yellow, well-balanced punchy flavour.
• *'Sungold'*, yellow-orange, superb tomato flavour, very sweet.

Slicing tomatoes:
• *'Brandywine'*, large convoluted deep red fruits with thin skin. Well-balanced sweet tangy flavour.
• *'Evergreen'*, large convoluted fruits. Stunning green and yellow streaked skin, green flesh, even when ripe. Very good flavour.
• *'Golden Sunrise'*, medium-size yellow fruits. Juicy and sweet with some acidity.
• *'Shirley'*, medium-size smooth red fruits. Well-balanced sweet-sour flavour.
• *'Striped German'*, enormous convoluted fruits, spectacular red and yellow streaks throughout the skin and flesh. Taste as good as they look.

Plum tomatoes:
• *'Italian Gold'*, distinctive pear shape, smooth orange-red skin. Very sweet.
• *'Sheriff'*, smooth red skin. Well-balanced intense flavour.

Shopping notes
• Smell before buying – the best tomatoes have a rich flowery aroma.
• Look for vividly coloured fruits with taut skin and firm flesh, preferably with the green calyx still attached.
• Don't bother with squashy or split fruits.

assortment of heritage varieties with traffic-light colours and stunning textures. Look for the big bold slicing tomatoes in various colours (see **Varieties**), and vivid orange or yellow cherry tomatoes. Cut the big tomatoes into thick horizontal slices to show off their texture, and slice the cherry tomatoes in half vertically. Arrange them on a nice white plate, randomly rather than in tidy circles, and sprinkle with sea salt, cracked black pepper and some shredded purple basil if you have it. Sprinkle with olive oil and it's done.

An excellent **raw tomato sauce for pasta** can be made with 500g peeled and finely diced tomatoes, chopped garlic, olive oil and plenty of shredded basil, while a richly flavoured cooked tomato sauce is simply a matter of simmering peeled chopped tomatoes with a halved onion and a decadent amount of butter. **Grilled Tomato Sauce** made with tomatoes, onions and garlic (opposite) is excellent for perking up root vegetables or pasta.

For **tomato salsa**, to serve with grilled fish or chicken perhaps, combine 2 or 3 finely diced unpeeled but deseeded tomatoes with diced red onion, a smattering of chopped chilli, fresh lime juice, sea salt and a lavish amount of chopped coriander. Leave to stand for 30 minutes but enjoy it before the freshness fades. For an **Indian-style fresh chutney**, mix chopped tomatoes and cucumber with green chillies, lemon juice, salt and plenty of mint.

Served with a blob of luscious garlic mayonnaise, **char-grilled tomatoes** are a simple but delectable starter. Brush the cut side of large halved tomatoes with olive oil and grill them over white-hot coals for about 3 minutes a side until slightly blackened.

If you have a large quantity of plum tomatoes, try **oven-roasting** them. The flavour becomes wonderfully concentrated, so much so that even bland-tasting specimens benefit from the treatment. Pack a single layer of halved tomatoes cut-side up onto a roasting tray, sprinkle with olive oil, thyme, sea salt, freshly ground black pepper and a pinch of muscovado sugar, then bake at 150°C/gas 2 for 1½–2 hours or until shrivelled but still slightly moist. Serve as an antipasto with blanched baby broad beans, crumbled feta or Caerphilly cheese and plenty of mint, or use as a topping for pizzas and tarts (**Tomato Tart**, opposite). As long as the tomatoes are covered with oil they will keep in a covered container in the fridge for up to a week.

Storing

• Buy in small quantities and store at room temperature or, if not quite ripe, on a sunny windowsill.

• Ripe tomatoes will keep for a day or two; under-ripe ones for up to a week.

• Don't store in the fridge – the chill dulls the flavour and arrests the development of further sweetening and ripening.

Preparation

• Leave whole, slice or dice according to the recipe.

• Peeling is sometimes necessary for cooked dishes in which shreds of skin would be unwelcome. Put the tomatoes in a large bowl and cover with boiling water. Count to twenty, then drain and slip off the skins.

• To remove the seeds, slice in half horizontally to expose the cavities. If you slice vertically most of the seeds and juice remain encased in the flesh. Use a teaspoon or your little finger to scoop out the seeds.

Tomato Tart

Made with juicy oven-roasted tomatoes, this irresistible tart is packed with flavour.

Preheat the oven to 170°C/gas 3. Lightly grease a 28-cm loose-based tart tin. Roll out the pastry very thinly and use to line the tin. Press a rolling pin over the top of the tin to trim off surplus dough. Using the side of your forefinger, press the dough into the edge of the tin to raise it slightly above the rim. Line the base with foil and weigh down with baking beans, making sure they fill the base and go all the way to the edge. Bake blind for 15 minutes. Remove the foil and beans and bake for 10–15 minutes more until the pastry is pale golden. Remove from the oven and raise the temperature to 180°C/gas 4.

Arrange the tomato halves in the pastry case in concentric circles. Sprinkle the cheese evenly over the top. Beat the eggs lightly, then stir in the cream, herbs and sea salt flakes and black pepper to taste. Mix well, then pour into the pastry case. Bake for 20–25 minutes until puffy and golden. Serve hot or warm.

Variation

• If you don't have time to make oven-roasted tomatoes, use 8–10 fresh ones. Remove the peel and seeds (see **Preparation**). Cut the flesh into thin segments and arrange in overlapping circles in the pastry shell.

ready-made shortcrust pastry 375g
oven-roasted tomatoes (page 256) about 24 halves
hard cheese such as Gruyère or Lancashire, 150g, coarsely grated
eggs organic, 4
Jersey double cream organic, 125ml
oregano or **marjoram** leaves chopped to make 2 tbsp
sea salt flakes
freshly ground black pepper

Serves 8–10 as a snack or 6 as a light meal

Grilled Tomato Sauce

With the chillies included, this richly flavoured sauce perks up root vegetables or cooked grains such as barley or spelt (page 237).

Preheat a hot grill. Cut the onion across into 1-cm rings. Insert cocktail sticks horizontally from the outer edge to the centre to hold the rings in place. Brush lightly with olive oil and put in a grill pan with the garlic, chillies if you are using them, and tomatoes.

Place under the grill and cook, turning the tomatoes two or three times and the onion rings once, until the garlic feels soft and the rest of the vegetables are slightly blackened. Peel the garlic and chillies and remove the chilli seeds. Leave the tomatoes unpeeled.

Tip the lot into a food processor and whizz until smooth. Push through a sieve, pressing hard with the back of a wooden spoon to extract as much juice as possible.

Heat a frying pan over medium-high heat and add the 1 tablespoon of oil and then the sieved purée. Season with the salt and plenty of freshly ground black pepper, and cook for a few minutes until thickened. Stir in the butter and check the seasoning.

Cook's note

• If you prefer a thin sauce, dilute it with chicken or vegetable stock.

onion 1
olive oil 1 tbsp, plus more for brushing
garlic cloves 4, unpeeled
fresh red chillies (optional) 1–2
plum tomatoes 12
salt 1/2 tsp
freshly ground black pepper
butter a large knob

Makes about 600ml

Yellow Tomato Gazpacho

This is one of those lovely recipes in which simple ingredients combine to make a soup with real impact. As with all such dishes, it's the ingredients that count. You will need top-notch tomatoes and a flavourful cucumber and yellow pepper.

Cut the yellow tomatoes in half horizontally. Poke your finger into the cavities and scoop the seeds and juice into a bowl. Push through a sieve, pressing hard to extract as much juice as possible. Chop the tomato flesh and put in a bowl with the juice.

Set aside 4 tablespoons each of the diced cucumber and yellow pepper, and all of the chopped red cherry tomatoes.

Add the remaining cucumber and pepper to the yellow tomatoes in the bowl. Add the salad onions, chilli, vinegar and olive oil. Tip into a food processor and purée for at least 2 minutes, scraping down the bowl often, until the mixture is very smooth. Pour it back into the bowl.

Bash the sliced garlic with the sea salt flakes, using a mortar and pestle. When you have a smooth cream, stir this into the tomato mixture and season with the black pepper and sugar. Cover and chill for several hours until really cold.

Check the seasoning before serving – remember that chilling will dull the flavours. Ladle into cold bowls and top with the reserved chopped cucumber, pepper and the red cherry tomatoes. Add a slick of olive oil and a few shredded basil leaves. Serve with a bowl of garlic croûtons.

Cook's notes
• There is a reason for slicing the tomatoes horizontally – it exposes the seeds and the all-important flavourful jelly that surrounds them.
• There is no need to peel the tomatoes for the soup unless the skins are very leathery.

yellow slicing tomatoes 900g
cucumber $^1/_2$, peeled, deseeded and diced
yellow pepper 1, deseeded and diced
red cherry tomatoes 100g, deseeded and chopped
fat salad onions 3, weighing about 75g, trimmed and finely chopped
green chilli 1–2, deseeded and finely chopped
cider vinegar 2 tbsp
extra-virgin olive oil best quality, 3 tbsp, plus extra for drizzling
garlic cloves preferably 'green', 4, sliced
sea salt flakes $^1/_2$ tbsp
freshly ground black pepper $^1/_4$ tsp
sugar $^1/_4$ tsp
basil leaves a small handful, shredded, to garnish
Garlic Croûtons (page 112) to serve

Serves 4–6

Turkey

With its massive plumage and dangling snood, the turkey is a bizarre but truly magnificent sight – none the more so when allowed to roam freely, forage for food in open pasture and grow at an unhurried rate. Traditionally reared birds such as these are a million miles from mass-produced birds, grown for size in overcrowded conditions in the shortest possible time.

A fit and healthy free-range turkey produces rich, moist meat, thanks not only to careful rearing but also to sensitive slaughter and proper hanging – 7–14 days is the norm. Old-fashioned breeds (see **Turkey to look for**) are particularly prized for their eating quality. They may not have super-sized breast meat but they are well flavoured and juicy.

Birds like these do not come cheap, but if you buy direct from the farm and collect it yourself, the price may well be lower.

Cooking

Roasting is the best way to appreciate the flavour and succulence of a top-notch free-range turkey. As long as due care is taken with timing and temperature, it's not that different from roasting a large chicken. The trick is to get the legs cooked without drying the breast meat in the process. I have succeeded in this respect by **roasting turkey in a parcel** to seal in the juices. Place your prepared bird on a giant piece of heavy-duty foil, rub all over with oil, season with sea salt and freshly ground black pepper, and stuff the cavity with a couple of pierced lemons, an onion, thyme or rosemary sprigs and a few stalks of leafy celery.

Arrange a second piece of foil on top and crimp the edges to seal both sheets – don't encase the bird too tightly. Roast slowly on a rack at 180°C/gas 4, allowing 40 minutes per kilo. Remove the top piece of foil and increase the temperature to 240°C/gas 9. Basting with melted butter every 5 minutes, roast for about 30 minutes more, or until the turkey is browned and the juices run clear when you pierce the thickest part of the thigh. Leave to rest in a warm place for at least 20 minutes to allow the juices to flow back through the meat.

At times of year other than Christmas it is worth experimenting with dishes that will give you a fresh take on the bird. For everyday meals it's a good idea to use methods that benefit the different types of meat – casseroles and curries for the dark meat, and pan-frying for the white, for example. Try breast steaks in **Tandoori Turkey Tikka** (page 281) or use freshly minced turkey instead of pork in burgers (page 199).

Adventurous cooks will enjoy having a stab at *mole de guajalote*, a classic dish from Mexico in which marinated turkey joints are simmered in a spicy chilli sauce enriched with nuts, sweet spices and a small chunk of dark chocolate. It couldn't be more different from traditional roast turkey.

UK season
• *Free-range birds:* Christmas and Easter.

Turkey to look for
• *Bourbon Red:* rare breed, chestnut plumage. Broad breast, nutty flavour.
• *Cambridge Bronze:* rare breed, spectacular shimmering green-bronze plumage. Plump breast, rich gamey flavour.
• *Kelly Bronze:* modern breed, cross between Cambridge and Norfolk. Plump breast, excellent flavour.
• *Norfolk Black:* rare breed, striking black plumage. Narrow breast, meaty flavour.

Shopping notes
• Check that the bird has been dry-plucked and hung for at least 7 days.
• Look for plump smooth flesh with undamaged taut skin concealing a thin layer of fat.
• The skin should feel soft, smooth and powdery-dry to touch.

Storage
• Store on the bottom shelf of the fridge so raw juices cannot drip onto other food.
• Remove wrapping and store in a shallow dish, loosely covered with foil, for 2–3 days depending on 'use by' date.
• Remove giblets and store separately.

Preparation
• Remove from the fridge 2 hours before cooking.
• Wash inside and out, and pat dry with paper towels.
• After handling, wash and rinse hands and utensils in hot water, disinfect sinks and surfaces.
• *To defrost:* allow 4–6 hours per 450g in the fridge at 4°C. This may take up to 3 days depending on size. Regularly pour off any liquid, taking care not to splash it on worktops or other food.

Serving size
• Whole bird: 3kg serves 6–7; 4kg serves 8–9; 5kg serves 10–11; 6kg serves 12–13.

Turnips

A relative of the swede and the radish, turnips are a versatile vegetable harvested for their leafy tops as well as their bulbous root or stem. The tops, also known as broccoli raab and *cima di rapa*, have a rich, pungent and slightly bitter flavour that is not to everyone's taste, though they are highly sort-after by chefs. They are cooked just like kale or cabbage and go well with pasta, seafood and sweetish-tasting meat like duck or pork.

Turnips vary in shape – some are flat like spinning tops, others are spherical or elongated. Skin colours range from yellow and apricot to virginal creamy white, often tinged with purple, pink or green.

Though turnips are generally thought of as peasant food, nothing could be more elegant than the bunches of young bulbs that appear in early summer. They are such a pretty sight with their crisp green leaves and pearly skin so silky you want to stroke it. Later in the year the bulbs get bigger and the flavour more pungent, but they are still an attractive vegetable if bought in good condition.

Cooking

Turnips can usually be interchanged with swedes but need gentler cooking, particularly if young. Boil or steam them whole, halved or quartered, depending on size. Cook until just tender and serve tossed in melted butter and a generous shower of chopped flat-leaf parsley or chives, sea salt and freshly ground black pepper. Alternatively, sizzle just-cooked turnips in a syrupy glaze with black pepper and orange as in **Glazed Baby Turnips with Black Pepper and Orange** (page 262), or try them with duck breasts (**Duck Breasts with Young Turnips, Carrots and Cobnuts**, page 96) – rich sweet duck and slightly bitter turnips are a great mix of flavours.

Like most young root vegetables, turnips are very good cooked in a foil parcel with herbs and olive oil, either in the oven or on the barbecue (see **Beetroot**, page 32). The bulbs cook in their own steam, producing wonderfully concentrated flavours and fragrant oily juices. Very young turnips are excellent eaten raw like radishes either in a salad or as a crudité with a creamy dip.

Winter turnips can take more robust treatment. They are used all over the Middle East, stuffed, pickled, and in stews and soups. North African cooks use them to make spicy vegetable tagines, and in India they show up in pickles and curries.

Closer to home, turnips are good in a **creamy bubbling gratin** either alone or with potatoes or carrots. Slice and blanch medium-sized turnips, then layer them in a buttered baking dish, seasoning with sea salt, freshly grated nutmeg and black pepper as you go. Moisten with organic whipping cream and top with a layer of breadcrumbs and flat leaf parsley. Bake in a preheated oven at 180°C/gas 4 for about 20 minutes until the cream is thick and bubbling and the topping is golden.

UK season
• *Baby turnips:* May–June.
• *Winter turnips:* October–February.

Varieties to look for
• *'Golden Ball'*, heirloom winter variety, spherical bulbs, golden tender flesh. Rich buttery flavour, sweet and peppery.
• *'Market Express'*, small succulent white bulbs. Crisp and peppery. Use leaves in salads.
• *'Purple Top Milan'*, heirloom variety, flattened bulbs with pretty purple tops, tender fine-grained white flesh. Good turnip flavour.

Shopping notes
• Look for firm blemish-free turnips with smooth skin.
• Avoid those that are spongy or pitted.
• The leaves should be bright green and crisp.

Storing
• Store loosely wrapped in a paper bag in the fridge or in a cool well-ventilated shed.
• Turnip leaves will keep in a plastic bag in the fridge for 1–2 days.

Preparation
• Trim the tops and root end.
• If small there is usually no need for peeling as the skin is paper-thin.
• Peel larger specimens only if absolutely necessary – much of the flavour is concentrated in or near the skin.

Glazed Baby Turnips with Black Pepper and Orange

Turnips have a uniquely pungent flavour that is very good with black pepper and orange. Use tender young turnips with a smooth thin skin.

Plunge the turnips into a saucepan of boiling water. Boil for 7–8 minutes or until just tender, then drain and put in a bowl.

Pound the sugar, orange zest and peppercorns to a paste, using a mortar and pestle. Toss the turnips in the paste mixing with your hands until evenly coated.

Heat a non-stick frying pan in which the turnips will sit snugly in a single layer. Add the knob of butter over medium-high heat and, when sizzling nicely, slip in the turnips and any paste left in the bowl. Cook for about 7 minutes or until the turnips are beginning to colour.

Pour in the stock, season with sea salt flakes, add a squeeze of orange juice and swirl the turnip around. Simmer briskly until the liquid is reduced and syrupy. Add more salt if necessary. Sprinkle with the parsley just before serving.

Cook's note

• If the turnips are young they won't need peeling. The dish can be made with older specimens but they will need peeling and cutting into quarters or halves depending on size.

small turnips 450g, trimmed and unpeeled
sugar 1 tbsp
small orange finely grated zest of ½
black peppercorns ½ tsp
butter a large knob
vegetable or **chicken stock** 100ml
sea salt flakes
orange juice a squeeze
flat leaf parsley chopped to make 1 tbsp

Serves 2 as a side dish

Veal

Veal is back on the menu but there is still confusion about where it comes from, whether or not it's ethical to eat it and, once you've decided, how it should be cooked.

Veal is the meat from bull calves born to dairy cows. The calves are not considered up to the mark for beef production, so the practice has been to shoot them within hours of birth or export them to mainland Europe. Here, as has been well publicised, the calves were inhumanely reared in tiny wooden crates, kept permanently in the dark and fed reconstituted milk powder in order to meet the demand for tender white veal meat. I was once shown such a beast by a proud farmer in southwest France – it was a deeply disturbing sight.

The crate system has long been banned in the UK and more recently in the rest of Europe. Although rearing conditions in the UK vary, standards are generally higher than elsewhere. Nowadays, calves are legally required to be housed in spacious well-lit barns with straw bedding and given freedom to move around. They are fed on a mixed diet of whole milk and cereal-based feed. The resulting product is called rose veal, a term that acknowledges the colour of the meat, which in turn stems from the calves' natural needs for exercise and a balanced diet being met.

This about-turn in ethics means that veal is more widely available, its consumption championed mainly by producers but also promoted by the RSPCA and Compassion in World Farming (CIWF) as a relatively humane way of dealing with unwanted bull calves.

The pinkish-brown meat is as tender as white veal but it has a slightly fuller flavour and chewier texture. Rose veal comes in a vast range of cuts including chops, steaks, ribs, roasting joints and stewing veal, as well as the more familiar veal escalopes and osso bucco meat. More of the major supermarkets now stock it, but for the widest choice it's well worth buying direct from the farm or online (see **Resources**, page 284–286).

Cooking

Veal and beef come from the same animal, but it's worth remembering that they have different characteristics as far as cooking is concerned. It is better to treat veal like chicken or pork. Being naturally lean, the meat lends itself to moist methods such as pot-roasting, braising and stewing. It's also delicious grilled or fried but needs plenty of basting to stop it drying out.

For inspiration we need to look to Italy and France where veal dishes are commonplace. Veal is popular in Germany and Switzerland, too, but there it is usually cooked in a creamy sauce and served with noodles which do nothing for the slightly bland gelatinous nature of the meat. The best recipes include some kind of contrasting sharp or acidic element such as lemon or capers, or tomatoes as in **Veal Chops with Cherry Tomatoes, Mushrooms and Roasted Onion** (page 266). Good accompaniments are crisp-textured vegetables such as green

UK season
• Year-round.

Veal to look for
• Free-range or organic British rose veal.

Shopping notes
• Look for close-grained brownish-pink meat that is slightly moist but not wet.
• Avoid meat that looks dark, dry or sticky.
• Choose a cut suitable for the dish:
Stewing: neck, flank.
Braising and pot-roasting: shin, shoulder, breast.
Grilling and frying: best end cutlets, loin chops, escalopes, rump or fillet steak.
Roasting: boned and rolled loin, leg, best end of neck.

Storing
• Store on the bottom shelf of the fridge so raw juices cannot drip onto other food.
• Remove wrapping and store in a shallow dish, loosely covered with foil. Large joints will keep for 2–3 days; steaks and escalopes 2 days. Mince should be eaten within 24 hours.
• If vacuum-packed or in a rigid plastic container, leave unopened until ready to cook.

Preparation
• Remove from the fridge 1–2 hours before cooking. The meat will heat and brown more evenly if it starts off at room temperature.
• Snip the fat on chops and steaks at intervals to stop it shrinking and curling.

Serving size
Boneless: 250g serves 1.
Bone-in: 375g serves 1.

beans, cabbage or sprouting broccoli.

A favourite dish is **escalopes with lemon** (*scaloppine al limone*), often served in old-style Italian restaurants and none the worse for that. Place 4 escalopes between 2 layers of cling film and flatten them by bashing with a rolling pin. Heat 1 tablespoon of rapeseed oil and a good knob of butter in a large frying pan until sizzling. Dredge the escalopes with flour and slip them into the pan. Cook for 2–3 minutes each side, then move to a warm plate. Deglaze the pan with the juice of half a lemon, stirring in the tasty sediment from the base of the pan. Swirl in a small knob of butter and the juices from the veal. Put the veal back in the pan, season and turn briefly in the sauce. Sprinkle with finely chopped flat leaf parsley and serve with chunks of lemon.

Another classic is *osso bucco* in which hefty chunks of shin meat and marrow bone are slowly stewed in a fragrant stock with carrot, onion and celery. The dish is served with a colourful *gremolata* of chopped flat leaf parsley, lemon zest and garlic. The best bit, for some, is slurping nuggets of marrow from the bones.

Other delicious options are to poach a leg of veal and serve it with piquant caper sauce as in **Poached Leg of Mutton with Caramelised Onions and Caper Sauce** (page 157), or roast the best end of neck like the **Roast Rack of Lamb** (page 158).

Of the cheaper cuts, diced stewing veal is lovely fried in a Mediterranean mix of onion, garlic, red peppers, chilli and tomatoes. It's also a traditional ingredient in meat pies. Minced veal, on its own or combined with pork or beef, makes excellent meatballs – good with pasta and **Grilled Tomato Sauce** (page 257).

Veal Chops with Cherry Tomatoes, Mushrooms and Roasted Onions (page 266)

Veal Chops with Cherry Tomatoes, Mushrooms and Roasted Onion

This is big-time eating – huge chops with succulent juices, crushed tomatoes, fried mushrooms and caramelised onion.

Snip the fat surrounding the chops at 2-cm intervals to stop it curling. Brush the chops on each side with olive oil and season with plenty of freshly ground black pepper. Set aside.

Cut the onion horizontally into 1.5-cm slices. Keep the rings in place by inserting 2 or 3 wooden cocktail sticks from the outside to the centre. Brush each side with oil and place in a pan under a preheated grill for 5–7 minutes on each side or until beginning to blacken round the edges. Remove the cocktail sticks and set the onion rings aside.

Fry the mushrooms in 3–4 tablespoons of hot oil for about 5 minutes or until they start to give up their juices. Add the garlic, season with salt and black pepper, and fry for another minute or until the garlic just starts to colour. Drain on paper towels and set aside.

Heat a heavy-based non-stick frying pan, large enough to take the chops in a single layer. Add 3 tablespoons of oil. Dust the chops with flour and fry with the rosemary for about 8 minutes over medium heat. Turn two or three times so the chops brown evenly. Transfer to a plate and keep warm.

Pour off most of the oil. Raise the heat to medium-high and pour in the wine, stirring in all the tasty sediment from the base of the pan. Let the wine bubble and thicken for a few minutes, then swirl in the butter.

Add the cherry tomatoes, crushing them with the back of a wooden spoon. Fry for a minute or so, then add the mushrooms and onions and heat through. Finally, return the chops to the pan along with any juices that have flowed from them. Moisten with a little chicken stock and heat through briefly, turning them in the juices.

Arrange the chops in a warm serving dish and tip the vegetables and all the juices over the top.

Cook's note
• Take care not to overcook the chops or they will become tough and dry. The meat should be slightly pink inside.

veal chops 4, bone-in, each weighing about 280g, cut 2cm thick
olive oil
freshly ground black pepper
onion 1
mushrooms 175g, sliced
garlic clove 1, finely chopped
salt
plain flour for dusting
rosemary leaves finely chopped to make 1 tbsp
white wine 150ml
butter a knob
cherry tomatoes 16
chicken stock 5–6 tbsp

Serves 4

Venison

Venison is the term used for meat from various types of deer. In the UK the four most common species are roe, fallow, red and sika. There are also muntjac and Chinese water deer. Fallow, muntjac, roe and sika meat are considered the best; red deer meat is tougher and coarser.

Deer are raised in the wild, in the semi-wild in protected parkland, or on dedicated deer farms. Being free to roam and grazing almost entirely on natural forage, deer produce exceptionally lean, low-cholesterol, iron-rich meat.

Once the meat of kings, venison is now widely available and becoming more popular as people cotton on to its health benefits. Depending if and for how long the meat has been hung, the flavour varies from mildly gamey to intensely so. The texture is dense and finely grained, and the colour an unmistakable dark red.

The meat comes in a wide choice of cuts such as haunch (leg), saddle, loin and fillet, as well as shoulder, neck and breast. There are also venison burgers, sausages, pies and pâté. The quality and flavour of the meat may vary, but if you buy from a farm shop or traditional butcher you can find out about the type of deer and its source.

Cooking

Venison is distinctive-tasting meat often associated with decadent amounts of cream and brandy, which rather misses the point of its nutritional credentials. Though both are fine ingredients in themselves, sometimes a simpler treatment works better. Venison can of course be marinated for additional flavour or to tenderise wild venison that might be tough, but it is not always necessary if the meat is young and of good quality. For traditional dishes, choose a rich marinade based on red wine or port, olive oil, onions, garlic, herbs and spices; use olive oil and lemon juice for a lighter flavour that doesn't detract from the venison.

Classic ingredients to go with venison are gin, port and gutsy red wine, sharp-tasting fruit such as redcurrants, morello cherries and Seville oranges, and strongly aromatic herbs and spices – think rosemary, sage, thyme, juniper and lots of black pepper.

Steaks and medallions cut from the fillet can be **pan-fried**, but resist the temptation to overcook; the meat toughens and is much better rare or medium-rare. The meat should be at least 2cm thick. Brush with oil and season with sea salt and a good coating of coarsely ground black pepper. Sear in a preheated hot frying pan in a little oil and butter for 3–4 minutes depending on how you like your meat. Turn over and cook the other side for 2–3 minutes. Remove from the pan and keep warm on a plate. Deglaze the pan with a little game or meat stock and let it bubble until slightly thickened. If you like, you can add a spoonful of redcurrant jelly or a slug of cognac to enrich the sauce further. Stir for 2 minutes, adding any juices that have flowed from the meat and serve right away. Good accompaniments are slightly bitter caramelised chicory as in **pigeon with salsify, chicory and wet walnuts** (page 193) or **Pan-Fried Jerusalem Artichokes** (page 146).

UK season
• *Wild and semi-wild:* May–February, depending on type of deer and gender.
• *Farmed:* year-round.

Venison to look for
• *Fallow:* strong well-flavoured meat.
• *Muntjac:* small deer, highly prized for its dark gamey meat.
• *Roe:* truly wild, considered the finest venison. Milder tasting than most.
• *Sika:* strong gamey flavour, at its best in autumn.

Shopping notes
• Look for close-grained dark red meat with a velvety texture. It should not be sticky or wet.
• Choose a cut suitable for the dish:
Stewing: neck, shoulder, shin.
Braising and pot-roasting: shoulder, shoulder chops.
Grilling and frying: best end cutlets, loin chops, cutlets, fillet, haunch steaks.
Roasting: boned and rolled loin, haunch (leg), saddle, rack.

Storing
• Store on the bottom shelf of the fridge so raw juices cannot drip onto other food.
• Remove wrapping and store in a shallow dish, loosely covered with foil for up to 2 days.
• If vacuum-packed or in a rigid plastic container, leave unopened until an hour before cooking.

Preparation
• Remove from the fridge 1–2 hours before cooking. The meat will heat and brown more evenly if it starts off at room temperature.
• Remove vacuum-packed venison from the pack and allow to breathe for an hour.

Serving size
• *Boneless:* 250g serves 1.
Bone-in: 375–450g serves 1.

Thinly sliced, the tender fillet can be used in **Venison Stroganoff** (below). The meat cooks in minutes and a slightly sharp soured cream sauce keeps everything moist and well-flavoured.

Joints such as loin, sirloin and saddle from young animals are the ones to use for roasting. Some people like to bard the meat with bacon to prevent drying but I think this adds an unwelcome flavour. Far better is a light marinade of oil and lemon juice, and attentive basting during cooking.

For a magnificent festive dish, try using a **saddle of venison** instead of wild boar in **Roast Saddle of Wild Boar with Chestnuts, Shallots and Kumquats** (page 277). Haunch can also be roasted and is said to have a better flavour. However, it can sometimes be dry so pot-roasting is usually a better option.

Of the tougher cuts, the shoulder, neck and breast make richly flavoured stews and casseroles, and can be substituted for beef in most recipes. Cut the meat into decent-sized chunks so that it doesn't disintegrate. The meat is robust enough to stand up to, and indeed benefits from, strong sharp flavours as in the fiery **Venison Vindaloo** (opposite). Minced venison offers plenty of possibilities too. It is a world apart from its beefy counterpart and makes superb pasta sauce, shepherd's pie, chile con carne and burgers.

Venison Stroganoff

Venison gives an unmistakable richness to this timeless sixties classic, usually made with beef or pork. Farm shops often sell the meat ready sliced, so the dish can be on the table in very little time.

Spread out the meat on a board and sprinkle with the $^1/_2$ teaspoon of black pepper, massaging it well into the meat.

Heat a large heavy-based frying pan over medium-high heat. Add the rapeseed oil and half the butter, and when it sizzles, fry the onion for a few minutes until beginning to colour.

While the onion is cooking, heat a separate frying pan, add the remaining butter, and fry the mushrooms for about 7 minutes or until they start to give up their juices.

Stir the meat into the onions and season with the paprika, dill and salt to taste. Cook until the meat has lost its red colour, then add the mushrooms. Stir everything together and season with more salt and black pepper. Cook for 3–4 minutes more.

Pour in the soured cream, stir well to mix and cook until heated through. Check the seasoning, then pour into a warm dish. Sprinkle with a little parsley before serving.

Cook's note
• This is best served with plainly cooked white rice and a green vegetable such as Swiss chard (page 64), buttered kale (page 148) or cabbage (page 51).

venison fillet 500g, sliced into 1 x 4cm strips
freshly ground black pepper $^1/_2$ tsp, plus extra
rapeseed oil 1 tbsp
butter 50g
onion 1 small, finely chopped
mushrooms 250g, thinly sliced
paprika 2 tsp
dill seed 1 tsp
salt
soured cream 300ml
flat leaf parsley roughly chopped, to garnish

Serves 4

Venison Vindaloo

Brought by the Portuguese to Goa in southwest India, vindaloo is normally made with pork, but venison is a perfect match for the strident flavours – vinegar, garlic and chillies. Don't be put off by the long list of ingredients for the spice paste – many of them are standard store-cupboard items that you are already likely to have. Spices can usually be found in the larger farm shops.

First make the spice paste: dry fry the coriander and cumin seeds without any oil for a minute or two until they smell fragrant. Immediately remove from the heat. Crush to a powder with the cloves, cardamom seeds and peppercorns, using a mortar and pestle. Tip into a blender with the remaining spice paste ingredients and whizz to a smooth paste.

Put the venison in a bowl and stir in the spice paste, massaging it into the meat with your hands. Set aside for 20 minutes.

Heat the rapeseed oil in a heavy-based casserole over medium heat and fry the potatoes until browned on all sides. Remove from the casserole and set aside.

Reduce the heat a little and gently fry the onions for about 10 minutes or until browned.

Add the meat to the casserole, scraping in all the spice paste and juices. Fry for 10 minutes, turning occasionally, until browned.

Return the potatoes to the casserole. Pour in 500ml of the stock. Bring to the boil, then reduce the heat and simmer, uncovered, for 1 hour, stirring occasionally, until the meat is very tender and the sauce reduced and thickened. If the meat starts to look dry, add some more stock. Stir in the chopped coriander just before serving.

stewing venison 900g, cubed
rapeseed oil 4 tbsp
potatoes 8 small, halved
onions 2, finely chopped
stock made with bouillon powder, 500–600ml
coriander leaves chopped to make 2 tbsp

for the spice paste
coriander seeds 2 tbsp
cumin seeds 2 tsp
cloves 6
green cardamom seeds from 4 pods
black peppercorns $\frac{1}{2}$ tsp
ground cinnamon 1 tsp
cayenne pepper 1–2 tsp
ground turmeric 2 tsp
sugar 1 tsp
salt 1 tsp
fresh ginger root 4-cm piece, finely chopped
garlic cloves 12, finely chopped
green chillies 2–4, deseeded and finely chopped
malt vinegar 6 tbsp
vegetable oil 4 tbsp

Serves 4–6 as a main course with rice

Walnuts

Long ago walnut orchards were a common sight in Britain but, sadly, they have died out over the centuries. The trees that are left struggle with the climate, and supplies of home grown nuts are rare or intermittent at best; most are imported from France, Italy and California. Fortunately, thanks to changing weather conditions, UK farmers are beginning to plant walnut orchards again. Supplies of nuts remain patchy but there is a good chance of coming across them in farm shops.

Late June and early July is the time to look for 'green' pickling walnuts, traditionally eaten with cheese and cold meats. At this stage, the shells and kernel are undeveloped and encased in a thick fleshy green coating. The main crop is harvested in October at the 'wet' stage. These choice specimens are easily cracked to reveal two immaculate halves of moist milky nutmeat with a golden papery skin. In this pristine state they last for only a few days, and quickly become mouldy. Walnuts sold later in the year are dried and therefore keep better. The nutmeat has an altogether different quality; the kernels are less plump and creamy, and the papery husk is darker and somewhat bitter (see **Preparation**).

Cooking

Walnuts are big and meaty with a flavour to match. I cannot resist adding them, preferably freshly cracked, to peppery and fruity salads such as **Kohlrabi, Apple and Watercress Salad with Walnut** (page 155), and **Roasted Peppered Pear Salad with Sheep's Cheese, Honey and Walnuts** (page 183). They just seem so right.

Their mild bitterness is also good with duck and game (**Warm Duck Breast Salad with Watercress, Walnuts, Sugar Snap Peas and Bean Sprouts**, page 94, and **Warm Salad of Pheasant Breasts with Wet Walnuts and Bacon**, page 189) and, with port, Stilton and crisp celery, they are exactly what's needed after a festive meal.

Finely ground fresh walnuts add substance and velvety richness to sauces to serve with grilled meat or fish. Greek cooks whizz them with breadcrumbs, garlic, olive oil, lemon juice, salt and white pepper. In Syria and the Lebanon they make **muhamara**, a vibrant spicy red sauce or dip for serving with pitta bread. Purée a deseeded and chopped red pepper in a food processor, pulsing a few times until very smooth. Mix the purée with 150g very finely chopped fresh walnuts, 75g slightly stale breadcrumbs, 1 tablespoon of tomato purée, 1 teaspoon of crushed cumin seeds, a good pinch of dried chilli flakes, a pinch of sugar and salt to taste. When everything is well mixed, whisk in 150ml olive oil. You can put the whole lot in a food processor if you like but I prefer a slightly chunky texture.

Walnuts are equally delicious in sweet dishes. Try them in the exquisitely rich **Walnut and Chocolate Tart** (page 272) or **Sweet Puffy Pancakes with Walnuts** (page 103). They also make excellent cakes, biscuits and pastry. For a heavenly breakfast, mix freshly shelled wet walnuts with clear honey and add to fruit or yogurt.

UK season
- Green walnuts: June–July.
- Wet walnuts: September–October.

Walnuts to look for
- Green for pickling.
- Wet for eating straight away.

Shopping notes
- Look for nuts with pale brown shells that feel heavy for their size.
- Don't bother with nuts that rattle, are broken or streaked with dark mould.

Storing
- Store unshelled in a cool larder or the fridge for 2–3 weeks.
- Shell as needed and eat right away. Once shelled the nutmeat deteriorates quickly and becomes rancid because of high oil content.

Preparation
- Crack the shell and prize out the creamy two–part kernel.
- The papery husk encasing the kernel is edible but worth removing as it can be bitter. To loosen it, toast shelled nuts in the oven at 180°C/gas 4 for about 5 minutes or until just golden. Rub with a dry cloth to remove the skins.

Walnut and Chocolate Tart (page 272)

Walnut and Chocolate Tart

Known in Italy as *torta nera* (black tart), this is adapted from a traditional recipe given to me by an Italian friend. The tart is utterly addictive – dense, dark and sweet with a slightly chewy texture. I prefer to eat it at room temperature rather than hot, and it tastes better the day after making when the flavours have settled. It's perfect for late autumn entertaining.

Preheat the oven to 170°C/gas 3. Lightly grease a 24-cm x 4-cm deep loose-bottomed tart tin. Mould the pastry into a thick disc, roll out into a circle and use to line the tin. Pass a rolling pin over the top to trim excess dough. Using the side of your forefinger, press the dough into the corner of the tin to raise it slightly above the rim.

Grind the walnuts and one-third of the sugar to a powder in a food processor.

Beat the eggs with the rest of the sugar until the beaters leave a faint trail when lifted from the bowl. Beat in the walnut mixture. Add the remaining ingredients one by one, beating well after each addition.

Spoon the filling into the pastry case. Bake for 45 minutes or until a knife comes out clean when inserted into the middle. Leave to cool in the tin for 15 minutes before turning out.

Cook's notes
• If you are using ready-shelled walnuts, make sure they are well within their 'best before' date and do not taste rancid.
• Sweet shortcrust pastry is quite fragile. You may have to patch up a few cracks but they disappear once cooked.
• It's fine to use ordinary shortcrust pastry if you prefer the tart to be less sweet.

ready-made sweet shortcrust pastry 375g
shelled walnuts 225g (see **Cook's notes**)
sugar 175g
eggs organic, 3
plain flour 1/2 tbsp
amaretti biscuits 60g, roughly crushed
unsalted butter 50g, melted
plain chocolate (85% cocoa solids) 85g, grated
instant coffee granules 1 tbsp
almond extract 2–3 drops (optional)

Serves 8–10

Watercress

Historically one of our oldest salad crops, watercress grows mainly in the chalk belts of Hampshire, Dorset and Wiltshire. Though once gathered wild from streams and rivers, it is now produced in hygienic gravel beds fed by pure spring water from artesian wells and boreholes.

Watercress is a member of the feisty brassica family that includes broccoli, cabbage, rocket and radishes. It is packed with essential nutrients: iron, vitamin C and health-promoting phytochemicals (plant compounds) and antioxidants with cancer-fighting potential. The flavour is complex, peppery and long-lasting, the heat coming from mustard oils that are released as you chew the leaves, perking up the taste buds in the process.

The tastiest watercress is sold in bunches; you'll find it freshly harvested in farm shops situated near watercress beds. It is highly perishable and loses its full earthy flavour after a day or two.

Cooking

Watercress brings refreshing vigour to all kinds of dishes, both hot and cold, but I think it is at its best raw and unadulterated. A sprightly sprig or two make the most pleasing garnish for grilled meat or oily fish, offsetting the richness, though people invariably push it to one side, which rather misses the point.

Far better to make watercress the key ingredient in a salad, perhaps with shaved fennel and pine nuts, or glacial strips of Belgian chicory and walnuts, or slivers of red onion and immaculately sliced oranges. My favourite combination is **Radish Sprout Salad with Watercress and Pink Grapefruit** (page 244).

I have a distant childhood memory of watercress sandwiches for Sunday tea. They were a bit of a treat and made me feel all was well with the world. By no means dainty, they were made with halved slices of farmhouse bread thickly spread with unsalted butter and filled with 'plenty of watercress so that it bursts cheerfully out at the sides', as the late food writer Jane Grigson so rightly recommended.

As well as adding pep to sandwiches and salads, watercress works well with eggs; chop it roughly and add to omelettes, quiches or scrambled eggs. I also like it chopped very finely, mixed with softened butter and rolled into a cylinder to keep in the fridge ready for slicing over grilled meat or fish.

Watercress is milder when cooked but still retains some of its bite. It loses bulk in the same way as spinach but because of its powerful flavour you don't need vast amounts. Wilted watercress can be stirred into pasta and risotto, or try it with mushrooms in tasty **Watercress and Mushroom Pâté** (page 274). It also makes very good soup, either with potato and cream as in the classic French *potage cressonière* or with leeks (**Watercress and Leek Soup**, page 274).

UK season
• Year-round. Best September–April.

Shopping notes
• Buy watercress in bunches rather than trimmed. It lasts longer and the leaves have a better flavour.
• Look for glossy deep green leaves. Avoid any that are limp or yellowing.

Storing
• Wrap unwashed bunched watercress in wads of damp paper towels and store in a sealed plastic bag in the salad drawer of the fridge for up to 24 hours.

Preparation
• Trim tough stalks but don't throw them out; they're handy for soup or stock.
• Wash the sprigs in several changes of water, drain well, dry in a salad spinner and blot on paper towels.

Watercress and Mushroom Pâté

A pretty green-flecked pâté with a delicate, slightly peppery flavour. Serve it chilled on thin toast or crackers.

Heat a medium-to-large frying pan over medium-low heat. Add the butter and, when it sizzles, the salad onions and coriander seeds. Gently fry for 5 minutes until the onions are soft but not coloured.

Raise the heat to medium-high and add the mushrooms. Stir for 2 minutes, then season with sea salt and freshly ground black pepper. Add the watercress and quickly cook until just wilted. Remove from the heat and leave to cool for a few minutes.

Tip the mixture into a food processor along with the curd cheese and Tabasco. Whizz to a purée, then scrape into a bowl, cover and chill.

Variation
• For a meatier version, replace the mushrooms with 125g chicken livers, cleaned and chopped.

unsalted butter 25g
salad onions 3 large, chopped
coriander seeds 1 tsp, toasted and crushed
flat mushrooms 85g, finely chopped
sea salt flakes
freshly ground black pepper
watercress 2 bunches, coarse stalks removed
curd cheese 100g
Tabasco sauce a few drops

Serves 3–4 as a snack or starter

Watercress and Leek Soup

This vibrant green soup is based on a recipe by food writer Colin Spencer. The watercress is added at the last minute so it keeps its bright colour.

Melt the butter in a large saucepan. Add the leeks and potatoes and cook gently, covered, for 10 minutes or until beginning to soften. Pour in the bouillon, bring to the boil, then simmer for 20 minutes, with the lid askew.

Purée half the soup in a food processor or blender and pour it back into the pan. Whizz the milk and watercress together, and add this to the pan too. Reheat gently. Season to taste with sea salt and a small amount of freshly ground black pepper, bearing in mind the pepperiness of the watercress.

Cook's note
• It's best to add the milk and watercress mixture just before reheating and serving, otherwise the colour will go sludgy green.

butter a knob
leeks 450g, chopped
potatoes 450g, cut into small chunks
vegetable bouillon or mild chicken stock 800ml
whole milk organic, 300ml
watercress 1 bunch, roughly chopped
sea salt flakes
freshly ground black pepper

Serves 6

Wild Boar

Most wild boar in the UK are farmed – the term 'wild' refers to the breed rather than the way of life. They were hunted to extinction about three hundred years ago, though there are signs that wily escapees from boar farms are re-establishing genuinely wild populations in parts of southern England and Herefordshire.

Farmed wild boar have the freedom to roam in woodlands and pastures where they feed on greenery, acorns, insects and fungi, supplemented with root vegetables. The meat is a bit like pork but is darker and denser with a rich nutty flavour that reflects the all-natural diet. The meat is lean – only 5g of fat per 100g portion compared with 23g of fat for pork. It is also lower in saturated fat and cholesterol, and higher in protein.

Baby boar are slow to mature, taking 18 months as opposed to 6 months for pigs. Some farmers cross wild boar with pigs to bump up productivity, but the resulting flavour is different from true wild boar.

Wild boar are popular in Eastern Europe, Italy and France where they are known as *marcassin* if less than one year old, and *sanglier* if older. Young boar are preferable for eating; older ones can be tough and sometimes excessively gamey.

The meat is hung for up to three weeks to improve the flavour and texture before it is butchered into various cuts such as saddle, loin, haunch and shoulder. You can also buy cubed or minced haunch and shoulder for stews and casseroles, tasty wild boar sausages and excellent salami.

It's best to buy from a specialist boar farm where the boar are slaughtered while young. If you come across wild boar in a farm shop it's worth trying to find out the age and source. It may have been shot in the wild and the texture and flavour can be unpredictable.

Cooking

Wild boar tastes similar to pork and can usually be substituted for pork in recipes. The meat needs careful cooking to prevent it drying or becoming tough: quick cooking over high heat for steaks and medallions, moist cooking at medium heat for other cuts. Marinading is not essential but you can do so for extra flavour or to lubricate joints for roasting and pot-roasting.

In ancient times, a boar's head with the obligatory apple in its mouth had pride of place on the festive table. Equally baronial is **Roast Saddle of Wild Boar with Chestnuts, Shallots and Kumquats** (page 277) – an impressive and unusual dish for a special occasion and not that difficult to cook.

Chops are one of the most popular cuts, particularly delicious moistened in a creamy sauce and seasoned with **lemon zest, crushed juniper and black pepper**. Crush 1 teaspoon of juniper berries and 2 teaspoons of black peppercorns with the finely grated zest of 2 lemons and a good pinch of sea salt. Mix the resulting paste with 1 tablespoon of olive oil and rub this over 4 thick loin chops. Marinate at room

UK season
- *Farmed:* year-round.
- *Wild:* no closed shooting season, which means they can be shot at any time – even pregnant and lactating sows.

Shopping notes
- Meat from young boar is pinker with smaller bones. Meat from mature boar is dark red and close-grained.
- Choose a cut suitable for the dish:
Stewing: shoulder.
Braising and pot-roasting: shoulder, haunch.
Grilling and frying: tenderloin, boneless loin, loin steaks.
Roasting: saddle, loin, haunch.

Storing
- Store on the bottom shelf of the fridge so raw juices cannot drip onto other food.
- Remove wrapping and store in a shallow dish, loosely covered with foil for up to 2 days.
- If vacuum-packed, leave unopened until an hour before cooking.

Preparation
- Remove from the fridge 1–2 hours before cooking. The meat will heat and brown more evenly if it starts off at room temperature.
- Remove vacuum-packed boar from the pack and allow to breathe for an hour.
- Before pot roasting, marinade shoulder and haunch joins for 2 hours at room temperature or up to 24 hours in the fridge.

Serving size
- Boneless: 250g serves 1.
- Bone in: 375–450g serves 1.

temperature for 2 hours or more if possible. Heat a large frying pan over medium-high heat. Add a good knob of butter, then sear the chops on both sides until nicely browned. Move to a plate and keep warm. Pour a little stock or a slug of gin into the pan and stir to scrape up any sediment. Add 2 finely chopped shallots and 425ml game or chicken stock. Bring to the boil, then simmer for a few minutes. Add 5 tablespoons of double cream and simmer until slightly reduced. Put the chops back in the pan along with any juices that have accumulated. Cover and cook over low heat for 25–30 minutes, turning two or three times, until the chops are tender. Check the seasoning. Put the chops in a warm serving dish and strain the sauce over the top. Delicious served with gleaming green kale and sautéed potatoes.

The haunch or shoulder is superb in a **slowly cooked stew**. Cut 1kg meat into largish chunks so that it doesn't disintegrate. Dust with seasoned flour and brown in oil. Add diced celery, carrots, onion and garlic, and season with fresh bay leaves, thyme and a little salt. Soften over medium heat, then pour in a glass of fruity red wine and cook for a few minutes until the alcohol has evaporated. Stir in two 400g cans chopped tomatoes, bring to the boil, then reduce the heat to a gentle simmer and cook for 2 hours. Just before serving, season with a lavish amount of freshly ground black pepper and stir in a handful of chopped flat leaf parsley. Excellent with pasta or boiled potatoes.

Roast Saddle of Wild Boar with Chestnuts, Shallots and Kumquats

A baronial dish for a very special occasion. The meat needs to be carved with due ceremony (see **Cook's notes**).

To make the marinade, grind the first six ingredients to a paste using a mortar and pestle. Pat the meat dry, make a few slashes in the flesh and place in a shallow dish. Massage all over with the paste, pushing it into the slashes. Sprinkle with the 3 tablespoons of olive oil and the balsamic vinegar, rubbing them evenly into the meat. Cover loosely with foil and leave to marinate in a cool place for 2 hours, or in the fridge for up to 24 hours, turning occasionally.

Preheat the oven to 230°C/gas 8. Heat a large frying pan over medium-high heat. Add 1 tablespoon of olive oil and the knob of butter. When the butter is foaming sizzle the shallots for a few minutes, then sprinkle with the sugar. Once the shallots are nicely browned, add 200ml of the stock, the chestnuts and kumquats, and season with sea salt and freshly ground black pepper. Simmer for a few minutes until slightly reduced.

Meanwhile, put the meat in a roasting tin with 2 tablespoons of olive oil and roast for 15 minutes. Reduce the temperature to 170°C/gas 3. Pour the shallot mixture round the meat and roast for 50 minutes, basting frequently, until the juices run clear. Stir in a little more stock if things start to look dry. Lift the meat from the tin and leave to rest in a warm place for 15 minutes.

Remove the shallots, chestnuts and kumquats with a perforated spoon and keep warm. Boil up the pan juices and stir in 250ml stock, the vinegar, redcurrant jelly and any juices from the meat. Simmer for a minute or two, check the seasoning and strain into a jug.

Transfer the meat to a warm serving platter, surround with the shallots, chestnuts and kumquats and serve with the sauce.

Cook's notes
• Remove the meat from the fridge 2 hours before cooking; it needs to be at room temperature.
• *To carve the saddle:* using a sharp knife cut down one side of the backbone to separate the eye of the loin from the bone. Carve horizontally from the side to the centre of the saddle to make 1-cm slices. Repeat on the other side. Turn the saddle upside-down. Slice along one side of the backbone and lift out the fillet in a single piece. Repeat on the other side. Carve the fillets across the grain into 1-cm slices.

wild boar 1 saddle, weighing about 1.6kg
olive oil
butter a knob
shallots 12, peeled
sugar 1 tsp
game stock or **meat stock** preferably home-made, 450–600ml
peeled chestnuts 225g
kumquats 9, halved lengthways
sea salt flakes
freshly ground black pepper
balsamic vinegar 1 tbsp
redcurrant jelly 1 tbsp

for the marinade
salt 1 tsp
juniper berries 1 tsp
black peppercorns 1 tsp
orange finely grated zest of ½
garlic clove 1, crushed
rosemary finely chopped to make 1 tsp
olive oil 3 tbsp
balsamic vinegar 2 tbsp

Serves 6

Yogurt

Once associated with beards and birkenstocks, yogurt is now on most people's shopping lists. It has become a dairy staple both as a food in its own right and as an ingredient. It is the most well-known of fermented milks, made with harmless live bacteria that set the milk into creamy curds and convert most of the innate sugars (lactose) into lactic acid. It is this that gives yogurt its characteristic sharpness, though the type of milk and its fat levels also have an effect, as do additional sweeteners and flavourings.

In the UK most yogurt is made with cow's milk though sheep, goat and buffalo milk yogurts are becoming widely available. Sheep and buffalo milk yogurts are thick, creamy and pleasantly yeasty, but also clean-tasting with no hint of the animal from which the milk comes. Goat milk yogurt is tangier and tastes undeniably of goat – perhaps not to everyone's liking, though people with allergies find it helpful.

Yogurt found in farm shops is invariably of good quality and additive-free, whether plain or flavoured. It may be made with organic cow's milk, often from local herds, or one of the more esoteric milks. The flavour and texture can vary slightly depending on the season and where the animal has been grazing.

See also **Milk** (page 164)

Cooking

Yogurt is a key ingredient in the cuisines of Eastern Europe, the Middle East and India. It smoothes the flavours of strident curries, adds richness to casseroles and soups, and forms the basis for numerous sauces, salad dressings and dips. Yogurt is also invaluable for marinating lean dense-textured meat as in **Tandoori Turkey Tikka** (page 281).

A refreshing sauce to calm a curry or serve with grilled meat or fish is made with **yogurt, cucumber and mint**. The sauce is well-known from Greece to India and beyond, and there are numerous variations. For a basic recipe use 250ml organic plain yogurt – sheep's yogurt is excellent – and 1 or 2 small seedless cucumbers. If you can't find these, a run-of-the-mill cucumber will do but use half only, and first slice it lengthways and scoop out the seeds. Remove alternate strips of skin with a swivel peeler – the remaining green gives a bit of colour to an otherwise pale sauce. Slice the flesh fairly thinly, then stack the slices and chop them into quadrants. Toss in a colander with salt, then place a weighted plate on top and leave to drain for an hour. (If you're short of time you can dispense with this but the sauce will become more watery as the cucumber exudes its liquid.) Toss the cucumbers in a bowl with the yogurt, black pepper, a handful of chopped mint and a tablespoon of olive oil to give it gloss. Check the flavour and add more salt if necessary.

Yogurt lightens and sharpens mayonnaise-based sauces – add it to the dressing for **celeriac rémoulade** (page 59). It's also good in a **spicy spinach and yogurt sauce** (page 239), and in a creamy **lemon yogurt dressing** that goes well with crunchy raw vegetables. Mix 6 tablespoons

Yogurt to look for
• *Whole milk organic yogurt:* smooth and buttery, full flavour.
• *Organic sheep's yogurt:* exceptionally thick and creamy, slightly tangy, appetising crust on the surface.
• *Buffalo milk yogurt:* for the health-conscious – excellent source of calcium, very low in cholesterol.

Shopping notes
• Make sure yogurt is properly chilled and within its 'use by' date.
• Check that the container is clean and the seal unbroken.

Storing
• Store in the fridge for up to 2 weeks depending on the 'use by' date.
• The flavour becomes more tangy with age.

Preparation
• If intended for a hot dish, use whole milk rather than low-fat yogurt, and bring to room temperature before heating. Add to the dish towards the end of cooking.
• To prevent curdling during lengthy cooking, yogurt needs to be stabilised: blend 1 tablespoon of plain flour with 250ml whole milk yogurt before adding to the dish.

of organic plain yogurt with 2 tablespoons of organic whipping cream and 1 tablespoon of extra-virgin olive oil. Stir in 1 teaspoon each of Dijon mustard and lemon juice, and a little sea salt. Excellent with **Red Slaw with Radish Sprouts, Smoked Cheese and Lemon Yogurt Dressing** (page 53).

Top-notch yogurt – Greek, for example, or organic whole milk – can be served with desserts instead of cream. Combined with well-flavoured fruit, it is rich and smooth enough to make delectable ice cream. Try **Plum and Yogurt Ice with Raisin Syrup** (below).

Yogurt is the perfect breakfast for those who aren't up to crunching toast or cereal at that time of day. It is positively ambrosial drizzled with honey and mashed with a ripe banana or sprinkled with bulging blueberries. For a speedier and more liquid start to the day, whizz up yogurt with strawberries or diced mango in a blender and drink through a straw, or try Indian *lassi* – a froth of yogurt and iced water seasoned with salt, pepper and spices.

Plum and Yogurt Ice with Raisin Syrup

Thick-set Greek yogurt makes surprisingly good ice cream even though it is relatively low in fat. It goes well with strongly flavoured fruit such as the plums used here. Cherries or blackcurrants are also good.

Cut each plum round the indentation through to the stone. Twist the two halves in opposite directions to loosen the stone, then scoop it out with a small knife. Slice the flesh lengthways into thin segments and place in a bowl.

Put the water, sugar and orange zest in a saucepan. Heat gently until the sugar has dissolved, then raise the heat and boil for about 10 minutes until syrupy. Immediately pour over the plums and leave to cool. Strain the syrup and set aside.

Finely chop about a quarter of the plums. Whizz the rest to a purée with the lemon juice in a food processor. Tip into a large bowl and add the chopped plums. Stir in the brandy if you're using it, then fold in the yogurt and 200ml of the reserved syrup. Chill for at least 2 hours.

Churn and freeze in an ice cream machine. Once thickened, store in the freezer to harden.

To make the raisin syrup, put the raisins in a small saucepan with the rest of the reserved syrup. Bring to the boil, then boil rapidly for 3 minutes until slightly reduced. Remove from the heat and leave to cool.

Scoop the ice cream into dessert glasses and spoon over the raisin syrup.

Cook's note
• If you don't have an ice cream machine, follow the directions for still-freezing Quince and Ginger Sorbet (page 213).

dark-skinned plums 500g
water 600ml
sugar 200g
orange finely grated zest of 1
lemon juice 2 tsp
brandy or port (optional) 2 tsp
plain Greek yogurt organic, 225g
seedless raisins 40g

Makes about 1 litre

Tandoori Turkey Tikka

Yogurt is a key ingredient in this spicy marinade which protects the meat from the intense heat of the grill.

Slice the turkey steaks into cubes and put in a shallow dish. Mix the salt, black pepper, cayenne and lemon juice in a small bowl and pour over the turkey, turning the cubes with your hands. Cover and leave for 30 minutes.

Combine the marinade ingredients in a blender and whizz to a purée. Mix with the turkey, making sure the cubes are well coated. Cover and leave in the fridge for at least 2 hours or up to 24 hours. Remove from the fridge 1 hour before you are ready to cook.

Thread the turkey cubes on to 4 skewers, alternating them with bay leaves and the large outer pieces of red onion (use the smaller bits in a salsa). Brush with rapeseed oil on all sides and place on a baking tray under a preheated hot grill, about 10cm from the heat source, or cook on a barbecue. Grill for 10–12 minutes, turning from time to time, until the turkey is cooked through and slightly charred at the edges.

Transfer to a serving platter, sprinkle with coriander and strew with wedges of lime.

turkey breast steaks 4, each about $1\frac{1}{2}$ cm thick, weighing 500g in total
salt $\frac{1}{2}$ tsp
black peppercorns $\frac{1}{2}$ tsp, coarsely ground
cayenne pepper $\frac{1}{2}$–1 tsp
lemon juice of $\frac{1}{2}$
fresh bay leaves 12
small red onions 3, quartered lengthways
rapeseed oil for brushing
coriander leaves chopped to make 1 tbsp
lime wedges to garnish

for the marinade
thick plain yogurt organic, 175ml
fresh ginger root 5-cm piece, chopped
garam masala 1 tsp
cayenne pepper $\frac{1}{2}$–1 tsp
salt 1 tsp
lime juice of $\frac{1}{2}$
rapeseed oil 4 tbsp

Serves 4

Resources

Farms shops and Pick-Your-Own farms

www.farmshop.uk.com Farm shops, farmers' markets, events and b&b accommodation.

www.farmshopping.net Interactive map of farm shops, PYO farms, news and information.

www.farmshops.org.uk Farm shops, specialist retail outlets and farm gate sales.

www.pickyourown.info PYO farms by region, what's in season.

www.pick-your-own.org.uk Soft fruit PYO farms in the Midlands and Northern England.

www.thefoody.com/regionalproduce.html Farm shops by region, details of produce sold.

Festivals

www.britishasparagusfestival.org Asparagus Festival, Worcestershire.

www.commonground.org.uk Internationally recognised charity supporting local diversity. The driving force behind Apple Day, community orchards and Tree Dressing Day.

www.lythdamsons.org.uk Westmorland Damson Association. Damson Day, Westmorland.

www.wakefield.gov.uk Festival of Rhubarb, Wakefield, Yorkshire.

www.watercress.co.uk Alresford Watercress Festival, Hampshire.

www.wightonline.co.uk Garlic Festival, Isle of Wight.

Food information

Dairy products

www.britishcheese.com Portal for all things related to British cheese.

www.buffalomilk.co.uk All you need to know about buffalo milk.

www.thecheeseweb.com Website of Juliet Harbutt, cheese diva and driving force behind the British Cheese Awards.

Fish

www.fishonline.org Lists which fish are endangered and which to eat.

www.mcsuk.org Marine Conservation Society. In-depth information on all issues associated with eating fish.

www.msc.org Marine Stewardship Council. International charity promoting certification of sustainable fisheries. Lists sustainable fish, suppliers, recipes.

Fruit

www.brogdale.org.uk Brogdale Horticultural Trust, home of the National Fruit Collections. Largest collection in the world of fruit tree and plant varieties: apples, pears, cherries, plums, damsons, quinces, nuts.

www.dorset-blueberry.com Detailed information on blueberries, health benefits, recipes.

www.fruitforum.net Website and blog of Joan Morgan, one of the best-known figures in the British fruit community.

www.orangepippin.com Comprehensive information on apples and orchards.

Game

www.britishwildboar.org.uk News and views on all issues concerning wild boar in Britain.
www.gct.org.uk Game & Wildlife Conservation Trust. Promotes the conservation of game in the UK.

Meat

www.goat-meat.co.uk All you need to know about goat meat.
www.muttonrenaissance.org.uk Dedicated to the promotion of mutton. Detailed product information.
www.rbst.org.uk Rare Breeds Survival Trust. Dedicated to promoting and conserving Britain's native livestock.
www.waterbuffalo.co.uk Information about water buffalo in Warwickshire.

Nuts

www.kentishcobnutsassociation.org.uk Kentish Cobnuts Association. Promotes regeneration of cobnuts and holds events such as the Annual Nutters Supper.

Poultry

www.geese.cc British Goose Producers' website.

Vegetables and fungi

www.british-asparagus.co.uk Asparagus growers and suppliers nationwide.
www.mushroom-uk.com Promotes cultivated mushrooms sold in the UK.
www.mushrooms.org.uk Visual catalogue of wild mushrooms found in the UK.
www.reallygarlicky.co.uk Detailed information on unusual types of garlic.

Local food producers

www.bigbarn.co.uk Local food producers, what's in season.
www.foodloversbritain.com Website of Henrietta Green, champion of small food producers and local food.
www.localfoodadvisor.com Award-winning producers and suppliers.

Useful organisations

www.farma.org.uk FARMA (National Farmers' Retail and Markets Association). Supports sustainable development of farm shops, PYO farms, farmers' markets, box schemes. Promotes high ethical standards. Inspects and accredits farm shops. Organises FARMA Local Food Awards with categories for Best Farm Retailer, Best On-Farm Butchery, Best PYO Farm, Best On-Farm Café-Restaurant, Environmental Retailer of the Year. Well worth checking if you are planning a visit to a farm shop.
www.farmsunday.org LEAF-accredited network of demonstration farms that anyone interested in food production can visit.
www.leafmarque.com LEAF (Linking Environment And Farming), a charity dedicated to promoting a better understanding of British farming.

www.nfuonline.com National Farmers Union. Represents farmers and producers in England and Wales. Promotes successful and socially responsible agriculture, horticulture and long-term viability of rural communities.

www.redtractor.org.uk Assured Food Standards (AFS), the initiative behind the Red Tractor logo. Accredited foods are guaranteed to come from British farms and meet high standards of production relating to food safety, hygiene, animal welfare and environmental protection.

www.slowfood.org.uk. UK arm of the international Slow Food movement, dedicated to preserving artisan foods and regional traditions. Lists local groups or 'convivia', events, campaigns, projects.

www.soilassociation.org.uk Soil Association. Campaigns to raise awareness of benefits of organic food and farming. Local food links, organic certification, advice on organic growing.

www.sustainweb.org SUSTAIN: the alliance for better food and farming. Lists projects, campaigns and events.

Bibliography

Ayrton, E. *The Cookery of England.* Penguin Books, London 1977

Bissell, F. *The Organic Meat Cookbook.* Ebury Press, London 1999

Brillat-Savarin, J-A. *The Philosopher in the Kitchen.* Penguin Books,London 1970

British Tourist Authority and Boyd, L. (editor) *British Cookery (second edition).* Christopher Helm, Kent 1988

Brown, C. *Broths to Bannocks.* John Murray, London 1991

Bunyard, E. *The Anatomy of Dessert.* Dulau and Company, London 1929

Carrier, R. *Great Dishes of the World.* Thomas Nelson, London 1963

Clarke, B. *Good Fish Guide.* Marine Conservation Society, Ross-on-Wye 2002

Clifford, S. and King, A. *The Apple Source Book.* Hodder and Stoughton, London 2007

Clusells, S. *Cooking on Turning Spit and Grill.* Arthur Barker, London 1961

Corbin, P. *The River Cottage Preserves Handbook.* Bloomsbury, London 2008

Costa, M. *Margaret Costa's Four Seasons Cookery Book.* Sphere Books, London 1972

Davidson, A. *The Oxford Companion to Food.* Oxford University Press, Oxford 1999

Dowding, C. *Organic Gardening the Natural No-Dig Way.* Green Books, Totnes, Devon 2007

Dowding, C. *Salad Leaves for All Seasons.* Green Books, Totnes, Devon 2008

Fearnley-Whittingstall, H. *The River Cottage Meat Book.* Hodder and Stoughton, London 2004

Fearnley-Whittingstall, H. and Fisher, N. *The River Cottage Fish Book.* Bloomsbury Publishing, London 2007

Feasey, M. *Eat Dorset.* Parnham Press, Beaminster, Dorset 2005

Freeman, S. *The Real Cheese Companion.* Time Warner, Northamptonshire 2003

Fresh Produce Consortium. *Re:fresh Directory: 2007.* Peterborough 2007

Grigson, J. *Charcuterie and French Pork Cookery.* Penguin Books, London 1978

Grigson, J. *Good Things.* Penguin Books, London 1973

Grigson, J. *Jane Grigson's Fruit Book.* Penguin Books, London 1983

Grigson, J. *Jane Grigson's Vegetable Book.* Penguin Books, London 1980

Harbutt, J. (editor) *British Cheese Directory 2008.* Juliet Harbutt, Oxfordshire 2008

Harbutt, J. *A Cook's Guide to Cheese.* Anness Publishing, London 2004

Kimball, C. (editor) *Cook's Illustrated magazine (various editions).* Boston Common Press, Massachusetts 2003-8

Kiple, K.F. and Ornelas, K.C. *The Cambridge World History of Food.* Cambridge University Press, Cambridge 2000

Leeman, A. *A Taste of Devon.* Redcliffe Press, Bristol 2007

Leeman, A. *A Taste of Somerset.* Redcliffe Press, Bristol 2007

Mason, L. and Brown, C. *The Taste of Britain*. HarperCollins, London 2006

McFadden, C. *Healthy Fruit Desserts*. Little, Brown and Company, London 1996

McFadden, C. and Michaud, M. *Cool Green Leaves and Red Hot Peppers*. Frances Lincoln, London 199

Milk Marketing Board. *The Dairy Book of British Food*. Ebury Press, London 1988

Moore, I. and The Food Foundation. *The Food Book*. BBC Worldwide, London 2002

Muir, J. A *Cook's Guide to Grains*. Conran Octopus, London 2002

Nelson, S. (editor) *NW Fine Food Lovers Guide 2007*. North West Fine Foods, Skelmersdale, Lancashire 2007

Ortega, S. and I. *1080 Recipes*. Phaidon Press, London 2007

Oxford Symposium on Food and Cookery. Hosking, R. (editor) *Eggs in Cookery*. Prospect Books, Totnes, Devon 2007

Oxford Symposium on Food and Cookery. Walker, H. (editor) *Milk: Beyond the Dairy*. Prospect Books, Totnes, Devon 2000

Raichlen, S. *How to Grill*. Workman Publishing, New York 2001

Roach, F.A. *Cultivated Fruits of Britain: their origin and history*. Basil Blackwell, Oxford 1986

Roden, C. *The Book of Jewish Food*. Viking, London 1997

Roux, M. *Eggs*. Quadrille, London 2007

Stein, R. *Guide to the Food Heroes of Britain*. BBC Books, London 2003

Stocks, C. *Forgotten Fruits: a guide to Britain's traditional fruits and vegetables*. Random House, London 2008

The Goose: history, folklore, ancient recipes. Könemann, Köln, Germany 1998

The Guardian. *The Guardian and Observer Guides to Growing Your Own: part 1 vegetables*. London 2008.

The Guardian. *The Guardian and Observer Guides to Growing Your Own: part 2 salad and fruit*. London 2008.

The Silver Spoon. Phaidon Press, London 2006

Vaughan, J.G. and Geissler, C.A. *The New Oxford Book of Plants*. Oxford University Press, Oxford 1997

Willan, A. *Reader's Digest Complete Guide to Cookery*. Dorling Kindersley, London 1989

UK seasonal produce availability

This is an approximate guide to availability since weather conditions vary according to region. With the exception of forced rhubarb, the chart includes outdoor-grown crops only.

	Jan	Feb	Mar	Apr	May	Jun	Jul	Aug	Sep	Oct	Nov	Dec
Apples	*	*	*	*					*	*	*	*
Asparagus					*	*						
Beetroot						*	*	*	*	*	*	
Blackberries							*	*	*	*		
Blackcurrants						*	*	*				
Blueberries							*	*	*			
Broad beans						*	*	*	*			
Brussels sprouts	*	*	*							*	*	*
Cabbage (spring)				*	*	*						
Cabbage (red)	*	*	*	*	*	*		*	*	*	*	*
Cabbage (white)	*	*	*	*	*	*	*	*	*	*	*	*
Cabbage (winter)	*	*	*								*	*
Carrots						*	*	*	*	*	*	*
Cauliflower		*	*	*	*			*	*	*	*	*
Celeriac	*	*	*	*						*	*	*
Celery							*	*	*	*		
Chard	*	*	*	*		*	*	*		*	*	*
Cherries						*	*	*				
Chestnuts										*	*	
Chillies							*	*	*	*		
Cobnuts								*	*			
Courgettes						*	*	*	*	*		
Cucumber							*	*	*	*		
Damsons									*			
Garlic (green)					*	*	*					
Garlic (wild)				*	*							
Globe artichokes					*	*	*	*	*	*	*	
Gooseberries (cooking)					*	*	*					
Gooseberries (dessert)							*	*				
Green beans (French)						*	*	*	*			
Green beans (runner)							*	*	*	*		
Greengages								*	*			
Herbs (tender annuals)					*	*	*	*	*			
Horseradish							*	*	*	*		
Jerusalem artichokes	*	*	*							*	*	*
Kale	*	*	*	*						*	*	*
Kohlrabi						*	*	*	*	*	*	
Leeks	*	*	*						*	*	*	*
Mushrooms (wild)					*				*	*	*	
New Zealand spinach	*	*	*	*	*	*	*	*	*	*	*	*
Onions (main crop)**									*	*		
Onions (pickling)						*	*	*				
Parsnips	*	*	*	*					*	*	*	*

	Jan	Feb	Mar	Apr	May	Jun	Jul	Aug	Sep	Oct	Nov	Dec
Pears	*								*	*	*	*
Peas					*	*	*	*	*			
Plums							*	*	*			
Potatoes					*	*	*	*	*	*	*	*
Pumpkin/winter squash									*	*	*	
Quinces										*	*	
Radishes	*				*	*	*	*	*	*	*	*
Raspberries						*	*	*	*	*		
Redcurrants						*	*	*				
Rhubarb (forced)	*	*										
Rhubarb (early outdoor-grown)			*	*	*							
Rhubarb (main crop)					*	*	*	*	*			
Salad (chicory/endive)	*	*	*							*	*	*
Salad (lettuce)					*	*	*	*	*	*		
Salad (micro-leaves)	*	*	*	*	*	*	*	*	*	*	*	*
Salad (oriental leaves)							*	*	*	*	*	
Salad (rocket)				*	*	*	*	*	*	*	*	*
Salsify/scorzonera	*	*	*	*						*	*	*
Shallots	*	*	*									*
Spinach					*	*	*	*	*	*		
Sprouting broccoli		*	*	*	*							
Sprouting beans/seeds	*	*	*	*	*	*	*	*	*	*	*	*
Strawberries						*	*	*	*			
Swede	*	*	*	*	*		*	*	*	*	*	*
Sweetcorn							*	*	*	*		
Tomatoes							*	*	*	*		
Turnips	*	*			*	*				*	*	*
Walnuts (green)						*	*					
Walnuts (wet)										*	*	
Watercresss	*	*	*	*	*	*	*	*	*	*	*	*

** Cold storage October–July

UK game availability

The chart shows the open season for fresh game. Frozen meat is usually available at other times.

	Jan	Feb	Mar	Apr	May	Jun	Jul	Aug	Sep	Oct	Nov	Dec
Grouse								*	*	*	*	*
Hare	*	*						*	*	*	*	*
Partridge	*								*	*	*	*
Pheasant	*									*	*	*
Venison***	*	*			*	*	*	*	*	*	*	*
Wild boar	*	*	*	*	*	*	*	*	*	*	*	*
Wild duck (mallard)	*								*	*	*	*
Wild duck (teal/widgeon)	*	*								*	*	*

*** Depending on type of deer
    and gender

Recipe index

Acknowledgements

Writing this book has brought me in contact with so many good-hearted producers and farmers with stories to tell and information to share.

It has been a privilege to write and I am deeply indebted to Meg Avent and Jon Croft of Absolute Press for asking me to take on the project. My sincerest thanks also to the following:

Jim Armstrong, Littlebredy, for helpful advice and lovely lamb.

Patricia and John Barker, Bride Valley Farm Shop, for Longhorn beef, oxtail and other tasty meat.

Cristian Barnett for inspiring photography.

Pat Bowcock, Ourganics, Litton Cheny, for constant support and immaculate salads.

Tim and Julie Garry, Modbury Farm Shop, for bantam eggs and very fresh vegetables.

David Hammerson, Everleigh Farm Shop, for outstanding eggs of many kinds.

Simon Holland, Washingpool Farm Shop, for helpful advice, very fresh vegetables and sourcing difficult-to-come-by produce.

Matt Inwood, art director at Absolute Press, for unfailing good humour and patience.

Joy and Michael Michaud, Peppers By Post, for chillies and constant encouragement.

Nichola Motley for generously sharing her knowledge of Dorset food producers.

Andrea O'Connor at Absolute Press for compiling the index and unending unsung help that kept the project on track.

Carol Ridley, Ridley's Fish and Game in Northumberland, for information about squirrel and supplying samples for cooking.

Anne Sheasby for meticulous editing.

Claire Siggery at Absolute Press for patiently dealing with corrections.

Linda Tubby for preparing the food for photography.

I am also deeply indebted to my family and friends for bearing with me during the many months when the book took over my life.